This book applies rigorous economic analysis to the question of sustainable development. It considers the inter-relationship between growth and sustainability showing that one does not necessarily exist to the detriment of the other. Sustainability may be measured and defined in national accounting terms and the contributors explore a potentially powerful theoretical definition. Case studies on Morocco and China examine some of the domestic policy requirements of sustainability, revealing the desirability of quite complex combinations of policies. International policy aspects of sustainability are considered, such as technology transfer and the establishment of workable agreements to reduce global pollution. The volume demonstrates the need to build the sustainability debate on sound economic foundations, and the ability of economists to provide such foundations.

The economics of sustainable development

OECD Development Centre

The OECD Development Centre was established in 1962. Its main activities are research, external relations, in particular with research and training institutes in the world, and the organisation of informal meetings with high-level representatives of Member and non-Member countries to discuss economic issues of mutual concern.

In its research activities, the Development Centre seeks to identify issues that will become the subject of growing concern in the near future, and whose implications are of vital interest to both Member and non-Member countries. It also seeks to suggest policy directions for dealing with these issues.

The Centre maintains numerous contacts in the field of development and encourages the world-wide exchange of experience and knowledge. It thereby contributes to the flow of information on development and to the bridging of differences between OECD Member and non-Member countries in the perception and analysis of problems and policies relating to development and interdependence.

The opinions expressed in this volume are those of the authors and not necessarily those of the OECD Development Centre, the OECD or the governments of their Member countries.

The Centre for Economic Policy Research

The Centre for Economic Policy Research is a network of over 200 Research Fellows, based primarily in European universities. The Centre coordinates its Fellows' research activities and communicates their results to the public and private sectors. CEPR is an entrepreneur, developing research initiatives with the producers, consumers and sponsors of research. Established in 1983, CEPR is already a European economics research organisation with uniquely wide-ranging scope and activities.

CEPR is a registered educational charity. Institutional (core) finance for the Centre is provided through major grants from the Economic and Social Research Council, the Esmée Fairbairn Charitable Trust, the Bank of England, Citibank, the Baring Foundation, 33 other companies and 14 other central banks. None of these organisations gives prior review to the Centre's publications, nor do they necessarily endorse the views expressed therein.

The Centre is pluralist and non-partisan, bringing economic research to bear on the analysis of medium- and long-run policy questions. CEPR research may include views on policy, but the Executive Committee of the Centre does not give prior review to its publications, and the Centre takes no institutional policy positions. The opinions expressed in this volume are those of the authors and not those of the Centre for Economic Policy Research.

The economics of
sustainable development

Edited by

IAN GOLDIN

and

L. ALAN WINTERS

CAMBRIDGE
UNIVERSITY PRESS

Published by the Press Syndicate of the University of Cambridge
The Pitt Building, Trumpington Street, Cambridge CB2 1RP
40 West 20th Street, New York, NY 10011-4211, USA
10 Stamford Road, Oakleigh, Melbourne 3166, Australia

First published 1995

Printed in Great Britain at the University Press, Cambridge

A catalogue record for this book is available from the British Library

Library of Congress cataloguing in publication data
Economics of sustainable growth / edited by Ian Goldin and L. Alan Winters.
    p.   cm.
Includes index.
ISBN 0 521 46555 9. – ISBN 0 521 46957 0 (pbk.)
1. Sustainable development.   2. Environmental policy.
3. Economic policy.   I. Goldin, Ian, 1955– .   II. Winters, L. Alan.
HC79.E5E2835   1995
338.9 – dc20   94-27994   CIP

ISBN 0 521 46555 9   hardback
ISBN 0 521 46957 0   paperback

CE

Contents

List of figures   *page* xiii
List of tables   xv
Preface   xvii
Acknowledgements   xviii
List of conference participants   xix

1 Economic policies for sustainable development   1
Ian Goldin and L. Alan Winters
  1   Is growth sustainable?   1
  2   The economy-wide dimension: from mess to macro   2
  3   The effects of growth   4
  4   Definition and measurement   6
  5   Domestic policies for sustainable growth   9
  6   International policies for sustainable growth   11
  7   Conclusions   13

PART ONE: GROWTH AND THE ENVIRONMENT

2 Pollution and growth: what do we know?   19
Gene M. Grossman
  1   Data and estimation   23
  2   Air quality   27
  3   Water quality   35
  4   Conclusions and policy implications   41
    Discussion   47
  Gilles Saint-Paul
  1   Introduction   47
  2   The model   47

3   Does sustainability require growth?   51
    Richard Baldwin
    1   Introduction   51
    2   Demographic and ecologic transitions   53
    3   Where the world is today   63
    4   A simple-minded extrapolation: constant income growth   71
    5   Sustainability and policy implications   73
    6   Summary, conclusions and future research   76
    Discussion   78
    Daniel Cohen

PART TWO: SUSTAINABILITY

4   What sustains economic development?   83
    Maurice Scott
    1   Some definitions   83
    2   Environmental concerns and sustainability   91
    3   The role of government   97
    5   Conclusions: what sustains economic development?   102
    Discussion   106
    Constantino Lluch
        1   Scott versus the profession   106
        2   On the evidence   108
        3   On sustainability   108

5   Optimal development and the idea of net national product   111
    Partha Dasgupta
    1   Introduction   111
    2   What are environmental resources?   112
    3   Social objectives: 1 – sustainable development   115
    4   Social objectives: 2 – optimal development, discount rates
        and sustainability   117
    5   Second-best optima, global warming, and risk   121
    6   Project evaluation and the measurement of net national
        product   123
    7   The Hamiltonian and net national product   126
    8   Biases in technological adaptation   127
    9   Environmental accounting prices: the valuation problem   128
    10 Conclusions   130
    Appendix: NNP in a dynamic economy   130
    Discussion   143
    Philippe Aghion

6 **Sustainable growth and the Green Golden Rule**   147
   Andrea Beltratti, Graciela Chichilnisky and Geoffrey Heal
   1 Introduction   147
   2 A model of growth with environment   151
   3 The discounted utilitarian solution   155
   4 The Green Golden Rule   158
   5 Optimal sustainable paths   159
   6 An example of a sustainable optimal path   160
   7 Conclusions   162
      Discussion   166
      Alistair Ulph

PART THREE: DOMESTIC POLICY

7 **Economic policies for sustainable resource use in Morocco**   175
   Ian Goldin and David Roland-Holst
   1 Introduction   175
   2 Practical issues in Moroccan water allocation   176
   3 Methodological issues   179
   4 The Moroccan CGE model   182
   5 Simulation results   187
   6 Conclusions   191
      Appendix: results of sensitivity analysis   192
      Discussion   197
      Jaime de Melo

8 **Energy pricing for sustainable development in China**   200
   Rosemary Clarke and L. Alan Winters
   1 Optimal abatement   202
   2 Marginal benefits of abatement   204
   3 Marginal abatement costs   206
   4 The simulations   209
   5 Conclusions   219
      Appendix 1: definitions   220
      Appendix 2: base prices   221
      Appendix 3: flow matrix, China, 1985   222
      Appendix 4: commodity demands and parameters   223
      Appendix 5: the model   224
      Discussion   230
      Athar Hussain

PART FOUR: INTERNATIONAL POLICY COORDINATION

9 **Carbon abatement, transfers and energy efficiency**   239
   Jean-Marc Burniaux, John P. Martin, Joaquim Oliveira-Martins and Dominique van der Mensbrugghe
   1 Introduction   239
   2 Brief overview of GREEN   240
   3 The role of the AEEI parameter in the BaU scenario   245
   4 Energy productivity and catch-up   248
   5 Two scenarios of international recycling of carbon tax
      revenues   250
   6 Conclusions   259
   Appendix: energy efficiency, emissions and real income in
      GREEN   260

10 **Policy coordination for sustainability: commitments, transfers,
   and linked negotiations**   264
   Carlo Carraro and Domenico Siniscalco
   1 Introduction   264
   2 Stable environmental coalitions   266
   3 Expanding coalitions through transfers and commitment   269
   4 Linking environmental negotiations   274
   5 Conclusions   280
   Discussion   283
   Marcus Miller and Lei Zhang
      1 Outline and summary   283
      2 Key features of the CS model   283
      3 Externalities in abatement   284
      4 Charging for emissions   286
      5 Conclusions   288

11 **Industrial competitiveness, environmental regulation and direct
   foreign investment**   289
   Ravi Kanbur, Michael Keen and Sweder van Wijnbergen
   1 Introduction   289
   2 The basic model   290
   3 Environmental competition: the Nash equilibrium   292
   4 International coordination of environmental regulation   297
   5 Summary and conclusions   300
   Discussion   302
   Jean-Claude Berthélemy

   Index   307

Figures

		page
2.1	Urban air quality	29
2.2	Air quality and local income across the US	30
2.3	Faecal contamination of rivers	37
2.4	Heavy metals in rivers	39
2.5	The oxygen regime in rivers	42
D2.1	Emissions and income levels	49
D2.2	Effects of growth on emissions and prices	50
3.1	Schematic demographic transition	54
3.2	Demographic data versus income levels	56
3.3	Phase diagram of endogenous growth and fertility	58
3.4	Schematic ecologic transition	61
3.5	Population and population growth rates	64
3.6	Population and birth rates by age groups	65
3.7	Demographic transition with cross-country data	67
3.8	*Per capita* emissions versus average income, 1989	68
3.9	Air pollution and population for 120 countries	70
3.10	Demographic and ecologic transitions, 1989	71
3.11	Air pollution levels with constant population growth	73
6.1	Stationary states of the utilitarian solution are intersections of the line and the curve	154
6.2	The path which maximises $\lim \inf u(C, A)$ approaches (A^*, C^*), the point giving the highest sustainable utility level	159
6.3	Dynamics of the utilitarian solution for the simple case of one state variable, A	163
8.1	Optimal Chinese abatement	203
9.1	Production functions of GREEN	243
9.2	World emissions under alternative AEEI assumptions, 1985–2050	248

9.3	Energy production levels, BaU scenario	249
9.4	Energy productivity levels, global tax scenario	259
D10.1	Abatement externalities and the incentive to cooperate	286
D10.2	How coalition size increases with the externality	287
11.1	Best responses	293
11.2	The Nash equilibrium	295
D11.1	Nash equilibrium in environment policy	304

Tables

		page
2.1	World Health Organisation guideline values based on effects other than cancer or odour/annoyance	28
3.1	OLS analysis on a cross-section of total fertility rates, 96 countries, 1985	74
7.1	Formal structure of the Morocco model	184
7.2	Social accounting matrix for Morocco, 1985	188
7.3	Estimates of structural parameters	189
7.4	Aggregate simulation results	189
7.5	Sectoral simulation results	191
7A.1	Results for varying factor substitution elasticity	193
7A.2	Results for varying water prices	194
8.1	Greenhouse gas emissions	201
8.2	Fuel prices for China, 1985	208
8.3	Shares of sales at state prices	210
8.4	Emission factors	212
8.5	Simulation results	215
8.6	Alternative results	218
9.1	Key dimensions of the GREEN model	241
9.2	World carbon emissions by region and type of fuel, BaU scenario	247
9.3	Summary statistics for the international recycling of carbon tax revenues scenario	252
9.4	Transfers and AEEI in the recycling of an OECD carbon tax scenario	253
9.5	Summary statistics for the implementation of a global carbon tax scenario	256
9.6	Transfers and AEEI in the implementation of a global carbon tax scenario	257

Preface

The OECD Development Centre and the Centre for Economic Policy Research share a desire to stimulate economic analysis with policy applications. Sustainable development has come to the top of the international and domestic policy agendas. The broad commitments have proved difficult to implement, however, not least because the meaning of 'sustainable development' and its implications for economic policy making remain poorly understood.

This volume aims to clarify the relationship between economic and environmental policies. It breaks new ground in approaching environmental policies from an economy-wide perspective. In addition to addressing the broad question of the relationship between growth and sustainability, it considers specific domestic and international economic policies which support sustainable development as well as the need to clarify the measurement and definition of sustainable growth.

The volume represents the results of the joint Development Centre/CEPR Conference on Sustainable Economic Development: Domestic and International Policies, held in Paris in May 1993. We expect it to provide a timely contribution to those engaged in the vital task of designing national and international policies which ensure that development is indeed sustainable.

July 1994

Jean Bonvin
President, OECD Development Centre
Richard Portes
Director, Centre for Economic Policy Research

Acknowledgements

The editors and publishers acknowledge with thanks permission from the following to use copyright material.

World Bank, for data in figures 3.2, 3.5–3.7, from the World Bank data base, and in figure 8.2, from *China: The Energy Sector* (1985).

Oxford University Press, for figure 3.8 and table 8.1, from World Resources Institute, *World Resources, 1992–1993* (1992).

MIT, for figure 2.1, from P. Garber (ed.), The US–Mexico Free Trade Agreement (1993).

World Health Organisation, for data in table 2.1, from *Air Quality Guidelines for Europe* (1987).

Royal Institute of International Affairs, for data in table 8.4, from M. Grubb *et al.*, *Energy Policies and the Greenhouse Effect*, vol. 2 (1991).

List of conference participants

Philippe Aghion (*EBRD and CEPR*)
Richard E. Baldwin (*Graduate Institute of International Studies, Geneva, and CEPR*)
Andrea Baranzini (*Université de Genève*)
Andrea Beltratti (*Università degli Studi di Torino and Fondazione Eni Enrico Mattei, Milan*)
Jean-Claude Berthélemy (*OECD Development Centre*)
Jean Bonvin (*OECD Development Centre*)
Colin Bradford (*OECD Development Centre*)
Carliene Brenner (*OECD*)
Jean-Marc Burniaux (*OECD*)
Carlo Carraro (*Università degli Studi di Venezia and CEPR*)
Graciela Chichilnisky (*Columbia University*)
Rosemary Clarke (*University of Birmingham*)
Daniel Cohen (*Ecole nationale supérieure, Paris, Université de Paris I and CEPR*)
Partha S. Dasgupta (*University of Cambridge and CEPR*)
Jaime de Melo (*World Bank, Université de Genève and CEPR*)
Ian Goldin (*World Bank*)
Gene M. Grossman (*Princeton University and CEPR*)
Geoffrey M. Heal (*Columbia University*)
Athar Hussain (*LSE*)
Constantino Lluch (*OECD*)
John P. Martin (*OECD*)
Marcus Miller (*University of Warwick and CEPR*)
Joaquim Oliveira-Martins (*OECD*)
Richard Portes (*CEPR and Birkbeck College, London*)
Lucrezia Reichlin (*Observatoire français des conjonctures economiques, Paris, and CEPR*)
David Roland-Holst (*OECD Development Centre*)

Gilles Saint-Paul (*DELTA and CEPR*)
Maurice Scott (*Nuffield College, Oxford*)
Albert Simantov (*International Policy Council on Agriculture and Trade, Paris*)
Domenico Siniscalco (*Università degli Studi di Torino and Fondazione Eni Enrico Mattei, Milan and CEPR*)
Andrew Steer (*World Bank*)
Alistair M. Ulph (*University of Southampton and CEPR*)
Dominique van der Mensbrugghe (*OECD Development Centre*)
Sweder van Wijnbergen (*World Bank and CEPR*)
L. Alan Winters (*University of Birmingham and CEPR*)

1 Economic policies for sustainable development

IAN GOLDIN and L. ALAN WINTERS

1 Is growth sustainable?

Sustainable development has come to the top of the international and domestic policy agendas. However, while the notion of 'sustainability' is widely accepted, its precise content has remained elusive. 'Sustainable development' is often defined as development that meets the needs of present generations without compromising the ability of future generations to meet their needs. This and similar definitions of sustainable development underline the intergenerational responsibilities placed on the earth's inhabitants. However, the concept of needs is one of the most complex in economics, and to imbed it in the definition of sustainability is to make intractable an already complex definition. Accordingly, it is necessary to narrow the definition of sustainable development to refer to an economy in which future growth is not compromised by that of the present.

This volume examines the economics of sustainable development. It is concerned with the interaction of economic policies, growth and the environment: in particular with the question: is growth sustainable? The volume draws on economic theory to provide fresh perspectives on this issue. It provides an indication of the 'state of the art' in the economic analysis of sustainability issues, and then extends the economic literature by stretching the theory to incorporate sustainability issues. In line with our comparative advantage and to keep the volume manageable, however, we confine ourselves to the interface of economic theory and sustainability, and thereby neglect a range of elements which are integral to sustainable development. These include considerations of equity, gender, education, civil rights, culture and other aspects of human development. Development cannot and should not simply be associated with economic growth alone and sustainability cannot be confined to main-

1

taining growth. However, the link between sustainable resource use and growth is, perhaps, the key economic question.

The literature on sustainable development has necessarily focused on resource use. However, it is ironic that, while economics is often defined as the science of the allocation of scarce resources, economists have been marginal to the sustainability debate. A review of the growing literature on sustainable development reveals the dearth of formal economic analysis; this stems mainly from environmentalists' general scepticism towards economists and the resulting limited extent of the latter's participation in the debate. Among those economists who have contributed, two groupings may be identified. One is the individuals who have distanced themselves from the mainstream and rejected neoclassical economics on the grounds that it is part of the problem not the solution. In this vein, Daly (1990) and others argue that development cannot be premised on comparative advantage and growth, and that orthodox economic theory is incompatible with sustainable development.

The other set of contributors has sprung to the defence of orthodox economic principles. They comprise a growing group of microeconomists who, under the rubric of environmental or resource economics, have sought to adapt the neoclassical framework to place greater emphasis on environmental degradation. Dasgupta and Heal (1979), Pearce and Turner (1990), and others have sought to demonstrate how the development of appropriate incentives and regulatory structures is not only compatible with sustainable development, but contributes towards it.

The work of this heterogeneous but basically orthodox school has gone a long way in drawing sustainability into the mainstream of microeconomics. However, this progress stands in contrast to the virtual absence of macroeconomic analysis of sustainability issues. This volume aims to redress this imbalance by examining sustainability in the context of economic growth, fiscal policy and the open economy. The volume analyses the relationship between growth oriented economic policies and sustainability. While a number of the contributors are well known for their contributions to the growth debates, the sustainability dimension is for the first time addressed in this volume.

2   The economy-wide dimension: from mess to macro

Until recently the economic analysis of environmental impacts was principally associated with adaptations of traditional cost-benefit analysis. Cost-benefit captures the direct effects of investments on a defined population. It may be extended to account for environmental externalities by the imaginative integration of non-market impacts. However the usefulness of this approach is confined to assessing the direct effects of specific microeconomic actions or projects.

Economists have become increasingly aware that the assessment of the impact of direct interventions needs to be complemented by the analysis of the overall and systemic effects of economy-wide policies. The influence of the economy-wide dimension on policy making has been highlighted in recent years by the introduction of supply-side and structural adjustment policies which include exchange rate, trade and fiscal reforms, which seek to correct relative prices and incentives. The establishment of an appropriate economy-wide incentive framework, together with a facilitating regulatory and institutional structure, is now widely accepted as a central pillar of economic policy in both rich and poor countries.

The effects of economy-wide policies on production and consumption have been explored mainly with respect to agriculture and food. Recent studies by Krueger, Schiff and Valdes (1991), Goldin and Winters (1992) and Goldin (1993) have shown that macroeconomic policies may be more important than sectoral policies. Similarly, the Uruguay Round has stimulated a renewed focus on the interaction of trade reforms and sectoral performance (Goldin, Knudsen and van der Mensbrugghe, 1993). The Uruguay Round has also turned analytic attention to the examination of the links between trade reform and the environment. Low (1992) and Anderson and Blackhurst (1992) have shown that environmental protectionism is misplaced and that it tends to compound environmental degradation, while trade liberalisation facilitates less pollution intensive growth. This work suggests that economy-wide policy distortions may have a significant impact on the environment. Hyde *et al.* (1991) and the 1992 *World Development Report* (World Bank, 1992) have highlighted the need for greater attention to be paid to the economy-wide dimension and such analyses are likely to become ever more frequent given the increasing clamour for more sustainability in economic policies. An indication of this trend may be gleaned from the recent US Congress review of the funding for the World Bank where one witness 'recommended that starting in FY95, appraisals for all structural and sectoral adjustment loans contain "predictions" of how the conditions would affect the natural environment and the poor' (US Congress, 1993).

Unfortunately, economists have neither the theoretical tools nor the empirical data to predict how economy-wide policy reforms impact on the environment. Indeed, the necessary theoretical and empirical analysis is only now being initiated. This volume aims to stimulate such analysis. It is a first step and as befits a new subject area, improvements may be expected as the 'dismal science' of economics evolves through its usual complex and lengthy process of debate and investigation. It is to these theoretical debates and empirical investigations that we now turn.

3   The effects of growth

Following this introductory chapter, this volume is divided into four parts. Part I is devoted to a consideration of the effects of growth, Part II to the analysis and measurement of sustainable development, Part III to domestic economic policies to promote sustainable growth and Part IV to the international economic policy dimension of sustainable growth.

In Chapter 2, Gene Grossman addresses the key question of the relationship between pollution and growth, seeking to examine whether more growth means more pollution or, equivalently, whether anti-pollution objectives imply that growth should be restricted. Drawing on a rich international data set, Grossman reviews the comparative evidence on the relationship between indicators of air and water quality and the scale of economic activity. He finds that economic growth does not always contribute to degradation of the environment. Much hinges on the composition of output; changes in the composition of output towards more environmentally friendly methods of production can more than compensate for higher levels of economic activity.

To the extent that economic growth is linked to environmental degradation, Grossman shows that incomes are also important. For most pollutants, an inverted 'U' or bell-shaped relationship between income and the environment is identified; environmental quality deteriorates in the early stages of economic growth but at higher levels of *per capita* income improvements are evident. The turning points are estimated for the different pollutants, and vary considerably. For example, the levels of suspended solids and toxic metals in air or water increase rapidly as *per capita* incomes approach middle income levels but then improve. Other pollutants continue to rise, before declining at the approach to high income levels. For carbon dioxide and nitrous oxide, the turning points appear to be well beyond the levels of income currently attained by the richest countries.

Whereas the link between *per capita* incomes and environmental quality is made in the chapter, the transmission mechanism is not simply related to composition of output by which higher growth automatically increases the share of cleaner technologies through their substitution for older, dirtier processes. Rather, the link between income and pollution appears to be driven by the demands of the citizens of richer countries for policy changes. This policy dimension is a cause for some optimism as it indicates that the articulation of greater pressure can yield a cleaner environment. The development of cleaner technologies in the richer countries and their transfer to the poorer countries is also potentially a key element; such transfers should be seen as part of a strategy to shift the turning points downwards as later generations of economies achieve development. Development, the chapter shows, is sustainable, but urgent steps are necessary to ensure that poorer countries get over the pollution hump as quickly as possible. Higher incomes and technologies provide one of the keys, but the other is greater voice. This particularly contributes to measures to limit local pollutants which have a direct and immediate effect on health. By contrast, even the richest countries are only now awakening to the threat posed by slower and more indirect threats, such as arise from high carbon dioxide emissions and other cross-border and delayed environmental externalities of economic growth.

The demographic dimension of the growth–environment linkage is the focus of Chapter 3. Richard Baldwin's argument, in a nutshell, is that people make pollution and poverty makes people. Current population growth rates are unsustainable environmentally, so that reducing fertility should be a key element in sustainable development policies. In linking pollution to economic growth, Baldwin notes that while many developing countries are near the end of the explosive stages of their demographic transitions, they appear to be at the beginning of their rapid-emission-growth phases. Consequently, global environmental damage is likely to increase before it declines. However, slowing economic growth would exacerbate the problem, because it would accelerate population growth and slow the adoption of cleaner technologies, with severely negative consequences, particularly in the poorer countries.

Adding the demographic dimension highlights the fact that rising average income and output levels will not be an unmitigated blessing for the environment. The extent to which developing country growth will be associated with a worsening environment depends critically on policy. Policies which reduce demographic pressures are a vital element in sustainable growth. Higher incomes are important, but so too are policies which reduce personal risk and the need for large families. Improvements in the security of employment, education and training, pension policies, social security and the employment of women are especially important in this regard, for in Baldwin's view they entail significant and hitherto largely unaccounted positive externalities for the environment. Population growth has been shown to be inversely related to levels of income; hence economic policies which promote growth and equity will reduce the long-term population–pollution threat to sustainable development.

4   Definition and measurement

Part I highlights the need for better measurement and definition. This is the subject of Part II. Maurice Scott, in Chapter 4, provides a broad perspective on sustainable development. The meaning of 'economic development' has been a subject of continual debate within the economics profession, but in terms of the widely accepted Hicksian definition, economic growth requires that income and consumption be expanded. Maintenance costs, defined very broadly, are incurred in producing income, and if all required maintenance is undertaken, income will not fall through time. Population growth, however, necessitates investment expenditures sufficient to generate at least enough new income to keep *per capita* income constant. The demographic explosion means that the rate of investment necessary to maintain constant *per capita* incomes is high and rising. This, together with increased trans-national interdependence and risk, is placing greater responsibilities on governments. The higher the level of environmental degradation, the greater the pressure on maintenance.

Scott notes that the use of natural resources is part of economic development. It poses a problem from the perspective of economic development only if the required investments derived from these resources or the maintenance required to overcome environmental degradation are not accounted for. The concern is that the costs of environmental maintenance are greater than have been experienced historically, and that future growth of *per capita* income may have to be abandoned. Scott suggests, however, that while there *has* been an increase in the required level of maintenance, it still remains small in relation to world output. Expenditures on environmental maintenance are expected to grow but, even at their peak, they should not be expected to slow world growth significantly. The more serious threats arise from the unknown. These are either in the hands of governments or are largely beyond human control, as in the case of droughts, floods and earthquakes.

Government policies which facilitate growth are vital to ensure sustainable development. Increasingly, governments have to respond to the pressures of higher levels of environmental degradation and to overcome the national and trans-border externalities which are associated with private economic behaviour. From the point of view of sustainable development, governments have an even greater responsibility. Scott reminds us that wars and civil unrest pose at least as severe a threat to economic development as do current environmental preoccupations. In addition to their devastating short-run impact, wars have severe long-run environmental consequences, as may be witnessed in their continued toxic and radioactive fallout. Nuclear, chemical, bio-chemical and other power-generating, industrial and military facilities continue to pose a severe threat. While this has been recognised for many years, so that its articulation no longer appears intellectually exciting or innovative, it is important to remember that these older concerns remain the major cause of instability and risk and, as such, the major threat to sustainable development.

Government action and intergovernmental coordination will be necessary to meet these challenges but, to date, have remained elusive. Indeed the failure to measure and define the global maintenance requirements stands in marked contrast to the various threats posed by environmental degradation.

In Chapter 5 Partha Dasgupta offers a means to incorporate the idea of sustainable development into the measurement of income. By drawing on the theory of welfare economics this chapter provides perspectives on the optimal patterns of resource use over time. Dasgupta identifies the failure of current estimates of net national product (NNP) to measure and deduct the depreciation of environmental resources as a key failure of the orthodoxy. This amounts to imputing the depreciation of environmental capital to be zero. Environmental resources are scarce goods, with positive shadow prices; accounting prices need to reflect this. The failure adequately to price environmental resources means that the private profits attributed to activities that degrade the environment are higher than the social profits they generate. This biases investments and technological choices. If full account were taken of environmental depreciation, profits and national output would be lower. In Costa Rica, for example, it is estimated that, in 1989 alone, the depreciation of the forests, soil and fisheries amounted to around 10 percent of gross domestic product and over a third of gross capital accumulation. Biases such as this have severe consequences everywhere, but are particularly pernicious in poor countries where small fluctuations in levels of income and growth can spell the difference between famine and survival. Equally, the biases in research and development and in demand, which arise from the failure to account for environmental resources, have particularly acute developmental consequences in poor countries.

Dasgupta defines the valuation of environmental accounting prices in terms of the sum of their use value and their option value. The use value captures the value of environmental resources as inputs into the production of tradeable goods and in household production. However, the shadow value of a good may exceed its use value because of its intrinsic worth (for example, the blue whale or a waterfall) or because of uncertainty regarding its future use value and concerns regarding irreversibility (for example, genetic materials). The introduction of option values covers this additional worth. Better measurement and definition, including the incorporation of use and option values into environmental prices would go a long way to focusing economists on the issues of sustainable development.

Andrea Beltratti, Graciela Chichilnisky and Geoffrey Heal tackle another issue of measurement in Chapter 6. They observe that any objective function which discounts future income or welfare relative to current levels leads to a dictatorship of current and near-future generations over distant future ones. In these circumstances sustainability very nearly ceases to be an issue, because in making current policy decisions agents, or more likely governments, can effectively ignore the distant future. The authors propose an alternative objective function which captures the notion of sustainability more directly. Their lim inf criterion, very roughly, seeks the lower limit of the stream of income or utility in the very distant future and seeks to maximise it. It is related to, but not identical to, Rawlsian notions of justice between generations. Beltratti, Chichilnisky and Heal then propose that outcomes should be ranked according to a linear combination of the usual discounted utilitarian objective and the lim inf. This, they argue, allows a balance between current and future generations.

Beltratti, Chichilnisky and Heal are also innovative in the terms of their environmental concern. Their model allows the environment to regenerate itself provided that the 'stock of environment' does not fall below some lower limit, or rise above some maximum amount. The environment is used in production, as a substitute for capital, and also confers direct utility benefits. Its degradation is related to the latter, not the former. Along steady-state growth paths many different combinations of consumption and the stock of environment are feasible. Surprisingly, however, when we use a discounted utilitarian objective function, higher rates of time discount lead to *higher* stocks of environment in steady state. Higher discount rates lead to lower investment and capital stock and thus increase the need for environmental inputs in production, so increasing the steady-state stock of environment.

Confronting this model with the lim inf criterion leads to a 'Green Golden Rule' which equates the marginal rates of transformation and substitution between consumption goods and the environment across steady-state growth paths. The marginal rate of transformation reflects the fact that as consumption, and hence output, rises, environmental damage occurs which, through the regenerative process, reduces the stock of environment all along the steady-state path. The optimal path thus reflects the trade off between consumption and the environment. Optimal consumption lies below the maximal sustainable level because the direct utility benefits of the environment make it attractive to surrender some consumption for more environment.

The mathematics of lim inf are complex, especially if combined with a utilitarian objective, and the environmental model used here is quite specialised (see Alistair Ulph's Discussion), but Beltratti, Chichilnisky and Heal provide an intuitively attractive way of conceptualising sustainability.

5   Domestic policies for sustainable growth

Whereas Parts I and II of the volume address the conceptual and broad analytic issues associated with the economics of sustainable development, Part III aims to provide two concrete examples of how sustainability concerns may be addressed at the country level.

Increasingly, water is perceived as a serious and fixed constraint to development. African, Middle Eastern and Asiatic countries face the prospect of water shortages sharply attenuating their development process. For these countries, sustainable development requires the putting in place of alternative policies for water production and allocation. In Chapter 7, Ian Goldin and David Roland-Holst illustrate the differential effects of direct and indirect policies to influence water use patterns, including changes in water prices and international trade reforms. The results indicate that there is considerable scope for substitution between the two sets of policies and that a combination of economy-wide and direct economic policies may ensure that water use is compatible with sustainable economic growth.

The novel introduction of water into a computable general equilibrium (CGE) model facilitates the analysis of the relationship between natural resources, economic incentive and trade policies, as an example of the interaction of economy-wide and sector specific reforms. The sustainability of water resources in Morocco is shown to be dependent upon a more rational approach to resource use in general. Sustainable water resource development is predicated upon a reallocation of water resources away from irrigated agriculture, which currently consumes over 90 percent of all Morocco's water. Whereas higher water charges are shown to yield considerable water savings, they also serve to slow economic growth and increase rural poverty. Greater efficiency in water use, on the other hand, and the reallocation of water to higher-value production is shown to be facilitated by economy-wide policy reforms and notably by trade liberalisation. In combination, the stimulus of trade reform plus the water-saving effects of water charges offers an attractive and sustainable policy package.

In Chapter 8, Rosemary Clarke and L. Alan Winters explore a similar set of issues for China. Here the issue is global sustainability in the face of the warming effects of greenhouse gas emissions. China is likely to become the world's greatest emitter of carbon dioxide in the next century and a major source of methane. To date, China has avoided commitments to abate her greenhouse gas emissions, but has started to question her very heavy use of coal because of its local adverse effects such as acid rain and particulate related health problems. An added complication in China is that, at least until very recently, China had highly distorted extremely inefficient energy markets, which led to extremely inefficient fuel use and losses of national income. Clarke and Winters briefly describe the relevant institutions of the Chinese economy. They then use a CGE model to explore whether carbon taxes or general pricing reforms allow welfare improvements, taking into account not only production/consumption decisions but also local and global pollutants.

A simple and small-scale CGE model cannot produce precise predictions of the effects of different policies, but the broad policy messages are clear. China can reduce her carbon dioxide emissions quite significantly while increasing her own welfare. The latter effect, however, arises only from the fact that curtailing energy use and, more particularly, switching away from coal reduces other noxious emissions. The authors consider sulphur dioxide, the nitrous oxides and particulates, and even using fairly conservative estimates of their harmful effects find that a carbon tax has sufficient benefits in these emissions to compensate for the loss of output it induces. Correspondingly policies designed to curb these emissions could have beneficial effects on carbon emissions, but only if they operate on overall fuel use rather than introducing cleaning technologies. The latter worsen carbon dioxide emissions, for they reduce the thermal efficiency of fuels.

Clarke and Winters also ask whether correcting the distortions in fuel markets would reduce pollution. The answer, so far as 'generic' policies are concerned, is 'no', because while some fuels are subsidised others, notably electricity, are effectively heavily taxed. Thus, for example, equating all consumer prices to marginal production costs reduces direct coal and oil use strongly but increases their indirect consumption by stimulating private electricity use. Similar factors beset 'getting industrial prices right', coupled with the fact that before acting on the prices of industrial inputs one must ensure that industries pass on the corrective price shocks to their customer industries in a constructive fashion. Thus while China could devise tax packages that abate carbon dioxide emissions strongly these would have to be more complex than the mere removal of price distortions. On the other hand, such abatement will not be costly overall because of its strong secondary benefits on other, local pollutants.

6   International policies for sustainable growth

Policies for sustainable development raise problems of international coordination in two fashions. First, global or trans-border pollutants such as carbon dioxide or nuclear fallout cause direct negative externalities with all the well-known problems of free-riding in policy decisions. In their most extreme form these are reflected in the tension between OECD countries' desires that developing countries should curb their emissions of greenhouse and ozone-depleting gases, and the latter's understandable concerns not to do anything that might jeopardise their developmental objectives. Second, even if pollutants are wholly local, there are international implications to the extent that sustainability spills over into industrial competitiveness. If exports or direct foreign investment generate rents, non-cooperative environmental policies will be set at non-optimal levels if they have any impact on such flows.

Jean-Marc Burniaux, John Martin, Joaquim Oliveira-Martins and Dominique van der Mensbrugghe consider some of these issues in Chapter 9. They use the global model GREEN to explore the prospects of obtaining global agreement on greenhouse gas abatement. Abatement by the OECD countries alone will not reduce emission levels over the next century sufficiently to affect global warming materially. However, to date the developing countries have not shown much enthusiasm for abatement because they perceive it as being inimical to their development aspirations. To bring them into a global agreement, therefore, seems likely to require significant financial and/or technological transfers. Burniaux *et al.* use GREEN, with its fully articulated sub-models of international trade and carbon dioxide emission, to explore the feasibility of such transfers supporting an agreement. Their conclusions are sobering.

First, they ask what level of technical progress in energy use would be required in developing countries in order to stabilise emissions by 2050. It is implausibly high. That is, energy use in efficiency units will have to fall if stability is to be achieved. Second, an OECD carbon tax coupled with revenue transfer to developing countries is unlikely to induce sufficient technical change to achieve stability. Even if all transfers were devoted to efficiency-improving investment, only a relatively small proportion of developing countries' capital stocks would be updated and even these benefits would be partly offset by the positive income effect of transfers on energy use. Third, and more optimistically, a global carbon tax with revenue transfers would achieve a sizable abatement without imposing an excessive burden on developing countries. According to GREEN, the former Soviet Union and the Central and East European Countries will gain from such a policy (because the tax will offset their existing fuel distortions), but for nearly all other countries there will be a loss, albeit of manageable proportions.

Chapter 10 also considers agreement over carbon dioxide emissions and technology. Carlo Carraro and Domenico Siniscalco explore the theory of linked international agreements among sub-sets of countries. Their starting point is that for purely global pollutants, while coalitions of countries may agree to abate emissions, those coalitions will be very small. The problem is essentially one of free-riding. They then ask whether a coalition could expand by buying new members in by means of transfers while still remaining better off themselves. If countries are symmetric the answer is 'no'. Imagine we have achieved an equilibrium coalition in the absence of transfers: each country in the coalition is better off than it would be if it left the coalition and each outsider better off than if it joined the coalition. If countries are all identical, if one outsider joined the coalition it would pay one of the original members to leave it to restore the optimum size. Clearly no original member is going to pay money, i.e. offer a transfer, to bring this situation about, so *without commitment among existing members*, transfers cannot enlarge the coalition.

Introducing commitment of various kinds can allow transfers to enlarge a coalition, but apparently not by much. Hence Cararro and Siniscalco suggest linking two sets of negotiations. If in the new negotiation for, say, sharing the fruits of research and development, countries can be excluded if they fail to sign the environmental agreement, the environmental coalition can be greatly enlarged, quite possibly to include all countries. Chapter 10 formalises this argument and proves the stability and optimality of the resulting coalitions.

Chapter 11, by Ravi Kanbur, Michael Keen and Sweder van Wijn-bergen, concentrates on local pollutants and shows that if environmental standards affect industry profits, the resulting competition between regulatory regimes will generally lead to too little environmental protection. Where a small country and a large country interact over environmental standards, the former will have an incentive for laxer standards than the latter. By lowering standards the small country government will harm its citizens directly by exposing them to more pollution, but it will also benefit them by attracting inflows of rent-generating investment from the large country. Under plausible conditions the small country will attract a larger inflow from the large country per 'unit of laxity' than the large country can attract from the small. Hence the offsetting profits to environmental laxity are greater and the standards set are weaker in the small country. Kanbur, Keen and van Wijnbergen show that environmental standards set in this non-cooperative way are laxer than either country wishes. They also observe that increasing integration between the two countries exacerbates the problems: as other barriers to firm and goods mobility are reduced, such flows become more sensitive to differences in environmental standards.

The usual solution proposed for these problems is to harmonise standards across the two countries somewhere between the two initial standards chosen. This, however, is unlikely to work because it *always* reduces the small country's welfare below its non-cooperative level! Suppose they harmonise at the large country's non-cooperative environmental standard: clearly this harms the small country because in the absence of constraints it chose a different best response to the large country using this value. Now consider relaxing the common standard from that level: the small country suffers more pollution, but now gets no investment advantage and so becomes even worse off. The larger country can benefit from harmonisation provided that the common standard is close enough to its own non-cooperative level. To get a Pareto-improving common standard, however, requires that a 'tight' standard be adopted and that the large country compensate the small – not a very likely prospect, one might think, in the light of the Rio Summit.

A more constructive approach exists, however – to set common minimum standards. The small country will adopt these while the large country will probably opt for tighter ones. The minimum standard defuses the destructive tit-for-tat in standards and thus neutralises the worst effects of the strategic interaction. It is probably also easier to negotiate than harmonisation and so Chapter 11 ends on a relatively optimistic note.

7   Conclusions

A number of themes have emerged from the research described in this book. First, while it is important to assess and provide for maintenance costs in the world economy, these do not appear to be unduly high. In most cases minor changes in techniques of production or life-style seem likely to be sufficient to preserve options for future generations, and the total cost should be equivalent to a reduction in GDP of no more than a few percent. There is no reason to believe that long-run economic growth will be adversely affected by environmental policies and, indeed, growth could even be enhanced as new technologies are explored. Overall, economic growth and development are perfectly consistent with environmental protection, as is trade liberalisation.

Second, several chapters make clear the importance of prices and incentives in pursuing environmental objectives. They stress, however, that it will be up to governments to initiate policy changes and that there will be increasing pressure for them to do so. Both in channelling that pressure constructively and in intergovernmental relations political economy and institutional design will be important factors. By understanding the ways in which players interact we should be able to avoid creating the poor institutions that generate poor policy.

Third, environmental issues must be tackled on a wide front with attention paid to their causes as well as their symptoms. For example, chapters in this volume note the importance of both security issues and of social policy.

Fourth, environmental protection does not entail trade protectionism. Indeed environmental efficiency will be enhanced by taking advantage of the opportunities for specialisation offered by trade liberalisation. One must recognise, however, that trade and environmental distortions may interact and that careful analysis should consider both.

More research will be needed to provide greater precision to the relationships between economic policies and sustainable development. In highlighting a number of the crucial linkages this volume indicates the breadth and significance of the economy-wide dimension to environmental management. Public demand has placed sustainability at the top of the political agenda, but the economics profession has generally been slow to respond. This volume reveals the frontier and provides a point of departure for further analysis. It is hoped that it will provide the basis for a lively debate and stimulate further research in order to advance our understanding of the economics of sustainable development.

REFERENCES

Anderson, K. and Blackhurst, R. (eds.) (1992) *The Greening of World Trade Issues*, Hemel Hempstead: Harvester Wheatsheaf
Daly, H. (1990) 'Toward some operational principles of sustainable development', *Ecological Economics*, 2
Dasgupta, P. and Heal, G. (1979) *Economic Theory and Exhaustible Resources*, Cambridge: Cambridge University Press
Goldin, I. and Winters, L.A. (eds.) (1992) *Open Economics: Structural Adjustment and Agriculture*, Cambridge: Cambridge University Press
Goldin, I., Knudsen, O. and van der Mensbrugghe, D. (1993) *Trade Liberali-*

sation: Global Economic Implications, Paris: Organisation for Economic Cooperation and Development (OECD) and Washington, DC: World Bank

Goldin, I. (ed.) (1993), *Economic Reform, Trade and Agricultural Development*, London: Macmillan

Hyde, W. *et al.* (1991) 'Forest economics and policy analysis: an overview', *World Bank Discussion Paper*, **134**, Washington, DC: World Bank

Krueger, A., Schiff, M. and Valdes, A. (1991) *The Political Economy of Agricultural Pricing Policies*, Washington, DC: World Bank

Low, P. (ed.) (1992) 'International trade and the environment', *World Bank Discussion Paper*, **159**, Washington, DC: World Bank

Pearce, D. and Turner, R. (1990) *Economics of Natural Resources and the Environment*, Hemel Hempstead: Harvester Wheatsheaf.

US Congress (1993), Evidence on the Replenishment of the IDA, Washington, DC: *US Congressional Record*

World Bank (1992), *World Development Report: 1992: Development and the Environment*, Washington, DC: World Bank

Part One
Growth and the environment

2 Pollution and growth: what do we know?

GENE M. GROSSMAN

There is growing concern that continued expansion of the world economy will cause irreparable damage to the earth's environment and a reduced quality of life for future generations. This fear rests on two intuitive notions: first, that more output requires more inputs and so the earth's 'sources' (of natural resources) inevitably will be depleted by continued growth of production and consumption; and second, that more output means more emissions and wastes, and so the earth's 'sinks' inevitably will become overburdened by continued economic growth. Those who are most alarmed by this scenario see the possibility that economic activity will eventually exceed the 'carrying capacity' of the biosphere (see, e.g. Daly, 1977), with dire consequences for human and animal welfare. To avoid such a tragic outcome, they argue, it is necessary for global economic expansion to cease and for humankind to make the transition to a steady-state economy.

Others have noted that the *scale* of economic activity is but one determinant of the rate of depletion of natural resources and the rate of production of waste materials and gases (see, e.g. World Bank, 1992; Radetzki, 1992). Equally important are the *composition* of economic output and the *techniques* used to produce it. If, along with economic growth, there comes a transformation in the structure of the world economy, as well as the substitution of cleaner and resource-conserving technologies for dirtier, resource-using technologies, then growth can continue to provide ever higher standards of material living without threatening the nonmaterial aspects of human wellbeing.

A simple decomposition can be used to make this point clear. Let Y_t represent the scale of economic activity (i.e. GDP) at time t, s_{it} the share of output deriving from sector i, and a_{it} the amount of waste (or pollution) generated per unit of output in sector i. Then, by definition, total emissions of some pollutant at time t are given by

$$E_y = \Sigma_i a_{it} s_{it} Y_t. \tag{1}$$

Over time, emissions will evolve according to

$$\hat{E} = \hat{Y} + \Sigma_i \lambda_i s_i + \Sigma_i \lambda_i \hat{a}_i, \tag{2}$$

where λ_i is the share of the total amount of emissions of the pollutant generated by economic activity i, and a 'hat' over a variable denotes a rate of change. The first term in equation (2) represents the scale effect feared by environmental pessimists: *all else equal*, an increase in output means an equiproportionate increase in pollution. But this effect may be offset by two others. The second term on the right-hand side of (2) is a composition effect: emissions may fall if the shares in GDP of relatively cleaner economic activities rise over time. The third term represents the technique effect: if technological progress, market-induced substitution, or government regulation cause less-polluting technologies to replace dirtier ones, then the rate of emissions may fall over time. Finally, we should note that the relationship between the flow of emissions and the stock of the pollutant in the biosphere hinges on the regenerative capacity of the environment; for example, we might have

$$P_t = P_{t-1} + E_t + N + \delta(P^* - P_{t-1}) \tag{3}$$

where P_t is the stock of the pollutant at time t, N represents baseline emissions per unit time from nonanthropogenic sources, P^* is the amount of the pollutant to which the stock would tend to converge absent any new emissions, and δ reflects the speed of convergence to the natural level. With this regenerative process, P_t approaches a constant so long as E_t does, but environmental degradation may continue for a while even after emissions have levelled off (or even fallen).

There is some scope for optimism, at least with respect to some types of environmental risks. This is especially true for marketed, nonrenewable resources such as metals, minerals, and energy, where the evidence does not support the view of increasing economic scarcity. Rather, perceived shortages – be they potential or actual – have generated sharp price hikes and thereby created powerful incentives for substitution of other inputs and for resource-saving technological developments. The most pressing environmental problems today involve instead the regenerative but currently nonmarketed resources; that is, resources for which property rights are difficult to define or simply are poorly established or enforced under current institutional arrangements. For these 'shared' resources, the users do not face the true scarcity value that gives appropriate private incentives for conservation.

As concerns these currently nonmarketed resources, there are some reasons to hope that continued economic growth may be *part* of the solution to the problem in some cases, rather than being the source of the problem itself. First, the 'pattern of development' that has been documented by Syrquin (1989) suggests that the structural transformations that accompany growth have beneficial side-effects on the environment. Countries typically follow a path that entails an initial shift of resources from agriculture to industry, but a subsequent shift from industry to services. Once the turning point is reached, the share of services in GDP rises monotonically over time, at least within the range of experience that we have witnessed so far in the wealthiest countries. Of the three broad categories of economic activity, it would seem (and the evidence reviewed below corroborates this) that services do the least damage to the environment. Furthermore, within the industrial sector, we have seen increasing shares of high-tech production, which seem to involve less intensive use of many materials and natural resources than the types of industrial activities that came before.

Second, growth and development in the low- and middle-income countries often involves the replacement of old capital equipment by new, and the replacement of older technologies by newer ones. Due to the increased awareness of environmental problems in the developed countries, these new capital goods and newer technologies tend to be more environmentally friendly than previous generations of capital goods and production methods. This may impart a pro-environment bias to the growth process in the developing world.

Finally, and most importantly, economic growth generates increased prosperity, almost as a matter of definition. As *per capita* incomes rise, citizens may express greater demands for a cleaner and healthier environment. This is not to say that the poor have a greater tolerance for pollution or a different taste for clean water, clean air, or for preserving that habitat for future generations. Rather, the smaller budgets of these individuals forces upon them a more difficult and unpleasant trade off between providing subsistence goods for themselves and their families and expressing demands for the nonmaterial aspects of their welfare.

For some initially nonmarketed resources, availability may appear limitless when the level of economic activity is quite low. Then it may not seem necessary for the government to define and enforce property rights or to introduce regulations and controls. In such cases, growth is bound to be resource-using in its initial stages, because private agents will see little personal benefit from conserving on the use of common property. For some of these resources, it will be possible to establish property rights as their scarcity increases, and institutions may respond to the changing perception of the need for these rights (Radetzki, 1992). But for other types of resources it may be impossible to enforce property rights. Then the government must be called upon to introduce taxes or regulations, so that negative externalities can be internalised. While there is no guarantee that governments will respond in this way to increased demand by the populace for a clean environment, it is certainly possible that this will be the case.

Several factors combine to determine whether a certain type of environmental degradation intensifies with greater economic activity, or is alleviated by either the changed composition of output or the greater prosperity that attends economic growth, or first one and then the other. Among these are the salience of the environmental damage, the cost of avoiding such damage, and the degree to which the harm inflicted by the pollution coincides in its geographic and temporal extent with the political jurisdiction of the bodies empowered to establish property rights and enforce regulations. Political demands for regulation are likely to be focused first on those forms of pollution that have obvious and immediate health impacts, and those that can be abated at relatively low cost. On the other hand, there may be less political will to control environmental damage when the adverse effects are perceived as uncertain or when the costs of that damage will be borne by individuals living in a different political jurisdiction or in a different era. We would expect, therefore, that output growth may impart continuing harm to the environment along those dimensions where the adverse consequences will be shared widely by peoples in different regions or countries, or where the effects on health and welfare will not be evident until well into the future. Other considerations that enter into the relationship between growth and a particular form of pollution include the extent to which the pollutant is produced jointly with others and the extent to which the pollutant is produced intensively in sectors whose share of GDP tends to rise or fall over time.

In the remainder of this chapter I will review the empirical evidence on the relationship between economic output and various dimensions of air and water quality. In section 1, I describe the various data sets that are available for examining the relationship between environmental quality and growth and the methodology that has been used in addressing this issue. Sections 2 and 3 focus on air and water quality, respectively. In each case I review the anthropogenic sources of the various pollutants, the environmental risks that they pose, and the method and scope of abatement. I then discuss what is currently known about the relationship between that pollutant and growth. Section 4 discusses some policy implications of this body of research.

1   Data and estimation

1.1   Data sources

In order to study the relationship between the scale and composition of economic activity and the extent of damage to the environment it is necessary to have observations on environmental quality in different geographic locations or different points in time (or both) that have been measured or estimated by comparable methods. Several interesting data sets exist for this purpose, which have only recently attracted the attention of economists.

One important source of data is the Global Environmental Monitoring System (GEMS), a joint effort of the World Health Organisation (WHO) and the United Nations Environmental Program (UNEP).[1] GEMS was initiated in 1974 as a means to promote and coordinate the collection of environmental data in different countries. The GEMS air monitoring project focuses on air quality in urban settings. Frequent measurements are taken of concentrations of sulphur dioxide (SO_2) and suspended particulate matter in a network of monitoring stations.[2] These stations are located in a changing sample of cities in a variety of developed and developing countries. Many cities have monitoring stations in more than one location and the participating cities have been chosen to be fairly representative of the geographic conditions that exist in different regions of the world. The data span the period from 1977 to the present, with 42 countries represented in the sample of SO_2 and 37 in the sample for suspended particles. The data are published by WHO in the series *Air Quality in Selected Urban Areas*, and form the basis for some of the analysis reported in Grossman and Krueger (1993a, 1993b).

Water quality has been monitored at selected rivers, lakes, and groundwater aquifers that are major sources of water supply for municipalities, irrigation, livestock, and selected industries. By January 1990, a total of 488 monitoring stations in 64 countries had participated in the project, with 423 stations in 58 countries still active. Of these, 287 were river stations, 60 lake stations, and 76 were stations monitoring groundwater. The data set includes measures for the period from 1979 through 1990 for 13 basic physical, chemical and microbiological variables, as well as globally significant variables comprising such pollutants as heavy metals and pesticides and a variety of site specific optional variables. The data are available from WHO's Collaborating Centre for Surface and Groundwater Quality in the Canada Centre for Inland Waters, Burlington, Ontario, and are published triennially in a series entitled *GEMS/Water Data Summary*. Grossman and Krueger (1993a) use these data to study the relationship between economic growth and water quality.

The advantage of the GEMS data is that they provide actual measurements of environmental quality, i.e. concentrations of pollutants detected by sophisticated monitoring equipment. The disadvantage of these data is that they relate to local conditions at a limited number of specific locations. Moreover, despite the intentions of the GEMS organisation, there may be reasons to suspect the representativeness of these data. It seems likely that there will exist a bias in the selection process toward the monitoring of sites where pollution is deemed to be an actual or potential problem. The econometric problems associated with sampling that is based on the size of the dependent variable are well known. Data on countries' aggregate emissions of pollutants would not suffer from these problems. Unfortunately, emissions from all sources cannot be directly measured, nor are there comparable surveys for different countries that would allow total emissions to be estimated. Instead, emissions must be estimated from production data using *ad hoc* assumptions about the technological relationships in different countries between the amount of the pollutant emitted and outputs of various types of goods.

The World Resources Institute (1990) publishes estimates of emissions of various air pollutants for a wide sample of countries which have been calculated by multiplying aggregate national consumption of several types of fuel by coefficients that reflect the contemporaneous abatement practices in each country. Figures are available for many different pollutants, with over 100 countries represented in the data, but unfortunately only a few pollutants have estimates spanning a period of 10 years and coverage of more than a few low- and middle-income countries. These pollutants – sulphur dioxide, suspended particulates, oxides of nitrogen, and carbon monoxide – form the basis of the analysis in Selden and Song (1992). A similar method has been used by Oak Ridge National Laboratory (1992) to estimate emissions of carbon dioxide in a panel of 197 countries and territories for the period from 1951 to 1986. Oak Ridge applies emissions coefficients to national data for consumption of different types of fuel, and also estimates the CO_2 released in the course of cement manufacture. The relationship of national income to estimated CO_2 emissions has been studied by Holtz-Eakin and Selden (1992).

Finally, a large panel data set exists for measures of concentrations of six criteria air pollutants at monitoring stations across the US. The Aerometric Information Retrieval System coordinated by the US Environmental Protection Agency contains data from approximately 6000 monitoring stations going back in most cases to the mid-1970s, and in some cases as far as 1957. Most of these stations were established by the states prior to coordination by the EPA, although many of the stations now participate in the State and Local Air Monitor System (SLAMS) that was put into effect in 1981. The SLAMS stations must meet common federal requirements for siting, sampling methods, and administrative procedures. In many ways, the US data are least suitable for the purposes at hand. First, many of the stations were set up explicitly to monitor the highest concentrations expected to occur in an area, or to determine the impact on ambient pollution levels of significant sources or source categories (e.g. power stations).[3] Second, the data relate to narrow geographic areas, whereas regulatory policy often is set at the state or even the federal level. Third, the variance in income levels among the counties represented in the sample is relatively small. One advantage of these data, however, is that they can be linked to data on the composition of output taking place in the county in which the monitor is located, so that the effects of economic structure on pollution outcomes can be examined. This has been the focus of an ongoing study by Grossman *et al.* (1994).

1.2   Estimation methods

The recent studies of the relationship between growth and pollution use a common (and simple) methodology. The time-series and cross-section data on the concentration or estimated emissions of the pollutant are regressed on a function of the real *per capita* GDP for the area to which the observation applies, plus a number of other explanatory variables. Usually, a cubic function of the level of real *per capita* income has been used, although in some cases other functions (such as a cubic in the log of income) has been tried as well. Most of the studies have allowed for a lagged effect of income on pollution, inasmuch as (1) the concentration of the pollutant in the water or air may be slow to adjust to the current level of emissions, and (2) it may take a while for the demands for improved environmental quality that result from an increase in income to translate into government policy measures and then to change the behaviour of households and firms.

The question that has been posed – what is the observed relationship between the scale of economic activity and pollution? – suggests a reduced-form approach. That is, we are interested in both the direct and indirect consequences of economic growth. Therefore, the various studies (with one exception, to be described below) omit explanatory variables that may affect pollution outcomes but that themselves evolve in the course of economic development. The independent variables that have been included, besides ones relating to the scale of economic activity, are those exogenous factors that can help to explain why measured pollution at one monitoring station may differ from that at another, even if the scale and nature of the nearby economic activity is similar. For the regressions that used air quality measures as the dependent variable, the regressors include (where available) a measure of the population density of the city or country where the station is located, an indication of whether the monitoring station is located in a city, suburban or rural location, an indication of whether the land near the station is used for residential, commercial, or industrial purposes, and variables that reflect the particular characteristics of the monitoring station (such as the height of the measuring probe, the type of instrument used, the elevation of the station, and the proximity of the station to a coastline or a desert). For the regressions seeking to explain water quality, the explanatory variables included a measure of the average water temperature at the monitoring station, which has in most cases a significant effect on the concentration of the various pollutants, and which happens to be correlated with the income variable. All of the studies also include one or more time variables (either a linear time trend or a dummy variable for each year) to allow for the possibility that the relationship between GDP and pollution may be changing over time. This time dependence may stem from an increased awareness of environmental problems or from technological improvements that reduce the cost of abatement.

Despite the inclusion of variables intended to capture location specific characteristics that might affect the concentration of a particular pollutant at a given monitoring station or the aggregate emissions of a pollutant in a given country, there are likely to be other omitted site or country specific factors that influence the level of pollution in a particular location. These factors may not change (or may change only very slowly) over time. In the event, the residual term in the various regressions will not be independently distributed: rather, there will be a positive correlation in the prediction errors for a particular monitoring station or country over time. These considerations argue for a random-effects model that allows for a site specific component of the error term. Some of the results reported below have been estimated by the method of generalised least squares, in recognition of these random effects.

One study (Grossman et al., 1994) computes a set of regressions (for six criteria air pollutants at monitoring stations across the US) that includes the composition of economic activity as an explanatory variable. In particular, these authors have used the share of income generated in an exhaustive set of 11 different economic sectors for the county in which the monitoring station is located. The reason for including these variables was twofold. First, it is possible to examine whether the composition of activity in fact matters for environmental outcomes, as *a priori* reasoning suggests that it should. Second, by comparing the regressions that include and exclude the variables describing the composition of economic activity, it is possible to draw some tentative conclusions about the relative importance of the different channels through which economic growth may affect environmental quality (i.e. is improvement in environmental quality mostly due to a change in the composition of output or mostly due to a change in techniques?).

2   Air quality

2.1   Urban and local air pollution

Urban air pollution is among the most salient forms of environmental degradation. The pollution is densely populated areas is often visible, is obviously man-made, and poses clear and immediate health risks to many people living in a concentrated geographic area. It would seem, therefore, that citizens might demand of their leaders that attention be turned to this problem relatively early on, once a modest standard of material living has been achieved.

Perhaps the most serious health problems stem from exposure to *suspended particulate matter* (SPM). These health consequences include a high incidence of respiratory diseases such as coughs, asthma, bronchitis and emphysema, and increased mortality rates among children and the elderly, especially for those who are already weak. Particulates, especially the finer ones, can also carry heavy metals (many of which are poisonous and/or carcinogenic) into the deepest, most sensitive parts of the lungs (Worldwatch Institute, 1990). Anthropogenic sources of SPM include the sooty smoke from incomplete fuel combustion, and vehicle exhaust, particularly from diesel engines. Liquid particulates can be caused by various chemical reactions in the atmosphere involving gaseous pollutants, such as SO_2, and water. Particulate emissions can readily be reduced by installing control equipment (such as dust removal equipment in coal-fired utilities) and by switching to fuels other than coal. Table 2.1 shows the WHO's recommended standards for this and the other air pollutants.

Grossman and Krueger (1993a, 1993b) studied the relationship between concentrations of SPM and real *per capita* GDP using the GEMS/Air data. Some typical findings for 'dark matter' – the finer and more hazardous form of SPM – are reproduced in figure 2.1. In this and subsequent figures, we show the 'extra' concentration of the pollutant that one would expect to find (based on the regressions) in a location with the *per capita*

Table 2.1. *World Health Organisation guideline values based on effects other than cancer or odour/annoyance*

Pollutant	Time-weighted average	Average time
Dark matter	50 μg c^2	1 year
Airborne lead	0.5–1.0 μg c^2	1 year
Sulphur dioxide	50 μg c^2	1 year
Carbon monoxide	10 μg c^2	8 hours
Nitrous dioxide	150 μg c^2	24 hours

Source: World Health Organisation (1987).

GDP given along the horizontal axis, as compared to a hypothetical location with a *per capita* GDP of zero and all other independent variables the same. The figures also report mean observations in our samples (so that the magnitude of the predicted effects of income variation can be gauged) and label *per capita* income levels at turning points in the relationship between income and pollution.

For both the median and 95th percentile of daily observations, concentrations of SPM were found to rise with the scale of economic activity until a *per capita* income level of approximately $5000 (1985 US$) is reached, but to fall with further increases in GDP beyond that point. Since these results make use of the Summers and Heston (1991) income data that correct for differences in purchasing power, the turning point corresponds to a level of income such as in Malaysia or Mexico in 1988. Selden and Song (1992) find a similar inverted U-shaped relationship between SPM and income using the data on estimated aggregate emissions *per capita*, but with a peak occurring at a *per capita* income level of just over $8000. They interpret the higher turning point as indicating that urban air receives more immediate attention in developing countries than air in rural areas, because pollution in cities poses more immediate health risks and because improvements in urban air quality can perhaps be achieved at relatively low cost by shifting some sources to less densely populated areas. While these interpretations are possible, we cannot rule out the possibility that the result may be an artifact of the way in which the data on estimated emissions are constructed.

Looking at data for monitoring stations in the US, we find that concentrations of SPM do not vary much with county output until income reaches about $17,000 (1987 US$), whereupon the concentrations do begin to fall (see figure 2.2).[4] We note, of course, that the levels of SPM in

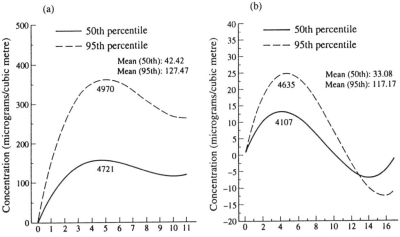

Figure 2.1   Urban air quality
(a) Suspended particulates (dark matter)
(b) Sulphur dioxide
Source: Grossman and Krueger (1993b).

most locations in the US are already well within suggested norms by WHO. Moreover, the major effect of income growth on air quality may come through federal and state regulations, rather than through policies implemented at the local level. Comparing the regressions that include and exclude the variables representing the composition of output in the country, we can conclude that the reduced concentrations of SPM in the highest-income counties probably reflect tighter government restrictions rather than a more benign mix of activities. The regressions do show, however, that the composition of economic activity matters for measured concentrations of SPM: particulates are highest in counties with a great deal of wholesale trade, transportation and public utilities, and FIRE (finance, insurance, and real estate), and lowest in counties that engage in farming, private services, government services, and retail trade.

Very significant health risks also are posed by *airborne lead*. High concentrations of lead are known to impair circulatory, reproductive, nervous, and kidney systems, and are suspected of causing hyperactivity and lowered learning ability in children (Worldwatch Institute, 1990). The primary source of airborne lead has been vehicular emissions, with about 10 percent due to industrial processes and stationary combustion sources (CFR, 1992).

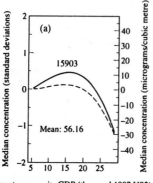

County *per capita* GDP (thousand 1987 US$)

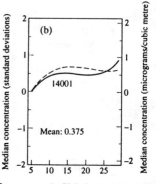

County *per capita* GDP (thousand 1987 US$)

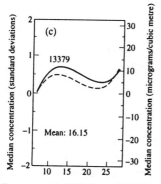

County *per capita* GDP (thousand 1987 US$)

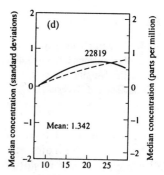

County *per capita* GDP (thousand 1987 US$)

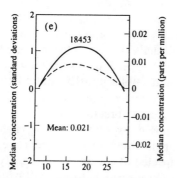

County *per capita* GDP (thousand 1987 US$)

——— Without output consumption

– – – With output consumption

Unfortunately, no international data are available for comparing the concentrations of airborne lead in countries at different levels of development. But an inverted U-shaped relationship similar to that for SPM is highly plausible inasmuch as middle-income countries have many more motor vehicles *per capita* than very poor countries, while the OECD countries have virtually solved the problem of lead in the air by applying increasingly strict standards that limit lead additives to gasoline. Such standards have recently been introduced in Malaysia, Mexico, and Thailand, but many other developing countries have yet to follow suit (World Bank, 1992).

Figure 2.2 shows the estimated relationship between concentrations of airborne lead and local income levels using the US data. As is evident, the scale of local economic activity has little effect on measured concentrations of lead, looking across counties in the US. This is probably because lead emissions now are only a small fraction of what they were in the early 1970s in all areas of the US, and because airborne lead is no longer perceived to be a serious environmental problem. The regressions show a statistically significant but quantitatively small effect of the composition of economic activity on lead concentrations, with lead pollution being most sensitive to the shares of mining, FIRE, and retail trade (the latter two probably because they are concentrated in urban centres).

Sulphur dioxide also poses local health risks, but perhaps not so grave as with SPM and lead. The negative health effects of SO_2 include a higher incidence of respiratory diseases such as coughs, asthma, bronchitis and emphysema. These effects are exacerbated by the presence of particulates. At high levels of concentration, SO_2 is also thought to cause increased death rates among individuals with heart and lung diseases (Conservation

---

◄ **Figure 2.2   Air quality and local income across the US**
   (a) **Suspended particulate matter**
   (b) **Airborne lead**
   (c) **Sulphur dioxide**
   (d) **Carbon monoxide**
   (e) **Nitrogen dioxide**

Note: All regressions estimated by ordinary least squares. All regressions include a cubic function of contemporaneous income and a cubic function of the average income in the three years prior to observation. Regressions for suspended particulates and airborne use median concentrations calculated from daily observations; regressions for sulphur dioxide, carbon monoxide, and nitrogen dioxide use median concentration calculated from hourly observations. Regressions use 'intermediate samples' described in Grossman, Krueger and Laity (1994).

Foundation, 1982). SO_2 also has more far-reaching impacts on the environment: it is a major cause of acid rain, which is known to do serious damage to trees, crops, buildings, and aquatic ecosystems.

Sulphur dioxide is emitted during the burning of fossil fuels, especially those with a high sulphur content. Other sources include automobile exhaust, nonferrous ore smelting, petroleum refining, and automobile exhaust. Emissions can be controlled by the installation of flue gas desulphurisation equipment (scrubbers) on polluting facilities, and by switching electricity-generating and home-heating capacity to lower sulphur grades of coal or away from coal altogether.

Figure 2.1 shows the relationship between concentrations of SO_2 and *per capita* income levels, as estimated using the GEMS/Air data for urban air quality by Grossman and Krueger (1993b). Both the median and 95th percentile of daily observations rise with the scale of economic activity until a country reaches a level of *per capita* income of between $4000 and $5000, and fall sharply thereafter. This finding is consistent with the World Bank (1992) perception that many middle- and high-income countries have been able to address the problem of SO_2 in the past decade, and that the problem now is worst in the low- (and some middle-) income nations. Again, Selden and Song (1992) find a somewhat higher turning point when they use data for aggregate emissions. Estimated emissions *per capita* appear to peak in a country with an income of $8643.

The results using the US data on SO_2 concentrations are shown in figure 2.2. These are broadly consistent with our findings for the other pollutants, i.e. that variation in local income has a smaller effect on environmental quality than does a similar range of variation in national incomes, and that the turning point comes later when looking across counties within the US than when looking across countries of the world. Here again the relationship is relatively flat, with concentrations of SO_2 rising with the scale of country GDP until output reaches about $13,000 *per capita*. Again the downturn appears not to be due to changes in the composition of output, so we can infer that government policy must play the major role.

Carbon monoxide interferes with the ability of the blood to absorb oxygen, thereby impairing perception and thinking, slowing reflexes, and causing drowsiness; if inhaled by pregnant women, it may threaten the growth and mental development of the foetus. Carbon monoxide contamination is due primarily to incomplete combustion of fossil fuels, especially by motor vehicles and industry. It is heavily concentrated near major roadways and at intersections with high traffic density and poor ventilation.

The GEMS/Air data do not include measures of concentrations of carbon monoxide. Cross-country analysis has therefore been limited to examination of estimated aggregate emissions. Selden and Song (1992) find a strong downward trend over time in emissions for the countries in their sample; but the turning point in the relationship between income and emissions comes at the relatively high level of $11,338. For counties in the US, concentrations of carbon monoxide rise with economic activity until an even higher level of local income is reached (see figure 2.2), although again the quantitative effect of cross-country variations in output is reasonably small.

Nitrous oxides comprise a range of gases, some of which (e.g. nitrogen dioxide) do harm to the respiratory system and can increase susceptibility to viral infections. Like SO_2, some oxides of nitrogen contribute to the formation of acidic compounds that harm animals and plants when they fall as acid rain. Sources include motor vehicles and various industrial processes, most notably power plants.

The estimates in Selden and Song (1992) show a very high turning point of $22,874 in the relationship between *per capita* income and estimated emissions of oxides of nitrogen (but with a standard error on this estimate of $14,153). Indeed, this turning point lies outside the range of national incomes in their sample. This finding is consistent with the observation in OECD (1991) that emissions of oxides of nitrogen show no clear trend in the OECD countries outside of Japan.

In this case, the data for the US do show a somewhat more quantitatively significant relationship between county GDP and measured concentrations of nitrogen dioxide (see figure 2.2). A county with a *per capita* income of $17,000 will, on average, have a higher mean concentration of NO_2 that is almost two standard deviations higher than that in a county with a *per capita* income of only $6000. Beyond $17,000, concentrations of NO_2 appear to fall with local activity. At least some of this relationship seems to stem from a changing composition of economic activity as county income rises.

2.2   Large-scale air pollution

Some of the potentially most serious forms of air pollution do not have adverse impacts that are concentrated in the area where the emissions take place. Moreover, the harmful effects of some types of emissions may not be felt for several decades. Here we speak of course of the emissions of sulphates and nitrates that cause acid deposition and those of the greenhouse gases that contribute to global and regional climate change.

It was first recognised in the early 1970s that sulphur pollution could travel long distances through the atmosphere and contribute to acidification of the environment in remote locales. Since then, the fact that many air pollutants can travel long distances, cross national borders, and contribute to degradation of the environment in far-away places is well established. Of course, the groups that generate the pollution may see little reason to alter their behaviour, especially if abatement is costly and if the costs of the environmental damage will be borne mostly by others. We have seen that income growth does appear to be associated with a reduction in one of the contributing factors to acidification of the environment – sulphur dioxide – once a country reaches the middle-income range. But this is probably because SO_2 causes significant local as well as global environment damage. For oxides of nitrogen, whose local health risks are less clearly established, the evidence is that emissions continue to grow with economic output over the full range of *per capita* incomes so far experienced in the world's wealthiest countries.

Recent research findings for *carbon dioxide*, the most important of the greenhouse gases, give similar cause for concern. Atmospheric concentrations of CO_2 have increased by about 25 percent since the industrial revolution. Carbon is oxidised and CO_2 is released to the atmosphere whenever fossil fuels are burned. Different fuels release different amounts of the gas per unit of thermal energy: coal releases more CO_2 than oil, which in turn releases more than natural gas. It is possible, although costly, for a country to reduce its CO_2 emissions by switching its fuel sources or by reducing its overall energy demand. Other human activities that cause CO_2 to be released to the atmosphere, and which in principle might be affected by policy intervention, include deforestation and the conversion of grasslands into farmlands.

Holtz-Eakin and Selden (1992) studied data on *per capita* emissions of CO_2 from fossil fuel consumption and cement manufactures in 130 countries. As noted before, these data are generated using estimates of emissions coefficients in different countries for different types of fuel. Holtz-Eakin and Selden estimated both quadratic and cubic relationships between *per capita* emissions and both the level and the log of *per capita* income. They find considerable evidence of a decreasing marginal propensity to emit CO_2 with increased economic activity, but very little evidence that carbon dioxide emissions actually will fall when incomes grow higher even in the richest of countries. For example, with their preferred specification – one that relates CO_2 emissions to a quadratic function of the level of *per capita* income – estimated emissions will continue to rise until a country's *per capita* income reaches more than $35,000 in 1985 US$. The authors caution that the estimated turning point must be taken with a grain of salt, both because it is sensitive to the exact functional form that is used in the regression and especially because it relies on the out-of-sample properties of the estimated relationships.[5] In any event, it seems that the forces that tend to cause societies to redress local environmental problems as their incomes grow are much muted in the case of problems that affect far-off populations or ones whose adverse effects are uncertain or much delayed.

3   Water quality

Freshwater pollution takes three main forms. Pathogens in raw sewage cause a variety of debilitating and sometimes fatal diseases. Heavy metals and synthetic organic compounds from industry, mining, and agriculture contaminate drinking water and accumulate in aquatic organisms. And excessive nutrients in sewage, agricultural runoff, and industrial discharge cause high rates of algae and bacterial growth, which eventually deplete the water's oxygen content, to the detriment of the ecosystem. Using the data from the GEMS/Water project, it is possible to explore the relationship between economic growth and each of these forms of environmental degradation.

3.1   Pathogenic contamination from faecal discharge

When untreated sewage is discharged into rivers and lakes, the human and animal faeces in the sewage transport a variety of bacteria and viruses that threaten the health of humans, animals, and aquatic life forms. Waterborne pathogens from human and animal waste are known to cause gastroenteritis, typhoid, dysentery, cholera, hepatitis, amoebic dysentery, schistosomiasis, and giardiasis, which are responsible for untold discomfort and millions of deaths each year.

This most serious of environmental problems is not one that stems directly from economic activity. Rather, contamination occurs any time raw sewage is discharged without adequate treatment, as is the case with 95 percent of urban sewage in the developing world (World Resources Institute, 1992). Primary (physical), secondary (biological), and advanced sewage treatment can dramatically reduce the presence of pathogens in sewage, but the building, operation, and maintenance of such treatment facilities requires substantial resources that many poor countries can ill afford. Human pathogens can be eliminated entirely by adding chlorine to treated water, and some countries now do this. However, since the chlorine reacts with organic chemicals to form carcinogenic chlorinated hydrocarbons, the procedure generates considerable controversy.

Typically, the number of pathogens in river or lake water is not measured directly. Instead, the GEMS/Water project and other water management teams monitor *faecal coliform*, which are bacteria found in human and animal faeces that, while not dangerous themselves, indicate the presence of pathogens. Faecal coliform are more plentiful than pathogens, stay alive for a longer time, and therefore are easier to measure in the laboratory.

The GEMS/Water data include measures of faecal coliform from monitoring stations located along rivers in 42 countries at widely differing stages of development. A quick look at these data reveals that it would be inappropriate to treat the level of faecal coliform in a water sample of a given size as the dependent variable in a regression analysis. The concentrations of faecal coliform in a few rivers – presumably those that have been exposed to discharges of untreated sewage – are several orders of magnitude higher than those in the great majority of others, although there is substantial variation in the counts even among the latter group. In other words, the distribution of the mean annual concentration in the GEMS sample is highly skewed to the right; whereas the fifth percentile observation has 2.6 organisms/100 ml, the median observation has 844 organisms/100 ml, and the 95th percentile observation has 438,832 organisms/100 ml. This consideration led us to relate $\log(1 + p)$ to a cubic function of current and lagged *per capita* income (where p is the mean concentration of faecal coliform), rather than p itself. As explanatory variables in this regression, we used (besides income) a time trend, the mean water temperature, and a dummy variable to reflect the method of measurement.[6]

The results of this analysis are shown in figure 2.3.[7] We estimate that concentrations of faecal coliform rise with real *per capita* output until a country's income reaches approximately $8300 (1985 US$). In this range, growth may contribute to water pollution because it promotes rural to urban migration. Subsequent growth appears to generate the wherewithal for investments in water treatment; concentrations of faecal coliform drop sharply in most cases.

Figure 2.3 also reports an estimated relationship between the concentration of *total coliform* and current and lagged *per capita* output for a sample of rivers in 22 countries. Total coliform are a broader class of bacteria that, unlike faecal coliform, include some that are found naturally in the environment. For this reason, the concentration of total coliform is considered to be an inferior indicator of faecal contamination. In any event, we find that concentrations of total coliform in the sample of rivers rise with national income over the entire range of incomes (up to $12,209) found in our sample.

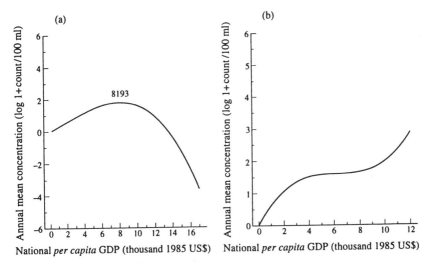

Figure 2.3   **Faecal contamination of rivers**
(a) **Faecal coliform**
(b) **Total coliform**

Note: All regressions estimated by weighted least squares. All regressions include a cubic function of contemporaneous income and a cubic function of the average income in the three years prior to observation. Graphs show long-run (current and lagged) effects of income. National income measures are from Summers and Heston (1991) and include correction for purchasing power of exchange rates.

3.2   *Heavy metals and toxic chemicals*

Heavy metals and toxic chemicals discharged by industry, mining and agriculture have become an increasingly serious environmental problem. The metals and toxics prove difficult to remove from drinking water by standard purification procedures and also bioaccumulate in fish and shellfish that are later ingested humans. Many of these substances accumulate into bottom sediment that is released slowly over time, long after the metals are initially deposited. The health hazards posed by these metals and toxics are many: lead causes convulsions, anemia, kidney and brain damage, cancer, and birth defects; mercury contributes to irritability, depression, kidney and liver damage, and birth defects; nickel causes gastrointestinal and central nervous system damage, and cancer; arsenic induces vomiting, poisoning, damage to liver and kidneys, and cancer; cadmium is suspected of causing tumours, renal dysfunction, hypertension, arteriosclerosis, itai-itai disease; and so on (Conservation Foundation, 1992).

The industrial sources of heavy metal pollution include smelting and heavy metal processing, the discharge of solutions used in plating, galvanising, and pickling, the discharge of compounds used in paints, plastics, batteries and tanning, and discharges from pulp and paper plants. Some metals and toxics also leach into groundwater from solid waste dumps. In many less developed countries, mining is a more important source of heavy metals in water than is industry. In all cases, pollution is best controlled by government regulations that reduce effluent discharges and that ensure proper disposal of sludge from treatment plants and toxic wastes.

The evidence from the GEMS/Water project on the relationship between economic growth and the concentrations of various heavy metals in rivers is decidedly mixed. Figure 2.4 shows the result of regressions of concentrations of five metals on current and lagged national income variables, plus water temperature, a time trend, and (in some cases) dummy variables for the type of measuring instrument. The results for two of these metals – *lead* and *cadmium* – are encouraging. The concentration of lead in rivers appears to fall sharply with economic growth in the poorest countries, and then level off when *per capita* income reaches about $8000. Income growth also appears to contribute to reduced concentrations of cadmium at low levels of national income, although the influence is less pronounced.

The patterns observed for *mercury, arsenic,* and *nickel* are more difficult to interpret. The GEMS/Water project has monitored concentrations of nickel in rivers in only 10 countries (and only three of these in the developing world), so perhaps these findings should not be taken too seriously. In the cases of mercury and arsenic, for which monitoring takes place in 28 and 17 countries respectively, the estimated pattern is one where concentrations rise with output in the early stages of development, fall with output through the middle-income range, and then rise again after *per capita* GDP reaches about $13,000. It is possible, of course, that

---

Figure 2.4   Heavy metals in rivers
    (a) Lead
    (b) Cadmium
    (c) Mercury
    (d) Arsenic
    (e) Nickel

Note: All regressions estimated by weighted least squares. All regressions include a cubic function of contemporaneous income and a cubic function of the average income in the three years prior to observation. Graphs show long-run (current and lagged) effects of income. National income measures are from Summers and Heston (1991) and include correction for purchasing power of exchange rates.

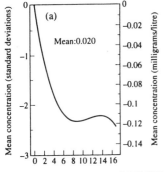

National *per capita* GDP (thousand 1985 US$)

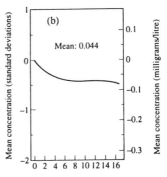

National *per capita* GDP (thousand 1985 US$)

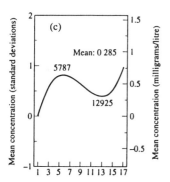

National *per capita* GDP (thousand 1985 US$)

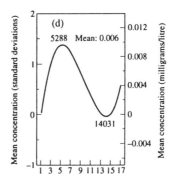

National *per capita* GDP (thousand 1985 US$)

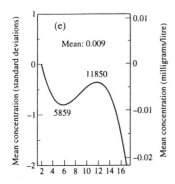

National *per capita* GDP (thousand 1985 US$)

the upturns represent imprecise measurement of the coefficients on the cubed income terms, especially since there are relatively few observations in the high-income range.[8] In any event, it is unclear whether greater income has so far given countries the wherewithal and the willingness to tackle the problems associated with industrial discharges of these dangerous metals.

3.3   The oxygen regime

The final type of freshwater pollution problem involves deterioration of the oxygen regime. Fish and shellfish require dissolved oxygen to metabolise organic carbon. Contamination of river and lake water by human sewage or industrial discharges (by, for example, pulp and paper mills) increases the concentration of organic carbon in forms usable by bacteria, which then demand greater amounts of dissolved oxygen. This reduces the amounts available for fish and other higher forms of aquatic life; at high levels of contamination, the fish population dies off and the entire ecosystem changes. A similar problem can arise when water is over-enriched by nutrients, such as are contained in runoff from agricultural areas where fertilisers are used intensively. Excess nitrogen and phosphorus promote algal growth. The decay of the dying algae also consumes oxygen that is lost to the fish population.

Although oxygen loss poses no direct health risk to humans, there may be indirect effects through the reduced availability of fish and shellfish and the loss of biodiversity. Depletion of the oxygen content of water can be prevented primarily by control of effluent discharges and by domestic waste-water treatment. Primary and secondary treatment of sewage can be used to remove between 35 and 85 percent of the pollutants in sewage, as well as 30 percent of the phosphorus and 50 percent of the nitrogen. More costly advanced treatment techniques can be used to reduce pollutant levels still further (World Resources Institute, 1990). Government regulation can also be used to limit the amounts of pollutants that industries discharge into particular bodies of water.

Some GEMS/Water stations directly monitor the level of dissolved oxygen in a river as an indication of the state of the oxygen regime. Other stations measure instead contamination by organic compounds as an indication of the competing demands for oxygen: one measure of this, called biological oxygen demand (BOD), is the amount of natural oxidation that occurs in a sample of water in a given period of time; another measure, called chemical oxygen demand (COD) is the amount of oxygen consumed when a strong chemical oxidant is added to the sample of water. Whereas dissolved oxygen is a direct measure of water quality,

BOD and COD are inverse measures, indicating the presence of contaminants that will eventually cause oxygen loss.

Figure 2.5 shows the relationship between these various measures of the state of the oxygen regime and the scale of economic activity. As before, we have allowed for both an immediate and a lagged effect of income, have controlled for mean water temperature, and have allowed for a common global time trend. The results for the different measures (which include a different sample of monitoring stations in overlapping but not identical sets of countries) are strikingly similar: the oxygen regime appears to deteriorate with greater economic activity until *per capita* output reaches somewhere between $8500 and $11,000, and to improve when economic growth pushes income beyond that point.

Figure 2.5 also shows the relationship between mean annual concentrations of *nitrates* and the level of real *per capita* GDP in the country in which a river is located. The presence of a high concentration of nitrates mainly reflects pollution from agricultural runoff, although municipal sewage and seepage from septic tanks also are sources. Concentrations of nitrates also exhibit an inverted U-shaped relationship to national income, with an estimated peak (of $9725) very similar to that for BOD, COD, and dissolved oxygen.[9]

4   Conclusions and policy implications

We have reviewed the evidence on the relationship between the scale of economic activity and measurable indicators of the state of the environment. We find that economic growth does not always contribute to degradation of the environment. In some cases, economic growth has been accompanied by a change in the composition of output and a change in the methods of production that more than compensates for the increased scale of activity.

Not all measures of environmental quality have been similarly affected by increases in output. Along some dimensions, as with the concentration of lead and cadmium in river basins and the concentration of coarse suspended particles in urban air, we have seen conditions improve monotonically with increased *per capita* output and the associated rise in standards of material living. For other pollutants we find an inverted U-shaped relationship with output; environmental quality deteriorates along these dimensions in the early stages of economic growth until a turning point is reached beyond which higher levels of *per capita* output are associated with improved measures of pollution. The estimated turning points vary substantially across the different pollutants that have been studied, with some typically coming early on in the develop-

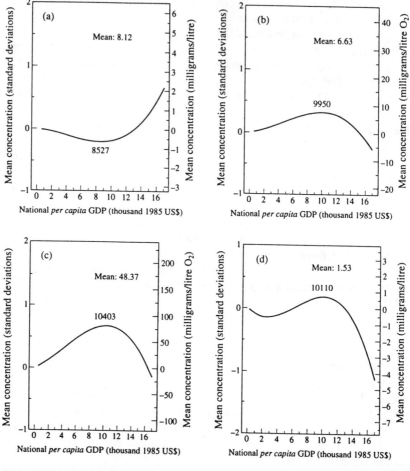

Figure 2.5   The oxygen regime in rivers
   (a) Dissolved oxygen
   (b) Biological oxygen demand (BOD)
   (c) Chemical oxygen demand (COD)
   (d) Nitrates

Note: All regressions estimated by weighted least squares. All regressions include a cubic function of contemporaneous income and a cubic function of the average income in the three years prior to observation. Graphs show long-run (current and lagged) effects of income. National income measures are from Summers and Heston (1991) and include correction for purchasing power of exchange rates.

ment process and others only much later. Finally, for some types of pollution there is no evidence at all that a turning point has yet been reached; estimated emissions of carbon dioxide and nitrous oxides have continued to rise with national output throughout the entire range of income levels observed in the richest countries of the world.

Several points should be emphasised concerning the interpretation of our findings. First, even for those dimensions of environmental quality where growth seems to have been associated with improving conditions, there is no reason to believe that the process has been an automatic one. In principle, environmental quality might improve automatically with growth if countries inevitably substituted cleaner technologies for dirtier ones as they moved up the income ladder, or if there were a very pronounced effect on pollution of the typical patterns of structural transformation. However, a case-by-case review of instances of improved environmental quality suggests that the strongest link between income and pollution in fact is via an induced *policy response*; as nations or regions experience increased economic prosperity, their citizens demand of their leaders that greater attention be paid to the natural habitat. The richer countries, which tend to have relatively cleaner urban air and relatively clean river water also have relatively stricter environmental standards and tougher enforcement of their environmental laws than the middle-income and poorer countries that still have many pressing environmental problems to address.

Second, it is possible (as the Discussant, Gilles Saint-Paul, suggests) that downward-sloping and inverted U-shaped patterns might arise because, as countries develop, they cease to produce certain pollution intensive goods, and begin instead to import these products from other countries with less restrictive environmental protection laws. If this is the main explanation for the (eventual) inverse relationship between a country's income and pollution, then future development patterns could not mimic those of the past; developing countries will not always be able to find still poorer countries to serve as havens for the production of pollution intensive goods. However, the available evidence does not point to cross-country differences in environmental standards as an important determinant of the global pattern of international trade (see, e.g., Tobey, 1990; Grossman and Krueger, 1993b). While some 'environmental dumping' may take place, the volume of such trade is almost surely too small to account for the reduced pollution that has been observed to accompany past episodes of economic growth.

Finally, it should be stressed that there is nothing at all inevitable about the relationships that have been observed in the past. These patterns reflected the technological, political, and economic conditions that existed at the time. The low-income countries of today have a unique opportunity to learn from this history and thereby avoid some of the mistakes of earlier growth episodes. With the increased awareness of environmental hazards and the development in recent years of new technologies that are cleaner than ever before, we might hope to see the low-income countries turn their attention to preservation of the environment at earlier stages of development than has previously been the case. Indeed, the studies that have been reviewed here give some cause for optimism in this regard; for nearly every pollutant that has been examined one finds a statistically significant and quantitatively meaningful negative time trend. That is, along most dimensions, environmental quality is likely to be higher for a country with a given level of *per capita* income today than it was for another that was at that same level of development a decade ago. Technology transfers to developing countries could almost surely be used to continue or accelerate these trends.

The pattern of findings for the different pollutants that have been examined also has implications for policy. We find that the turning point in the relationship between pollution and national output has, in the past, come soonest for those dimensions of environmental quality that have a direct and immediate connection to local health and wellbeing. In cases where the effect on human health is less clear and immediate, such as with the oxygen regime in rivers, economic growth may contribute to a worsening situation until reasonably high levels of income are reached. And in cases where the risks associated with damage to the environment threaten the health and welfare of populations living in far-off places, or that of generations as yet unborn, one finds little evidence that greater income generates an increasing willingness on the part of the polluting society to bear the costs of environmental protection. It is these cases of international externalities and delayed effects that will require the closest scrutiny by the international community in the coming years. Without increased international cooperation and leadership from far-sighted politicians, the potential exists for continued expansion of economic activity to bring harm to the earth that will be difficult or impossible to reverse at a later time.

NOTES

Much of this chapter reports on research that I am conducting jointly with my colleague, Alan Krueger. Jim Laity has provided us with extraordinary research assistance, while the OECD, the Ford Foundation, and the Center for Economic Policy Studies at Princeton University have contributed partial financial support. I am grateful to Peter Jaffee for his tutoring on water quality and to Robert Bisson for providing the GEMS/Water data. Ian Goldin, Alan Winters and participants in the OECD Development Centre and CEPR Conference provided useful comments. All errors and opinions are my own.

1 UNESCO and the World Meteorological Organisation also participate in certain aspects of this international monitoring project.

2 Some stations, mostly in Europe, also monitor oxides of nitrogen. There are plans to incorporate more systematic monitoring of this pollutant in the future of the project.

3 The stations that participate in SLAMS are coded to indicate the monitoring objective: highest concentration, representative concentration in densely populated areas, general background concentration in low-density areas, and impact of particular sources. However, the data set contains relatively few observations for a relatively short time period for stations that can be considered 'representative'.

4 The relationship depicted here uses data in what Grossman and Krueger (1993c) refer to as the 'intermediate sub-sample': it excludes data from monitoring stations in the EPA network that are part of SLAMS and that were coded as being included to monitor highest-concentration areas, as well as those for stations that, from the description of their location, could be identified as being sited to monitor concentrations in the vicinity of a power plant. The relationships shown in figure 2.2 have been calculated using ordinary least squares; estimation of a random-effects model is currently in progress and will be reported (along with more information about the formation of the different sub-samples) in Grossman et al. (1994).

5 In the equation that uses a cubic functional form in the log of per capita income, the turning point in the relationship between emissions and income comes at less than $14,000; however, a quadratic form using the log of per capita income indicates a turning point something above $8 million!

6 In cases where water temperature was not available for a given station, we used instead the predicted value from an estimated relationship between temperature and latitude. All of the regressions using the GEMS/Water data included linear, quadratic and cubic terms for both contemporaneous income and for the arithmetic average of income during the three years prior to the measurement. The relationships were estimated using generalised least squares, with weights attached according to the number of individual observations that were used to calculate the mean concentration of the pollutant (see Grossman and Krueger, 1993a, for more detail).

7 The regression results shown in figures 2.3, 2.4 and 2.5 were calculated using weighted least squares (WLS), with weights reflecting the number of readings taken at the monitoring station per year. Grossman and Krueger (1993a) reports estimates of a random effects model that allows for site specific components in the error term for each observation. In most cases, the random-effects estimates are quite similar to the WLS estimates, although there are one or two of the heavy metals that are exceptions to this rule.

8 It should be noted that the estimated upturn in the relationship between arsenic and per capita GDP is much less pronounced when a random-effects specification is used (see Grossman and Krueger, 1993a).

9 We also examined the GEMS/Water data for mean annual concentrations of phenols in rivers, but found no statistically significant relationship between this form of pollution and national income. Phenols, which are discharged to rivers by foundries, have a high level of oxygen demand, and also are toxic to fish.

REFERENCES

Code of Federal Regulation (CFR) (1992) Title 40, Part 58, Appendix D (1 July): 158–72

Conservation Foundation (1992) *State of the Environment 1982*, Washington, DC: Conservation Foundation

Daly, H.E. (1977) *Steady-State Economics*, San Francisco: Freeman & Co.; 2nd edn, Washington, DC: Island Press (1991)

Grossman, G.M. and Krueger, A.B. (1993a) 'Economic growth and the environment', Princeton University, forthcoming

(1993b) 'Environmental impacts of a North American Free Trade Agreement', in P. Garber (ed.), *The US–Mexico Free Trade Agreement*, Cambridge, MA: MIT Press

Grossman, G.M., Krueger, A.K. and Laity, J.A. (1994) 'Pollution and growth: evidence from the United States', Princeton University, forthcoming

Holtz-Eakin, D. and Selden, T.M. (1992) 'Stoking the fires? CO_2 emissions and economic growth', NBER, *Working Paper*, **4248**, Cambridge, MA: NBER

Oak Ridge National Laboratory (1992) *Trends '91: A Compendium of Data on Global Change*, Oak Ridge, TN: Oak Ridge National Laboratory

Organisation for Economic Cooperation and Development (OECD) (1991) *The State of the Environment*, Paris: OECD

Radetzki, M. (1992) 'Economic growth and environment', in P. Low (ed.), *International Trade and the Environment*, World Bank, *Discussion Paper*, **159**, Washington, DC: World Bank

Selden, T.M. and Song, D. (1992) 'Environmental quality and development: is there a Kuznets curve for air pollution?', Syracuse University, mimeo

Summers, R. and Heston, A. (1991) 'The Penn Mark V World Table: an expanded set of international comparisons, 1950–1988', *Quarterly Journal of Economics*, **106** (May): 327–69

Syrquin, M. (1989) 'Patterns of structural change', in H. Chenery and T.N. Srinivasan (eds), *Handbook of Development Economics*, vol. 1, Amsterdam: North-Holland

Tobey, J.A. (1990) 'The effects of domestic environmental policies on patterns of world trade: an empirical test', *Kyklos*, **43**, 191–209

World Bank (1992) *World Development Report 1992: Development and the Environment*, Washington, DC: World Bank

World Health Organisation (1987) *Air Quality Guidelines for Europe*, WHO Regional Publications, European Series, **23**, Copenhagen, World Health Regional Office for Europe

World Resources Institute (1990) *World Resources 1990–91*, New York and London: Oxford University Press

(1992) *World Resources, 1992–93*, New York and London: Oxford University Press

Worldwatch Institute (1990) *State of the World 1990*, New York: Norton

Discussion

GILLES SAINT-PAUL

1   Introduction

In his chapter 2 Gene Grossman has provided interesting evidence on the correlation between *per capita* GDP and pollution. The main finding is that pollution follows a hump-shaped pattern: as income increases, pollution goes up and then down. Grossman then interprets this as evidence of increased awareness in richer countries. The chapter points toward the optimistic conclusion that as poorer countries get richer, they will eventually move along the downward-sloping portion of the curve, and aggregate emissions will hopefully be reduced, at least for some gases.

In my Discussion I want to suggest that the observed relationship may be (partly) due to the pattern of international specialisation, so that the optimistic conclusion that growth is good for the environment may not be guaranteed. The idea is that as frontiers open to international trade, countries will try to import pollution intensive goods rather than produce them, thus pushing their price up. In equilibrium the countries that will produce pollution intensive goods in response to this price hike are those for which the marginal utility of income is higher, that is to say the poor countries. This pattern of specialisation is likely to generate a hump-shaped curve as evidenced in Grossman's chapter. Nevertheless when some countries move down the hump-shaped curve, the world price of pollution intensive goods will increase, which triggers a positive supply response. As a result, aggregate emissions need not go down, and can well go up.

2   The model

To make this point formally let us consider the following simple model.

In each country there is a representative consumer with the following utility function:

$$U = \theta \log c_p + (1 - \theta) \log c_c - \beta e$$

where c_p is consumption of good p, c_c consumption of good c, and e the emission level. Here p is the pollution intensive good. Its production is associated with emissions. More specifically I assume:

$$e = x_p$$

where x_p is output of good p.

The production possibility frontier in any given country is linear, and is given by:

$$x_p + x_c = H$$

where H is the total capital stock of the country (including human capital, etc.). The frontier is assumed to have the same slope of 1 in each country. I therefore neutralise all comparative advantage considerations, thus isolating the effect of pollution on trade.

The last assumption I make is that in each country there exists a system of taxes and transfers which allows the government to implement the first-best allocation.

Let us first consider the solution in the absence of trade. One must have $c_p = x_p$ and $c_c = x_c$ so that the solution maximises:

$$U = \theta \log x_p + (1 - \theta) \log(H - x_p) - \beta x_p.$$

The first-order condition is given by:

$$\theta / x_p + (1 - \theta)/(H - x_p) - \beta = 0.$$

It is clear from the previous equation that:

$$\partial e / \partial H = \partial x_p / \partial H > 0 \; \forall \; H.$$

Therefore there is no hump-shaped response: emission levels monotonically increase with output.

Let us now consider what happens when a large number of countries are able to trade with each other. Let p be the world price of good p. Then each individual country maximises U subject to:

$$c_c + pc_p = x_c + px_p = R$$
$$x_p + c_c = H$$
$$e = x_p.$$

Conditional on R, maximisation of U implies $c_c = (1 - \theta)R$ and $c_p = \theta R/p$. One then has $U = \log R - \beta e + \text{constant} = \log(H + (p - 1) x_p) - \beta x_p + \text{constant}$. Maximising that expression with respect to x_p yields the following solution:

1 If $H \geq (p - 1)/\beta$ then $x_p = 0$. The country fully specialises in the 'clean' good and imports the pollution intensive good.
2 If $(p - 1)/(p\beta) \leq H \leq (p - 1)/\beta$ then $x_p = 1/\beta - H(p - 1)$. The country produces both goods, and in that range one has $\partial e / \partial H = \partial x_p / \partial H = -1/(p - 1) < 0$. In that range of income levels one will

observe a falling emission level as income rises. This is because in that range it pays to give up part of extra income to produce less pollution intensive goods.

3   If $H \leq (p - 1)/(p\beta)$ then $x_p = H$. The country fully specialises in the p good. It will produce more of it as it gets richer, so that $\partial e/\partial H > 0$.

Therefore, one will observe the hump-shaped response as depicted in figure D2.1. The key point is that this curve depends on the world price p of the pollution intensive good. When it increases the curve shifts upwards and its peak moves rightwards, as indicated by the dashed line in figure D2.1.

The model is closed by the determination of p. The world supply of the p good must be equal to its world demand. Algebraically this is equivalent to:

$$\text{Supply} = \int_0^{(p-1)/(p\beta)} Hf(H)\,dH + \int_{(p-1)/(p\beta)}^{(p-1)/\beta} (1/\beta - H/(p-1))f(H)\,dH$$

$$= \text{Demand} = \int_0^{(p-1)/(p\beta)} \theta Hf(H)\,dH + \int_{(p-1)/(p\beta)}^{(p-1)/\beta} \theta(p-1)/(p\beta)f(H)\,dH$$

$$+ \int_{(p-1)/(p\beta)}^{+\infty} \theta H/pf(H)\,dH$$

where f is the density of the world distribution of income.

What happens when a country (or a set of countries) moves along the downward-sloping portion of the hump-shaped locus in figure D2.1? It

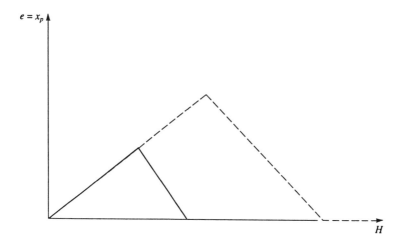

Figure D2.1   Emissions and income levels

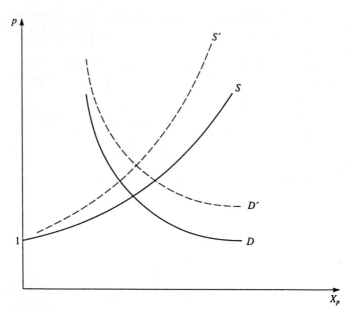

Figure D2.2   Effects of growth on emissions and prices

will tend to increase its specialisation in the clean good. As a result the world supply of the p good will shrink, pushing the price up. Simultaneously, as it gets richer, its demand for both goods increases. As a result the world demand for the p good increases. The net result, illustrated in figure D2.2, is a shift in both the supply curve and the demand curve of the pollution intensive good. The main implications are (i) the world price of that good unambiguously increases, so that one will observe a shift in the hump-shaped curve, and (ii) the aggregate level of emissions, which we can read from the abscissa of the equilibrium point in figure D2.2, may either increase or decrease. If θ, the expenditure share on the p good is low, it will decrease. If it is high, it will increase.

I conclude from that exercise that the emergence of an empirical hump-shaped response may partly be due to the pattern of trade, so that one should be cautious in inferring from such a hump shape that economic development is likely to reduce pollution.

3 Does sustainability require growth?

RICHARD BALDWIN

1 Introduction

'Sustainable development' is often defined as development that meets the needs of the present without compromising the ability of future generations to meet their own needs. The conveniently flexible word 'needs' renders this definition inoperable. To economists 'sustainability' suggests a steady state and this is the interpretation that will be used here. One of the many issues surrounding sustainability is the growth controversy. Some analysts argue that the world has already reached its limits of growth and that further growth will take the planet further away from sustainability. Indeed Daly (1990) argues that 'sustainable growth' is a contradiction in terms. The line of reasoning advanced by this school is often eclectic. For instance, Goodland and Daly (1992) argue that 'the North should stabilize its rate of resource consumption to free resources for the South and to free up ecological space as well'. It is not exactly clear which resources and space are being referred to, but the authors go on to state that 'the North can continue to develop but must cease increasing throughput growth. If the expanding global economy is bounded by a finite inexpandible [*sic*] ecosystem, then . . . the traditional view becomes impossible.' The 'traditional view' is characterised as one in which Northern growth is essential to alleviate Southern poverty. Other researchers, such as MacNeill (1989), argue that growth is greatly needed to further development and prevent environmental degradation. The World Resources Institute (1992) argues that 'alleviating absolute poverty also has important practical consequences for sustainable development, since there are close links between poverty, environmental degradation, and rapid population growth'.

This chapter attempts to make a simple, empirically-based argument for the growth-is-necessary school of thought. Although the conclusion is far from novel, the analytic and empirical approaches adopted hopefully are useful. To put it bluntly, people make pollution and poverty makes people. The simple fact is that current population growth rates, if they were maintained, would lead to an unsustainable world population. Getting the demographics right, therefore, must be part of any planetary environmental strategy.

Higher average output and income in the developing world, however, are not without environmental costs. There is now evidence that *per capita* emission rates rise at low levels of income, but fall at higher levels (Grossman and Krueger, 1991). The concept of an 'ecologic transition', which has many similarities with the well known demographic transition, is introduced to analyse the implications of this emerging empirical regularity. This analytic framework decomposes actual pollution into two quantities: incipient pollution and abatement. 'Incipient pollution' is defined as the level of pollution a country would produce at its current level and composition of output, if environmental costs were zero. Abatement is the difference between this and actual pollution. It is argued that incipient pollution and abatement follow very different paths during industrialisation, leading to three phases of emission rates. Phase I is marked by a steady, low level of average emission maintained by low levels of output and an environmentally-friendly sectoral composition (see figure 3.1). Phase II is identified with rising *per capita* pollution flows due to a rapid rise in polluting activities accompanied by a much slower rise in abatement activities. Phase III is characterised by a low emission rate stemming from a shift into services and, in the remaining industrial activity, a high incipient pollution rate that is offset by a high abatement rate.

This chapter argues that the world finds itself in an awkward position. While most less-developed countries (LDCs) are near the end of the explosive phase of their demographic transitions, they appear to be right at the beginning of the rapid-emission-growth phase of their ecologic transitions. As a consequence, global environment damage is likely to increase before it declines. Despite this inevitable deterioration of the envirionment, stopping economic growth would be exactly the wrong prescription. Such medicine would simply replace industrial pollution with more Malthusian deteriorations of the environment, especially in the poorest countries.

The chapter is organised in six sections. Following the introductory section, section 2 presents the analytics of the demographic and ecologic transitions, together with some supporting evidence. Section 3 examines evidence on where the world is today in terms of these two transitions. Section 4 studies a thought experiment that suggests that sustainability requires growth. Section 5 looks at sustainability and policy issues. Section 6 presents a summary, policy approaches and directions for future research.

2 Demographic and ecologic transitions

2.1 Theory of the demographic transition

The notion that a society's population growth progresses in three stages is well known.[1] In Phase I, called the premodern phase (see figure 3.1a), fertility is unchecked by economic or other considerations.[2] However mortality – especially among the old and the young – does respond directly to economic conditions. Life expectancy is low on average and fluctuates widely as land, food and clean water scarcities lead to famines and epidemics. Mortality fluctuates more than fertility. The population of a premodern society rises to the point where living standards are low enough to equilibrate the high birth rate with an equally high death rate. Phase II has two parts. In the first, the death rate drops quickly but the birth rate stays constant or even rises. The drop in the death rate is due to productivity growth (mainly in agriculture) that removes the economy from the brink of starvation and, perhaps even more important, to technical advances in public health and medical care. These factors reduce deaths but do not directly alter reproductive behaviour or birth rates. Indeed, since more women survive to the end of their reproductive years, fertility may even increase. The wedge between birth and death rates leads to a rapid rise in the population, especially at the low end of the age profile. Additionally, life expectancy doubles. The net result is a rapid expansion of population and a built-in population momentum. The latter stems from the natural rise in the average birth rate as the bulge of population in its prereproductive years reaches its fertile phase. This raises the share of the population in its fertile years, so even with no change in fertility per women the average birth rate rises.

During the latter part of Phase II, fertility declines faster than mortality, so population growth begins to stabilise. The fertility decline is driven largely by socioeconomic factors such as rising levels of education, real income and life expectancy levels as well as higher female labour force participation rates.

Phase III is marked by a stable population at a high living standard, which is supported by low birth and death rates, and a high life expectancy at birth. Fertility fluctuates more than mortality.

(a)

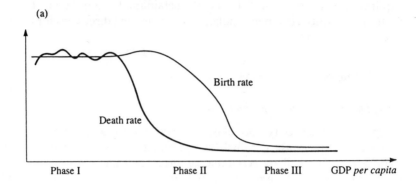

(b)

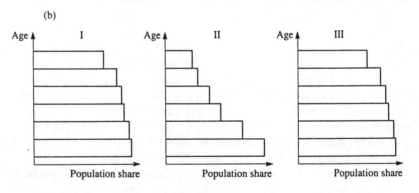

Figure 3.1   Schematic demographic transition
      (a) Phase I, II and III
      (b) Age profiles in the three phases

2.1.1 Analytic content of the demographic transition framework
The three phases presented above fit the facts in many countries; however, they are without analytic content *per se*. In order to use the framework for policy analysis, it is necessary to formulate models of the birth and the

death rate. The death rate is by far the easiest. Apart from minor causes such as accidents and idiosyncratic events such as warfare and natural disasters, people die of diseases. For this reason, the age profile of death is U-shaped in all countries, reflecting the susceptibility of the very young and the old to illnesses (figure 3.1b). At all levels of development, high incomes and high levels of education tend to suppress death rates, especially at the extremes of the age spectrum. At the young end (by far the most important to demography since the old are past their reproductive years) infant mortality is closely linked with *per capita* income. This can be seen in figure 3.2a. Education and public health are also important determinants of mortality at low levels of income. As can be seen in figure 3.2b, the link between a broader measure of mortality (life expectancy at birth) and income becomes very weak or nonexistent beyond a certain level of development. For the purposes of this chapter, we assume that the death rate is determined by public health policy, which is in turn exogenously chosen. Although this is a simplification, it does shift attention to fertility, which is the part of population growth most amenable to governmental influence.

The average number of births per thousand people depends upon the total fertility rate (expected births per woman) and the number of women in their fertile phase of life. Since the fertile interval begins around 15, the number of women in it is dictated by past events and so is largely exogenous at any given moment. The fertility rate, however, is directly and indirectly influenced by policy and economics. In particular it varies inversely with *per capita* income, as figure 3.2c suggests, although the relationship is highly nonlinear. Education, especially of women, also has a strong negative effect on fertility.

2.1.2 Becker–Murphy–Tamura theory of human capital, growth and fertility

Becker, Murphy and Tamura (1990) present a theory of fertility and growth that focuses on human capital. In their model, the level of human capital is the primary determinant of fertility. The human capital–fertility link involves a simple economic trade off. Child bearing and rearing are time-consuming activities that provide parents with some vicarious utility. Since parents always have the alternative of boosting their utility via direct consumption of goods, higher wages induce a substitution effect away from fertility. This accounts for the negative correlation between *per capita* GDP and fertility. Additionally, the model contains a second link between fertility and economic conditions. Parents vicariously value the consumption of their progeny; however, the discount rate applied by the present generation to the utility of future generations falls as fertility rises.

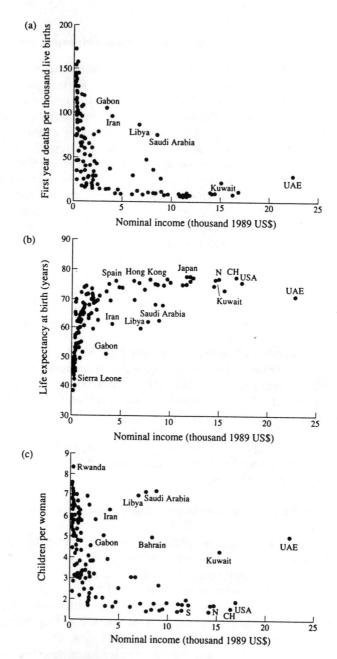

Figure 3.2   Demographic data versus income levels
    (a) Infant mortality
    (b) Life expectancy
    (c) Fertility
Source: World Bank data base

The implication of this assumption is that the marginal utility of investing in the human capital of children diminishes as the number of children rises. Finally, sustained economic growth – that is to say, ever-rising wages – is assumed to be driven by the ceaseless accumulation of human capital.

The movement of fertility in the classic theory of the demographic transition can be explained in terms of the Becker–Murphy–Tamura model. The model assumes that the rate of return on human capital is low for low stocks of human capital, but raises the stock of human capital up to some given constant rate of return. The dynamics implied by this assumption can be illustrated in figure 3.3, which is taken from Becker, Murphy and Tamura (1990). The curved line h-h shows the optimal H_{t+1} for each level of H_t. Points along the 45 degree line show where there is no growth in H. There are three steady states shown in figure 3.3. The two zero growth equilibria occur where the curve line h-h crosses the 45 degree line. The positive growth equilibrium occurs for any H_t that is greater than $\hat{H}$.

Consider first the steady state with $H = 0$. Here the low level of human capital implies that the cost of bearing and rearing children is low, so fertility is consequentially high. The high rate of fertility, in turn, implies that the discount rate on consumption of future generations is high because of the assumption made above. In fact, if this effect is strong enough, the discount rate would exceed the rate of return on investment in human capital at $H = 0$. This makes $H = 0$ a steady state. Clearly this is the classic poverty trap: average *per capita* human capital and GDP are low, while fertility is high. Since average incomes are very low, we can suppose that the population is approximately stable since high mortality offsets high fertility, although mortality is not formally explored in the Becker–Murphy–Tamura model. This steady state corresponds to the premodern phase in the demographic transition. In figure 3.3, any initial level of H below $\hat{H}$ would lead the system to converge to the low-H/high-fertility steady state at $H = 0$.

The second stable steady state involves the continual accumulation of human capital. If H starts out above $\hat{H}$, then fertility is low enough to imply a discount rate that makes investment in human capital worthwhile. Since the return to H rises with the stock (up to a point), the H stock continues to rise. Clearly as H rises, *per capita* income and parents' opportunity costs rise, so fertility falls. Given sufficient convexity in the utility derived from the consumption of agents' progeny, fertility will not drop to zero. Detailed calculations by Becker, Murphy and Tamura demonstrate that sustained growth is possible as long as the return to H asymptotes to a constant.

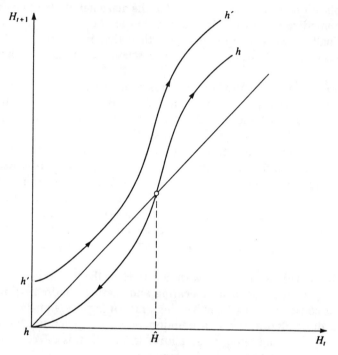

Figure 3.3   Phase diagram of endogenous growth and fertility

In this model, the demographic transition could be induced by a shift up in the *h-h* line, to *h'-h'*. This sort of shift deletes the low-income/high-fertility steady state, triggering a persistent rise in *H* and a fall in fertility rates. In terms of figure 3.1, this transitional dynamics corresponds to Phase II of the demographic transition. Policies that could accomplish this sort of shift in the *h-h* schedule fall into those that exogenously increase the return to accumulating *H* and those that lower the discount rate. An exogenous rise in technology and the opening of new markets for the country's products are some examples of the former; policies that directly reduce fertility constitute examples of the latter. Either change would imply that even at *H* = 0, the return to human capital investment exceeded the discount rate, so agents would begin to invest in *H*. As *H* began to rise, parents would tend to substitute away from having children, thereby reducing the fertility rate. Alternatively, a policy-led education drive that forced *H* from *H* = 0 to a point above *Ĥ* would spark a take off in incomes and a fall in fertility.

2.2 Ecologic transition

It is useful to think of pollution as the environmentally harmful by-product of economic activity. However there is not an immutable connection between pollution and value added. Casual empiricism suggests that *per capita* pollution varies systematically with *per capita* income. Environmental conditions in cities such as New Delhi and Mexico City bear little resemblance to those in Stockholm and Geneva. To formalise this affiliation between income *per capita* and pollution *per capita*, I introduce a framework that I call the ecologic transition.

2.2.1 Incipient pollution and abatement

It is useful to think of actual pollution as the difference between two fictitious quantities: incipient pollution and abatement or negative pollution. 'Incipient pollution' is here defined as the amount of pollution a particular activity would have produced using a technology that would have been optimal if the private cost of pollution were zero. The size of this 'lowest-cost unit pollution coefficient' or LCUPC clearly varies across economic activities – compare mercury refining to teaching economics. It also varies according to factor prices; on average US farmers use 2 kg of pesticides per hectare a year, while Thai farmers use only 0.6 kg (World Resources Institute 1992). Of course, this lowest-cost pollution coefficient may never be observed in activities where agents face some cost of polluting.

'Abatement' is defined as the difference between incipient and actual pollution; thus abatement can be thought of as the production of 'negative pollution' that stems from the implementation of pollution abating techniques or technology. One could roughly quantify these two variables by the following formulae:

$$\begin{pmatrix} \text{Incipient} \\ \text{pollution} \end{pmatrix} = (\text{LCUPC}) \times (\text{output})$$

$$(\text{Abatement}) = \begin{pmatrix} \text{Actual} \\ \text{pollution} \end{pmatrix} - \begin{pmatrix} \text{Incipient} \\ \text{pollution} \end{pmatrix}. \tag{1}$$

2.2.2 The per capita incipient pollution curve

In societies with very low levels of *per capita* income, people are engaged primarily in subsistence agriculture, which uses few chemical inputs. Thus by the nature of the economic activities pursued, very poor economies are likely to have a relatively small average LCUPC. Moreover, since they produce little output, the *per capita* emissions of very poor societies are likely to be small. Rising incomes are typically associated with both a higher average LCUPC and a higher output per person. The rise in the LCUPC stems from the typical shift from low LCUPC activities such as subsistence farming towards higher LCUPC activities such as mining and industry. This shift directly raises the average unit pollution coefficient for the economy. Moreover, as land and labour prices rise, agricultural techniques tend to become much more polluting in that they rely on pesticides, chemical fertiliser, irrigation and mechanised implements. The same is true of many industrial processes. As labour becomes expensive, chemical treatments and energy-consuming devices or processes are substituted for workers. At very high levels of income, services (which usually have low unit pollution coefficients) start to displace agriculture and, to a lesser extent, industry. This results in a reduction in the average unit pollution coefficients. This is shown schematically in figure 3.4a.

The incipient pollution *per capita* is the simple product of the average LCUPC and output per person. This hypothetical incipient pollution curve is plotted in figure 3.4b. The lazy-S shape of the curve is due to two distinct factors: a composition factor and an output factor. As economies move up the development ladder, they first move into activities that are inherently more polluting and then later move into services that are inherently less polluting. This explains the bell shape of the LCUPC. The second factor is that of total output per person, which obviously rises with *per capita* GDP. By construction, it would not be possible to observe data on incipient pollution. However given sufficiently detailed engineering knowledge of specific industrial techniques, it should be possible to construct 'what if' data for actual economies.

Evidence   Of the two hypothesised factors behind the lazy-S shape of the incipient pollution curve, there appears to be only causal empiricism to support the technique factor (i.e. bell-shaped LCUPC curve). What would be required is a study of how the pollution intensity of production techniques varies with the level of development. Fortunately, there is direct evidence supporting the composition factor (i.e. that economies shift to first more- then to less-polluting activities as they become richer). Evidence for a 'pollution Kuznets curve' is provided by Hettige, Lucas and Wheeler (1992). They find that the share of heavily-polluting activity first rises and then falls with *per capita* income. In particular the bell-shaped relationship applies to an index of the sectoral composition of industry weighted by the pounds of toxic material released by each sector.

2.2.3 The per capita abatement curve
For a variety of reasons, societies tend to increase their efforts to abate pollution as they get richer. Reasons for this stylised fact abound. One

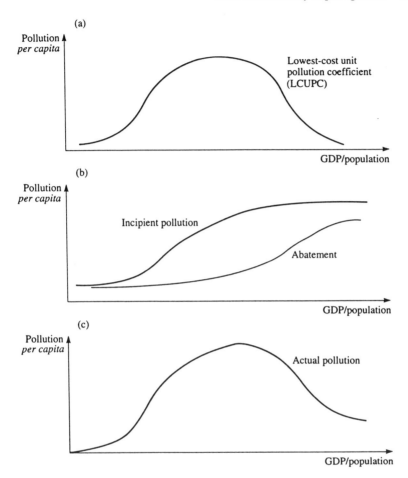

Figure 3.4   Schematic ecologic transition
       (a) Lowest-cost unit pollution coefficient
       (b) Incipient pollution and abatement
       (c) Actual pollution

simple explanation focuses on the demand for environmental quality: environmental concern has an income elasticity greater than unity. A more popular way of phrasing this is that only rich societies can afford to worry about the environment; poor societies must direct most of their expenditure to the basic necessities of life. Another explanation is that only rich countries have the advanced social, legal and fiscal infra-structures that are essential to enforcing environmental regulations and promoting 'green awareness'. Whatever the reasons, causal empiricism suggests that at early stages of industrialisation, abatement does rise more slowly than incipient pollution for many types of pollutants. Just as a drop in fertility lags behind a drop in mortality, abatement typically lags behind the rise in incipient pollution that accompanies rapid industrialisation. This is shown schematically in figure 3.4b.

Evidence   Direct evidence on abatement would require engineering studies. The task would be complicated by the fact that one cannot automatically take the most-polluting technology observed in the world as the LCUPC for all countries. The point is that many factor prices – the price of labour in particular – vary radically between more-developed countries (MDCs) and less-developed countries. As a consequence, they are unlikely to share LCUPCs. Doing a job with manual labour tends to be less polluting than doing it with more advanced techniques; think of weeding a plot of land by hand versus weeding it with herbicides, or stripping paint manually versus stripping it chemically.

2.2.4 Per capita pollution curve
The shape of the actual pollution curve, shown in figure 3.4c, follows necessarily from the relative levels of the incipient pollution and abatement curves. At early stages of economic development a country produces little output per person and that output consists of mostly environmentally-friendly products. As development progresses, a gap opens between incipient pollution and abatement, leading to a rising flow of *per capita* pollution. *Per capita* emissions reach a peak at an intermediary level of income. At higher levels of income, abatement rises faster than incipient pollution, leading to a falling level of *per capita* emissions.

Copeland and Taylor (1992) present a simple theoretical model that captures some aspects of the ecologic transition presented above. Their model assumes a continuum of goods that are distinguished by their intrinsic pollution intensity. Production of each good allows a trade off between more labour and more pollution. Governments are assumed to impose a pollution tax and firms optimally choose the degree of abatement in which to engage. As wages rise, the abatement undertaken falls for a given level of the pollution tax. The Copeland–Taylor model is not rich enough to capture the observed shift of rich economies into services; it does, however, capture one part of the LCUPC curve, namely the rising part. The Copeland–Taylor study also captures the general shape of the abatement curve by assuming that welfare-maximising governments endogenously raise pollution taxes as the country gets richer. As a consequence, firms in richer countries find it optimal to engage in more abatement.

The Copeland–Taylor model does not have endogenous growth; it is, however, easy to imagine how the Becker–Murphy–Tamura model could be wedded to the Copeland–Taylor model in order to produce an ecologic transition. In the Copeland–Taylor model, countries' endowment of labour is fixed. However if the amount of effective units of labour rises, say through the accumulation of human capital, wage rates rise. This forces the country up their LCUPC curve and their abatement curve. As long as we ruled out feedback from pollution to human capital accumulation and fertility, we could append the Copeland–Taylor model to the Becker–Murphy–Tamura model as a set of side equations.

Evidence   Actual emissions of pollution are observable, so the shape of the actual pollution curve is immanently testable and has been eminently tested. Selden and Song (1992) find a bell-shaped relationship between *per capita* GDP and *per capita* emission of SO_2, NO_2, suspended particulate and carbon monoxide. Holtz-Eakin and Selden (1992) find a similar relationship for *per capita* carbon dioxide emissions. Grossman and Krueger (1991) provided the first analysis of this type, although they focused on levels of pollutants rather than emissions (obviously the two are closely related under certain reasonable assumptions). The Grossman–Krueger study used a cross-country panel of data on levels of three types of air pollutants as monitoring stations in urban areas. For sulphur dioxide and smoke, they found that air concentrations tend to increase with *per capita* income at low levels, but decrease at higher levels.
   The turning point for the various pollutants varied widely. Grossman and Krueger (1991) found that for SO_2 and smoke, the peak of the actual pollution curve was approximately $5000 *per capita*. (For the third contaminant, suspended particulate, they found pollution decreased monotonically with *per capita* income at all levels of development; see also Chapter 2 in this volume.) Selden and Song (1992) found the top of the curve at $8000–$9000 for *per capita* emissions of SO_2 and suspended particulate. For oxides of nitrogen and carbon monoxide, they found that the curve crested at much higher levels, $23,000 and $11,000 respectively. Holtz-Eakin and Selden (1992) found that the *per capita* emissions of CO_2 turned down only at an extremely high level of income of $35,000. This point is almost twice as high as the highest income observed in their sample, so it must be viewed with caution.

3   Where the world is today

3.1   Demographics

We start with *per capita* income, population and population growth. Figure 3.5 clearly shows two unsurprising facts. Most people are very

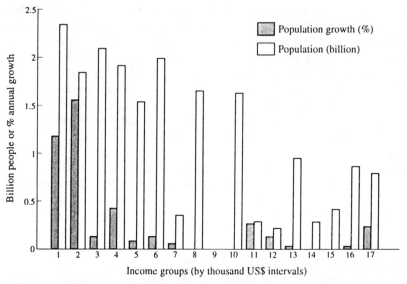

Figure 3.5   Population and population growth rates
Source: World Bank data base.

poor and the poor – especially the very poor – are reproducing at a much higher rate than the rich. More than half of the world's population has a real *per capita* income of less than $2000.[3] Population growth rates in these countries are at least two to three times higher than those in Europe and North America. The doubling time (at current rates) for the poorer half of the world's 5.5 billion people is approximately 35 years. Figure 3.6a shows that about a third of the people in LDCs have yet to reach the fertile phase of their lives. Figure 3.6b shows that the current high population growth rates in poor countries are likely to continue and perhaps even to increase. Unless something changes the current pattern of fertility, poor populations will expand very rapidly for decades as the very young in poor countries move into their highest fertility periods of life. Note that the age profile in the more developed countries is much flatter, as is typical of societies in the third phase of the demographic transition.

A rough idea as to the position of the world's population in the demographic transition can be had from figure 3.7a. This graphs World Bank 5-year average data (1985–90) for births and deaths per 1000 people for 131 countries. Cubic approximations to the data were fitted to ease inspection. It is clear that both birth and death rates decline rapidly with *per capita* income. Birth rates appear to decline more rapidly than death rates, although for all income levels fitted births exceed fitted deaths.

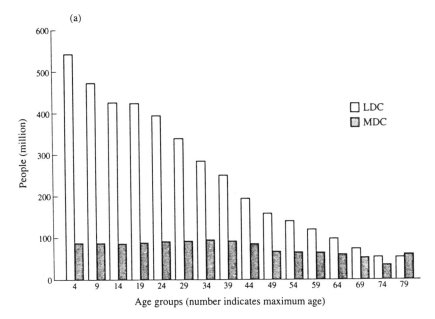

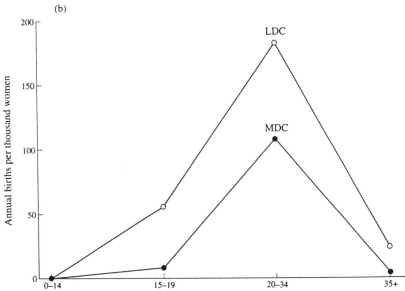

Figure 3.6   Population and birth rates by age groups
   (a) Age profiles of population, 1990
   (b) Birth rates by age groups, 1985–90 average
Source: World Bank data base.

Figure 3.7b presents exactly the same data, including the fitted line, but zooms in on poor countries (those with incomes below $3000 per person). This close-up shows that the birth rate line fitted to data for the 131 countries follows the poor country data fairly well, although there is some suggestion that the curve should be falling even faster at the lowest levels of income. In contrast, the fitted line for death rates clearly understates the rate at which death falls with income in the poorest countries. Nonetheless for income level beyond $500, the fitted curve broadly captures the true relationship between death rates and material living standards. Notice that India and especially China are below the fitted curve.

In summary, more than half of the world population is very poor, very young and in the rapid growth phase of the demographic transition. Cross-country data suggests that virtually all countries in the world are currently in the latter part of Phase II of their demographic transitions (see figure 3.1). Consequently, income growth will reduce birth rates by more than it will lower death rates. This is especially true for the poorest (countries with *per capita* incomes less than $2000) that account for about half of the world's population.

3.2   *Pollution*

Due to data limitations, this chapter concentrates on air pollution even though other forms of environmental degradation are at least as important. In particular, population pressures place a heavy strain on land and water resources. Human-induced soil degradation due to overgrazing and the intensification of agriculture on marginal land are forms of environmental damage that are likely to impact quite directly on the sustainability of economic activity in poor countries. Deforestation, often driven by population pressures, poses similar problems, as does water pollution stemming from untreated sewage and industrial activites. Finally, reduced biodiversity bears important costs, even if they are difficult to quantify. This omission is quite serious, since these are the sorts of environmental damage that will most directly affect the citizens of poor countries. More to the point, these are the effects that should be foremost in the minds of policy makers in poor nations when considering the advantages of population control.

Figure 3.8a and b plots *per capita* CO_2 emissions against real *per capita* income for 120 countries. Although there is no clear bell shape in the 1989 data (figure 3.8a), Holtz-Eakin and Selden (1992) did find one using a fixed-effects estimator (with both year and country specific fixed effects); they found that the apex of the curve occurs at $35,000. According to the

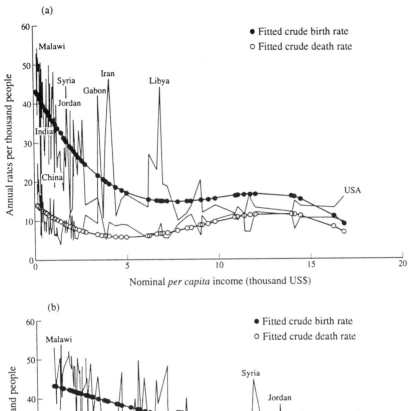

Figure 3.7 Demographic transition with cross-country data
    (a) All countries
    (b) Close-up of poor countries
Source: World Bank data base.

(a)

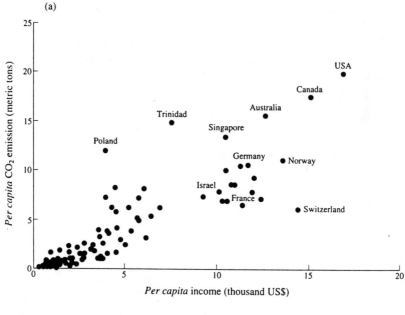

(b)

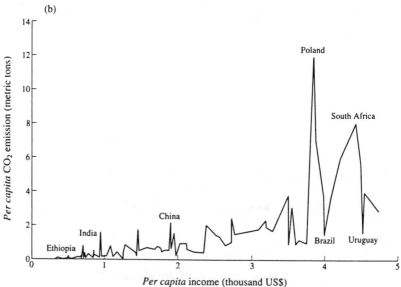

Figure 3.8   *Per capita* CO$_2$ emissions versus average income, 1989
   (a) All countries
   (b) Close-up of poor countries
Source: WRI (1992).

Holtz-Eakin–Selden analysis, all or most of the people in the world are on the upward sloping section of the bell-shaped pollution curve.

Figure 3.9a shows that although the rich countries account for a very disproportionate share of the carbon dioxide emitted, the poor account for a very significant fraction. The point is that although the poor have very low *per capita* emission rates, they number between 2 and 3 billion.

The bell-shaped *per capita* pollution curves estimated by Selden and Song (1992) are plotted in figure 3.9b against the actual range of incomes observed in the world.[4] Annual *per capita* emissions of carbon monoxide, nitrogen dioxide, sulphur dioxide and suspended particulants are measured in kilograms. To get an idea of which parts of the bell-shaped curve are most important, we plot the population of countries (in 10 million) (figure 3.9b). It is plain that most of the countries and most of the world's population are facing the most steeply rising section of the curves.

In summary, poor countries, which account for most people in the world, emit very little air pollution *per capita*; however, their incomes are at such a level that growth in income will rapidly increase their *per capita* pollution. The figures suggest that the poor countries are in fact in the first part of their Phase II in the ecologic transition (see figure 3.1). That is, their incomes lie in a range where incipient pollution rises more quickly than abatement. This suggests that income growth will lead to accelerating *per capita* emissions, although the relative flatness of the pollution curve implies that the acceleration will be quite moderate in terms of absolute levels.

3.3 Interaction of the demographic and ecologic transitions

Figure 3.10 combines data on world population, birth rates, death rates and emissions. It suggests that many of the world's poor are at an income level that puts them in the ending stages of their demographic transition, although the two lowest income groups are still in the rapid expansion stage. By contrast, most of the world has average incomes that suggest rapidly rising emission rates. If incomes continue to grow, the heavy mass of population in the $0–2000 range will shift rightwards, experiencing lower population growth but rising pollution flows. The obvious conclusion is that if nothing is done to close the demographic gap (between birth and death rates) and the ecologic gap (between incipient pollution and abatement), the world will experience rapid increases in pollution flows until the LDCs get much richer. The nightmare scenario is that income growth in the poorest LDCs would stall at the point where they are in the high-emission stage, but not quite out of high-growth stage of their demographic transition. This would be likely to produce population

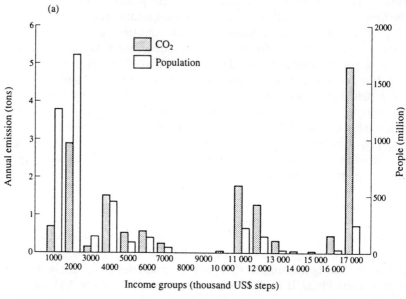

(a)

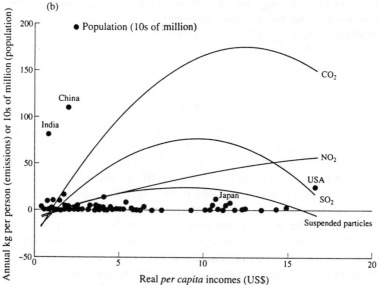

(b)

Figure 3.9   Air pollution and population for 120 countries
(a) CO₂ emissions versus population
(b) Selden-Song *per capita* emission curves versus population

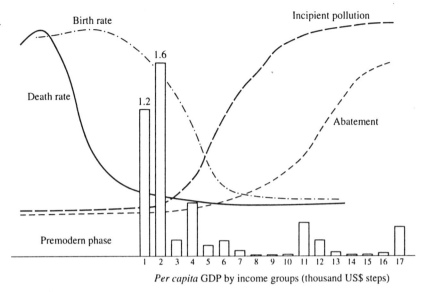

Figure 3.10 Demographic and ecologic transitions, 1989
Bars show world population by income group (billion)

growth that puts unsustainable strains on domestic resources and emission growth that puts unsustainable pressure on the global atmosphere.

Figure 3.10 can be used to argue for bringing down the birth rate curve and bringing up the abatement curve, especially in the $0–2000 range. It would appear that the demographic problem is the more pressing of the two. These thoughts are explored further in section 5.

4   A simple-minded extrapolation: constant income growth

With the simple analytic frameworks presented in section 2 and the simple data presented in section 3, we are ready to address the question posed by this chapter's title: does sustainability require growth? The answer is a fairly obvious 'Yes', if one takes seriously the links between *per capita* income and demographics on the one hand, and *per capita* income and pollution on the other. To see this, suppose that average incomes in all nations were somehow frozen. While this is an extraordinarily unlikely event, it proves to be a useful thought experiment. According to the pollution curve, per-person emissions would stay constant. According to the demographics, the number of people would continue to grow. The results of this thought experiment are presented in figure 3.11. In particular we add the four per-person emission rates from the Selden–Song fitted pollution curves (corrected by constants to eliminate negative emission rates) and the actual *per capita* CO_2 figures from figure 3.9b. All rates are measured in kg per person. Each country's *per capita* air pollution rate is multiplied by its total population to yield total air pollution per country. Figure 3.11 shows these country totals, summed by income group. The population of each country is increased over 20 year periods using historical (1985–90) population growth rates. Using this simple extrapolation, world population reaches 14.9 billion by 2049. This is much greater than the World Bank's baseline forecast of 9 billion since the extrapolation freezes all countries at their 1989 position in the demographic transition.[5]

The leftmost bar for each income class in figure 3.11 shows the actual pollution in 1989. In 1989, LDCs had much lower *per capita* pollution rates than MDCs. Indeed, the rates were so much lower that, despite the much greater population in the LDCs, the MDCs accounted for the bulk of the world's air pollution. Each bar further to the right shows the total air pollution corresponding to the higher populations in 2009, 2029 and 2049. The growth of poor countries' population far outstrips that of the rich countries for the simple reason that their populations are assumed to continue growing faster. The numbers are impressive. The $1000–$2000 income class generated only 150 billion kg of the five air pollutants in 1989. By 2049 they emit half a trillion kg, or five times more than the US (which is the only country in the highest income class).

It is not possible to defend the actual numbers shown in figure 3.11 as being realistic. They should not be construed as a forecast. Indeed, this is the crux of the matter. Accelerating annual emissions of air pollution are not sustainable. Given almost any reasonable assumption on the world's ability to break down pollutants, an accelerating inflow leads to an ever-rising stock of pollution. This violates every definition of sustainability.

The implication is straightforward. Unless people – especially the very poor – get richer, they are likely to continue to have children at an unsustainable pace and thus produce pollution at an unsustainable pace.

The thought experiment focuses on air pollution; however, the same sorts of calculations would show unsustainable increases in food production, fresh water consumption, deforestation and fish stock depletion. This is the sort of thing that the Reverend Thomas Malthus had in mind in 1803 when he wrote, 'An Essay on the Principle of Population'. To put it simply, sustainability requires growth because if people do not get richer, they will continue to produce children at an unsustainable rate.

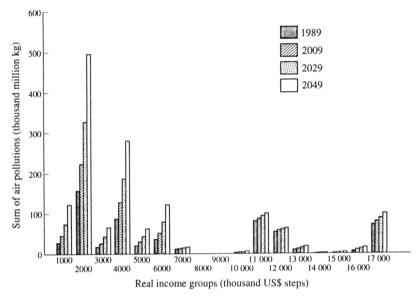

Figure 3.11 Air pollution levels with constant population growth
Source: Author's calculations.

5   Sustainability and policy implications

If we take 'sustainability' to mean achievement of a steady state in the environment, we can conclude that an ever-rising flow of pollution is not sustainable since the flow of pollutant that the world is able to break down must be finite. By definition, total world pollution is the product of the world's average *per capita* pollution and world population. Consequently, sustainability requires that the sum of population growth and the growth of the average *per capita* pollution coefficient be zero (or at least approach zero at a sufficiently rapid rate). The analytic frameworks presented above, the demographic and ecologic transitions, help us to focus more closely on how the nonrising flow of pollution can be achieved. In terms of the demographic transition, sustainability requires that all of the world's population get past the second stage of the demographic transition into the few-births–few-deaths stage. In terms of the ecologic transition, sustainability requires that all countries get to the point where abatement offsets incipient pollution.

In figure 3.10, this would require all countries to have real incomes that are on the far right-hand side of the scale. This, of course, is highly unlikely to occur any time in the near future. Fortunately, raising incomes is not the only way to reduce population and *per capita* pollution growth.

Table 3.1. *OLS analysis on a cross-section of total fertility rates, 96 countries, 1985*

C	Primary enrolment	Female primary enrolment	Secondary enrolment	GDP *per capita*	R^2
Data in levels					
1. 8.0	0.01	− 0.02	− 0.06	0.00004	0.77
(15.1)	(0.6)	(− 1.2)	(− 8.7)	(1.1)	
Data in logs					
2. 2.3	1.29	− 0.99	− 0.37	− 0.13	0.63
(2.7)	(2.0)	(− 1.9)	(− 4.1)	(− 2.1)	

Note: *t*-statistics shown below point estimates.
96 country sample, 1985 data. Dependent variable is total fertility rate from World Bank database; enrolment data from same source. Real *per capita* GDP from Summers and Heston (1991).

The relationships between *per capita* GDP and demographics, on the one hand, and between *per capita* GDP and pollution, on the other, are not immutable. They can be affected by policy. The goal of the policy should be twofold: first to get the fertility curve down closer to the death curve, especially in the most populous nations, and second to get the abatement curve up to the incipient pollution curve, again especially for the most populous countries.

We turn first to demographics – fertility in particular. Simple cross-sectional regression analysis of total fertility rates suggests that education is an important policy tool that can be used to reduce fertility. Table 3.1 shows the results of OLS analysis on a cross-section of total fertility rates from 96 countries in 1985. The explanatory variables include various measures of educational investment and *per capita* GDP (as measured by Summers and Heston, 1991). The regression performed on the data in levels indicates that the secondary enrolment rate is the only significant variable. In particular, *per capita* real income is not significant. Although this result confirms the well-known Barro (1991) result, it is quite unsatisfactory. The point is that even the most casual inspection of the data suggests that any relationship between *per capita* GDP and fertility must be highly nonlinear.

To reflect this, we re-ran the regression in log-log form. The results, which are shown in the second line of table 3.1, are quite different. Allowing for simple nonlinearities in the relationships, we see that all five regressors are statistically different from zero at the 10 percent level.

Notice that two of the three measures of investment in human capital –
primary education for females and secondary education in general – have
a strong negative influence on fertility. *Per capita* GDP also has a fairly
strong dampening effect on fertility. These results line up very well with
the predictions of the simple Becker–Murphy–Tamura model. The positive and significant sign of total primary enrolment rates is somewhat of a
puzzle. Inspection of the data, however, reveals that primary enrolment is
fairly close to 100 percent for all countries with incomes above $1200,
while secondary enrolment increases for all levels of income. Thus,
loosely speaking, the positive sign on primary enrolment may be acting as
a proxy for more complicated nonlinearities in the relationships.

Population scientists would certainly include many more variables in a
fertility regression, such as the availability of contraception, the presence
of birth control programmes, etc. Moreover, they would certainly break
down the total fertility rate into fertility by age group. Nonetheless, the
rough model of fertility estimated above serves to make our basic point.
Fertility rates can be brought down by policies other than simple
increases in *per capita* GDP. Indeed, extra effort placed on education is
likely to yield double dividends since there is strong evidence (Mankiw,
Romer and Weil, 1992) that *per capita* GDP is positively linked to the rate
of investment in human capital. Given that the data suggest that a very
large fraction of the world's population is about to enter a high-fertility
phase, it would seem that policies to control population growth should be
given a high priority on the sustainability agenda.

There is little doubt that government policy can curtail *per capita*
pollution. Many policies – such as the introduction of unleaded petrol –
curb *per capita* pollution quite directly. Others, such as taxes on fuels and
automobiles, do so less directly, but just as effectively. For most countries
and most industries, stricter environmental standards imply an increase in
costs. Thus, each government is faced with a trade off between stimulating economic activity and curbing pollution. Historically, richer countries
tend to opt for higher environmental standards. This has forced firms
based in rich countries to develop abatement technologies such as cata-
lytic converters and smoke scrubbers. The fact that such technologies are
subject to the usual increasing returns of information intensive industries
– large fixed costs of R&D with low marginal costs of production –
suggests that international transmission of abatement technology should
play a role in decreasing global pollution.

Figure 3.9b suggests that a large share of the world's population is on the
verge of industrialising. Unless effective abatement technologies are made
available at a reasonable price, it seems likely that the governments of the
poor countries will tend to lean towards the economic stimulus side of the

pollution–industrialisation trade off. This suggests that another important item on the sustainability agenda should be the transfer of 'green' technologies.

6 Summary, conclusions and future research

Expressed in its most Spartan form, the thesis of this chapter is that people produce pollution and severe poverty produces people at an unsustainable rate; *ergo*, sustainability necessitates *per capita* income growth, at least among the world's poor. Since more than half the world's population currently lives in severe poverty, the issue of population growth is inexorably tied up with planetary environmental considerations. Raising the level of education, which raises incomes and reduces fertility, would be a natural way to achieve such growth.

Raising average income and output in the developing world, however, will not be an unmitigated blessing for the environment. The fundamental problem is that while most LDCs are near the end of the explosive phase of their demographic transitions, they appear to be right at the beginning of the rapid-emission-growth phase of their ecologic transitions. As a consequence, global environment damage is likely to increase before it declines. Despite this inevitable deterioration of the environment, stopping economic growth would be exactly the wrong prescription. Such medicine would simply swap industrial pollution for more Malthusian degradations of the environment, especially in the poorest countries. Alarmist prognoses are generally unhelpful, and that is not the intent of this chapter. Rather, the purpose is to suggest that the generous attention paid to schemes for reducing *per capita* pollution in rich countries may be missing the proverbial forest for the trees.

Two complementary policy approaches are suggested. First, countries should continue and increase their efforts to shorten the explosive phase of their demographic transitions. The fact that the atmosphere is a shared resource suggests that it would be in the best interest of rich countries to assist poor countries in this effort. Several countries, India and China most notably, have quickly lowered their birth rates, thus bringing their population growth rates closer to a sustainable level. Clearly, then, policy efforts to alter demographic forces are not fruitless. Similarly, it should be possible for countries to institute policies that would compress the gap between rising incipient pollution and rising abatement. While part of this ecologic transition is due to the shifting composition of output that is typically observed in the development process, much of it has to do with the slow adoption of abatement technologies. The former would be quite difficult to alter, but it would seem that the latter is largely a matter of diffusion of technologies that exist in the West. Good policy, such as technology transfers and correct factor prices, in rich and poor nations could help close the gap between incipient pollution and abatement. Understanding of the economic and technological determinants of the incipient pollution curve and the abatement curve are rather under-developed. Indeed apart from some general platitudes about elasticities of substitution in production and the Kuznets curve, the microeconomics of the ecologic transition – and the bell-shaped, *per capita* emission curve that it provides – is nonexistent. In particular, it would be important to disentangle the roles of the production composition and production technique factors. Furthermore it would be interesting to study differences among the ecologic transitions experienced in different countries, with special emphasis on the role of policy.

NOTES

I gratefully acknowledge the help of Rikad Forslid, Mario Gehring, Thomas Selden, Kym Anderson, Gene Grossman, Ian Goldin and Alan Winters.
1 The French demographer Adolphe Landry introduced the theory in his famous book *La Revolution Demographique* (1934).
2 'Fertility' here is defined as the crude birth rate, i.e. number of births per 1000 citizens.
3 In 1985, using Summers and Heston (1991) data.
4 The Selden–Song estimates allow for country specific and year specific effects that are not incorporated into figure 3.9b. Presumably the negative emissions would disappear if they were included.
5 Of course the World Bank's forecast is based on a judgement that growth will continue. Nevertheless, it is interesting to note that income plays no role whatsoever in the World Bank's forecast. Birth and death rates are assumed to fall in an exogenous way, following a logistic function of time.

REFERENCES

Barro, R. (1991) 'Economic growth in a cross-section of countries', *Quarterly Journal of Economics*, 106(2): 407–44
Becker, G., Murphy, K. and Tamura, R. (1990) 'Human capital, fertility and economic growth', *Journal of Political Economy*, 98(5): S12–S37
Copeland, B. and Taylor, S. (1992) 'North–South trade and the environment', University of British Columbia, mimeo
Daly, H.E. (1990) 'Toward some operational principles of sustainable development', *Ecological Economics*, 2: 1–
Goodland, R. and Daly, H.E. (1992) 'Why Northern growth is not the solution', in R. Goodland, H.E. Daly and S. Serafy (eds.), *Population, Technology and Lifestyle*, Washington, DC: Island Press

Goodland, R., Daly, H.E. and Serafy, S. (eds.) (1992) *Population, Technology and Lifestyle*, Washington, DC: Island Press

Grossman, G. and Krueger, A. (1991) 'Environmental impacts of a North American Free Trade Agreement', CEPR, *Working Paper*, **644**, London: CEPR

Hettige, H., Lucas, R. and Wheeler, D. (1992) 'The toxic intensity of industrial production: global patterns, trends and trade policy', *American Economic Review*, **82(2)**: 478–81

Holtz-Eakin, D. and Selden, T.M. (1992) 'Stoking the fires? CO_2 emissions and economic growth', NBER, *Working Paper*, **4248**, Cambridge, MA: NBER

MacNeill, J. (1989) 'Strategies for sustainable economic development', *Scientific American*, **261**: 154–65

Mankiw, G., Romer, D. and Weil, D. (1992) 'A contribution to the empirics of economic growth', *Quarterly Journal of Economics*, **107**: 407–37

Nerlove, M. (1991) 'Population and the environment: a parable of firewood and other tales', *American Journal of Agricultural Economics*, **73(5)**: 1334–47

Overbeek, J. (1976) *The Population Challenge*, London: Greenwood Press

Selden, T.M. and Song, D. (1992) 'Environmental quality and development: is there a Kuznetz curve for air pollution', Syracuse University, mimeo

Summers, R. and Heston, A. (1991) 'The Penn Mark IV Data Table, an expanded set of international comparisons, 1950–1988', *Quarterly Journal of Economics*, **106** (May): 327–59

World Bank (1992) *World Population Projections*, 1992–1993 edn., Washington, DC: Johns Hopkins University Press

World Resources Institute (1992) *World Resources 1992–93*, New York and London: Oxford University Press

Discussion

DANIEL COHEN

The key point of Richard Baldwin's Chapter 3 is the following: if poor countries were to become rich, they would pollute more on account of the increased number of goods produced, but less on account of their enhanced concern for air quality. Can one argue that a big push of the wealth of nations could reduce the level of pollution? This is the modern version of the anti-Malthusian view. Getting rich did not lead European nations in the 19th century to have more children but instead to raise the quality of their lives. In the same vein, it could happen that getting rich will lower rather than raise the degree of pollution that today's poor countries will be led to.

There is a theoretical point and an empirical point to the argument. The theoretical point can mimic the children's paradigm: when rich the marginal benefit of reproducible goods declines with respect to non-reproducible ones (time to childbearing for children for the demographic transition, fresh air for the ecologic transition). Empirically, this amounts to assuming that fresh air is a luxury good, and to calculating its elasticity with respect to *per capita* income. One would then write:

$$P = (P/Q)(Q/N)N$$

in which P/Q is pollution per output, Q/N is output *per capita*, and N is the population. Call $y = Q/N$, assume that $P/Q = f(y)$, with $f' < 0$, and further take it that $N = N(y)$, with $N' < 0$ (a simple-minded version of the Malthusian hypothesis which encompasses the demographic transition). Then the dependency of pollution over *per capita* income can be written:

$$P'(y) = y f'(y) N(y) + f(y) N(y) + y f(y) N'(y).$$

When $y = 0$, pollution will rise along with $f(0) N(0)$. Both $f(0)$ and $N(0)$ are maxima: very poor countries have very large (asymptotic) populations, and $f(0)$ is also at the highest point, because poor countries have no concern over pollution. When y is very large, $y f'(y) N(y) + y f(y) N'(y)$ is highly negative, and the empirical question amounts to deciding whether this effect dominates $f(y) N(y)$ which measures the per output supply of pollution of a rich country. If the answer is 'yes', as it seems to be when one looks at the numbers, then the pollution curve will be an inverted U-shaped. Then the empirical question is twofold. For which world *per capita* income is the maximum level of pollution reached? Theoretically, this will be at the point where the sum of the two elasticities of f and N is equal to -1. Second, if the world stands today to the left of that threshold, will the minimum level that can be reached to the right of that threshold (for infinite *per capita* income) be above or below the current level?

Chapter 3 argues that we are at the very early stage of industrialisation for the poor countries, so that we are about to climb that inverted U-shaped curve, and yet it also argues that it would be foolish to stop economic growth in the name of the environment, because demographics would make things worse. Having no competence to judge the empirics, I can only regret that the one part that I know best, the dynamics, and the analysis of the time to reach one state from another, are not exploited. If the wealth of nations is a very slow-moving process (as argued in the new growth theory), how long will it take before we reach the peak of the inverted U-shaped curve, and before we get back below current levels? What are then the implications for the 'stock' of pollution of that slow motion?

Part Two
Sustainability

4 What sustains economic development?

MAURICE SCOTT

1 Some definitions

The chapter starts (in this section) with an attempt to clarify the meaning of certain concepts relevant to 'sustained economic development'. It needs to be said that the definitions have been chosen for their analytic convenience, and that they do not have any direct implications for policy. For example, defining income in one way does not imply that it should be kept constant or be made to grow or decline at any particular rate. Definitions are only definitions. It is hoped that the ones given here do help to clarify the issues subsequently discussed, namely, environmental concerns (section 2), the role of government (section 3), and the main conditions for continuing growth in real *per capita* income (the concluding section 4).

Other chapters in this book are concerned with *optimal* growth, but my concern is with whether sustained growth is *feasible*. It has been argued in recent years that the effects of growth on the environment are such that, in the not too distant future, growth must cease. While environmental concerns must be taken seriously they are not, I believe, the most important ones. Nor is another one often mentioned in this context, namely, whether present generations are sufficiently interested in the welfare of future generations. The view that people save and invest only for themselves and not for their descendants is, to my mind, a caricature of the truth (see Scott, 1989: 221–4). Instead, I believe that continuing future development mainly depends on the ability of different nations, and of different groups within nations, to coexist peaceably and to organise collective action effectively. This consideration has taken me beyond my role as an economist into territory with which I am less familiar; it is hard to avoid this if one is to answer the question posed in the title of this chapter.

1.1   The meaning of economic development

Throughout this chapter I shall confine myself to a narrow definition of economic development, namely, growth in real *per capita* income more or less as conventionally measured. Many of the most interesting and controversial questions can be adequately discussed with this definition, and its use serves to sharpen some points that may otherwise be blunted by vagueness or complexity. Nevertheless, a few remarks on wider definitions are offered here, if only to show awareness of them (see Beckerman, 1974, for a valuable analysis).

The chief difficulty with conventional measures of real *per capita* income is that they leave out of direct consideration some of the most important determinants of human happiness. Many studies have shown that family and other personal relationships are what matter most, and some studies suggest that, beyond a reasonably prosperous level, further increases in *per capita* income do not increase happiness at all (see Lane 1991, part VII, and the studies referred to therein). Arthur Lewis (1955: 420–1) roundly asserted that:

> The advantage of economic growth is not that wealth increases happiness, but that it increases the range of human choice . . . We certainly cannot say that an increase in wealth makes people happier . . . We do not know what the purpose of life is, but if it were happiness, then evolution could just as well have stopped a long time ago, since there is no reason to believe that men are happier than pigs, or than fishes. What distinguishes men from pigs is that men have greater control over their environment; not that they are more happy. And on this test, economic growth is greatly to be desired. The case for economic growth is that it gives man greater control over his environment, and thereby increases his freedom.

Despite this, I do not know that anyone has attempted to measure 'control over [the] environment', power or freedom in any direct way. Some have sought to widen the scope of measurement to include indicators of things which, one might think, influence happiness, such as leisure time, longevity, educational attainment, access to beautiful countryside and preservation of species. There are also indicators of bads, such as suicide rates, divorce rates, crime rates, and measures of air, water or noise pollution.

Estimates for the US which do not stray as far as this from conventional ones, but which improve them as indicators of 'measureable economic welfare', have been made by Nordhaus and Tobin (1972), and estimates which bring in more allowances for damage to the environment have been made by Daly and Cobb (1989). Nordhaus (1992) has brought these two sets of estimates together, provided a critique of Daly and Cobb's estimates, and attempted an estimate of Hicksian income for the US using them both and also drawing on Eisner's (1989) estimates. I refer to this very interesting study below.

One can only applaud attempts to widen and improve conventional estimates of income. As supplies of conventional goods and services become more plentiful in richer countries, more attention should be given to the other indicators of goods and bads mentioned above. Despite that, in numerous poorer countries the level of conventionally measured *per capita* income is low enough to be of great concern, and is likely to remain so for many years. If Lewis is right, even wealthier people will continue to want their incomes to grow. Without further apology I therefore confine myself to growth in *per capita* income, which requires me to clarify what I mean by it, and by some related concepts.

1.2 The meaning of income

I follow Hicks (1946, ch. XIV) in defining income as the maximum real rate of consumption which it is expected can be sustained 'indefinitely'. As I have discussed this (and other terms defined below) elsewhere (Scott, 1989: ch. 1, 1990), I will be as brief as possible. It is obvious that no mortal can expect to achieve any level of consumption *indefinitely*. However, most mortals are interested in the fates of their offspring, and the subject-matter of much of history and economics is the fate of societies. It is therefore useful to define income as accruing to a stable demographic group. Societies, as well as individuals, are subject to extinction, and this and other catastrophes are discussed below. Ignoring them for the moment, income for a society may be defined as the maximum level of consumption which it could have achieved from 'now' onwards if it had been given a long period of notice that, from now onwards, both economic and demographic growth were to cease. The long period of notice is needed so that the production of investment goods can be converted to production of consumption goods. If one assumes, as a first approximation, that the factors producing each £1 of investment goods can be converted to produce £1 of consumption goods, then income equals the sum of consumption and investment. That is the conventional definition, which is both welcome and convenient.

1.3 The meaning of maintenance and investment

Maintenance costs are those incurred in producing income. Generally speaking they restore existing assets (e.g. repairing a fence or a road), or protect them from wear and tear (painting a fence, oiling an engine), or replace assets that have worn out or been consumed (restoring depleted inventories, replanting forests). If the whole of *required maintenance* is undertaken, income will not fall. It is all those expenditures needed in the hypothetical static society mentioned above.

By contrast, *investment* expenditures are those incurred to *increase* income, and so go beyond maintenance. Investment is the cost, measured by consumption foregone, of changing (hopefully of improving) economic arrangements. It includes the large category of human investments (education, training and the cost of moving workers from lower to higher paid jobs), as well as what I call 'material' investment, consisting of all the usual items such as expenditures on buildings and other constructions, on machinery, equipment and vehicles, and on increases in inventories. It also includes the cost of increasing and improving stocks of farm animals, of trees and of fields and pastures. It is wider than the conventional definition in including, for example, R&D expenditures, and some advertising, financial and managerial expenditures. One way or another it therefore includes all the costs of acquiring knowledge, whose importance in development has been emphasised by so many. I have argued elsewhere (Scott, 1989: ch. 1, 1990) that, at least for developed countries, *net* investment for a whole country is better approximated by human investment plus conventional *gross* material investment than by this minus so-called capital consumption, which gives conventional net investment. Very briefly, the reason for this is that *depreciation* (capital consumption) of material assets is due almost entirely to obsolescence and *not to physical deterioration*, and is offset by an equal and opposite *appreciation* of human assets as real wage rates rise. The latter is omitted from conventional accounts, which are therefore biased downwards.

1.4   Sustainable development in the light of the above

It follows from these definitions that, so long as there is positive investment (which implies that required maintenance is being undertaken) with a positive yield, and so long as population is constant, *per capita* income will grow. If population grows, some investment is required merely to keep *per capita* income constant, the amount depending on the marginal productivity of labour and on the yield of investment. This then provides a starting point from which we can begin to consider what sustained economic development is. Before launching into this, however, three issues which can create confusion need to be dealt with: the so-called 'natural' capital stock, technical progress, and catastrophes.

1.5   The irrelevance of the 'natural' capital stock

The concept of the 'natural' capital stock has been given prominence by David Pearce and others (Pearce and Turner, 1990; Pearce, Barbier and Markandya, 1990). In a discussion of the conditions for sustainable development (Pearce et al., 1990: 4) the authors:

> summarize the key necessary condition as 'constancy of the natural capital stock'. More strictly, the requirement is for non-negative change in the stock of natural resources and environmental quality. In basic terms, the environment should not be degraded further but improvements would be welcome.

Pearce et al. discuss the meaning of a constant natural capital stock, but conclude with no definition of it. They reject the notion of keeping every item in the stock constant, since they believe it is sensible to use many exhaustible resources. They also reject keeping the economic value of the stock constant, or keeping the real price of natural resources constant. It is then rather difficult to know what they mean by this 'key necessary condition'.

Furthermore, they do not provide a clear definition of 'natural resources' which are presumably the constituents of the natural capital stock. Many environmentalists are concerned to preserve the beautiful English countryside, but by far the greater part of it has been shaped by human activities, and so is presumably not natural. Have our ancestors then degraded England because they have not handed down to us the primeval forests that used to cover it? I suspect that many are grateful for the enormous toil and effort they expended, and are glad they did not preserve the natural capital stock of their time.

This is not to deny that, for example, the depletion of forests or minerals, or the pollution of rivers or seas, may all be relevant to future consumption possibilities and hence to *maintenance*. But in my preceding discussion I did not need to mention *any* aggregate capital stock, let alone a 'natural' one. Even when the concept of economic development is widened, that does not seem necessary. Pearce et al. mention 'access to resources'. Perhaps some sort of stock concept is relevant there. Stocks of *particular* assets are also relevant in evaluating sustainable rates of, for example, fishing or logging. But for the rest it does not seem necessary, and is confusing, to introduce concepts of aggregate capital which are difficult to define.

1.6   Technical progress is not manna from heaven

A strict interpretation of the orthodox neoclassical production function implies that output can increase without there being any increase in employment or in society's capital stock. This occurs because technical progress shifts the production function as time passes, increasing output per unit of all inputs taken together. Since there is no need for investment in working methods, many empirical estimates appear to imply that increases in total factor productivity have been large and have accounted for a large part of increases in total output.

If all this were true, it would have important implications for the measurement of income as defined above. Assume for simplicity no growth of population or employment. *Per capita* income would increase, because of technical progress, even if investment were zero. The maximum sustainable rate of real consumption would then exceed the sum of consumption and investment, since it would be possible to sustain output with *negative investment*. The loss of output due to that would be offset by the gain due to technical progress. Were one to accept the estimates of this gain mentioned above, the extent to which investment could be negative would be very large. Nordhaus (1992) draws attention to this possibility.

Unfortunately, no such conclusion is warranted. The idea that there is costless technical progress which increases output without there being any investment is, in my view, substantially untrue, and is not supported by empirical evidence in the manner alleged. I have stated my reasons for this view many times (e.g. Scott, 1976, 1989, 1991a, 1992a, 1992b) and have yet to see them convincingly challenged (see Denison, 1991, together with my reply, Scott, 1991b, for what I regard as an unconvincing challenge). It would take too long to repeat them here; if I am right, my earlier conclusion that Hicksian income is, to a reasonable approximation, the sum of consumption and investment, holds good.

1.7   Catastrophes and the meaning of income

Examples of catastrophes are climatic changes, diseases, earthquakes and wars. The causes of some of these are outside the control of the countries concerned, while others may be wholly or partly within their control. Another distinction is between events which are more or less foreseen and those which are not foreseen. Yet another is between those which damage a country's economic output while leaving its population more or less intact, and those which destroy the population. How should such events be allowed for in defining income? In searching for answers, I try to find a definition which is both useful and as close as possible to conventional usage.

We can best proceed by taking examples. Suppose one could confidently expect a gradual rise of the sea level by 5 cm per decade over the next 100 years, subsequently coming to an end in some predictable way. This would be a very serious matter for populations living in various coastal areas such as in Bangladesh, Britain or the Netherlands. Suppose that the best way of dealing with this was to strengthen sea defences at a predictable total cost spread over the same period. This cost would be part of required maintenance. If these countries wished to consume as much as they could, at a static level, indefinitely (our definition of income), then the best they could do (by assumption) would be to strengthen their sea defences, and it would be only after they had met that cost that they could consume what was left of their output. The actual cost might be spread unequally over the years. Income should then be calculated by subtracting an annuity with the same present value as the total cost. The correct discount rate to use in computing the annuity would be the marginal real rate of return to investment. To achieve the static rate of consumption, while incurring unequal expenditures on sea defences, it would be necessary to invest in some years (when expenditures on sea defences were low) and to disinvest in others (when they were high) and it is the marginal rate of substitution between outputs at different times that is relevant. The life of the annuity should be the same as that implicit in the definition of income. However the precise length of life makes a negligible difference to the size of the annuity if it is over, say, 100 years and if the discount rate is over, say, 3 percent per annum. The simplest procedure will therefore generally be to assume an infinite life so that the annuity is a perpetuity.

It makes no difference in this example if the catastrophe is controllable or not. What matters is the actual course of action taken. However, the fact that the outcome can be controlled does open up different possibilities. Thus suppose a world authority could choose between strengthening sea defences and stopping the sea level rising by reducing greenhouse gas emissions. If it chose the latter, it would be the cost of that action which would form part of required maintenance, and the cost of strengthening sea defences would become irrelevant.

What if the catastrophe is not foreseen? Something unforeseen cannot influence one's expectation about maximum sustainable consumption. One cannot anticipate it by allowing for extra required maintenance. One can only treat the catastrophe, when it occurs, as a windfall loss, which reduces income.

In between these polar cases of certainty and ignorance will come a great many cases where there will be uncertainty about both the timing and extent of the damage caused by the catastrophe. Fire damage is a familar example. The cost of insurance against it is treated as a current cost, and so implicitly as part of maintenance. A fire should then not significantly affect the incomes (net of insurance premiums) of those insured. Uncertain catastrophes can be handled similarly, although where very little is known about the risks the size of the 'premiums' will themselves be very uncertain.

What if the catastrophe eliminates people as well as output? To take an extreme example, suppose that there was a known probability in any year that the Earth would be struck by a meteor sufficiently large to destroy humanity. Humanity's income might then best be defined by analogy with that of a pensioner who is subject to the risk of death in any year. The pension is commonly referred to as 'income'. It is an annuity which is larger than the interest on its purchase price, since it includes some capital repayment – the more the greater the risk of death. One could equally estimate humanity's income, when subject to the risk of extinction by meteorite, as being somewhat greater than its income assuming indefinite existence. If the risk of extinction is very small, however, the difference would be negligible, given the uncertainty in all these estimates.

In the example of the meteorite I assume that there is nothing that can be done to avoid extinction. War is an example in which extinction for a particular population can be avoided, or at least its risk reduced. Countries try to protect themselves against these risks in various ways, and notably by defence expenditure. Perhaps (as some have suggested) this expenditure should not form part of income, but should be netted out like fire insurance premiums, thus forming part of maintenance. There is a difference compared with fire insurance, however. If a fire occurs, compensation is paid. In the event of war, that is unlikely. Wars are therefore treated as windfall losses, like unforeseen catastrophes. Building up a compensation fund through provisions for maintenance seems impracticable, since that too would be at risk.

1.8   Conclusions on income, maintenance and investment

We have seen that neither the maintenance of the 'natural' capital stock nor 'free' technical progress need concern us. Apart from reducing current estimates of income to allow for foreseeable catastrophes (other than wars) in the way described above, and apart from deducting defence expenditures, and apart from further improvements proposed in the works cited earlier, we are left with the sum of consumption and (gross) investment as a reasonable first approximation to the concept of income as maximum sustainable consumption in a static society. However, income should be net of maintenance, and there is little doubt that some forms of environmental deterioration are not properly allowed for in conventional accounts. Fears have been expressed that environmental maintenance costs are rising and will continue to do so as population and output grow. To these concerns we now turn.

2   Environmental concerns and sustainability

2.1   Some forebodings

During this century in most countries, and for still longer in some, there has been sufficient positive investment, not merely to make total income grow, but to make *per capita* income grow as well. This has occurred while population has increased at unprecedented rates. The yield of investment has not fallen, despite a very long period of capital accumulation. Indeed, it has probably risen (Scott, 1989, ch. 7 and 10). Nevertheless, some fear that it will fall in the future and, as well, that the cost of required maintenance will rise. If this were to happen on a sufficient scale, further growth of *per capita* income could prove increasingly costly, and might have to be abandoned.

The idea of 'limits to growth', set by the finite resources available to us, is an old one. It was revived in a book of that title published in 1972 as a report for the Club of Rome (Meadows *et al.*, 1972). Its message, that resources were fast running out, seemed to be confirmed by the oil shock of 1973. Although that book was heavily criticised (see e.g. Beckerman, 1974, and Cole *et al.*, 1973) some of the ideas put forward in it are still very much alive. Thus, according to a report in *The Times* of 20 November 1992, a declaration signed by 1575 scientists, including 99 Nobel Prize winners, stated that:

> The Earth is finite. Its ability to absorb wastes and destructive effluent is finite. Its ability to provide for growing numbers of people is finite. And we are fast approaching many of the Earth's limits. Current economic practices . . . cannot be continued without the risk that global systems will be damaged beyond repair. Pressures from unrestrained population growth puts demands on the natural world that can overwhelm any efforts to achieve a sustainable future.

The phenomenon of constant exponential growth can make the past a poor guide to the future, given the existence of finite limits. As the absolute size of requirements (e.g. for food, energy, materials or waste disposal) grow, they become larger and larger in relation to the finite size of the resources available to satisfy them. The fact that it has always proved possible to satisfy them in the past does not imply that it will prove possible in the future. Furthermore, the limits may be approached, not gradually, thus giving time for adjustment, but very rapidly. It is like the old puzzle of the lily in the pond. The lily starts off very small, and doubles in area every day. In 1000 days it has covered half the pond. In how much longer will it cover the rest of the pond? Answer: 1 day.

The implication of this line of thought seems to be that exponential growth of both population and output must be brought to an end. In fact, Meadows *et al.* argued that unless both were brought to an end soon there would be not merely a forced halt to the growth of population and output, but a sharp collapse of both. Population and output would have reached levels which were no longer sustainable, and so would have to plunge to much lower levels. Meadows *et al.* (1992) consider that the world economy has already passed sustainable rates of output, and is heading for decline.

2.2 *More sanguine views*

Despite the above concerns, there is a large and influential body of opinion which maintains that further growth in *per capita* output is sustainable. This is the view, for example, of the authors of the *World Development Report 1992* (World Bank 1992) and of *Scanning the Future* (Netherlands Centraal Plan Bureau, 1992). These studies do not deny that if present trends were to continue unchanged – 'business as usual' – there would indeed be increasingly severe environmental problems, especially in poorer countries. Rapidly growing populations are putting pressure on resources and, over the next decades, over 90 percent of the increase in the world's population is expected to occur in developing countries. However, the reports argue that there are ways of dealing with these problems while keeping *per capita* income growing. In fact, further growth of income makes it more likely that the problems will be tackled successfully, as they already have been to some extent in the richer countries. Thus Beckerman (1992), after reviewing evidence on air pollution, water supply and sanitation, concludes: 'On the whole, there is a strong positive correlation between income level and environmental quality – at least as measured by the particular environmental factors noted here'. Beckerman points out that there is nothing *automatic* about this. It is the result of measures taken, especially by governments, to deal with the relevant problems. This issue is further discussed in chapter 2 in this volume.

Let us now consider the reasons given in the above-mentioned reports for believing that environmental problems can be tackled successfully, and their estimates of the costs.

2.2.1 Shortages of fossil fuels and other minerals
Over the coming decades, fuel costs may rise as oil and gas become scarcer. Nevertheless, we are nowhere near the limits of energy supplies directly available from sunlight. The cost of converting this energy into usable forms has fallen greatly in recent years, and it is reasonable to expect that it will continue to fall. If so, it could replace fossil fuels at costs not far removed from their current levels (World Bank, 1992, p. 123), with the further advantage that greenhouse gas emissions would be drastically cut. According to the *World Development Report*, shortages of metals and other materials are not a worry. Methods of production must change in response to changing relative scarcities, as they have for centuries. Renewable energy sources must be developed, and research expenditure should be diverted from nuclear power to other renewable forms, perhaps especially to photo-voltaic and other direct energy production from the sun's rays.

The Netherlands Centraal Plan Bureau states that fuel prices have risen 'in real terms' at about 2 to 3 percent per annum on average from 1950 to 1990. Prices of other exhaustible resources (mainly metals) have risen more slowly – less than 1 percent per annum on average over the same period. Continuation of these trends over the next 25 years would, assuming an optimistic 4 percent per annum growth in the world economy, and making conservative assumptions about new discoveries, still leave the world with 15 to 40 years of *economic* reserves of the scarcest metals and of oil at 2015. The higher real prices would stimulate the search for new sources of supply, and for more efficient ways of extracting them. It would encourage the continuation of a long-established trend to reduce the material intensity of output. As with direct use of sunlight, which provides a backstop technology which promises virtually limitless amounts of energy at costs not far removed from current levels for oil, so for other resources there will probably be backstop technologies using substitute materials in virtually limitless supply which will set upper limits to the costs of substitution. The Bureau therefore concludes that there will probably be no catastrophic exhaustion of resources of the kind envisaged by Meadows *et al.* (1972), even beyond 2015 and for an indefinite period into the future: 'we do not believe that the cumulative consumption of exhaustible resources ... need necessarily be viewed as a "plundering" of our planet which might seriously limit the chances for development of generations living after 2015' (1992: 121).

2.2.2 Other environmental problems
The OECD Report on the *State of the Environment* (OECD, 1991) provides estimates of expenditure on pollution and abatement control in

the mid-1980s in 11 member countries. These vary from about 1 to 1.5 percent of their GDPs. They also report on attempts to measure some of the benefits of these expenditures, which are generally appreciably higher. The indirect economic effects are judged to have been small, but the Report warns that 'there is certainly concern that both damage and abatement costs in the future may increase significantly, in particular with regard to some global issues such as climate change' (1991: 256).

The *World Development Report 1992* provides a table of estimates of the annual costs of environmental programmes in developing countries of dealing with the problems of water and sanitation, controlling emissions from power stations, vehicles and industry generally, problems related to agriculture and forestry (soil conservation, afforestation, extension, training, research and surveys), and family planning and increased education for girls. These annual costs refer to the year 2000 and are estimated to come to between 1.25 and 1.5 percent of the GDP of all developing countries in that year. The costs are called 'investment', and many of them do lead to improvements, e.g. in water supplies and sanitation, and in education. However, many could reasonably be classed as maintenance costs, since they do no more than prevent or offset losses due, e.g. to pollution, soil degradation, and deforestation. Even the water and sanitation programmes could be regarded as merely restoring conditions which people enjoyed in the past when good water supplies were less scarce and when the growth of towns and cities had not aggravated the problems of sanitation. Nevertheless, if, at the worst, all of these costs are regarded as increases in required maintenance, they imply a reduction in income levels of less than 2 percent, and would be much more than offset by the growth in output which the World Bank projects for developing countries between 1990 and the year 2000. In fact they would amount to only 3 or 4 percent of the projected growth over that period.

The above programmes do not include the cost of preventing global warming or offsetting its bad effects. It seems realistic to suppose that it is the richer countries who will incur most of the costs of reducing emissions, and of further research needed to make better estimates of their likely effects. Some studies have put the costs of adapting to a doubling of carbon dioxide concentrations in the USA at about 1 percent of its GNP. One study (Cline, 1991) put the cost much higher, 6 percent of GNP, when allowance was made for higher concentrations over a much longer period (250 years). However, in neither case are these costs appreciable assuming that even modest growth in *per capita* income can be sustained. Despite such estimates, the *World Development Report 1992* considers it would be prudent, in view of the very great uncertainties, to put in hand certain measures which, without costing very much, could turn out to be very useful should the climate spring a surprise on us. Further research into climatic change and its effects, and into the development of alternative sources of energy, are obvious candidates, as are the elimination of subsidies, and protection given, to sources of energy (such as coal) which result in emissions. Replacement of some inefficient taxes by carbon taxes is another possibility, as are measures to encourage energy efficiency.

The Netherlands Centraal Plan Bureau (1992: 133), while expressing due caution, presents its estimates of the costs of achieving sustainable growth in a different way but, as I interpret it, with much the same conclusion:

> Combining information on the impact of (far-reaching) national abatement programmes, with information supplied by model studies on the abatement of the greenhouse effects, provides support for the conclusion that the *total* costs, in terms of production growth, are relatively moderate: probably between 0.25 and 0.5% annually.

I interpret this to mean that required maintenance costs will rise by an amount which, if it all reduced investment, would cause the rate of growth of the world economy to fall by the above amount. The implied increase in required maintenance depends on the rate of return assumed for investment. On certain assumptions if, for example, the average return on the investment in question was 10 percent per annum, then the increase in required maintenance would be around 5 percent of world income, which is of the same order of magnitude as the other estimates quoted above.

Nordhaus (1992) provides estimates of corrections to be made to conventional US GNP to allow for pollution, depletion of non-renewable resources, and long-term environmental damage due to greenhouse gas emissions. For 1986 he puts these at 6.4 percent of GNP, which is lower than in 1965 (7.5 percent) or 1950 (9.1 percent). The fall in this percentage is mainly due to a fall in the absolute cost of air pollution. Other forms of environmental cost have risen in absolute terms, but only a little faster than GNP on average, from 4.3 percent in 1950 to 5.1 percent in 1986.

2.2.3 Food supplies

From 1970 to 1990 world population grew at 1.8 percent per annum and world food production at 2.3 percent per annum. *Per capita* food production rose in both developed and developing countries, each considered as a separate region. However, *per capita* food production fell over this period in Sub-Saharan Africa, and it also stagnated in the world as a whole from 1985 to 1990 (Netherlands Centraal Plan Bureau, 1992: 136, 177). There are food surpluses in developed countries, and their populations will increase by only about 0.5 percent per annum over the next 25 years, according to UN projections. By contrast, *per capita* food consumption is already low in Africa, and its population is expected to double in this period. There are other areas of the world facing food supply problems, such as Bangladesh, and there has been serious soil degradation in many areas of the world, including in the former Soviet Union, a region which is a potential food exporter (World Resources Institute, 1992: ch. 8). The scope for increasing food output by bringing more land under cultivation is very limited and, indeed, the fertility of some land is being lost. The world as a whole can probably produce enough food for the projected increase in population (Netherlands Centraal Plan Bureau 1992: 140), but the places where the food can be best produced are not those where the increased populations will be. If the latter can produce manufactures or traded services in exchange for food, this could solve the problem. The alternative of greatly expanding food production in, for example, Sub-Saharan Africa is likely to prove difficult, and to put still more stress on the environment (see further below).

2.3   Conclusion on environmental concerns and sustainability

The main message I obtain from the above is that there has been an increase in required maintenance for the whole world economy, but that it is not very big in relation to world output. There seems to be no *environmental* reason why growth in *per capita* income should not continue. Expenditures of the kinds mentioned above will be needed to prevent or to offset various worsenings. These expenditures will be well worth incurring, just as are other maintenance expenditures.

They will, however, mostly differ from other maintenance expenditures in one important respect. Whereas for most others one can rely on private individuals or enterprises to decide on their worthwhileness, and to undertake them when they are worthwhile, this is less often the case for environmental expenditures. Collective action, involving central or local government, is usually needed for water and sanitation, for controlling pollutant emissions and waste disposals – and, depending on land tenure systems, for preventing soil degradation and deforestation. It is also usually needed for promoting agricultural research and extension, family planning and education. In all these cases there are important *externalities*, either beneficial or harmful, which mean that private benefits or costs are a poor measure of social ones. The pervasiveness of externalities is one of the hallmarks of environmental economics.

Another hallmark is the long-term nature of many of the effects involved. The slow accumulation of carbon dioxide and other greenhouse gases in the atmosphere is an extreme example of the point. This does not of itself necessarily imply a need for government as opposed to private action. As mentioned already, most people are concerned for the fate of their descendants. The problem is, first, that governments may be insufficiently concerned – a week is a long time in politics – and, secondly, that people are naturally sceptical as a result of too frequent prophecies of doom round the corner. The result is that, where collective action is needed, it is taken later than would be optimal, often in response to a crisis.

For these reasons, government action to deal with environmental issues is both necessary and yet often difficult to secure. In developed countries, where there is a free press that prevents concealment of impending environmental catastrophes and gives expression to popular concerns, and where governments are reasonably competent, there is less fear that problems will be neglected. The greatest difficulty is perhaps to secure collective action to tackle problems which cross international boundaries.

However, comforting conclusions about sustainable growth for the world as a whole, or for developed countries as a whole, may be of little relevance to many people of the world. As already noted, it is in the developing countries that environmental problems are likely to be most acute in the coming years. Many of their governments, and those of the former Soviet Bloc countries, have not been exposed to a free press, have intervened too much in attempting to foster industry, and have sometimes hindered agriculture as well by ill-chosen schemes of collectivisation and the like. In these ways government intervention has gone too far, sometimes with disastrous results. But there is a time and place for all things, and government action is needed to protect the environment. The question is whether governments in some countries, whose past record in the control of industry and agriculture is so bad, are likely to be able to deal with the environmental problems which press increasingly for attention.

3   The role of government

3.1   Over past centuries

The economic historian, E.L. Jones, has pointed out (1988) that the view (probably still that of many laymen) that economic growth began, rather suddenly, with the so-called industrial revolution in Britian in the 18th century is mistaken. In the first place, the 'revolution' was really a gradual evolution over a long period, and one which occurred in other parts of Europe as well as Britain. Secondly, there were other times and regions of the world in which real *per capita* income probably grew for long periods, albeit very slowly compared with modern times. These included the Sung dynasty in China (10th–13th centuries AD), Tokugawa Japan (1600–1868), and possibly the Abbasid Caliphate which, at its peak in the 9th century, stretched from North Africa to the Indus and to the Pamirs, and whose capital, Baghdad, may have been the largest city then in the world.

Jones argues that the propensity to improve one's lot is sufficiently widespread that the question should be asked, not what causes the 'take off' to sustained growth, but what stops growth? The ending of growth in *per capita* income in China (and possibly in the Middle East) in the early 13th century can be attributed to the Mongol invasions. These did not penetrate as far as Western Europe or Japan, which suggests that those regions' subsequent success may be connected with that escape. Nevertheless, more has to be explained, since the economy of China did recover from the invasions and yet failed to deliver growth in *per capita* income for some centuries afterwards. Jones points out that there was, all the same, considerable growth in population in China, probably at a roughly constant *per capita* income – what he calls *extensive* growth, as opposed to *intensive* growth when *per capita* income rises. Consequently, the Chinese economy was changing considerably. Forests were cleared, people moved South, new crops were introduced and probably new techniques spread more widely. That growth was not intensive Jones seems to attribute to a lack of interest by the central government in promoting it, and to a deterioration in government efficiency. Taxation does not appear to have been unduly heavy. In some other regions of the world, the Middle East and India in particular, taxation was often very heavy, and this, plus corrupt and arbitrary administrations, must have discouraged private investment. The situation was different in Europe and in Britain in particular, where the law of property was developed and gave protection to mercantile interests, and where, indeed, these interests were able to exert a considerable influence over governments.

One gets the impression from Jones' book that political factors were the key ones determining whether growth occurred or not. He plays down the importance of cultural and other institutional factors, while not denying that religions, guilds, caste systems and the like did matter. While there is much uncertainty about all this, given the lack of data, so far as it goes the historical evidence (according to Jones) does suggest that growth will occur if governments permit it to, and perhaps if they help it along a bit as well.

3.2   Comparison of the two Germanies and the two Koreas

Turning to more recent history, there are many examples of the importance of political regimes in determining rates of economic growth. In studies of the role of education as a determinant of individual economic success, comparisons have been made of the performance of genetically identical twins who have received different educations. In this way the effect of education can be separated from that of genetic endowment. An analogous study in macroeconomics would be to take two countries with the same endowments of natural resources and capital, the same culture and institutions, but subjected at some date to different policy regimes. By comparing their economic performance over subsequent years one might hope to isolate the effects of the different policy regimes on growth. Unfortunately, there is no precise counterpart of identical twins in countries of the world. Nevertheless an approximation to what is needed is provided by the experiences of East and West Germany, following the Second World War, and those of North and South Korea, following the Korean War.

According to Michael Kaser (1987):

> In 1936 the GNP per capita of the Western part of Germany was on average the same as that of the Eastern part (only 7% greater) but by 1980 it was, on the purchasing power calculations just cited, 2.3 times that of the Eastern state: for West Germany it was $13,590 per capita and for the GDR $5910 (the 'purchasing power calculations' were those of Marer, 1985, a study commissioned by the World Bank).

One could attribute some part of the better performance of Western Germany not to the difference in regimes but to the fact that it received a great deal of aid from the USA after the Second World War. But there is a further consideration which works the other way, namely, the collapse in output in Eastern Germany that followed the collapse in its regime. The experience of the whole Eastern Europe and the former USSR shows that the communist regimes were indeed not sustainable, and the cost of their collapse is part of the cost of following the track they took.

The communist regime in North Korea has not, thus far, collapsed. I do not know of a careful comparison of North and South Korea's real *per capita* GNP. It seems likely that, before the Second World War, when the whole of Korea was controlled by Japan, the North had a higher *per capita* GNP than the South. It was more industrialised and had more minerals. The UN has published estimates, for 1989, of *per capita* Net Material Product in the North of $897, and of *per capita* GDP in the South of $5029 (*per capita* GNP is barely 1 percent less, see United Nations, 1991). This exaggerates the difference between them, since Net Material Product is a narrower concept than GDP, excluding many services. Nevertheless, it seems certain that comparable *per capita* output in the North is well below that of the South. Again, it is true that South Korea, unlike North Korea, received a great deal of aid from the US following the Korean War. It is also true that the cost of transforming North Korea into a non-communist regime has yet to be met.

3.3   Rapidly growing countries in the Far East

Ian Little (1979) has compared the economic performance of South Korea, Japan, Taiwan, Hong Kong and Singapore in the period between the Second World War and 1975 with those of other developing countries. The rates of growth of the former were extraordinarily high, and Little considers a great many possible explanations. He points out that they suffered a relative lack of *per capita* cultivable land, and of minerals, and that geography hardly favoured the first three, although it may have favoured Hong Kong and Singapore. Korea and Taiwan have spent a great deal on defence, but the others little. All suffered defeat or occupation in the Second World War, and Korea suffered immense loss of life and destruction in the Korean War. Of factors *not* directly related to government and economic policy, Little singles out two as being probably important: these countries were ethnically and culturally homogeneous within themselves, and their people had a tradition of hard work. However, he points out that these favourable factors had existed for centuries without resulting in rapid economic growth. He concludes that, for their recent success: 'the main part of any explanation must come from government and economic policies' (1979: 465). Much of the rest of Little's study is an analysis of the policies which were so successful.

3.4   Sub-Saharan Africa

Let us turn now, by way of contrast, to the record of Sub-Saharan African countries from about 1945 to the 1980s, which has been analysed by David Fieldhouse (1986) amongst others. Many of these countries achieved independence from colonial powers in the early part of this period, starting with Ghana in 1957. The postwar years before independence saw rates of growth which were high compared with prewar experience, and these relatively high rates continued until the early 1970s. However, the oil shock then adversely affected many countries (while benefiting the country with much the largest population, Nigeria), and some were also hit by falling commodity prices. By the early 1980s, several countries had become heavily indebted, and these were badly affected by rising real interest rates. On average, growth slowed down markedly and, in *per capita* terms, became about zero in the 1970s, and negative (about − 1 percent per annum) in the 1980s. Agricultural growth failed to keep pace with population from 1965 to 1990 (World Bank, 1992).

While much was achieved, this performance disappointed initial hopes, and does not appear thus far to have led to sustained development. That could be attributed to international conditions, to the inherent difficulties of African development (geophysical and cultural), or to bad policies of African governments.

Despite the deterioration of international economic conditions after 1973, Fieldhouse does not think it possible to blame limitations in African development simply on adverse external factors (1979: 121). World developments in the period 1960–75 were, on the whole, unusually favourable for most countries, yet for some the deterioration in performance began quite early on. Thus in Ghana, growth in *per capita* output declined from 1.9 percent per year in the 1950s to 0.7 percent per year in the 1960s, in Senegal from 4.4 to 1.6 percent per year and in Zambia from 2.7 to 0.5 percent per year. For these countries the finger of blame points to bad economic policies, including heavy taxation of the export sector, inefficient attempts at industrialisation or at restructuring agriculture, and elaborate systems of control beyond the administrative capacities available and open to corruption. Nigeria, which gained greatly from the oil boom, failed to invest the gains wisely and raised public expenditure to unsustainable levels, incurring large debts as oil prices fell back. *Per capita* output, which is estimated to have grown at the high rate of 3.4 percent per year in 1965–80, *fell* at 1.7 percent per year in 1980–90.

Fieldhouse accepts that there were adverse geophysical factors, such as poor soil, lack of minerals (in most, but not all, countries), tropical diseases and variable weather, including severe droughts, all of which made expansion of agricultural output in particular very difficult. It is also possible that the attitudes and customs of some African farmers were hard to change and not helpful to rapid development. There was a severe shortage of skilled workers, and there was an extraordinarily rapid rate of population growth. For all these reasons the expectations of rapid development held by many at the start of independence were unrealistic, and this may have contributed to the adoption by governments of over-ambitious attempts at structural change.

However, as well as this, governments used their powers to divert income into the hands of their supporters, for example by taxing farmers and subsidising favoured industries or paying relatively high public sector wages. One reason they did this is the reverse of Ian Little's point about the ethnic and cultural homogeneity of Korea, Japan, etc. These African countries were not ethnically and culturally homogeneous, and had little history of nationhood. Governments, initially backed by anti-colonial sentiment, had to establish legitimacy and keep in power. They sought to do so by distributing favours to powerful groups. But, as Usher (1981) has argued in a very stimulating book, this can destabilise a democracy, especially one lacking homogeneity. In many countries political cohesion could not be secured, and destructive civil wars took place. In such circumstances sustained growth could not be achieved.

3.5   Conclusion on the role of government

The phenomenon of ethnic, cultural and religious divisions leading to unrest and war, and economic decline, is of course not confined to Africa:

> By one accounting, there have been 127 wars and violent internal conflicts since 1945, all but two of them in the developing world, although often with industrial countries' direct involvement. Such conflicts have a direct effect on economic performance and development. One study found that most precipitous declines in economic growth could be traced to serious political disturbances and civil or international violence. A partial list of victims in just the last decade is long: Sudan, Ethiopia, Chad, Somalia, Nigeria, Uganda, Mozambique, Angola, Afghanistan, Iran, Iraq, Lebanon, Haiti, Peru, El Salvador, Nicaragua, Cambodia, and Myanmar. That these are amongst the world's poorest countries and also rank relatively low in human development is no accident. (World Resources Institute 1992: 11)

Whether, then, one considers the long sweep of history, or only the most recent period, it seems clear that a prerequisite of growth has been political stability, together with policies which at least did not stop growth in its tracks, whether by unduly heavy taxation or by inhibiting investment or rendering it grossly inefficient in other ways.

4   Conclusions: what sustains economic development?

Maintenance expenditures are required to sustain existing rates of output. For by far the greater part of its existence, humanity has consisted of hunter–gatherers, and then most maintenance could be left to nature. But when population grew and settled down to static farming a great deal of investment was needed to provide maintainable systems of cultivation. Forests were cleared, fields marked out and drained, and buildings constructed. Maintenance now had to include fertilising the soil, storing seeds and replenishing herds. When people congregated into towns and cities still more investment and still more maintenance were needed for buildings, roads, water supply and sanitation.

When people lived in small bands widely spaced apart, relations between them needed no overarching government. Codes of behaviour between bands evolved, and were of some importance, but they concerned the individual for only a small part of his or her existence, which was much more to do with relations within the band. There were no professional armies and no property worth seizing. Hobbes' vision of life as 'nasty, brutish and short' was the reverse of the truth. Compared with his own day life, for most people, was probably more enjoyable, leisurely and lasted longer (see, e.g. Cashdan, 1989: 22–3). However, today's populations could not exist like the hunter–gatherers, even if they wanted to. Although it is still true that what matter for most people are their relations within small groups, since human nature has not changed much, we are thrust into contact with great numbers of others in our daily lives, and we depend upon people we hardly know for the essentials of life. The system could not function without a vast array of government officials, and it requires the protection of professional armies and police, together with the existence of important legal, educational, medical and other institutions. Its maintenance costs, compared with the old days, have become gigantic.

The increase of required maintenance is then nothing new, and while environmentalists are right to point out new ways in which it will go on increasing, the estimates quoted earlier suggest that these extra costs will amount to only a few per cent of total world output. Nevertheless, there are new dangers and difficulties. Modern man's capacity to damage the environment has increased, and damage arising from action in one country is not necessarily confined to it, a dramatic example being the Chernobyl explosion. The pace at which populations are growing in so many countries, and the even faster pace at which cities are growing, is unprecedently high. The rate of investment needed to match requirements, at a constant level of *per capita* income, is likewise high, compared with the past; and the task of organising it efficiently, which involves coordinated action, and participation by governments, becomes more difficult.

Still more investment is needed if *per capita* income is to grow, but less is needed the greater its efficiency. Experience suggests that, for much of investment, decentralised decision making coordinated by the market, and with a system of private property which allows the investor to keep an appreciable part of the gains, results in sustainable growth. This has proved to be more efficient, and more sustainable, than attempts by government to control most investment. All the same, a great deal of investment has been directed or financed by government in most countries: in roads and other communication systems, in power networks, in water supply and sanitation, in health, education and research.

The role of government has been of crucial importance in maintenance as well as in investment. Without it, the market system could not survive. In recent years there has been a reaction against 'big government' and the growing tax burden imposed by the welfare state, and attempts have been made to cut it down to size. But the cost of government may well be a component of maintenance that is set to grow. Environmental concerns, and the externalities involved, are one reason for this. Another is the increasing ability of quite small numbers of people to cause destruction. Mainteinance of law and order has always been the most basic need which governments can satisfy.

Nations consisting of heterogeneous linguistic, ethnic and religious groups often lack cohesion, but the same can be said of the nations of the world. The dangers are so obvious and so unpleasant that one is inclined to forget them. That they have to be guarded against perhaps goes without saying. All the same, if I am asked to list conditions for sustained development I do not want to leave this unsaid. It seems to me that we have learned a great deal about the other requirements of development, but we still do not know how peace can be kept and reasonably good government achieved in many countries of the world.

NOTES

I am grateful for comments by Dennis Anderson, Wilfred Beckerman, David Fieldhouse, Eric Jones, Rachael Scott, Constantino Lluch and the editors of this volume, none of whom is necessarily in agreement with the views expressed here nor bears responsibility for mistakes which may remain.

REFERENCES

Beckerman, W. (1974) *In Defence of Economic Growth*, London: Jonathan Cape (1992) *Economic Development and the Environment: Conflict or Complementarity?*, background paper for the *World Development Report 1992*, Washington, DC: World Bank

Cashdan, E. (1989) 'Hunters and gatherers: economic behaviour in bands', ch. 2 in S. Plattner (ed.), *Economic Anthropology*, Stanford: Stanford University Press

Cline, W. (1991) *Estimating the Benefits of Greenhouse Warming Abatement*, Washington, DC: Institute of International Economics

Cole, H.S.D., Freeman, C., Jahoda, M. and Pavitt, K.L.R. (1973) *Thinking About the Future: A Critique of the Limits to Growth*, London: Chatto & Windus for Sussex University Press

Daly, H.E. and Cobb, J.B. Jr. (1989) *For the Common Good*, Boston: Beacon Press

Denison, E.F. (1991) 'Scott's *New View of Economic Growth*: a review article', *Oxford Economic Papers*, **43**

Eisner, R. (1989) *The Total Incomes Systems of Accounts*, Chicago: University of Chicago Press

Fieldhouse, D.K. (1986) *Black Africa 1945–1980: Economic Decolonisation and Arrested Development*, London: Allen & Unwin

Hicks, J.R. (1946) *Value and Capital*, 2nd edn, Oxford: Clarendon Press

Jones, E.L. (1988) *Growth Recurring: Economic Change in World History*, Oxford: Clarendon Press

Kaser, M.C. (1987) 'The economic dimension', ch. 9 in E. Moreton (ed.), *Germany between East and West*, Cambridge: Cambridge University Press in association with the Royal Institute of International Affairs

Lane, R.E. (1991) *The Market Experience*, Cambridge: Cambridge University Press

Lewis, W.A. (1955) *The Theory of Economic Growth*, London: George Allen & Unwin

Little, I.M.D. (1979) 'An economic reconnaissance', ch. 7 in W. Galenson (ed.), *Economic Growth and Structural Change in Taiwan: the Postwar Experience of the Republic of China*, Ithaca: Cornell University Press

Marer, P. (1985) *Dollar GNPs of the USSR and Eastern Europe*, Baltimore: Johns Hopkins University Press

Meadows, D.H., Meadows, D.L., Randers, J. and Behrens III, W.W. (1972) *The Limits to Growth: A Report for the Club of Rome's Project on the Predicament of Mankind*, London: Earth Island Press Ltd

(1992) *Beyond the Limits*, Post Mills, VT, Chelase Green Publishing Co.

Netherlands Centraal Plan Bureau (1992) *Scanning the Future: A Long-Term Scenario Study of the World Economy 1990–2015*, The Hague: Sdu Publishers

Nordhaus, W.D. (1992) 'Is growth sustainable? Reflections on the concept of sustainable economic growth', paper presented to the International Economic Association, Varenna, Italy (October), mimeo

Nordhaus, W.D. and Tobin, J. (1972) 'Is growth obsolete?', in National Bureau of Economic Research Fiftieth Anniversary Colloquium, *Economic Growth*, New York: NBER

OECD (1991) *The State of the Environment*, Paris: OECD

Pearce, D. and Turner, R.K. (1990) *Economics of Natural Resources and the Environment*, Hemel Hempstead: Harvester Wheatsheaf

Pearce, D., Barbier, E. and Markandya, A. (1990) *Sustainable Development: Economics and Environment in the Third World*, Aldershot: Edward Elgar

Scott, M.F.G. (1976) 'Investment and growth', *Oxford Economic Papers*, **28**

(1989) *A New View of Economic Growth*, Oxford: Clarendon Press

(1990) 'Extended accounts for national income and product: a comment', *Journal of Economic Literature*, **28**

(1991a), 'A new view of economic growth: four lectures', *World Bank Discussion Paper*, **131**, Washington, DC: World Bank

(1991b) 'A reply to Denison', *Oxford Economic Papers*, **43**

(1992a) 'Policy implications of *A New View of Economic Growth*', *Economic Journal*, **103**

(1992b) 'A new theory of endogenous economic growth', *Oxford Review of Economic Policy*, **8**

United Nations (1991) *National Accounts Statistics: Analysis of Main Aggregates, 1988–9*, and *Main Aggregates and Detailed Tables, 1989, Part I*, New York: UN

Usher, D. (1981) *The Economic Prerequisites to Democracy*, Oxford: Basil Blackwell

World Bank (1992) *World Development Report 1992: Development and the Environment*, Washingon, DC: World Bank

World Resources Institute (1992) *World Resources 1992–93*, New York and London: Oxford University Press

Discussion

CONSTANTINO LLUCH

I have long been impressed by the power of Scott's ideas on growth, investment and employment, and equally impressed by the professional neglect towards them. In my view, Scott is right and the profession is wrong. Better put, Scott is useful, much more so than the profession, for the analysis of how economic policies affect growth. In this note, I shall justify my belief in Scott's brand of growth economics. In so doing, I shall discuss chapter 4 by focusing on Scott's fundamental growth equation (Scott, 1989: 171) on the payoff of good policies in terms of higher growth in *per capita* output; and on the issues of 'sustainability' that are central to any discussion of this topic.

1   Scott versus the profession

For the purpose of this discussion, the 'profession' is represented by three propositions:

Proposition 1
It is possible to increase output permanently without changing inputs.

Proposition 2
In a stationary economy (one with constant output per worker) the rate of output growth is not affected by the investment ratio.

Proposition 3
Proposition 2 is false, because investment in human capital affects the rate of technical progress.

Propositions 1 and 2 stand for a neoclassical growth theory, where technical progress is costless and steady growth possible as long as such progress comes in the form of 'labour augmentation'. Proposition 3 stands for the new growth theory of Romer (1986) and Lucas (1988), that distinguishes sharply between material investment and investment in human capital.

Admittedly, this is a caricature of the 'profession'. Work by Mundlak (1992) clearly shows that within the professional tradition there has been a great advance in issues of choice of technique, aggregation and the nature of the production of knowledge. Yet, the advance appears to be based on increased complexity, and it pays to go back to the origin, propositions 1–3 above, and see whether, and how, Scott's contribution represents a new departure.

Propositions 1–3 lead to growth accounting equations with the contributions of primary inputs (typically weighted by their shares in value added); and the contribution of technical change, the 'residual', either unexplained or explained in terms of added factors of production (like accumulated knowledge).

Scott's fundamental growth equation stands in sharp contrast to all of this. It is not an accounting equation. Rather, it reflects optimising behaviour on the part of a representative firm. Its derivation and use reflect three other propositions that do away with many neoclassical principles.

Proposition 4
If the contribution of changes in capital to changes in output is measured correctly, the 'residual' disappears. The residual is a mistake.

Proposition 5
Changes in output, rather than output levels, are all that need to be explained.

Proposition 6
Long-term growth and its changes can be analysed in terms of episodes of growth equilibrium. Along one such episode, the cycle is ignored and four magnitudes are constant: the output growth rate, the rate of (quality-adjusted) employment growth, the labour shares and the investment ratio.

Propositions 4–6 put the empirical examination of economic growth in a new and very productive light. This is not the time or place to elaborate on them. I only want to emphasise that the fundamental growth equation has two terms only: the rate of (quality-adjusted) employment growth, weighted by the ratio of the labour share to the share of consumption; and the investment ratio, weighted by the efficiency of investment, which can be estimated. Underlying such growth equation is the Investment Programme Contour (IPC) map (Scott, 1989, figure 6.2: 162 and figure 6.4: 168). For each investment ratio there is one such contour. The change in output and employment is then such that wages grow at the same rate as (quality-adjusted) productivity. The choice of the investment ratio is determined by adding one relationship: the equality of the marginal real rate of return of investment to the rate of discount of consumption at the margin. The task of growth economics is then to explain each one of the factors in the fundamental growth equation. The production function is gone, replaced by the IPC.

Why is this so useful? In economics, everything depends on everything else, as the saying goes. Yet, for policy, the line of causation from investment and employment to growth is much more fruitful than the opposite line of causation: the command 'grow to employ' is a recipe for disaster; the command 'remove obstacles to the growth of investment and employment' is much more attuned, in my view, to the need of the times. Furthermore, the efficiency of investment is as important, and as problematic, as the efficiency of labour.

2   On the evidence

In a bold stroke, Scott divides more than 100 years of growth (up to 1973) in the UK, the US and Japan into 19 episodes of equilibrium growth; adds the period 1955–62 for seven other countries; and uses the resulting 26 observations to estimate his fundamental growth equations. The period since 1973 is the subject of separate chapters (Scott, 1989: chs. 10 and 16). A large part of the variation in growth rates is captured by his equation, there is no room for an intercept team representing technical progress, and coefficient estimates accord with theory.

Lal (1990) has used the estimated growth equation by Scott, together with his estimates for 21 developing countries, to assess the impact of a decline in the OECD investment ratio upon growth in the OECD and in LDCs, over the period 2000–25. The OECD decline has partly happened already and may go on due to the aging of populations. The result, at odds with conventional growth theory, yields a drastic fall in the equilibrium rate of output growth in both the OECD and LDCs.

Even if one accepts that the word 'evidence' in the heading of this section may be too strong, it appears that Scott's procedure of using growth episodes as the unit of observation is very promising. Attention shifts automatically to applications like the one by Lal, and to asking what causes breaks across episodes, and thus to the influence of policy. This is particularly so in the area of 'sustainable development', with which this Discussion is concerned.

3   On sustainability

Suppose that episodes of equilibrium growth are accepted as useful stylised facts on which to build the theory of growth and the analysis of growth policies. The question of growth limits then poses itself. Is the exhaustion of some finite stock (natural resources, the atmosphere) threatening growth? Will equilibrium growth episodes be characterised by ever-lower growth rates in *per capita* output, down to zero and beyond?

Nothing guarantees sustained growth, and finite stocks may be one reason for stagnation. Indeed, in many parts of Africa it appears that soil depletion is an important reason for economic decline. But, then, why is soil depleted? Population growth coupled with bad policies and institutions must surely be the answer.

I have little to add to Scott's treatment of sustainability. His emphasis on distinguishing maintenance from depreciation and using maintenance as a key concept in a stationary economy and, by extension, in a growing one, is very much to the point. Also to the point is that little is to be gained, from the problem at hand, by trying to enlarge the concept of capital. The notion of 'natural' capital is a blind alley, directing effort to a measure at the end controversial and most probably useless. We only need to know what is necessary to maintain indefinitely a given consumption flow (income in the Hicksian sense). It may be that it takes an increasing amount of resources, and that there is a systematic downward bias in the allocation of resources to maintenance. There certainly was in the centrally-planned economies. It may also be that, for now and for the foreseeable future, maintenance expenditure is likely to remain small, as Scott says, quoting work at the World Bank and the Netherlands Centraal Plan Bureau among others: 'small' in the sense that it does not need to interfere with growth in *per capita* income.

Nevertheless, I am less sanguine on this, for two reasons. The first is that the brakes on growth are already very powerful, so that problems with maintenance get added on to a fragile growth environment. Inefficiencies and rigidities of all sorts damage investment and employment prospects. For example, with taxation reaching 30–40 percent of GDP, the power of bad tax systems to do damage is very large indeed. Again, let me refer to Scott (1991: ch. 14). More generally, the productivity slowdown since 1973, and the current recession, makes the OECD countries wonder where to turn to resume sustainable growth and reduce unemployment. 'Perestroika in the West' was a term coined at the OECD and too soon forgotten and yet OECD countries need to turn away from paths of growth that have proven quite unsustainable. The welfare state has failed in its extreme forms and it has produced quite large transfer systems in others, to the detriment of incentives to invest and to work. But to deal with the issue of 'efficiency versus equity' is proving extremely difficult.

The second reason is the combination of population growth with the growing perception that mankind may now be causing atmospheric change (not only global warming, but also ozone depletion and acid rain). On this subject, speculation is rampant, the science developing and the uncertainties large. Yet, the problem, if any, will be the more severe if population growth does not get accompanied quickly with (quality-adjusted) extra employment, efficient investment, and adequate maintainence expenditure. The prospects for this are not encouraging and the gloom that pervades pp. 102 and 104 of chapter 4 strikes a chord.

At the end, an equilibrium growth episode is an event with intensity and duration. So far, work has concentrated on intensity (why do growth rates differ?), and this is of course very important. But effort is also needed to understand duration. What can be said about the forces stopping an episode, on the way to higher (or lower) growth? How are those forces related to policies and institutions? Is it possible to abstract from the cycle, and to stick to the assumption of a constant ratio of output to capacity? Since 1973, this is very doubtful. I wish I had answers to these questions. I do not. But Scott has opened doors that have to be opened, if advance is to be made towards the answers. Perestroika, both in the East and the West; economic development world-wide; and global environmental issues are all urgent problems waiting for these answers.

REFERENCES

Lal, D. (1990) 'World saving, prosperity and growth II: saving and growth in developing countries', *Rivista di Politica Economica*, **70(12)** (December): 101–23

Lucas, R.E. (1988) 'On the mechanics of economic development', *Journal of Monetary Economics*, **22(1)** (July): 3–42

Mundlak, Y. (1992) 'Agricultural productivity and economic policies: concepts and measurements' (May), OECD Development Centre, mimeo

Romer, P.M. (1986) 'Increasing returns and long-run growth', *Journal of Political Economy*, **94(5)** (October): 1002–37

Scott, M.F. (1989) *A New View of Economic Growth*, Oxford: Clarendon Press

5   Optimal development and the idea of net national product

PARTHA DASGUPTA

1   Introduction

The idea of sustainable development is associated with the Brundtland Report (World Commission, 1987). A large literature has followed in its wake. Unhappily, a good deal of it has been uninformed by an older literature that addressed a more general notion – that of optimal development. Among other things, this earlier literature drew upon modern theories of distributive justice to illuminate the nature of optimal public policies. It also was able to draw a sharper set of prescriptions even while studying a wider range of analytical models. In this chapter I shall make use of the theory of optimal development to draw conclusions about the idea of net national product (NNP) and its use for identifying optimal policies.

When anyone talks of 'sustainable development', it is usually in conjunction with thoughts on the management of the environment. It is therefore as well to begin with an identification of 'environmental resources'. This will help us to see that environmental economics in large measure falls within the realm of capital theory.

For expositional ease, it will pay to ignore the any number of information, transaction, and institutional constraints that should ideally inform our discussion (on this see Dasgupta, 1993). We will be able to obtain clean formulae for NNP by this contrivance. Furthermore, I shall abstract from those kinds of nonconvexities that would make it wrong to rely exclusively on changes in NNP as a way of assessing changes in aggregate well-being (on this see Dasgupta and Mäler, 1993). In the presence of significant nonconvexities, we will need more than one index. It is a matter of significance that we determine what this set should be. But little progress has been made in recent years to move beyond the few remarks that I shall be able to make about it. While the analysis that I will develop here will be general, many of my illustrations will be motivated by environmental problems that the rural poor face in poor countries. I shall do this partly because of their obvious importance, but partly also for the purpose of redressing the prevailing imbalance in the literature, which in great part has studied environmental problems in rich communities.

2 What are environmental resources?

Environmental problems are almost always associated with resources that are regenerative (we could call them *renewable natural resources*), but that are in danger of exhaustion from excessive use.[1] The earth's atmosphere is a paradigm of such resources. In the normal course of events, the atmosphere's composition regenerates itself. But the speed of regeneration depends upon, among other things, the current state of the atmosphere and the rate at which pollutants are deposited. It also depends upon the nature of the pollutants. (Smoke discharge is different from the release of chemicals or radioactive material.) Before all else, we need a way of measuring such resources. In the foregoing example, we have to think of an atmospheric quality index. The net rate of regeneration of the stock is the rate at which this quality index changes over time. Regeneration rates of atmospheric quality are complex, often ill-understood matters. There is a great deal of synergism associated with the interaction of different types of pollutants in the atmospheric sink, so that, for example, the underlying relationships are almost certainly non-linear, and, for certain compositions, perhaps greatly so. What are called 'non-linear dose-response relationships' in the ecological literature, are instances of this.[2] But these are merely qualifications, and the analytical point I am making here, that pollution problems involve the degradation of renewable natural resources, is both true and useful (see Ehrlich, Ehrlich and Holdren, 1977).

Animal, bird, plant, and fish populations are other examples of renewable natural resources, and there are now a number of studies addressing the reproductive behaviour of different species under a variety of 'environmental' conditions, including the presence of parasitic and symbiotic neighbours.[3] Land is also such a commodity, for the quality of arable and grazing land can be maintained only by careful use. Population pressures can result in an extended period of overuse. By 'overuse' I mean not only an unsustainable shortening of fallow periods, but also deforestation, and the cultivation and grazing of marginal lands. This causes the quality of land to deteriorate, until it eventually becomes a wasteland.

The symbiotic relationship between soil quality and vegetation cover is central to the innumerable problems facing Sub-Saharan Africa, most especially the Sahel.[4] The management of the drylands in general has to be sensitive to such relationships. It is, for example, useful to distinguish between, on the one hand, a reduction in soil nutrients and humus and, on the other, the loss of soil due to wind and water runoff. The depletion of soil nutrients can be countered by fertilisers (which, however, can have adverse effects elsewhere in the ecological system), but in the drylands, a loss in topsoil cannot be made good. (In river valleys the alluvial topsoil is augmented annually by silt brought by the rivers from mountain slopes. This is the obverse of water runoff caused by a lack of vegetation cover.) Under natural conditions of vegetation cover, it can take anything between 100 and 500 years for the formation of 1 cm of topsoil. Admittedly, what we are calling 'erosion' is a redistribution of soil. But even when the relocation is from one agricultural field to another, there are adjustment costs. Moreover, the relocation is often in the oceans and non agricultural land. This amounts to erosion.[5]

Soil degradation can occur if the wrong crops are cultivated. Contrary to general belief, in sub-tropical conditions most export crops tend to be less damaging to soils that are cereals and root crops. (Groundnuts and cotton are exceptions.) Many export crops, such as coffee, cocoa, oil palm, and tea, grow on trees and bushes that enjoy a continuous root structure and provide continuous canopy cover. With grasses planted underneath, the rate of soil erosion that is associated with such crops is known to be substantially less than the rate of erosion associated with basic food crops (see Repetto, 1988: table 2). But problems are com-pounded upon problems in poor countries. In many cultures, the men control cash income while the women control food. Studies in Nigeria, Kenya, India and Nepal suggest that, to the extent that women's incomes decline as the proportion of cash-cropping increases, the family's nut-ritional status (most especially the nutritional status of children) deterio-rates (Gross and Underwood, 1971; von Braun and Kennedy, 1986; Kennedy and Oniang'o, 1990). The indirect effects of public policy assume a bewildering variety in poor countries, where ecological and technological factors intermingle with norms of behaviour that respond only very slowly to changing circumstances.

The link between irrigation and the process by which land becomes increasingly saline has also been much noted in the ecological literature (see Ehrlich, Ehrlich and Holdren, 1977). In the absence of adequate drainage, continued irrigation slowly but remorselessly destroys agri-cultural land owing to the salts left behind by evaporating water. The surface area of agricultural land removed from cultivation world-wide through salinisation is thought by some to equal the amount added by irrigation (see United Nations, 1990). Desalinisation of agricultural land is even today an enormously expensive operation.

The environment in poor countries is affected by the fact that the rural poor are particularly constrained in their access to credit, insurance and capital markets. Because of such constraints, domestic animals assume a singularly important role as an asset.[6] But they are prone to dying when rainfall is scarce. In Sub-Saharan Africa farmers and nomads, therefore, carry extra cattle as an insurance against droughts. Herds are larger than they would be were capital and insurance markets open to the rural poor. This imposes an additional strain on grazing lands, most especially during periods of drought. That this link between capital and credit markets (or rather, their absence) and the degradation of the environmental resource base is quantitatively significant (World Bank, 1992) should come as no surprise. The environment is itself a gigantic capital asset. The portfolio of assets that a household manages depends on what is available to it. Both theory and evidence suggest that the many activities a poor rural household is typically engaged in are interlinked. These links are in part forged by it and in part imposed upon it, and they come about because households face severe constraints in economic transactions: markets that typically function in advanced industrial economies are often absent in rural communities of poor countries (and when present, they often function badly). In short, households link their decisions in different spheres of life as a means of circumventing the limitations they face in transaction possibilities. To cite an example, children in poor households are not only 'consumer goods', they also play a role in providing their parents with labour and old-age security. From these observations one can even argue that the fertility rate is related to the extent of the local environmental resource base, such as fuelwood and water sources (see Dasgupta and Mäler, 1991, 1993; Nerlove and Meyer, 1992).

Underground basins of water have the characteristic of a renewable natural resource if they are recharged over the annual cycle. The required analysis is a bit more problematic, in that we should be interested in both its quality and its quantity. Under normal circumstances, an aquifer undergoes a self-cleansing process as pollutants are deposited into it. (Here, the symbiotic role of microbes, as in the case of soil, is important.) But the effectiveness of the process depends on the nature of pollutants and the rate at which they are discharged. Moreover, the recharge rate depends not only on annual precipitation and the extent of underground flows, but also on the rate of evaporation. This in turn is a function of the extent of soil cover. In the drylands, reduced soil cover beyond a point lowers both soil moisture and the rate of recharge of underground basins, which in turn reduces the soil cover still more, which in turn implies a reduced rate of recharge, and so on.[7] With a lowered underground water table, the cost of water extraction rises.

In fact, aquifers display another characteristic. On occasion the issue is not one of depositing pollutants into them. If, as a consequence of excessive extraction, the groundwater level is allowed to drop to too low a level, there can be saltwater intrusion in coastal aquifers, and this can result in the destruction of the basin.

Environmental resources, such as forests, the atmosphere, and the seas, have multiple competing uses. This accentuates management problems. Thus forests are a source of timber, bark, saps and, more particularly, pharmaceuticals. Tropical forests also provide a habitat for a rich genetic pool. In addition, forests influence local and regional climate, preserve soil cover on site and, in the case of watersheds, protect soil downstream from floods. Increased runoff of rainwater arising from deforestation helps strip soil away, depriving agriculture of nutrients and clogging water reservoirs and irrigation systems. The social value of a forest typically exceeds the value of its direct products, and on occasion exceeds it greatly (see Ehrlich, Ehrlich and Holdren, 1977; Hamilton and King, 1983; Anderson, 1987).

It is as well to remember that the kinds of resources we are thinking of here are on occasion of direct use in consumption (as with fisheries), on occasion in production (as with plankton, which serves as food for fish species), and sometimes in both (as with drinking and irrigation water). Their stock are measured in different ways, depending on the resource: in mass units (e.g. biomass units for forests, cowdung and crop residues), in quality indices (e.g. water and air quality indices), in volume units (e.g. acre-feet for aquifers), and so on. When we express concern about environmental matters, we in effect point to a decline in their stock. But a decline in their stock, on its own, is not a reason for concern. This is seen most clearly in the context of exhaustible resources, such as fossil fuels. Not to reduce their stocks is not to use them at all, and this is unlikely to be the right thing to do. In section 3 I shall appeal to modern welfare economic theory to study the basis upon which their optimal patterns of use should be discussed. But even a casual reading of the foregoing examples suggests that a number of issues in environmental economics are 'capital-theoretic'. The remainder of this chapter will be concerned with the structure of shadow (or accounting) prices that in principle can support optimal programmes.[8]

3   Social objectives: 1 – sustainable development

The idea of 'sustainable development' continues to be the focal point of much of the writings on the environment. It was noted earlier that the emerging literature has in great measure been developed independently of both intertemporal welfare economics and the theory of optimal development, two subjects that have provided for over 25 years a language in which we may usefully ask questions regarding intergenerational justice. In the event, most writings on sustainable development start from scratch and some proceed to get things hopelessly wrong. It would be difficult to find another field of research endeavour in the social sciences that has displayed such intellectual regress.

Much attention has been given to defining 'sustainable development'. Consider, for example, the following: 'we can summarize the necessary conditions for sustainable development as constancy of the natural capital stock; more strictly, the requirement for non-negative changes in the stock of natural resources, such as soil and soil quality, ground and surface water and their quality, land biomass, water biomass, and the waste-assimilation capacity of the receiving environments' (Pearce, Barbier and Markandya, 1988: 6). Or consider instead the passage cited by Solow (1991) from a UNESCO document: 'every generation should leave water, air and soil resources as pure and unpolluted as when it came on earth'.

Both passages involve a category mistake, the mistake being to identify the determinants of well-being (e.g. the means of production of well-being) with the constituents of well-being (e.g. health, welfare, and free-doms). But leaving that aside for the moment, the point is not that sustainable development, as it is defined by these authors, is an undesirable goal: rather, it is an impossible goal. In any event, the focus of concern should be present and future well-being, and methods of determining how well-being is affected by policy. History, introspection, and experience with analytical models since the early 1960s tell us that reasonable development paths would involve patterns of resource substitution over time.

To be sure, a number of authors writing on sustainable development have recognised that the starting point ought to be the realisation of well-being over time. But the thought that, barring exhaustible resources, a just distribution of well-being implies that all capital stocks ought to be preserved, retains an emotional pull. For example, elaborating on the notion of sustainable development, von Amsberg (1993: 15–16) writes:

> Under [the] guidelines for intergenerational resource distribution, the endowment of every generation would include the sustainable yield of the earth's natural capital plus the benefits from resource depletion of natural capital if adequate compensation is made to future generations . . . owning land would only include the right to harvest the sustainable yield of the land while leaving the capital value intact . . . the guidelines for intergenerational resource distribution could be implemented through a sustainability constraint . . . The purpose of the sustainability constraint is to ensure some minimum level of welfare of future gener-

ations and a guarantee that a basic stock of natural capital is passed on to the next generation.

Two constraints? No doubt *some* index of natural capital would have to be preserved if a minimum level of welfare for the future is to be guaranteed. Why then introduce it as an additional constraint? Preservation of the index ought to be derivable from the optimisation exercise.

A second weakness of the formulation is this: it offers no ethical argument for imposing either of the side constraints. A more general (and intellectually firmer) approach would be to allow future generations' well-beings to be reflected in a function that is defined over the well-beings of all generations. In other words, the idea is to appeal to an aggregate social well-being function. Such a tactic would enable us also to experiment with different degrees of substitutability between different generations' levels of well-being. The demands on the present generation could well be stiffer in this framework than that it be required merely to ensure that some minimum level of well-being is guaranteed for future generations.[9] This point of view was adopted by the late Tjalling Koopmans in his formulation of the problem of intergenerational justice. It will pay to review his findings.

4   Social objectives: 2 – optimal development, discount rates and sustainability

In a remarkable set of contributions, Koopmans (1960, 1965, 1967, 1972a, 1972b) conducted a series of thought experiments on intertemporal choice so as to see the implications of alternative sets of ethical assumptions in plausible worlds.[10] Underlying Koopmans' programme of research was the premise that no ethical judgement in such abstract exercises as those involving resource use should be taken as being decisive. We should instead play off one set of ethical assumptions against another within plausible scenarios, see what their implications are for the distribution of well-being, and then appeal to our varied intuitive senses before arguing policy. For example, Koopmans showed (1965, 1967) that we can have no direct intuition about the validity of discounting future well-beings unless we know something concrete about feasible development paths. As the set of feasible paths in a world with an indefinite future is enormously complicated, the reasonable thing would be to work with alternative discount rates on well-being and see what they imply.[11] Although seemingly innocuous, this suggestion represents a radical break with a philosophical tradition, stretching from Ramsey (1928) to Parfit (1984), that has argued against discounting future well-beings without first having studied distributional consequences across generations in plausible worlds. That this tradition is otiose was demonstrated by Mirrlees (1967) and Chakravarty (1969), who showed that in plausible economic models not to discount future well-beings could imply that the present generation be asked to save and invest around 50 percent of GNP. This is a stiff requirement when GNP is low.

For simplicity of exposition, let us assume that population size is constant over time (t), and that generation t's well-being is an increasing function of its level of consumption (C_t), which we denote by $W(C_t)$. We assume time to be continuous. Let Γ_C be the set of feasible consumption paths – from the present to the indefinite future – and let Γ_W be the corresponding set of well-being paths. I take it that there is no uncertainty, and that Γ_W is bounded. Imagine that there is an underlying ethical preference ordering defined over Γ_W. Alternative policies are therefore to be evaluated in terms of this ordering. Koopmans (1960) showed that under a plausible set of assumptions, this ordering can be represented by a numerical functional (which we may call *aggregate well-being*) possessing the 'utilitarian' form:

$$\int_0^\infty W(C_t)\exp(-\delta t)\,dt, \quad \text{where } \delta > 0.^{12} \tag{1}$$

Now (1) may look like classical utilitarianism, but it is not. There is nothing in the Koopmans axioms to force a utilitarian interpretation upon W. Moreover, (1) involves discounting future well-beings at a constant rate ($\delta > 0$). In short, positive discounting of well-being is seen to be an implication of a set of ethical axioms that, at face value at least, would appear to have nothing to do with discounting.

When conducting analytical experiments with alternative assumptions embedded in (1), it makes sense to go beyond the Koopmans axioms and allow for consideration the case where $\delta = 0$. It also makes sense to go beyond the axioms and to consider unbounded well-being functions. This way we are able to test models to see what all this implies for public policy and the choice of discount rates in social cost-benefit analysis. On the other hand, purposeless generality should be avoided. So we will assume that $W(C)$ is strictly concave, to give shape to the idea that intergenerational equity is valued as an ethical goal.[13]

It is as well to begin by noting that discount rates in use in social cost-benefit analysis (sections 5–7) are 'consumption discount rates'. In first-best situations, they equal 'income discount rates'. (They are also sometimes, misleadingly, called 'social discount rates', and are different from market interest rates in second-best situations, see below.) If consumption is expected to grow, then the discount rate used in cost-benefit analysis would be positive even if δ were taken to be zero. This follows from the strict concavity of $W(C)$. To see this, recall that, in discrete time the consumption rate of discount at time t is the marginal social rate of indifferent substitution between consumption at times t and $t + 1$ minus 1. This means that it is the percentage rate of decline in discounted marginal well-being over the interval $[t, t + 1]$. Let ρ_t denote this. Reverting to continuous time and the 'utilitarian' form in (1), it is an easy matter to confirm that

$$\rho_t = \pi(C_t) = \delta + a(C_t)[dC_t/dt]/C_t \qquad (2)$$

where $a(C_t) > 0$ is the elasticity of marginal well-being at t (see e.g. Arrow and Kurz, 1970). Moreover, along a full optimum, the consumption rate of discount equals the productivity of capital (i.e. the social rate of return on investment). This is the famous Ramsey Rule.

Iso-elasticity offers a simple, flexible form of $W(.)$. So let us assume that

$$W(C) = - C^{-a}, \quad \text{where } a \text{ is positive constant.} \qquad (3)$$

In this case the optimality criterion reflected in (1) depends upon only two parameters: a and δ. Obviously, the larger is δ, the lower is the weight awarded to future generations' well-beings relative to that of the present generation. The moral of Mirrlees' (1967) computations was that introducing this sort of bias would be a way of countering the advantages to be enjoyed by future generations, should the productivity of capital and technological progress prove to be powerful engines of growth in well-being.

Nevertheless, consider the case $\delta = 0$. As an example, let us assume that $a = 2.5$ (a not implausible figure if $W(C)$ were to be based on revealed preferences). If the rate of growth of optimum consumption at t is, say, 2 percent, then $\rho_t = 5$ percent. It will be noticed that the larger is a, the more egalitarian is the optimal consumption path. As $a \to \infty$, the well-being functional represented in (1) resembles more and more the Rawlsian maxi-min principle as applied to the intergenerational distribution of consumption (and thus well-being). This in turn means that, even in productive economies, optimal growth in consumption is slow if a is large. In the limit, as $a \to \infty$, optimal growth is zero. From (2), we can now see why the consumption rate of discount is bounded (and how it manages to equal the productivity of capital) even in these extreme parametric terrains. (On this, see Dasgupta and Heal, 1979: chs. 9–10.)

Social discount rates are percentage rates of change of intertemporal relative shadow prices. It follows that, unless the optimising economy is in a steady state, social discount rates typically depend upon the numéraire that has been adopted.[14] As (2) makes clear, the well-being discount rate differs from consumption rates of discount. This is not an obvious point, and it continues to be misunderstood in a good deal of the environmental literature that is critical of social cost-benefit analysis (see e.g. Daly and Cobb, 1991; Norgaard and Howarth, 1991). Modern philosophers writing on the matter make the same mistake and conflate well-being and consumption rates of discount. They argue that δ should be zero and then criticise the practice of discounting future flows of consumption in social cost-benefit analysis (see e.g. Parfit, 1984; Cowen and Parfit, 1992).

Although simple, the Koopmans formulation spans a rich variety of ethical considerations. Among other things, it tells us that consumption rates of discount do not reflect primary value judgements: they are derived notions. They are essential when we try to implement optimal policies by means of cost-benefit analysis of projects.

Notice that in (3), $W(C)$ is unbounded below. If $\delta = 0$, this ensures that very low consumption rates are penalised by the optimality criterion reflected in (1). On the other hand, if δ were positive, low consumption rates by generations sufficiently far in the future would not be penalised by (1). This means that unless the economy is sufficiently productive, optimal consumption will tend to zero in the very long run. As an illustration of how critical δ can be, Dasgupta and Heal (1974) and Solow (1974a) showed in a model economy with exhaustible resources that optimal consumption declines to zero in the very long run if $\delta > 0$, but that it increases to infinity if $\delta = 0$. It is in such examples that notions of sustainable development can offer some cutting power. If by 'sustainable development' we wish to mean that the chosen consumption path should as a minimum never fall short of some stipulated, positive level, then it follows that the value of δ would need to be adjusted downward in a suitable manner to ensure that the optimal consumption path meets with the requirement. This was the substance of Solow's remark (see Solow, 1974b) that, in the economics of exhaustible resources the choice of δ can be a matter of considerable moment.

On the other hand, by 'sustainable development' we could mean something else: we could mean that well-being (and, therefore, consumption) must never be allowed to decline. This is a stiffer requirement than the one I have just considered. If δ is less than the productivity of capital, the valuation criterion reflected in (1) ensures that the optimal consumption path will satisfy the requirement. This follows immediately from (2) and the Ramsey Rule. We may therefore conclude that the Koopmans programme is all-encompassing, and that concepts of 'sustainability' are useful in pruning out of consideration those consumption paths that are ethically indefensible on *prima facie* grounds. In sections 6–9 and the appendix I will study the implications of this framework for social cost-benefit analysis and national income accounting, both of which are central to the evaluation and choice of public policies.

5   Second-best optima, global warming, and risk

Analysing full optima (i.e. first-best allocations) helps fix ideas. In reality, a vast array of forward markets are missing (due to an absence of property rights, transaction costs, or whatever). It is a reason why, typically, market rates of interest are inappropriate for discounting future incomes in the social evaluation of projects and policies.   ·

The phenomenon of global warming offers a good instance of what this can imply. As we noted in section 3, the atmosphere is a global commons *par excellence*, and greenhouse emissions are a byproduct of production and consumption activities. In short, there is 'market failure'. Social cost-benefit analysis needs to be undertaken with these failures in mind. Consider then that a number of simulation studies on the economics of global warming (e.g. Nordhaus, 1990) have indicated that the social costs of doing much to counter the phenomenon in the near future would far exceed the benefits, because the benefits (e.g. avoiding the submergence of fixed capital in low-lying areas, and declines in agricultural outputs) would appear only in the distant future (100 years and more). Needless to say, the results depend crucially on the fact that in these studies future costs and benefits, when expressed in terms of income, are discounted at a positive rate over all future periods, even when doing nothing to combat global warming is among the options that are being considered.

These results, quite rightly, appear as something of a puzzle to many. They imagine that global warming will result eventually in declines and dislocations of incomes, production, and people; and yet they are informed that 'economic logic' has been shown to cast a damper on the idea that anything really drastic needs to be done in the immediate future to counter it. Perhaps then, or so it is on occasion thought, we ought, when deliberating environmental matters, to use social rates of discount that are different from those in use in the evaluation of other types of economic activity.

We have seen earlier why this would be an incorrect thought. On the other hand, using a constant discount rate for the purposes of simulation in the economics of global warming is not sound either. If global warming is expected to lead to declines in (weighted) global consumption over some extended period in the distant future, then the logic underlying (2) would say that over this same extended period, consumption rates of interest could well be *negative*. If this were so (and it would certainly be so if $\delta = 0$), then from our current viewpoint future losses due to global warming could well be amplified; they would not be reduced to negligible figures by the relentless application of a constant and positive discount rate. It is then entirely possible that far more aggressive policies are warranted to combat global warming than are implied by current simulation models.

Introducing risk into the theory of optimal development raises additional questions, and avoiding future disasters that could arise from global warming provides another reason why more aggressive current action may be called for. Here lies another weakness of most numerical models of global warming (e.g. Nordhaus, 1990); all estimates are point estimates, and so the downside of risky situations does not get to play a role. The theory of rational choice under uncertainty (i.e. the von Neumann–Morgenstern–Savage theory) instructs us to expand the space of commodities and services by including in their description the event at which they are made available. It tells us that the appropriate generalisation of (1) is the expected value of the sums of flows of (possibly discounted) well-being.

Optimal development when future technology is uncertain has been much studied within this framework (see e.g. Phelps, 1962; Mirrlees, 1965, 1974; Levhari and Srinivasan, 1969; Hahn, 1970; Dasgupta and Heal, 1974; Dasgupta, Heal and Majumdar, 1977). Risk of extinction of the human race provides an additional reason for discounting future well-beings. If the possibility of extinction is judged to be approximately a Poisson process, then the modification is especially simple: it involves increasing the well-being discount rate by the probability rate of extinction (see e.g. Mirrlees, 1967; Dasgupta, 1969, 1982a). We will identify a number of the salient features of optimal development paths under uncertainty in the appendix.

Uncertainty about future possibilities and the fact that economic decisions can have irreversible impacts, together provide us with a reason to value flexibility (Arrow and Fisher, 1974; Henry, 1974). The underlying idea is that the present generation should choose its policies in a way that helps preserve future generations' options. Environmentalists have frequently interpreted the idea of sustainable development in this light.

One way of formulating the idea of keeping future options open is to study the structure of Γ_C (which, recall, is the set of feasible consumption paths, from the present to infinity) in terms of the resource and capital base a generation inherits from the past, and to consider only those actions on the part of the generation that, as a minimum, preserves Γ_C. Thus, writing by $\mathbf{K}$ and $\mathbf{S}$ the stocks of manufactured capital (including knowledge and skills) and environmental resources, respectively, let $\Gamma_C^t(\mathbf{K}, \mathbf{S})$ denote the set of feasible consumption paths defined over $[t, \infty)$.

To preserve future generations' options would be to insist that $\Gamma^t_C \subseteq \Gamma^{t+1}_C$ for $t \geq 0$. This idea was suggested by Dasgupta and Heal (1979: ch. 9) and subsequently explored by Solow (1991).

There are two problems with it. First, but for the simplest of economies (e.g. the one-good economy in Solow, 1956), $\Gamma^t_C(\mathbf{K}, \mathbf{S})$ is so complicated a set that nothing directly can be gleaned about the nature of policies that preserve options. Second and more importantly, it is an unsatisfactory approach to the notion of intergenerational justice, because it pays no heed to the *worth* of options. But worth cannot be measured except in terms of well-being. So we are back full circle to notions of aggregate well-being. To be sure, uncertainties about current stocks (e.g. numbers of species), and about future needs, wants, technology, climate, and so forth, need to be introduced; say, in terms of the expected value of aggregate well-being. But this is only to remind us of a central truth: the worth of keeping future generations' options open should be seen as a derived value. In other words, the worth should be assessed in terms of an overarching notion of aggregate well-being. The theory of option values (see section 9 and chapter 7 in this volume) is based on this insight.

6   Project evaluation and the measurement of net national product

There are two ways of assessing changes in aggregate well-being. One would be to measure the value of changes in the constituents of well-being (utility and freedoms), and the other would be to measure the value of the alterations in the commodity determinants of well-being (goods and services that are inputs in the production of well-being). The former procedure measures the value of alterations in various 'outputs' (e.g. indices of health, education, and other social indicators), and the latter evaluates the aggregate value of changes in the 'inputs' of the production of well-being (real national income). A key theorem in modern resource allocation theory is that, provided certain technical restrictions are met, for any conception of aggregate well-being, and for any set of technological, transaction, information, and ecological constraints, there exists a set of shadow (or accounting) prices of goods and services that can be used in the estimation of real national product. The index in question has the following property: small investment projects that improve the index are at once those that increase aggregate well-being.[15] We may state the matter more generally: provided the set of accounting prices is unaffected, an improvement in the index owing to an alteration in economic activities reflects an increase in aggregate well-being. This is the sense in which real national income measures aggregate well-being. Moreover, the sense persists no matter what is the basis upon which aggregate well-being is founded. In particular, the use of national income in measuring changes in aggregate well-being is *not* restricted to utilitarian ethics.

The theorem should be well known, but it often goes unrecognised in development economics, and today the use of real national income increment as an indicator of economic development is held in disrepute. For example, Anand and Ravallion (1993) criticise the use of national income in assessing relative well-beings in poor countries, on the grounds that income is a measure of opulence, and not of well-being (nor, as they say, of 'capability'; see Sen, 1992). They assert that using the former for the purposes of measuring the latter constitutes a philosophical error, and imply that development planners would have been better placed to make recommendations in poor countries if they had only read their Aristotle. The authors divide national income into personal income and public services, and show that there are a number of countries with a better-than-average personal *per capita* income that display worse-than-average social indicators, such as health and basic education.

But it has long been a tenet of resource allocation theory that public health and basic education ought not to be a matter of private consumption alone. One reason for this view is that they both display strong externalities, and are at once merit goods (Musgrave, 1959). Another reason is that the credit and savings market work especially badly for the poor in poor countries. In short, the theory has always informed us that a community's personal consumption would not tell us much about its health and education statistics. As this is standard fare in public economics, one can but conclude that if the majority of poor countries have a bad record in the provision of public services, it is not due to philosophical error on the part of their leaderships, nor a lack of knowledge of resource allocation theory: it is something else. In any event reliance on national income increments as indicators of increases in aggregate well-being does not reflect any particular brand of ethics. Its justification rests on a technical result in economics, and is independent of the ethical stance that is adopted.

To be sure, if real national income is to reflect aggregate well-being, accounting prices should be used. Recall that the accounting price of a resource is the increase in the maximum value of aggregate well-being if a unit more of the resource were made available costlessly. (It is a Lagrange multiplier.) Accounting prices are, therefore, the differences between market prices and optimum taxes and subsidies. This provides us with the sense in which it is important for poor countries to 'get their prices right'. Moreover, by real national product for an intertemporal economy, I mean real *net* national production (NNP). The accounting value of the depreciation of fixed capital (and by this we mean both manufactured and natural capital) needs to be deducted if the index of national product is to play the role we are assigning to it here (see Dasgupta and Heal, 1979; Dasgupta and Mäler, 1991; Mäler, 1991). Thus, NNP, when correctly measured in a closed economy, reads as follows:

> NNP = *Consumption + net investment in physical capital*
> *+ the value of the net change in human capital*
> *+ the value of the net change in the stock of natural capital*
> *− the value of current environmental damages.* (4)

I am regarding consumption as the numéraire in our measure of NNP. So the 'values' referred to in (4) are consumption values, and they are evaluated with the help of shadow prices. In the appendix I will present an account of how NNP ought ideally to be computed in an intertemporal economy. I will study an optimising economy there. The optimisation exercise enables one to estimate accounting prices. These prices can then in principle be used for the purposes of project and policy evaluation even in an economy that is far off the optimum (see e.g. Little and Mirrlees, 1974; Squire and Van der Taak, 1975). (The formula has to be suitably extended for an open economy. For example, if exhaustible resources are exported, then the net value of the year's exports should be deducted from the figure for NNP in equation (4).)

An alternative way is to think of public policy as a sequence of reforms. Accounting prices in this framework would be estimated from the *prevailing* structure of production and consumption (and not from the optimum). If the economy has a convex structure, then a sequence of such reforms would in principle take the economy ultimately to the optimum (see e.g. Dasgupta, Marglin and Sen, 1972; Ahmad and Stern, 1990). (4) reflects the correct notion of NNP in both frameworks.[16]

It is useful to note here that the convention of regarding expenditures on public health and education as part of final demand implicitly equates the cost of their provision with the contribution they make to aggregate well-being. In all probability, this results in an underestimate in poor countries.[17] We should note as well that current defensive expenditure against damages to the flow of environmental amenities ought to be included in the estimation of final demand. Similarly, investment in the stock of environmental defensive capital should be included in NNP.

By 'investment', I mean the value of net changes in capital assets, and not changes in the value of these assets. This means that anticipated capital gains (or losses) should not be included in NNP (see the appendix). An answer to the question as to how we should estimate NNP should not be a matter of opinion today: it is a matter of fact.

7　The Hamiltonian and net national product

The theory of optimal development enables us to obtain the idea of NNP. Let us begin by recalling the main features of intertemporal optimisation exercises.[18] The theory of intertemporal planning tells us to choose current controls (for example, current consumptions and the mix of current investments) in such a way as to maximise the current-value Hamiltonian of the underlying planning problem. As is well known, the current-value Hamiltonian is the sum of the flow of current well-being and the shadow value of all the net investments currently being undertaken. (The planning exercise generates the entire set of intertemporal shadow prices.[19]) It will be seen in the appendix that the current-value Hamiltonian measures the social return on the value of all capital assets. In short, it is a measure of the return of wealth. This provides us with the necessary connection between the current-value Hamiltonian and real net national product. NNP is merely a linearised version of the current-value Hamiltonian, the linearisation amounting to a representation of the current flow of well-being by the shadow value of all the determinants of current well-being. In the simplest of cases, where current well-being depends solely on current consumption, NNP reduces to the sum of the shadow value of an economy's consumptions and the shadow value of the changes in its stocks of real capital assets.

The Hamiltonian calculus in fact implies something more. It implies that the present discounted sum of today's current-value Hamiltonian is equal to the maximum present discounted value of the flow of social well-being (appendix, (A13)). Thus the current-value Hamiltonian is the maximum sustainable flow of social well-being. This was not seen immediately as an implication of the mathematical theory of programming, although it should have been transparent from the work of Arrow and Kurz (1970) and Solow (1974a). Each of these matters will be illustrated in our formal model.

Conventional estimates of NNP are biased because depreciation of environmental resources is not deducted from GNP. Stated another way, NNP estimates are biased because a biased set of prices is in use. Prices imputed to envirionmental resources on site are usually zero. This amounts to regarding the depreciation of environmental capital as zero. But these resources are scarce goods, so we know that their shadow prices are positive. Profits attributed to projects that degrade the environment are therefore higher than the social profits they generate. This means in turn that wrong sets of projects get chosen – in both the private and public sectors.

The extent of the bias will obviously vary from project to project, and from country to country. But it can be substantial. In their work on the depreciation of natural resources in Costa Rica, Solorzano *et al.* (1991) have estimated that, in 1989 the depreciation of three resources – forests, soil, and fisheries – amounted to about 10 percent of GDP and over a third of gross capital accumulation. Resource-intensive projects look better than they actually are. Installed technologies are usually unfriendly towards the environment.

8   Biases in technological adaptation

One can go further: the bias extends to the prior stage of research and development. When environmental resources are underpriced, there is little incentive on anyone's part to develop technologies that economise on their use. The extent of the distortion created by this underpricing will vary from country to country. Poor countries inevitably have to rely on the flow of new knowledge produced in advanced industrial economies. Nevertheless, poor countries need to have the capability for basic research. The structure of shadow prices there is likely to be different from those in advanced industrial countries, most especially for non-traded goods and services. Even when it is publicly available, basic knowledge is not necessarily usable by scientists and technologists, unless they themselves have a feel for basic research. Often enough, ideas developed in foreign lands are merely transplanted to the local economy; whereas they ought instead to be modified to suit local ecological conditions before being adopted. This is where the use of shadow prices is of help. It creates the right set of incentives both among developers and users of technologies. Adaptation is itself a creative exercise. Unhappily, as matters stand, it is often bypassed. There is loss in this.

There is further loss associated with a different kind of bias: that arising from biased demand. For example, wherever household demands for goods and services in the market reflect in the main male (or for that matter, female) concerns, the direction of technological change would be expected to follow suit. Among poor countries, we would expect techno-logical inventions in farm equipment and techniques of productions to be forthcoming in regions where cultivation is a male activity (there would be a demand for them); we would not observe much in the way of process innovations in threshing, winnowing, the grinding of grain in the home, and in the preparation of food. Thus, cooking in South Asia is a central route to respiratory illnesses among women: women sit hunched over ovens fuelled by cowdung, or wood, or leaves. It is inconceivable that improvements in design are not possible to realise. But entrepreneurs have little incentive to bring about such technological innovations. Household demand for them would be expected to be low.

The argument extends to collective activity in general, and State activity in particular. In poor communities, men typically have the bulk of the political voice. We should then expect public decisions over rural investment and environmental preservation also to be guided by male preferences, not female needs. Over afforestation in the drylands, for example, we should expect women to favour planting for fuelwood and men for fruit trees, because it is the women and children who collect fuelwood, while men control cash income. And fruit can be sold in the market. Such evidence on this as I am aware of is only anecdotal. But as it is confirmed by theory, it is reasonable to imagine that this must quite generally be true.

Such biases in NNP as I have identified here occur in advanced industrial countries as well. So then why should we stress their importance in the context of poor countries? The reason is that poor people in poor countries cannot cope with the same margin of error as people living in rich countries can: a 10 percent drop in the standard of living imposes greater hardship on a poor household than a rich one. Recall too that the rural poor are especially dependent upon their local environmental resource base. Losses in well-being due to an underpricing of this base are absorbed by them disproportionately. The estimation of accounting prices of environmental resources should now be high on the agenda of research in the economics of poor countries.

9 Environmental accounting prices: the valuation problem

How we should estimate accounting prices is a complex question. But it is not uniformly complex. There are now standard techniques of evaluation for commodities like irrigation water, fisheries, timber, and agricultural soil.[20] The same techniques can be used for estimating losses associated with waterlogging and overgrazing. They rely on the fact that the environmental resources in question are inputs in the production of tradeable goods. As long as the flow of all other inputs in production are held constant, the accounting value of changes in their supply can be estimated directly from the value of the resulting changes in output.

For commodities such as firewood and drinking and cooking water, the matter is more complex: they are inputs in household production.[21] This means that we need estimates of household production functions. As an example, transportation costs (in particular energy costs as measured in calories) for women and children would be less if the sources of fuelwood and water were not far away and receding. As a first approximation, the value of water or fuelwood resources for household production can be estimated from these energy needs.[22] In some situations (as on occasion with fuelwood), the resource is a substitute for a tradeable input (for example, paraffin or kerosine); in others (as with cooking water) it is a complement to tradeable inputs (for example, food grain). Such facts allow us to estimate accounting prices of non-marketed goods in terms of the accounting prices of marketed goods (see Mäler, 1974).[23]

The approach outlined above allows us to capture only the known use value of a resource. As it happens, its shadow price may well exceed this. Why? The reason is that there may be additional values embodied in a resource stock. One additional value, applicable to living resources, is their intrinsic worth *as* living resources. (It is absurd to suppose that the value of a blue whale is embodied entirely in its flesh and oil, or that the value of the 'game' in Kenyan safari parks is simply the present-discounted value of tourists' willingness to pay.) It is almost impossible to get a quantitative handle on 'intrinsic worth' (sometimes called 'existence value'). So the right thing to do is to take note of it, keep an eye on it, and call attention to it in public debate if the resource is threatened with extinction.

What is the point of basing shadow prices solely on use value when we know that resources often possess intrinsic value as well? It is that such estimates provide us with *biased* shadow prices, and this can be useful information. For example, in his classic study on the optimal rate of harvest of blue whales, Spence (1974) took the shadow price of these creatures to be the market value of their flesh, a seemingly absurd and repugnant move. But he showed that under a wide range of plausible parametric conditions, it would be most profitable commercially for the international whaling industry to agree on a moratorium until the desired long-run population size were reached, and for the industry to subsequently harvest the creatures at a rate equal to the population's sustainable yield.[24] In other words, preservation is recommended solely on commercial ground. But if preservation is justified when the shadow values of blue whales are estimated from their market prices, the recommendation would, obviously, be reinforced if their intrinsic worth were to be added. This was the point of Spence's exercise.

There is another source of value of environmental resources, which is more amenable to quantification. It arises from a combination of two things common to them: uncertainty in their future use values, and irreversibility in their use. (Genetic material in tropical forests provides a prime example.) The twin presence of uncertainty and irreversibility implies that, even if the aggregate well-being function were neutral to risk, it would not do to estimate the accounting price of an environmental resource solely on the basis of the expected benefit from its future use. Irreversibility in its use implies that preservation of its stock has an additional value – the value of extending society's set of future options. (I discussed this in a wider context in section 5.) Future options have an additional worth because, with the passage of time, more information is expected to be forthcoming about the resource's use value. This additional worth is often called an *option value*. The accounting price of a resource is the sum of its use value and its option value.[25]

10   Conclusions

In this chapter I have translated what I believe to be inchoate ideas on sustainable development in terms of an earlier, more developed notion, that of 'optimal development'. The theory of optimal control has for over 25 years provided us with an instrument for formulating notions of intergenerational justice. It has also made clear such derived concepts as social discount rates and their role in the cost-benefit analysis of projects and policies. It transpires, not surprisingly, that the theory also provides us with a rigorous foundation for the idea of net national product (NNP) and its use as a measure of intergenerational well-being. That NNP estimates ought ideally to take account of environmental degradation and the depletion of natural resources has been noted for quite some time, and in recent years much has also been written on it. What has been lacking is a formal demonstration of how we can decide what items of economic activity ought to be included in estimates of NNP. In the body of this chapter I have suggested how this can best be reached, and in the appendix that follows I present a formal model of a closed economy that is sufficiently general to bring out a number of special issues that can arise. Ideas of intergenerational justice, optimal (as well as sustainable) development, social discount rates, cost-benefit analysis, and NNP are all related to one another very closely. Much of the economic theory that was developed over the 1960s and 1970s showed the precise sense in which they are related. My main purpose in writing this chapter has been to remind environmental economists of this. I felt it needed doing because the large literature on environmental economics that has recently been developed has shown an alarming tendency not to be cognisant of it.

Appendix: NNP in a dynamic economy

NNP in a deterministic environment

In what follows, I shall consider a closed economy.[26] Let us assume that there is a multi-purpose, man-made, perfectly durable capital good, whose stock I denote by K_1. If L_1 is the labour effort combined with this, the flow of output is taken to be $Y = F(K_1, L_1)$, where $F(.)$ is an aggregate production function.[27] The economy enjoys in addition two sorts of environmental-resource stocks: clean air, K_2, and forests, K_3. Clean air is valued directly whereas forests have two derived values: they help keep the atmosphere (or air) 'clean', and they provide fuelwood, which too is valued directly (for warmth or for cooking). Finally, I take it that there is a flow of environmental amenities, Z, which directly affects aggregate well-being.

Forests enjoy a natural regeneration rate, but labour effort can increase it. Thus I denote by $H(L_2)$ the rate of regeneration of forests, where L_2 is labour input for this task, and where $H(.)$ is, for low value of L_2 at least, an increasing function. Let X denote the rate of consumption of fuelwood. Collecting this involves labour effort. Let this be L_3. Presumably, the larger is the forest stock the less is the effort required (in calorie requirements, say). I remarked on this in the text above. I thus assume that $X = N(K_3, L_3)$, where $N(.)$ is an increasing, concave function of its two arguments.

Output Y is a basic consumption good, and this consumption is also valued directly. However, we take it that the production of Y involves pollution as a byproduct. This reduces the quality of the atmosphere both as a stock and as a flow of amenities. I shall assume however that it is possible to take defensive measure against both these ill-effects. Firstly, society can invest in technologies (e.g. stack-gas scrubbers) for reducing the emission of pollutants, and I denote the stock of this defensive capital by K_4. If P denotes the emission of pollutants, we have $P = A(K_4, Y)$, where A is a convex function, decreasing in K_4 and increasing in Y. Secondly, society can mitigate damages to the flow of amenities by expending a portion of final output, at a rate R. I assume that the resulting flow of amenities has the functional form, $Z = J(R, P)$, where J is increasing in R and decreasing in P.

There are thus four things that can be done with output Y: it can be consumed (we denote the rate of consumption by C); it can be reinvested to increase the stock of K_1; it can be invested in the accumulation of K_4; and it can be used, at rate R, to counter the damages to the flow of environmental amenities. Let Q denote the expenditure on the accumulation of K_4.

Now, the environment as a stock tries to regenerate itself at a rate which is an increasing function of the stock of forests, $G(K_3)$. The net rate of regeneration is the difference between this and the emission of pollutants from production of Y. We can therefore express the dynamics of the economy in terms of the following equations:

$$dK_1/dt = F(K_1, L_1) - C - Q - R \qquad \text{(A1)}$$

$$dK_2/dt = G(K_3) - A(K_4, F[K_1, L_1])$$ (A2)

$$dK_3/dt = H(L_2) - X$$ (A3)

$$dK_4/dt = Q$$ (A4)

$$X = N(K_3, L_3)$$ (A5)

and

$$Z = J[R, A(K_4, F[K_1, L_1])].$$ (A6)

The current flow of aggregate well-being, W, is taken to be an increasing function of aggregate consumption, C; the output of fuelwood, X; the flow of environmental amenities, Z; and the quality of the atmosphere stock, K_2. However, it is a decreasing function of total labour effort, $L = L_1 + L_2 + L_3$. (As noted in the text, labour effort could be measured in calories.) We thus have $W(C, X, Z, K_2, L_1 + L_2 + L_3)$.

Stocks of the four types of assets are given at the initial date; the instantaneous control variables are C, Q, R, X, Z, L_1, L_2 and L_3. The objective is to maximise the (discounted) sum of the flow of aggregate well-being over the indefinite future; that is

$$\int_0^\infty W(C, X, Z, K_2, L_1 + L_2 + L_3) e^{-\delta t} dt, \text{ where } \delta > 0 \text{ (see section 3).}$$

Let us take well-being to be the numéraire. Letting p, q, r and s denote the (spot) shadow prices of the four capital goods, K_1, K_2, K_3 and K_4 respectively, and letting v be the imputed marginal value of the flow of environmental amenities, we can use (A1)–(A6) to express the current-value Hamiltonian, V, of the optimisation problem as:

$$
\begin{aligned}
V = \ & W(C, N(K_3, L_3), Z, K_2, L_1 + L_2 + L_3) \\
& + p[F(K_1, L_1) - C - Q - R] \\
& + q[G(K_3) - A(K_4, F[K_1, L_1])] \\
& + r[H(L_2) - N(K_3, L_3)] \\
& + sQ + v(J[R, A(K_4, F[K_1, L_1])]) - Z.
\end{aligned}
$$ (A7)

Recall that the theory of optimum control instructs us to choose the control variables at each date so as to maximise (A7).[28] Writing by W_C the partial derivative of W with respect to C, and so forth, it is then immediate that, along an optimal programme the control variables and the shadow prices must satisfy the conditions:

(i) $W_C = p$; (ii) $W_X N_2 + W_L = rN_2$; (iii) $W_Z = v$;
(iv) $W_L[qA_2 - vJ_2 - p]F_2$; (v) $W_L = -rdH(L_2)/dL_2$;
(vi) $p = vJ_1$; (vii) $p = s$.[29] (A8)

Moreover, the accounting prices, p, q, r, and s satisfy the auxiliary conditions:

(1) $dp/dt = -\partial V/\partial K_1 + \delta p$; (2) $dq/dt = -\partial V/\partial K_2 + \delta q$;
(3) $dr/dt = -\partial V/\partial K_3 + \delta r$; (4) $ds/dt = -\partial V/\partial K_4 + \delta s$. (A9)

Interpreting these conditions is today a routine matter. Conditions (A8) tell us what kinds of information we need for estimating shadow prices. (A9) are the intertemporal 'arbitrage conditions' the shadow prices must satisfy. We may now derive the correct expression for NNP from (A7): it is the linear support of the Hamiltonian, the normal to the support being given the vector of accounting prices.

It will pay us now to introduce time into the notation. Let us denote by $\mathbf{O}_t^*$ the vector of all the non-price arguments in the Hamiltonian function along the optimal programme at date t. Thus:

$$\mathbf{O}_t^* = (C_t^*, Z_t^*, Q_t^*, R_t^*, K_{1t}^*, K_{2t}^*, K_{3t}^*, K_{4t}^*, L_{1t}^*, L_{2t}^*, L_{3t}^*).$$

Write $I_{it} \equiv dK_{it}/dt$, for $i = 1, 2, 3, 4$. Consider now a small perturbation at t round $\mathbf{O}_t^*$. Denote the perturbed programme as an unstarred vector, and $d\mathbf{O}_t$ as the perturbation itself. It follows from taking the Taylor expansion around $\mathbf{O}^*$ that the current-value Hamiltonian along the perturbed programme is:

$$V(\mathbf{O}_t) = V(\mathbf{O}_t^*) + W_C dC_t + W_X dX_t + W_Z dZ_t$$
$$+ W_L(dL_{1t} + dL_{2t} + dL_{3t}) + pdI_{1t} + qdI_{2t} + rdI_{3t} + sdI_{4t}, \text{(A10)}$$

where $Z^* = J[R^*, A(K_4^*, F[K_1^*, L_1^*])]$.

(A10) tells us how to measure NNP. Let $\{\mathbf{O}_t\}$ denote an arbitrary intertemporal programme. NNP at date t, which we write as NNP_t, in the optimising economy, measured in well-being numéraire, is the term representing the linear support term in expression (A10). So,

$$\text{NNP}_t = W_C C_t + W_X X_t + W_Z J[R_t, A(K_{4t}, F[K_{1t} + L_{1t}])]$$
$$+ W_L(L_{1t} + L_{2t} + L_{3t}) + pdK_1/dt + qdK_2/dt$$
$$+ rdK_3/dt + sdK_4/dt.^{[30]} \quad \text{(A11)}$$

Notice that all resources and outputs are valued at the prices that sustain the optimal programme $\{\mathbf{O}_t^*\}$. (But recall the alternative framework mentioned in section 4, in which accounting prices are estimated from the prevailing structure of production and consumption.) To stress the points I want to make here, I have chosen to work with a most aggregate model. Ideally, (income) distributional issues will find reflection in the social well-being functional. These considerations can easily be translated into the estimates of shadow prices (see Dasgupta, Marglin and Sen, 1972).

Why should (A11) be regarded as the correct measure of net national product? The clue lies in (A10). Suppose we are involved in the choice of projects. A marginal project is a perturbation on the current programme. Suppressing the index for time once again, the project is the 10-vector $(dC, dX, dR, dL_1, dL_2, dL_3, dI_1, dI_2, dI_3, dI_4)$, where $I_i = dK_i/dt$, $(i = 1, 2, 3, 4)$; and dC, and so on, are small changes in C, and so forth. If the project records an increase in NNP_t (the increase will be marginal of course), it will record an increase in the current-value Hamiltonian, evaluated at the prices supporting the optimal programme. Recall that optimal control theory asks us to maximise the current-value Hamiltonian. Moreover, I am assuming that the planning problem is concave. So, choosing projects that increase NNP (i.e. they are socially profitable) increases the current-value Hamiltonian as well; and therefore, they should be regarded as desirable. Along an optimal programme, the social profitability of the last project is nil. Therefore, its contribution to NNP is nil. This follows from the fact that the controls are chosen so as to maximise (A7). This is the justification. All this is well known, and my purpose here is to obtain some additional insights. (A11) tells us:

(a)   If wages were to equal the marginal ill-being of work effort, wages would not be part of NNP. In short, the shadow wage bill ought to be deducted from gross output when we estimate NNP. (However, if labour is supplied inelasticity, it is a matter of indifference whether the wage bill in this optimising economy is deducted from NNP.) On the other hand, were we to recognise a part of the wage bill as a return on the accumulation of human capital, that part would be included in NNP.

(b)   Current defensive expenditure, R, against damages to the flow of environmental amenities should be included in the estimation of final demand (see the third term in (A9)).

(c)   Investments in the stock of environmental defensive capital should be included in NNP (see the final term of (A11)).

(d)   Expenditures which enhance the environment find expression in the value imputed to changes in the environmental resource stock. We may conclude that this change should not be included in estimates of NNP (notice the absence of sQ in (A11)).

(e)   The value of changes in the environmental resource base (K_2 and K_3) should be included in NNP. However, anticipated capital gains (or losses) are not part of NNP.

The Hamiltonian and sustainable well-being

Differentiate (A7) and use (A9) to confirm that along the optimal programme:

$$dV_t^*/dt = \delta(pdK_1/dt + qdK_2/dt + rdK_3/dt + sdK_4/dt)$$
$$= \delta(V_t^* - W_t^*), \tag{A12}$$

where W_t^* is the flow of optimal aggregate well-being.

This is a differential equation in V_t^* which integrates to:

$$V_t^* = \delta \int_t^\infty W_\tau^* e^{-\delta(\tau - t)} d\tau, \text{ and thus}$$

$$V_t^* \int_t^\infty e^{-\delta(\tau - t)} d\tau = \int_t^\infty W_\tau^* e^{-\delta(\tau - t)} d\tau. \tag{A13}$$

(A13) says that the present discounted value of a constant flow of today's current-value Hamiltonian measures the maximum present value of the flow of social well-being. Thus V_t^* is the maximum sustainable flow of social well-being.

Define $K \equiv pK_1 + qK_2 + rK_3 + sK_4$ as the aggregate capital stock in the economy. The first part of (A12) can then be written as:

$$V_t^* = \delta K_t. \tag{A14}$$

In short, the current-value Hamiltonian measures the 'well-being return' on the economy's aggregate capital stock, inclusive of the environmental-resource base.

Future uncertainty

I will now extend the analysis to incorporate future uncertainty. As an example, we could imagine the discovery and installation of cleaner production technologies that make existing abatement technologies less valuable. For simplicity of exposition, I will assume that such discoveries are uninfluenced by policy, for example, R&D policy.[31]

It is most informative to consider discrete events. We may imagine that at some random future date, T, an event occurs which is expected to affect the value of the then existing stocks of capital. We consider the problem from the vantage point of the present, which we denote by $t = 0$; where t, as always, denotes time. Let us assume that there is a (subjective) probability density function, τ', over the date of its occurrence. (We are thus supposing for expositional ease that the event will occur at some future date.) From this we may define the cumulative function Φ'.

I take it that the social good is reflected by the expected value of the sum of the discounted flow of future aggregate well-being (1). If the event in question were to occur at date T, the economy in question would enter a new production and ecological regime. Let us continue to rely on the notation developed in the previous section. As is proper, we use dynamic programming, and proceed to work backwards. Thus, let K_i^T (with $i = 1, 2, 3, 4$) denote the stocks of the four assets at date T. Following an optimal economic policy subsequent to the occurrence of the event would yield an expected flow of aggregate well-being. This flow we discount back to T. This capitalised value of the flow of well-being will clearly be a function of K_i^T. Let us denote this by $B(K_1^T, K_2^T, K_3^T, K_4^T)$. It is now possible to show that until the event occurs (i.e. for $t < T$), the optimal policy is to pretend that the event will never occur, and to assume that the flow of aggregate well-being is given, not by $W(.)$, as on p. 132, but by $(1 - \Phi')W(.) + \pi' B(.)$. (See Dasgupta and Heal, 1974.) Suppressing the subscript for time, we may then conclude from the analysis of the previous section that NNP at any date prior to the occurrence of the event is given by the expression:

$$\begin{aligned}
\text{NNP} = (1 - \Phi)\{W_C C + W_X X + W_Z J[R, A(K_4, F[K_1, L_1])] \\
+ W_L(L_1 + L_2 + L_3) + pdK_1/dt + qdK_2/dt \\
+ rdK_3/dt + sdK_4/dt\}.
\end{aligned} \tag{A15}$$

Notice that if the event isn't ever expected to occur, then $\pi' = 0$ for all t, and consequently, $(1 - \Phi') = 1$ for all t. In this case (A15) reduces to (A11). Notice that the shadow prices appearing in (A15) are Arrow–Debreu contingent commodity prices. Notice too that while we have used the same notation for the accounting prices in (A11) and (A15), their values are quite different. This is because future possibilities in the two economies are different.

NOTES

This chapter is in part an elaboration of joint work that I have conducted over the years with Geoffrey Heal and Karl-Göran Mäler, respectively, and I have borrowed liberally from Dasgupta and Heal (1974, 1979) and Dasgupta and Mäler (1991, 1993). I am most grateful to them for the many discussions that we have had on the subject matter of this chapter.

I have also gained much from the comments of Philippe Aghion, Ian Goldin, and Maurice Scott.

1 Minerals and fossil fuels are not renewable (they are a pristine example of exhaustible resources), but they raise a different set of issues. For an account of what resource allocation theory looks like when we include exhaustible resources in the production process, see Dasgupta and Heal (1979), Hartwick and Olewiler (1986) and Tietenberg (1988). For a non-technical account of the theory and the historical role that has been played by the substitution of new energy resources for old, see Dasgupta (1989).

2 The economic issues arising from such non-linearities are analysed in Dasgupta (1982a) and Dasgupta and Mäler (1993).

3 Ehrlich and Roughgarden (1987) is an excellent treatise on these matters.

4 Anderson (1987) contains an authoritative case study of this.

5 One notable, and controversial, estimate of world-wide productivity declines in livestock and agriculture in the drylands due to soil losses was offered in UNEP (1984). The figure was an annual loss of $26 billion. For a discussion of the UNEP estimate, see Gigengack *et al.* (1990). The estimate by Mabbut (1984), that approximately 40 percent of the productive drylands of the world are currently under threat from desertification, probably gives an idea of the magnitude of the problem. For accounts of the economics and ecology of drylands, see Falloux and Mukendi (1988) and Dixon, James and Sherman (1989, 1990).

6 See, for example, Binswanger and Rosenzweig (1986), Rosenzweig and Wolpin (1989), and Hoff and Stiglitz (1990). I have gone into this range of questions in greater detail in Dasgupta (1993).

7 See, for example, Falkenmark (1986, 1989), Olsen (1987), Nelson (1988), Reij, Mulder and Begemann (1988) and Falkenmark and Chapman (1989).

8 There are added complications, among which is that the impact on the rate of regeneration of environmental resources of a wide variety of investment decisions is not fully reversible, and in some cases is quite irreversible. The capital-theoretic approach guides the exposition in Clark (1976), who, however, concentrates on fisheries. See Dasgupta (1982a) for a unified capital-theoretic treatment of environmental management problems in the context of poor countries.

9 This issue was the focus of Dasgupta and Heal (1974) and Solow (1974a). See Dasgupta and Heal (1979, chs. 9–10) for an elaboration.

10 For a more detailed account of this programme, see Dasgupta and Heal (1979, chs. 9–10).

11 Dasgupta and Heal (1974) and Solow (1974a) provide exercises of this sort in economies with exhaustible resources.

12 Koopmans' theorems were proved under the assumption that time is discrete. In Koopmans (1972a, 1972b) the ethical axioms are imposed directly on Γ_C, and $W(.)$ is obtained as a numerical representation.

13 For simplicity of exposition, we will begin by focusing on a full optimum. In section 5, when commenting on cost-benefit analyses of policies to combat global warming, we will look at second-best situations. Social cost-benefit analysis in second-best circumstances was the subject of discussion in Dasgupta, Marglin and Sen (1972) and Little and Mirrlees (1974).

14 Therefore, unless the numéraire has been specified, the term 'social discount rate' is devoid of meaning.

15 See Dasgupta (1993, chs. *7 and *10). The technical restrictions amount to the requirement that the Kuhn–Tucker Theorem is usable; i.e. that both the set of feasible allocations and the ethical ordering reflected by the aggregate well-being function are convex (see the appendix, p. 132). The assumption of convexity is dubious for pollution problems (see e.g. Dasgupta, 1982a). Nevertheless, in a wide range of circumstances, it is possible to separate out the 'non-convex' sector, estimate real national income (or product) for the 'convex' sector, and present an estimate of the desired index as a combination of the real product of the convex sector and estimates of stocks and their changes in the non-convex sectors. This is a simple inference from Weitzman (1970) and Portes (1971).

16 For a simplified exposition of the connection between these two modes of analysis (reforms and optimisation), see Dasgupta (1982a, ch. 5).

17 If education is regarded as a merit good, and not merely as instrumental in raising productivity, then its accounting price would be that much higher.

18 The best economics treatment of this is still Arrow and Kurz (1970).

19 The current-value Hamiltonian will in general also contain terms reflecting the social cost of breaking any additional (second-best) constraint that happens to characterise the optimisation problem. As mentioned in the text, I am ignoring such additional constraints for expositional ease.

20 See, for example, Brown and McGuire (1967) for irrigation water; Clark (1976), Cooper (1977) and Dasgupta (1982a) for fisheries; Magrath and Arens (1989) and Repetto et al. (1989) for soil fertility; Newcombe (1984) and Anderson (1987) for forestry; and Solorzano et al. (1991) for the latter three.

21 The classic on household production is Becker (1981).

22 Here is a simplified model for illustrating how one would go about it. Consider fuelwood (or water) collection. We take the unit of analysis to be a household. Assume that a representative household's daily energy intake is c, and that x is its harvest of fuelwood (or water) per day. Denote by S the stock of fuelwood (or water) resources in the locality, and by $e(S)$ the energy cost of bringing home a unit of fuelwood (or water). Obviously, $e(S)$ is a decreasing function of S. Equally obviously, the household's production of goods and services (e.g. cooked food, heating) is an increasing function of x. It follows that household well-being is an increasing function of both the net energy intake $(c - e(S)x)$ and x. Write this as $W(c - e(S)x, x)$. Assume for simplicity that the household chooses x so as to maximise W. I write the maximised value as $V(c, S)$. It is the indirect well-being function.

Suppose next that there are M households that rely on the resource. For an additive aggregate well-being function (see section 3), the shadow price of the resource is simply $- M(dc/dS)_W = MV_S/V_c = - Me'(S)x$. (Here V_S and V_c denote the partial derivatives of V, and $(dc/dS)_W$ denotes the marginal rate of substitution between c and S in the indirect well-being function.) In a more detailed model, c will be endogenous, and the effect of Mx on future values of S will also be taken into account (see the Appendix).

23 A second approach to the estimation of accounting prices of environmental resources is based on contingent valuation methods (or CVMs). They involve asking concerned individuals to reveal their equivalent (or compensating) valuation of hypothetical changes in the flow of environmental services. CVMs are useful in the case of amenities, and their applications have so far been confined to advanced industrial countries. As I am not focusing on amenities in this chapter, I shall not develop the ideas underlying CVMs any further. The most complete account to date on CVMs is Mitchell and Carson (1989). See also the report on the NOAA Panel on Contingent Valuation (co-chaired by K.J. Arrow and R.M. Solow) in the *Federal Register*. **58(10)** (15 January 1993).

24 During the moratorium the whale population grows at the fastest possible rate. In his numerical computations, the commercially most profitable duration of the moratorium was found to be some 10–15 years.

25 The pioneering works are Arrow and Fisher (1974) and Henry (1974). See also Dasgupta (1982a), Fisher and Hanemann (1986) and Mäler (1989).

26 For the extension to an open economy, see Sefton and Weale (1992).

27 In what follows we assume that all functions satisfy conditions which ensure that the planning problem defined below is a concave programme. We are not

going to spell out each and every such assumption, because they will be familiar to the reader. For example, we assume that $F(.)$ is concave.

28 Notice that we have used (A5) to eliminate X, and so we are left with six direct control variables.

29 F_2 stands for the partial derivative of F with respect to its second argument, L_1; and as mentioned earlier, $L = L_1 + L_2 + L_3$. We have used this same notation for the derivatives of $N(.)$, $J(.)$ and $A(.)$.

30 We may divide the whole expression by W_C to express NNP in aggregate consumption numéraire. It should also be recalled that by assumption W_L is *negative*.

31 Research and development policy can be easily incorporated into our analysis (see Dasgupta, Heal and Majumdar, 1977). The following account builds on Dasgupta and Heal (1974), Dasgupta and Stiglitz (1981), and Dasgupta (1982b). These earlier contributions, however, did not address the measurement of NNP, our present concern.

REFERENCES

Ahmad, E. and Stern, N. (1990) *The Theory and Practice of Tax Reform for Developing Countries*, Cambridge: Cambridge University Press

Anand, S. and Ravallion, M. (1993) 'Human development in poor countries: on the role of private incomes and public services', *Journal of Economic Perspectives*, **7**

Anderson, D. (1987) *The Economics of Afforestation*, Baltimore: Johns Hopkins University Press

Arrow, K.J. and Fisher, A. (1974) 'Preservation, uncertainty and irreversibility', *Quarterly Journal of Economics*, **88**

Arrow, K.J. and Kurz, M. (1970) *Public Investment, the Rate of Return and Optimal Fiscal Policy*, Baltimore: Johns Hopkins University Press

Becker, G. (1981) *A Treatise on the Family* Cambridge, MA: Harvard University Press

Binswanger, H. and Rosenzweig, M.R. (1986) 'Credit markets, wealth and endowments in rural South India', *Report*, 59, Agriculture and Rural Development Department, Washingon, DC: World Bank

Brown, G. and McGuire, C.B. (1967) 'A socially optimal pricing policy for a public water agency', *Water Resources Research*, **3**

Chakravarty, S. (1969) *Capital and Development Planning*, Cambridge, MA: MIT Press

Clark, C.W. (1976) *Mathematical Bioeconomics: The Optimal Management of Renewable Resources*, New York: John Wiley

Cooper, R. (1977) 'An economist's view of the oceans', *Journal of World Trade Law*, **9**

Cowen, T. and Parfit, D. (1992) 'Against the social discount rate', in P. Laslett and J.S. Fishkin (eds.), *Justice Between Age Groups and Generations*, New Haven, CT: Yale University Press

Daly, H.E. and Cobb, J.B. (1991) *For the Common Good: Redirecting the Economy Towards Community, the Environment, and a Sustainable Future*, London: Greenprint

Dasgupta, P. (1969) 'On the concept of optimal population', *Review of Economic Studies*, **36**

(1982a) *The Control of Resources*, Oxford: Basil Blackwell

(1982b) 'Resources depletion, research and development, and the social rate of discount', in R. Lind (ed.), *Discounting for Time and Risk in Energy Policy*, Baltimore: Johns Hopkins University Press

(1989) 'Exhaustible resources', in L. Friday and R. Laskey (eds.), *The Fragile Environment*, Cambridge: Cambridge University Press

(1993) *An Inquiry into Well-Being and Destitution*, Oxford: Clarendon Press

Dasgupta, P. and Heal, G.M. (1974) 'The optimal depletion of exhaustible resources', *Review of Economic Studies*, Symposium on the Economics of Exhaustible Resources, **41**

(1979) *Economic Theory and Exhaustible Resources*, Cambridge: Cambridge University Press

Dasgupta, P. and Mäler, K.-G. (1991) 'The environment and emerging development issues', *Proceedings of the Annual World Bank Conference on Development Economics* (Supplement to the World Bank Economic Review and the *World Bank Economic Observer*).

(1993) 'Poverty and the environmental-resource base', in J. Behrman and T.N. Srinivasan (eds.), *Handbook of Development Economics*, vol. III, Amsterdam: North-Holland (forthcoming, 1994)

Dasgupta, P. and Stiglitz, J.E. (1981) 'Resource depletion under technological uncertainty', *Econometrica*, **49**

Dasgupta, P., Heal, G.M. and Majumdar, M. (1977) 'Resource depletion and research and development', in M. Intriligator (ed.), *Frontiers of Quantitative Economics*, vol. III, Amsterdam: North-Holland

Dasgupta, P., Marglin, S. and Sen, A. (1972), *Guidelines for Project Evaluation* New York: United Nations

Dixon, J.A., James, D.E. and Sherman, P.B. (1989) *The Economics of Dryland Management*, London: Earthscan Publications

Dixon, J.A., James, D.E. and Sherman, P.B. (eds.) (1990) *Dryland Management Economic Case Studies*, London: Earthscan Publications

Ehrlich, P. and Roughgarden, J. (1987) *The Science of Ecology*, New York: St Martin's Press

Ehrlich, P., Ehrlich, A. and Holdren, J. (1977) *Ecoscience: Population, Resources and the Environment*, San Francisco: W.H. Freeman

Falkenmark, M. (1986) 'Fresh water: time for a modified approach', *Ambio*, **15**

(1989) 'The massive water scarcity now facing Africa: why isn't it being addressed?, *Ambio*, **18**

Falkenmark, M. and Chapman, T. (eds.) (1989) *Comparative Hydrology: An Ecological Approach to Land and Water Resources* Paris: UNESCO

Falloux, F. and Mukendi, A. (eds.) (1988) *Desertification Control and Renewable Resource Management in the Sahelian and Sudanian Zones of West Africa*, World Bank, *Technical Paper*, **70**, Washington DC: World Bank

Fisher, A. and Hanemann, M. (1986) 'Option value and the extinction of species', *Advances in Applied Microeconomics*, **4**

Gigengack, A.R. *et al.* (1990) 'Global modelling of dryland degradation', in J.A. Dixon, D.E. James and P.B. Sherman (eds.) as above (1990)

Gross, D.R. and Underwood, B.A. (1971) 'Technological change and caloric cost: sisal agriculture in North-Eastern Brazil', *American Ahthropologist*, **73**

Hahn, F.H. (1970) 'Savings and uncertainty', *Review of Economic Studies*, **37**

Hamilton, L.S. and King, P.N. (1983) *Tropical Forested Watersheds: Hydrologic and Soils Response to Major Uses or Conversions*, Boulder: Westview Press

Hartwick, J. and N. Olewiler (1986) *The Economics of Natural Resource Use*, New York: Harper & Row

Henry, C. (1974) 'Investment decisions under uncertainty: the irreversibility effect', *American Economic Review*, **64**

Hoff, K. and Stiglitz, J.E. (1990) 'Introduction: imperfect information and rural credit markets: puzzles and policy perspectives', *World Bank Economic Review*, **4**

Kennedy, E. and Oniang'o, R. (1990) 'Health and nutrition effects of sugarcane production in South-Western Kenya', *Food and Nutrition Bulletin*, **12**

Koopmans, T.C. (1960) 'Stationary ordinal utility and impatience', *Econometrica*, **28**

(1965) 'On the concept of optimal economic growth', *Pontificiae Academiae Scientiarum Scripta Varia*, 28; reprinted in *The Econometric Approach to Development Planning*, Amsterdam: North-Holland (1966)

(1967) 'Objectives, constraints and outcomes in optimal growth models', *Econometrica*, **35**

(1972a) 'Representation of preference orderings with independent components in consumption', in C.B. McGuire and R. Radner (eds.), as below

(1972b) 'Representations of preference orderings over time', in C.B. McGuire and R. Radner (eds.), as below

Levhari, D. and Srinivasan, T.N. (1969) 'Optimal savings under uncertainty', *Review of Economic Studies*, **36**

Little, I.M.D. and Mirrlees, J.A. (1974) *Project Appraisal and Planning for Developing Countries*, London: Heinemann

Mabbut, J. (1984) 'A new global assessment of the status and trends of desertification', *Environmental Conservation*, **11**

Magrath, W. and P. Arens (1989) 'The costs of soil erosion in Java: a natural resource accounting approach', World Bank Envirionmental Department, *Working Paper*, **18**

McGuire, C.B. and Radner, R. (eds.) (1972) *Decision and Organization*, Amsterdam: North-Holland

Mäler, K.-G. (1989) 'Environmental resources, risk and Bayesian decision rules', Stockholm School of Economics, mimeo.

(1974) *Enviroinmental Economics: A Theoretical Enquiry*, Baltimore: Johns Hopkins University Press

(1991) 'National accounting and envirionmental resources', *Environmental Economics and Resources*, **1**

Mirrlees, J.A. (1965) 'Optimum accumulation under uncertainty', Faculty of Economics, University of Cambridge, mimeo

(1967) 'Optimal growth when technology is changing', *Review of Economic Studies*, **34**

(1974) 'Optimum accumulation under uncertainty: the case of stationary returns on investment', in J. Drèze (ed.), *Allocation under Uncertainty: Equilibrium and Optimality*, London: Macmillan

Mitchell, R.C. and Carson, R.T. (1989) *Using Surveys to Value Public Goods: The Contingent Valuation Method*, Washington, DC: Resources for the Future

Musgrave, R. (1959) *Theory of Public Finance*, New York: McGraw-Hill

Nelson, R. (1988) 'Dryland Management: the "desertification" problem', World Bank Enviroinmental Department, *Working Paper,* **8**

Nerlove, M. and Meyer, A. (1992) 'Endogenous fertility and the environment: a parable of firewood', in P. Dasgupta and K.-G. Mäler (eds.), *The Environment and Emerging Development Issues,* Oxford: Clarendon Press (forthcoming, 1994)

Newcombe, K. (1984) 'An economic justification of rural afforestation: the case of Ethiopia', *Energy Department Paper,* **16**, Washington, DC: World Bank

Nordhaus, W.D. (1990) 'To slow or not to slow: the economics of the greenhouse effect', Department of Economics, Yale University, mimeo

Norgaard, R. and Howarth, R. (1991) 'Sustainability and discounting the future', in R. Costanza (ed.), *Ecological Economics,* New York: Columbia University Press

Olsen, W.K. (1987) 'Manmade "drought" in Rayalaseema', *Economic and Political Weekly,* **22**

Parfit, D. (1984) *Reasons and Persons,* Oxford: Oxford University Press

Pearce, D., Barbier, E. and Markandya, A. (1988) 'Sustainable development and cost-benefit analysis', paper presented at the Canadian Assessment Workshop on Integrating Economic and Environment Assessment, Toronto

Phelps, E.S. (1962) 'The accumulation of risky capital: a sequential analysis', *Econometrica,* **30**

Portes, R. (1971) 'Decentralized planning procedures and centrally planned economies', *American Economics Review (Papers and Proceedings),* **61**

Ramsey, F. (1928) 'A mathematical theory of saving', *Economic Journal,* 38

Reij, C., Mulder, P. and Begemann, L. (1988) 'Water Harvesting for Plant Production', World Bank, *Technical Paper,* **91**

Repetto, R. (1988) 'Economic policy reform for natural resource conservation', World Bank Environment Department, *Working Paper,* **4**

Repetto, R. *et al.* (1989) *Wasting Assets: Natural Resources and the National Income Accounts,* Washington, DC: World Resources Institute

Rosenzweig, M. and Wolpin, K.I. (1985) 'Specific experience, household structure and intergenerational transfers: farm family land and labour arrangements in devleoping countries', *Quarterly Journal of Economics,* **100**

Sefton, J. and Weale, M. (1992) 'Natural resources in the net national product: the case of foreign trade', Department of Applied Economics, University of Cambridge, mimeo

Sen, A. (1992) *Inequality Reexamined,* Oxford: Clarendon Press

Solorzano, R. *et al.* (1991) *Accounts Overdue: Natural Resource Depreciation in Costa Rica,* Washington DC: World Resource Institute

Solow, R.M. (1956) 'A contribution to the theory of economic growth', *Quarterly Journal of Economics,* **70**

(1974a) 'Intergenerational equity and exhaustible resources', *Review of Economic Studies,* Symposium in the Economics of Exhaustible Resources, **64**

(1986) 'On the intergenerational allocation of ntaural resources', *Scandinavian Journal of Economics,* **88**

(1991) 'Sustainability – an economist's perspective', Department of Economics, MIT

Spence, A.M. (1974) 'Blue whales and optimal control theory', in H. Gottinger (ed.), *Systems Approaches and Environmental Problems,* Göttingen: Vandenhoek & Ruprecht

Squire, L. and Van der Taak, H. (1975) *Economic Analysis of Projects*, Baltimore: Johns Hopkins University Press

Starrett, D.A. (1972) 'Fundamental non-convexities in the theory of externalitis', *Journal of Economics Theory*, **4**

Tietenberg, T. (1988) *Environmental and Natural Resource Economics*, 2nd edn, Glenview, IL: Scott, Foresman

UNEP (1984) *General Assessment of Progress in the Implementation of the Plan of Action to Combat Desertification 1978–1984*, Report of the Executive Director, Nairobi: United Nations Environment Programme

United Nations (1990) *Overall Socioeconomic Perspectives of the World Economy to the Year 2000*, New York: UN Department of International Economic and Social Affairs

von Amsberg, J. (1993) 'Project evaluation and the depletion of natural capital: an application of the sustainability principle', World Bank Environment Department, *Working Paper*, **56**

von Braun, J. and Kennedy, E. (1986) 'Commercialization of subsistence agriculture: income and nutritional effects in developing countries', *Working Paper on Commercialization of Agriculture and Nutrition*, **1**, Washington, DC: International Food Research Institute

Weitzman, M.L. (1970) 'Optimal growth with scale-economies in the creation of overhead capital', *Review of Economic Studies*, **37**

World Bank (1992) *World Development Report: Development and the Environment*, Washington, DC: World Bank

World Commission (1987) *Our Common Future*, New York: Oxford University Press

Discussion

PHILIPPE AGHION

This is a very stimulating chapter. My Discussion reviews the various approaches to the notion of sustainable growth and locates Dasgupta's in relation to them; it then raises a few questions.

There are various approaches to constructing a measure of 'sustainable growth'. For example, Nordhaus has listed these various approaches, starting with the early environmentalist approach of the Brundtland Commission, which according to him emphasized the Pareto criterion. This defines 'sustainable growth' as meeting the needs of present generations without compromising the ability of future generations to meet their own needs. The Pareto criterion is satisfied by many paths, and if we want something narrower we should look elsewhere. The Rawlsian approach aims to maximise the wealth of the most disadvantaged. The most disadvantaged are the future generations, so in this approach you would want to ensure that the consumption of future generations will not decline. Consumption should include all kinds of goods, but if one includes social goods, such as health, nutrition, and education, one runs into the problem of constructing an index of social welfare.

The Hicksian approach is easier to deal with. It is defined as the maximum amount which can be spent by current generations without impoverishing future consumers. There are various ways of defining 'expenditure' – the simplest is to say consumption + investment – depreciation. The problem with the Hicksian notion of sustainable income is deciding what one wishes to keep intact. For example, is it capital, real money, or the purchasing power of future generations, and if it is capital how does one define it? When one talks about income does one talk about private or social income? The latter is a complicated issue. Finally, there is the approach of Dasgupta, which tries to integrate ordinary goods with those, like the environment, that cannot be priced easily, using shadow prices.

Now some questions about Dasgupta's approach, some of which also apply to other approaches to sustainable growth. The first is that all rely on a strong convexity assumption: I started to get interested in the environment as an economic question with the infamous World Bank memorandum of Larry Summers in 1992. Of course everybody wanted to find reasons why he was wrong to argue that poor countries might wish to have more polluted environments. One such argument was the fact that he assumed a convex world. For example, he could be interpreted as saying the rich countries are very polluted, the poor are not and everybody should be evenly polluted. But, there is a counter-example, suggested to me by John Flemming. Consider a country with two rivers, the Tigris and the Euphrates; you may want to have one river very clean, because it could be a vacation resource or because it will regenerate the rest of the country, and one river that you pollute. This may be much better than partly polluting two rivers.

The second point is that Dasgupta assumes full predictability of the future. Even when he introduces option values it is in a context where all future events are somehow forecastable. This allows no scope for Kreps' preference for flexibility. Ideally we want to go towards some kind of unforecastable events or incompleteness of contracts or markets, in order to make the option value really meaningful.

Another limitation is that Dasgupta follows a representative agent approach (via an aggregate utility function) but at the same time offers a very interesting argument that the poor, because they may not have access to credit markets, may have some special preferences – for example, when he emphasises their preference for maintaining cattle. But, if one could borrow and thereby have access to other kinds of goods, the case for maintaining cattle would probably become weaker. This implies that preferences, in particular the preferences of the poor, are affected by the fact that they do not have access to credit or insurance markets. These aspects should be developed. There is a whole new literature that works with dynamic models without representative agents. It would be useful to introduce the environment in these kinds of models. Doing so might perhaps move us back towards Rawlsian-type models.

Another feature, related to the previous one, is that this type of model makes stationarity assumptions about credit markets, technology, and political institutions. But these evolve and are endogenously determined. For example, at an early stage of development there may be certain kinds of political institutions that make it easier to implement environmental policies that are compatible with growth, whereas later, with the rise of a (voting) middle class, different policies may emerge, this should arguably be taken into account by people who maximise today. All this, however, takes one away from the assumption of a stationary environment.

Political institutions bring me to the last of my questions: the problem of implementability. Even if you have a well-defined optimal programme which you solve to find the relevant shadow prices, what do you do about implementation? What can be implemented through private systems and what requires the intervention of the government? And what about political institutions? Is democracy versus dictatorship a matter of indifference in the implementability of environmental policy? On one hand, we have the argument that democracy might, for current generations, entail less pollution. For example, now that the East European countries are democracies, maybe there will be better control of the environment. On the other hand, however, only the current generation vote (for themselves) today while future generations do not vote, so in that sense you could well say that democracy implies the dictatorship of the current generation over future ones.

Relatedly, one would also want to examine the dynamic aspects of pollution control. When you reason in stationary terms, for example, it leads to the situation where rich countries try to impose pollution norms on poor countries, which are much tighter than those they would impose upon themselves. If the poor countries could borrow freely or could be subsidised by the rich, this might not be such a problem, but since they cannot, the question is: if you insist that a poor country obeys the same norms that the rich countries apply to themselves now, but which they were not applying before, are you inhibiting the poor countries' growth? Should environmental norms be different depending on the stage of development? To what extent does the inability of poor countries to borrow on the international capital market and the fact that they need to rely essentially on their own resources, constrain them in the choice between growth and the preservation of the environment? These are questions that we would like to ask and I am afraid that if we want to stick to a model where we can have a nice stationary maximisation solution we may miss some aspects of such developmental issues.

NOTE

This comment was prepared by the editors from the transcript of Aghion's comments at the conference.

6 Sustainable growth and the Green Golden Rule

ANDREA BELTRATTI, GRACIELA
CHICHILNISKY and GEOFFREY HEAL

1 Introduction

1.1 The concept of 'sustainability'

The concept of 'sustainable growth' is an appealing but elusive one. There are two factors common to most discussions and definitions of sustainability. One is the need to follow development strategies consistent with the planet's endowments. A clear statement of this can be found in the Bariloche model (Herrera *et al.*, 1976; see also Chichilnisky, 1977), whose authors remarked:

> The underdeveloped countries cannot advance by retracing the steps followed in the past by the now developed countries: . . . not only because of the historic improbability of such a retracing being feasible . . . but . . . because it is not desirable. It would imply repeating those errors that have lead to the current situation of . . . deterioration of the environment . . . The solution . . . must be based on the creation of a society that is intrinsically compatible with its environment.

In economic terms, following development strategies consistent with the planet's endowments means recognising the importance of resource and environmental constraints and the limitations that they may impose on growth patterns.

A second common factor is an emphasis on equity, both within and between generations. The authors of the Bariloche model emphasised this through the introduction and analysis of the concept of the satisfaction of basic needs as a development priority. The Brundtland Report's (1987) reference to sustainable development includes an emphasis on needs and on intergenerational equity:

> Sustainable development is development that meets the needs of the present without compromising the ability of future generations to meet their own needs.

Both elements in the analysis of sustainability, resource and environment constraints and equity, have been analysed previously. Daly (1991), Forester and Meadows (Meadows *et al.*, 1972), the Bariloche model (Herrera *et al.*, 1976), Chichilnisky (1977), Hotelling (1931), all study the importance of resource constraints. This literature is summarised in Heal (1993a, 1993b). The issue of intergenerational equity was addressed *inter alia* by Ramsey (1928), Solow (1974) and others: this literature is summarised in Dasgupta and Heal (1974).

1.2   Equity between generations

It is probably fair to say that of these two factors, resource constraints and intergenerational equity, the issue of intergenerational equity is the one that is more inadequately treated in the existing literature. This literature is largely built around the discounted utilitarian approach to defining an optional path of resource use, and many authors have expressed reservations about the extent to which this approach strikes an appropriate balance between present and future. Cline (1992) and Broome (1992) have argued for the use of a zero discount rate in the context of global warming, and Ramsey and Harrod were scathing about the ethical dimensions of this approach in a more general context (see Heal, 1993b). Heal (1993b) has argued that a zero consumption discount rate can in fact be consistent with a positive utility discount rate in the context of environmental projects. It may be a fair summary to say that discounted utilitarianism dominates our approach to the subject more for lack of convincing alternatives than because of the conviction that it inspires.

A positive discount rate forces a fundamental asymmetry between present and future generations, particularly those of the future who are very far into the future. This asymmetry is troubling to many who are concerned with environmental matters such as climate change, species extinction and disposal of nuclear waste, as many of the consequences of these may be felt only in the very long run indeed. At any positive discount rate these consequences will clearly not loom large (or even at all) in project evaluations. In this context, one could point out that at a positive discount rate no-one would ever have built a Romanesque or Gothic cathedral: however, a strict utilitarian would perhaps not be displeased with this outcome. To pursue this point further, if one discounts present world GNP over 200 years at 5 percent per annum, it is worth only a few hundred thousand dollars, the price of a good apartment. On the basis of such valuations, it is clearly irrational to be concerned about global warming, nuclear waste, species extinction, and other long-run phenomena. Yet we are worried about these issues, and are actively considering devoting very substantial resources to them. There appears to be a part of our concern about the future that is not captured by discounted utilitarianism. Perhaps as much as anything it is this that is driving an interest in formalising the concept of sustainability. The emphasis on sustainability is calling for a more temporally symmetric approach to intertemporal welfare economics, one in which the interests of generations in the very far distant future are not annihilated by discounting.

1.3 Valuing the long run

Here we take a new approach to this issue, using a welfare criterion developed in Chichilnisky (1977), and explore the implications of an alternative formulation of intertemporal welfare criteria which places positive weight on the very long-run properties of a growth path. Technically speaking, it places positive weight on the limiting properties of a path. We feel that this formulation is in tune with the concerns of those who write about sustainability and our responsibilities to future generations.

This approach builds on the observation that selecting an objective function in intertemporal planning involves solving a social choice problem. This is the problem of deciding how to combine the preferences of different generations. The distinctive feature of this social choice problem is that there are infinitely many generations or potential 'voters'. It is a simple mathematical fact that in general you cannot in summing give equal weight to each of an infinite sequence of numbers and expect to derive a well-behaved function. To be sure of a well-behaved outcome, it is customary to give more weight to the near than to the far ones – i.e. to discount (see Heal, 1985).

In a companion paper (1993) Chichilnisky presents a set of axioms for intergenerational social choice which imply that positive weight be placed on the limiting properties of alternative utility streams, as well as on their properties over finite horizons. Her approach builds on her earlier axiomatisation of the social choice problem (1980) (combining continuity, equal treatment and respect of unanimity) with its application to infinite populations by Lauwers (1993) and Lauwers and van Liederkierke (1993). Chichilnisky introduces two axioms which underlie our approach: these are that neither 'the present' nor 'the future' should be dictated. Nondictatorship of the present means that it should not be possible to determine the ranking of any two utility streams by looking only at the finite numbers of their components. Nondictatorship of the future means that the ranking of two utility streams should not depend only on their limiting properties, but should be sensitive to their characteristics over finite horizons. These axioms suffice to characterise the valuation of utility streams as the sum of two terms, one that is a discounted integral of utilities and one that depends on the limiting properties of the stream.[1]

1.4   Earlier literature

Our approach is fully consistent with earlier discussions of sustainability, but is more formal and so lends itself to mathematical analysis and the derivation of precise, testable and implementable conclusions.

The basic idea of the analysis in the Bariloche model, echoed in the Bruntland Report, was that development is necessary to improve the living conditions of those who are disadvantaged today, but that its environmental and resource impact has to be managed in such a way as not to damage the future generations. A similar perspective recurs in Tietenberg (1988), according to whom 'the sustainability criterion suggests that future generations should be left no worse off than current generations', and also in Solow (1991), who defines sustainability as 'an obligation to conduct ourselves so that we leave to the future the option or the capacity to be as well off as we are' (see also Solow, 1992).

Other definitions are more specific, and refer to targets for clearly measurable physical objects. Pearce et al. (1990) suggest more precisely that 'sustainability' is to be measured in terms of constancy of capital stocks. They define sustainable development by the requirement that a vector of desirable social objectives like increases in real income per capita, improvements in health and nutritional status, etc. does not decrease over time. The key necessary condition for achieving such a goal is, in their opinion, constancy of the natural capital stock. Hammond (1993), in an interesting review of the concept, traces stationarity of capital stocks as an indicator of sustainability or its precursors back to the works of Daly (1991) and others in the 1970s, and relates sustainability to the Hicksian concept of income. Weitzman (1976) relates Hicksian income to the solution of a dynamic maximisation problem, and Mäler (1991) extends the framework to a model with environmental resources, defining a sustainable path as one that is compatible with a non-decreasing level of utility.

But constancy of the natural capital stock is not a necessary requirement for increasing welfare, and is not to be confused with the necessity of an infinitely-lived agent to maintain her stock of wealth constant. A neo-classical growth model may give rise to depletion of natural capital which is replaced by physical capital along a path that maximises the utility of the decision maker. This gives a counterexample to definitions that require constancy of 'natural' capital. In fact Pearce *et al.* (1990) mention irreversibilities and low substitutability as the main factors that motivate their requirement of constancy of natural capital, while Nordhaus (1992) is critical about the practical importance of such elements for the definition of sustainability.

1.5 Goals and conclusions

Our application of the Chichilnisky criterion is an optimal growth model with resource and environmental constraints leads naturally to the introduction and analysis of the 'Green Golden Rule', an extension to the environmental field of the Meade–Phelps–Robinson concept of the Golden Rule of Economic Growth (see Phelps, 1961). Such a connection should not be surprising: Phelps described the Golden Rule as the growth path that gives the highest indefinitely maintainable level of consumption per head. Clearly there is an implicit concept of sustainability here: the Golden Rule path is the best sustainable path. Our Green Golden Rule gives the highest indefinitely maintainable level of instantaneous utility, in a framework where environmental goods are valued in their own right, i.e. are a source of utility, and are used as inputs to the productive process. It is a generalisation of the earlier concept. It is an easily defined and operational concept which is an essential element in the task of making operational the concept of a sustainable optimal path. Generally, our goal is to make the concept of sustainability precise so that it can be operationalised in the manner in which the discounted utilitarian solution has so successfully been operationalised. This means *inter alia* deriving the implications of sustainable optimality for associated shadow prices and embodying these implications in rules for project evaluation.

2 A model of growth with environment

The economic model with which we work is an extension of Dasgupta and Heal (1974). We extend that model by adding a regeneration process for the natural resource, so that it becomes renewable rather than exhaustible: we take the renewable resource to be an environmental resource, such as a rain forest, the climate, species diversity, etc. This resource serves as a source of utility, as an input to production, and may serve as a complement to consumption. We include the stock of the resource as an argument of the utility function (as in Krautkraemer, 1985), and as an argument of the production function.

The significance of these extensions is as follows. The presence of a *renewable* resource means that it is possible in principle for a positive stock of the resource to be maintained indefinitely. The fact that, along with a good produced from capital and the resource, the resource is an argument of the utility function, captures the concern that environmental resources are an important determinant of the quality of life, and that our long-term successors may ultimately be deprived of this. The model also allows us to examine a tradeoff between consumption of the produced good (and indirectly use of the resource) and long-run valuation of the resource stock. Higher long-run consumption of the produced good implies lower long-run levels of the resource stock.

The basic framework with which we work is the following. The social valuation of the state of the economy at time t depends on the level of consumption of a produced good and on the existing stock of an environmental good. Formally,

Assumption 1

Instantaneous utility is given by the strictly concave continuously differentiable real value function $U(C_t, A_t)$ defined on consumption $C_t \in \Re$ and on the stock of an environmental good $A_t \in \Re$. We also assume, without any loss of generality, that $U(A, C)$ is bounded above. We assume that $\frac{\partial U}{\partial C} > 0$ always: U may show satiation in A so that $\frac{\partial U}{\partial A}$ may have either sign.[2]

Assumption 2

Production of the single produced good occurs according to the linear homogeneous production function $F(K_t, {}_t)$ where K_t is the stock of produced capital at time t. Capital accumulation is therefore described by the usual equation:

$$\dot{K}_t = F(K_t, A_t) - C_t. \tag{1}$$

Note that we are specifically assuming the production process to depend on the stock rather than the flow of the environmental resource. We are deliberately not considering the optimal use of an exhaustible resource such as oil or iron ore, for which it is the flow not the stock that matters: these cases have been adequately considered elsewhere (Dasgupta and Heal, 1979; Krautkraemer, 1985). We are interested in environmental goods whose stocks have value both in themselves and as inputs to production: examples, as already mentioned, are climate, species diversity, etc.

Assumption 3

The stock of the environmental good has the ability to renew itself: the rate of renewal is given by the function $R(A)$, satisfying $R(0) = 0$. However, the act of consuming output may deplete the environment, so that the net rate of change of the stock of the environment is

$$\dot{A}_t = -aC_t + R(A_t), \quad a \geq 0. \tag{2}$$

We assume that the renewal function R is bounded above (i.e. $\exists B$: $R(A) \leq B \forall A$). R may exhibit a threshold effect, i.e. $\exists H$: $R(A) = 0 \forall A \leq H$ and $R(A)$ is strictly concave for $A \geq H$. It is possible that above a certain level of A, $R(A)$ may be decreasing, i.e. $R'(A) < 0$ for $A > A_m$. This is always the case for the most commonly used reproduction function, the Pearl–Verhulst logistic model (see Dasgupta and Heal, 1979 and Wilen, 1985). In addition it is assumed that the set of attainable values of A is bounded above, so that there is a limit to the amount of the environment resource that can be accumulated. Such a situation is depicted in figure 6.1.

In addition, certain initial conditions and nonnegativity constraints are imposed:

$$K_0 = \bar{K}, \ A_0 = \bar{A}, \ K_t \geq 0, \ A_t \geq 0, \ C_t \geq 0. \tag{3}$$

Agents derive utility both from produced goods and from a reproducible environmental good. Because of (2) and the boundedness of $R(A)$, the depletion of the environment may exceed the environment's capacity to regenerate itself. It is possible to attain consumption levels that are not compatible with indefinite preservation of a positive stock of the environmental good.

Note from equations (1) and (2) and from the assumption about $R(0)$ that when the stock of environment is zero there may still be a positive production level if the environment is not essential (in the sense of Dasgupta and Heal, 1974) for production. The possibility of running down the stock of capital completely cannot be excluded *a priori* if capital is not essential: it might be optimal to deplete the capital stock gradually and produce from resources only by means of the function $F(0, A)$.

The Chichilnisky criterion for evaluating alternative growth paths (1993), referred to in section 1, depends both on the sum of utilities over time and on the long-run behaviour of utility values. In this chapter we use the specific form:

$$\theta \int_0^\infty U(C_t, A_t) e^{-\delta t} dt + (1 - \theta) \lim_{T \to \infty} \inf_{t \geq T} U(C_t, A_t). \tag{4}$$

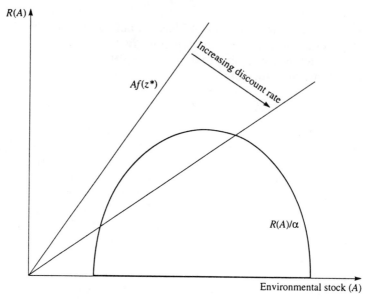

Figure 6.1   Stationary states of the utilitarian solution are intersections of the line and the curve

The lim inf of an infinite sequence of numbers is the largest number such that only a finite number of elements of the sequence are less than it. A ranking of this form is referred to below as a 'sustainable preference'. In effect what we are doing here is supplementing the conventional discounted utilitarian criterion with a term that depends only on the very long-run behaviour of utility sequences. The value of the term $\underset{T \to \infty}{\lim\inf}_{\,t \geq T}$ $U(C_t, A_t)$ is not affected by changes in the values of C_t or A_t for any finite t. The term only depends on the very long-run or limiting behaviour of utility values. The use in the criterion function of terms such as lim inf, lim and long-run average which depends on the very long-run behaviour of the instantaneous payoff function is common in dynamic programming and dynamic games (see Dutta, 1991 and Kannai, 1969). These are conventional elements of an intertemporal criterion function in situations where the very long-run matters. Returning to the perspective given by the sustainability debate, Chichilnisky's axioms allow us to capture a concern for sustainability – the capacity to generate welfare in the very long-run, for our distant successors – by including in the maximand (4) a term commonly used for valuing long-run characteristics of payoff sequences in game theory and dynamic programming.

The overall optimisation problem that we study is the maximisation of (4) subject to the constraints on capital accumulation (1), resource renewal (2) and to initial conditions (3). Our approach to solving this problem is to note that it is solvable by conventional methods in the extreme cases of $\theta = 1$ (pure discounted utilitarianism) and $\theta = 0$ (maximising the long-run value of utility), and then base a general argument on the solution in these two cases. First we consider the pure discounted utilitarian case in which $\theta = 1$.

3   The discounted utilitarian solution

Setting $\theta = 1$, our problem is

$$\max \int_0^\infty U(C_t, A_t) e^{-\delta t} dt, \quad \delta > 0 \tag{5}$$

subject to (1), (2) and (3). The Hamiltonian that can generate the necessary conditions is the following:

$$H = e^{-\delta t} U(C, A) + p e^{-\delta t}[F(K, A) - C] + q e^{-\delta t}[-aC + R(A)] \tag{6}$$

The first-order conditions are:

$$U_C = p + qa \tag{7}$$

$$\dot{p} - \delta p = -pF_K \tag{8}$$

$$\dot{q} - \delta q = -U_A - pF_A - qR_A \tag{9}$$

$$\lim_{t \to \infty} e^{-\delta t} pK = 0 \tag{10}$$

$$\lim_{t \to \infty} e^{-\delta t} qA = 0. \tag{11}$$

To write the necessary conditions in a compact way which allows us to keep track of dependence of the utility and production functions on various variables we define $z \equiv K/A \, F(K, A) = Af(z)$. A stationary solution to the necessary conditions (7)–(11) above must satisfy the following:

$$U_C(C, A) = p + qa \tag{12}$$

$$\delta = -F_K(z) \tag{13}$$

$$\delta q = U_A(C, A) + pF_A(z) + qR_A(A) \tag{14}$$

$$F(K, A) = C \tag{15}$$

$$aC = R(A). \tag{16}$$

According to equation (12) the marginal utility of stationary consumption has to be equal to a linear combination of the prices of the two stocks, in order to take into account the fact that consuming prevents capital accumulation and depletes the environment. According to equation (13) the capital–environment ratio in production has to make the marginal productivity of capital equal to the rate of time preference. Equation (14) yields the shadow price of the environment as a present discounted value of marginal utility and marginal productivity. (16) shows that in a stationary state the consumption of goods must be proportional to the regenerative capacity of the environment.

These conditions point to the following Proposition.

Proposition

If $R(A)$, the regeneration function for the environmental resource, has a threshold and is strictly concave above this (as in figure 6.1), then there may be zero, one or two stationary solutions with a positive level of A. These are characterised as solutions to:

$$aAf[f^{-1}(\delta)] = R(A).$$

Proof

A stationary solution can be shown to exist in the following way.

Given $A = A'$, (16) allows one to choose $C' + a^{-1}R(A')$. Given A' and C', (15) then determines the K' compatible with the production possibility set. So by this route we have for each value of A associated values of C and K.

In addition, (13) determines z, call it z^*, as a function of the pure rate of time preference, $\delta = F_K(K,A) = Af'(z^*)$, Given z^*, we have a second relationship between K and A. By setting $C = F(K,A) = Af(z^*)$ from (15) we have another relationship between C and A parameterised by δ. There will be a stationary solution if these two relationships are consistent.

The consistency or otherwise of these relationships is explored in figure 6.1, where we plot the relationship between C and A given by $C = F(K,A) = Af(z^*)$ and that given by $C = a^{-1}R(A)$. Where $R(A)$ is strictly concave there may be no intersection or one intersection; when $R(A)$ exhibits a threshold there may be zero, one or two intersections. This completes the proof. $\Box$

Note that $f(z) = F(K,A)/A$ is output per unit of the resource stock. If this is bounded above, as it is in the case of F, a CES function with elasticity of substitution at or near zero, then the slope of the line $C = Af(z)$ in figure 6.1 is bounded independently of the value of the discount rate δ. If this bound is sufficiently low, then there will always be a stationary solution with a nonzero value of the resource stock. Formally, assume that $f(z) \leq \bar{f}$ for all z. Then

Corollary 1
(a) If $R(A)$ shows a threshold effect, then there is at least one stationary solution with a positive value of A for any positive rate $\delta > 0$ if and only if $\bar{f} \leq \max_A \dfrac{R(A)}{Aa}$. (b) Otherwise, there is at least one stationary solution with a positive value of A for any discount rate $\delta > 0$ if and only if $\bar{f} \leq a^{-1} R'(0)$. (c) If $f(z)$ does not satisfy these bounds,[3] then there will be a stationary solution with a positive value of A if and only if $\delta \geq \beta$ for some number $\beta > 0$.

Proof
Parts (a) and (b) of the corollary are obvious. Part (c) follows from the fact that z^* decreases with δ.   □

Note that the bound on f is inversely proportional to a, the environmental impact coefficient of consumption: the lower is this impact, the higher is the permissible value of f. The corollary also shows the importance of the rate of time preference for the existence of stationary solutions: if $f(z)$ is not bounded, or not bounded tightly enough, then this must be 'high enough'. This might seem at first a surprising prediction: to have an equilibrium with a high level of environmental preservation one may need a high rate of time preference. The intuition is that a high δ implies a desire for immediate consumption and a low level of capital. Given the fact that A enters the production function and given the relation between the regenerative capacity of the environment and the level of consumption it is then necessary to have a high A to be able to produce and consume. Another interpretation of this result is to note that a high value of the discount rate δ leads to a low value of the capital–environment ratio K/A in the long run by equation (13).

To understand the dynamics of an optimal utilitarian path, we need not only to know whether stationary solutions to the first-order conditions exist, but whether they are dynamically approachable in the sense that from any initial conditions there are paths leading to a stationary solution. Because we are working with a system of four simultaneous differential equations, this is a complex mathematical issue. We address it in detail in Beltratti, Chichilnisky and Heal (1993), where we show that a stationary solution of the first-order conditions is always locally approachable if $R'(A) < 0$ at that solution, provided that a and F_A satisfy certain upper bounds. In figure 6.1, this result implies that the right-hand of the two stationary solutions will be locally approachable under the appropriate conditions.

4   The Green Golden Rule

Now we consider the case in which in (4) $\theta = 0$. In this case society is only concerned with the very long-run values of consumption and environment. We seek a path of consumption and capital accumulation that maximises $\lim_{T \to \infty} \inf_{t \geq T} U(C_t, A_t)$ over the set of feasible paths. The solution of the problem therefore requires that we find the indefinitely maintainable values of C and A which give the maximum utility level over all such levels. As indefinitely maintainable values of C and A satisfy $R(A) = aC$, this means that the problem

$$\max \lim_{T \to \infty} \inf_{t \geq T} U(C_t, A_t) \text{ over feasible paths satisfying (1)–(3)}$$

reduces to:

$$\max U(C, A) \text{ subject to } R(A) = aC. \tag{17}$$

The stock of capital is not a concern in this situation because any stock of capital can be accumulated given a sufficiently long period of time. The set of $\{C, A\}$ pairs satisfying the constraint in (17) is compact, so this problem is well defined. The maximum is characterised by the first-order condition:

$$\frac{U_A}{U_C} = \frac{R_A}{a}. \tag{18}$$

The solution given in the Proposition amounts to equality between the marginal rate of transformation and the marginal rate of substitution between consumption and environment across steady states. It can be depicted in graphical terms as the point of tangency between the indifference curve and the renewal function (see figure 6.2). It is clear that the solution to the problem of maximising the lim inf of utility values does not define a growth path for the economy: it merely defines a long-run or limiting configurations. There are many paths that will lead to this, some efficient, others inefficient. Amongst the efficient paths, some will give higher values of the integral of discounted utilities than others.

We term the configuration defined by (18) the 'Green Golden Rule', in reference to its relationship to the original Meade–Phelps–Robinson 'Golden Rule of economic growth' (Meade, 1962; Phelps, 1961; Robinson, 1962). That rule characterised the greatest indefinitely-maintainable consumption level: the Green Golden Rule (18) characterises the highest indefinitely-maintainable utility level. In a one-good growth model with increasing preferences the two concepts coincide: with an argument in addition to consumption in the utility function, they do not. The first-

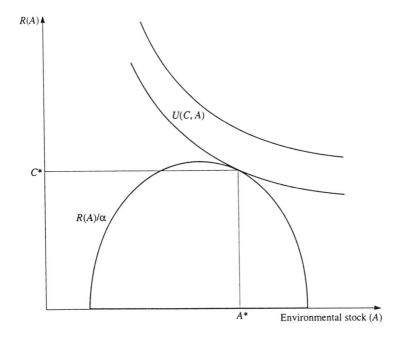

Figure 6.2   The path which maximises lim inf $u(C, A)$ approaches (A^*, C^*), the point giving the highest sustainable utility level

order condition (18) gives the optimal trade off between consumption and the environment. In the present model, the Green Golden Rule not only solves the problem of maximising the lim inf of the utility values along a plan: it also gives a maximum of any of lim, lim sup, or any increasing function of the limiting utility value.

It is worth pointing out the formal difference between the lim inf criterion and the Rawlsian criterion, which involves the maximisation of the inf rather than of the lim inf. This difference has a large impact on the results obtainable from the model. The Rawlsian criterion leads to unappealing solutions: in the context of a model with no natural resources Solow and others have shown that the Rawlsian criterion may require a society to remain at the initial configuration, without any accumulation of capital.

5   Optimal sustainable paths

The solution to the problem of maximising the lower bound to the long-run utility level may or may not coincide with the solution to the discounted utilitarian formulation of the problem. In general the two will not coincide, unless the rate of time preference is such that the intersection between the line and the renewal function that was referred to in the previous Proposition coincides with the point of tangency between the indifference curves and the renewal function. The example given in section 6 illustrates such a coincidence.

We therefore have to analyse the solution implied by the use of the 'sustainable preferences' introduced in section 2, i.e. we have to solve the problem:

$$\max \theta \int_0^\infty U(C_t, A_t) e^{-\delta t} dt + (1 - \theta) \lim_{T \to \infty} \inf_{t \geq T} U(C_t, A_t). \tag{19}$$

subject to (1)–(3).

A solution to this problem will be referred to as a 'sustainable optimal path'. We have so far solved this for the special cases in which $\theta = 0$ and $\theta = 1$: it remains to put these together. This is a mathematically complex task, which is analysed in its entirety in Beltratti, Chichilnisky and Heal (1993). Here we note only that any path which is a solution to the overall problem must satisfy the conditions necessary for a utilitarian optimum, namely equations (7)–(11). This follows from a straightforward argument which says that unless these conditions hold, it will be possible to make a small perturbation about the proposed path over a finite interval of time, leave the path unchanged outside of this interval, and raise the value of the integral of discounted utilities. As the path has been left unchanged outside a finite interval, the second term in the maximand has not been altered, and of course the first has been increased. This tells us how a solution to the overall problem behaves locally: what remains is to establish its asymptotic behaviour. This more complex task is carried out in Beltratti, Chichilnisky and Heal (1993). The existence of an optimal sustainable path can be assured by mild conditions on the optimal time path of consumption c_t: this issue is also reviewed in Beltratti, Chichilnisky and Heal (1993).

6   An example of a sustainable optimal path

To give precision to the ideas we have introduced in the earlier sections of the chapter, we illustrate them here by applying them to a simplified model in which some of the richness of the full model is lost, but which has the advantage of being readily analytically solvable. We treat the environmental resource as the only good, which may be consumed or allowed to reproduce. This formulation retains the conflict between current consumption and long-run maintenance, but gives us a model which has only one state variable. Its dynamics can therefore be studied graphically. The overall optimisation problems can now be stated as:

$$\max \theta \int_0^\infty U(C_t, A_t)e^{-\delta t} dt + (1 - \theta) \lim_{T \to \infty} \inf_{t \geq T} U(C_t, A_t).$$

subject to

$$\dot{A}_t = - C_t + R(A_t).$$

To be even more specific, we assume

$$U(C_t, A_t) = \ln C + \gamma \ln A$$

$$R(A) = rA - \frac{rA^2}{A^S}.$$

This reproduction function is logistic with A^S the carrying capacity of the environment. In this case the Hamiltonian of the system is:

$$H = [\ln C + \gamma \ln A] + q\left[- C + rA - \frac{r}{A^S} A^2 \right].$$

The first-order conditions for a utilitarian optimum are now:

$$\frac{1}{C} = q$$

$$\dot{q} - \delta q = -\frac{\gamma}{A} - q\left(r - \frac{2qr}{A^S} A\right)$$

$$\dot{A} = - C + rA - \frac{r}{A^S} A^2$$

$$\lim_{t \to \infty} e^{-\delta t} qA = 0.$$

The steady state of the two variables implied by these necessary conditions is:

$$A = \frac{A^S(\gamma r - \delta + r)}{2r + \gamma r}$$

$$C = \left[\frac{A^S(\gamma r - \delta + r)}{r(2 + \gamma)}\right]\left[\frac{r + \delta}{2 + \gamma}\right].$$

When $\gamma = 0$, corresponding to the case of no utility of the environment, we have that:

$$A = \frac{A^S}{2}\left(\frac{r - \delta}{r}\right) < \frac{A^S}{2}$$

and this means that the steady-state level of environment is lower than the one that gives the maximum sustainable yield. This result resembles the one obtained in standard growth theory, in which impatience prevents society from accumulating the stock of capital that maximises steady-state consumption. It is also possible to calculate that the steady-state level of the environment is larger than the one that allows maximum consumption only if:

$$\gamma > \frac{2\delta}{r}.$$

The lines along which values of A and C are constant are given respectively by

$$C = R(A)$$

$$R'(A) = \delta - \frac{\gamma C}{A}.$$

The characterisation of the dynamics of the discounted utilitarian solution is given in figure 6.3, which shows that the utilitarian stationary solution is a saddle point.

We can also characterise the lim inf solution to find that in that case the steady-state stock of environment is

$$A = \frac{rA^S + \gamma r}{2rA^S + \gamma r}.$$

This is in general larger than the value at the utilitarian stationary solution, although the two stationary states are equal if the discount rate is zero. Maximising an undiscounted sum of utilities also maximises the long-run utility level.

7   Conclusions

We have developed the implications of Chichilnisky's axiomatisation (1993) of the ranking of intertemporal utility sequences, an axiomatisation that places weight both on the characteristics of the sequence over any finite period and its very long-run or limiting characteristics. The criterion shows more intertemporal symmetry than the discounted utilitarian approach, which clearly emphasises the immediate future at the expense of the long run. In this respect our criterion captures some of the concerns of those who argue for sustainability and for a heightened sense of responsibility to the future.

The characterisation of optimal paths that emerges from this criterion is

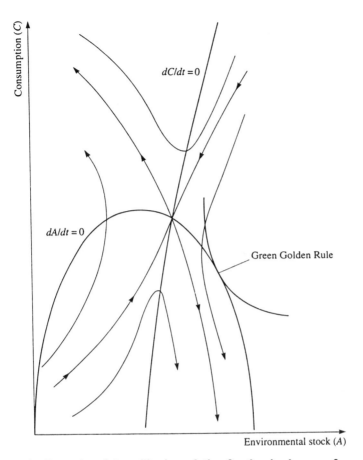

Figure 6.3 Dynamics of the utilitarian solution for the simple case of one state variable, A

eminently intuitive. Their long-run characteristics are a mixture of utilitarianism and the Green Golden Rule: locally, they always satisfy the utilitarian first-order conditions familiar from optimal growth theory.

Our objective function (4) has some point of contact with the Rawlsian approach to optimal resource use. The key distinction is that the Rawlsian approach ranks paths only the lowest of their utility values: we replace the lowest value of utility by the limiting lowest value (lim inf) and supplement this by the discounted integral of utilities along the path. This has two great advantages. One is that it avoids trapping an economy into low consumption levels because it has poor initial endowments (see Dasgupta and Heal, 1979; Solow, 1974). The other is that it ensures that any solution path is dynamically locally optimal because the path satisfies the local optimality conditions (see Heal, 1973).

NOTES

This work was funded in part by grants from the Fondazione ENI Enrico Mattei and NSF grants 92 16028 and 91 10460. An earlier version was presented at the CEPR–OECD Conference on Sustainable Economic Development, Paris (24–25 May 1993), and at the Universities of Bielefeld and Mannheim, as well as at the 1993 Stanford Institute for Theoretical Economics. We are grateful to Alan Winters, Ian Goldin and to the participants in these meetings for valuable comments.
1 A measure is countably additive if the measure of a countable family of disjoint sets is the sum of their measures. For a purely finitely additive measure, this property holds only for finite families of disjoint sets. In the theory of general equilibrium with infinitely many commodities, trouble is taken to ensure that only countably additive measures occur naturally – see Chichilnisky and Heal (1993).
2 One can conceive of having too much rainforest.
3 That is, if it is not bounded or if the bounds are too great.

REFERENCES

Beltratti, A., Chichilnisky, G. and Heal, G.M. (1993) 'Sustainable growth and the Green Golden Rule', *Working Paper*, Columbia Business School and Fondazione ENI Enrico Mattei
Broome, J. (1992) *Counting the Cost of Global Warming*, London: White Horse Press
Chichilnisky, G. (1977) 'Economic development and efficiency criteria in the satisfaction of basic needs', *Applied Mathematical Modeling*, 1 (September)
 (1980) 'Social choice and the topology of preferences spaces', *Advances in Mathematics*, 37(2): 407–8
 (1993) 'Symmetry between generations in the long run', paper presented at the 1993 workshop of the Stanford Institute for Theoretical Economics
Chichilnisky, G. and Heal, G.M. (1993) 'Competitive equilibrium in Sobolev Spaces without bounds on short sales', *Journal of Economic Theory*, 59(2) (April): 364–84
Cline, W.E. (1993) *The Economics of Global Warming*, Washington, DC: Institute for International Economics
Daly, H.E. (1991) *Steady-State Economics: Second Edition With New Essays*, Washington, DC: Island Press
Dasgupta, P.S. and Heal, G.M. (1974) 'The optimal depletion of exhaustible resources', *Review of Economic Studies*, Symposium on the Economics of Exhaustible Resources, 3–28
 (1979) *Economic Theory and Exhaustible Resources*, London: Cambridge University Press

Dutta, P. (1991) 'What do discounted optima converge to? A theory of discount rate asymptotics in economic models', *Journal of Economic Theory*, **55**(1) (October): 64–94

Hammond, P.J. (1993) 'Is there anything new in the concept of sustained development?', paper presented to the conference on 'The Environment after Rio', Courmayeur, Italy (10–12 February)

Heal, G.M. (19713) *The Theory of Economic Planning*, Amsterdam: North-Holland

—— (1985) 'Depletion and discounting: a classical issue in the economics of exhaustible resources', *American Mathematical Society, Proceedings of Symposia in Applied Mathematics*, **32**: 33–43

—— (1993a) *Classics in the Economics of Exhaustible Resources*, London: Edward Elgar

—— (1993b) *The Optimal Use of Exhaustible Resources*, vol. III of A.V. Kneese and J.L. Sweeney (eds.), *Handbook of Natural Resource and Energy Economics*, Amsterdam, New York, Oxford: Oxford University Press

Herrera, A.O., Scolnik, H.D., Chichilnisky, G. *et al.* (1976) *Catastrophe or New Society*, International Development Research Centre, Ottowa, Canada

Hotelling, H. (1931) 'The economics of exhaustible resources', *Journal of Political Economy*, **39**: 137–75

Kannai, Y. (1969) 'Countably additive measures in cores of games', *Journal of Mathematical Analysis and Applications*, **27**, 227–40

Krautkraemer, J.A. (1985) 'Optimal growth, resource amenities and the preservation of natural environments', *Review of Economic Studies*, **52**(168): 153–70

Lauwers, L. (1993) 'Infinite Chichilnisky Rules', *Discussion Paper*, Katholik Universtaet, Leuven (March)

Lauwers, L. and van Liederkierke, L. (1993) 'Monotonic Chichilnisky Rules with infinite populations', *Discussion Paper*, Katholik Universtaet, Leuven (March)

Mäler, K.-G. (1991) 'National accounts and environmental resources', *Environmental and Resource Economics*, **1**: 1–15

Meade, J.E. (1962) 'The effect of savings on consumption in a state of steady growth', *Review of Economic Studies*, **29** (June)

Meadows, D.H., Meadows, D.L., Randers, J. and Behrens III, W.W. (1972) *The Limits to Growth: A Report for the Club of Rome's Project on the Predicament of Mankind*, London: Earth Island Press

Nordhaus, W.D. (1992) 'Is growth sustainable? Reflections on the concept of sustainable economic growth', paper presented to the International Economic Association Conference, Varenna, Italy (October), mimeo

Pearce, D.W., Markandya, A. and Barbier, E. (1990) *Sustainable Development: Economy and Environment in the Third World*, London: Earthscan Publications

Phelps, E.S. (1961) 'The Golden Rule of accumulation: a fable for growthmen', *American Economic Review*, **51**(4): 638–43

Ramsey, F. (1928) 'A mathematical theory of saving', *Economic Journal*, **38**: 543–59

Robinson, J. (1962) 'A neoclassical theorem', *Review of Economic Studies*, **29** (June)

Solow, R.M. (1974) 'Intergenerational equity and exhaustible resources', *Review of Economic Studies*, Symposium on the Economics of Exhaustible Resources, 29–45

(1991) *Sustainability. An Economist's Perspective*, the Eighteenth Seward Johnson Lecture, Marine Policy Centre, Woods Hole Oceanographics Institution, Woods Hole, MA

(1992) *An Almost Practical Step Towards Sustainability*, invited lecture on the occasion of the Fortieth anniversary of Resources for the Future, Resources and Conservation Center, Washington, DC

Tietenberg, T. (1988) *Environmental and Natural Resource Economics*, 2nd edn, Glenview, IL: Scott, Foresman

Weitzman, M. (1976) 'On the welfare significance of national product in a dynamic economy', *Quarterly Journal of Economics*, **90**

Wilen, J.E. (1985) *Bioeconomics of Renewable Resource Use*, vol. I of A.V. Kneese and J.L. Sweeney (eds.), *Handbook of Natural Resource and Energy Economics*, Amsterdam, New York, Oxford: Oxford University Press

World Commission on Environment and Development (1987) *Our Common Future* (The Brundtland Report), Oxford: Oxford University Press

Yosida, K. (1974) *Functional Analysis*, 4th edn, Berlin, Heidelberg, New York: Springer Verlag

Yosida, K. and Hewitt, E. (1952) 'Finitely additive measures', *Transactions of the American Mathematical Society*, **72**: 46–66

Discussion

ALISTAIR ULPH

In chapter 6 the authors (hereafter BCH) discuss the implications of a new approach to analysing sustainable development captured by the use of a welfare function which is a convex combination of a discounted sum of a stream of instantaneous utilities and the lim inf of that stream of utilities. In the bulk of the chapter, this welfare criterion is applied to a model of renewable resources with capital accumulation, although in section 6 a special case without capital accumulation is solved. While the new welfare function is potentially interesting, the application with the capital accumulation has some features which I do not find compelling, while the example without capital accumulation seems to deliver fairly standard results. On the basis of these applications I find it difficult to assess how valuable this new criterion is going to prove, and I would like to see the criterion applied to a wider class of models before reaching a judgement. To amplify these points I will make some general comments about the welfare criterion and then discuss the particular applications.

The objection to the conventional discounted utilitarian welfare function is that it can sometimes produce outcomes which seem patently unjust to later generations. Consider a model with constant population, no technical progress, a nonrenewable resource which enters into a Cobb–Douglas aggregate production function. Dasgupta and Heal (1979) have shown that, with any positive utility discounting, along an optimal path consumption must tend to zero in the long run (i.e. the development plan is unsustainable). This is despite the fact that there exist other growth paths where consumption can either be maintained constant, or rise indefinitely. In this particular case, then, discounting utility produces outcomes which most people would believe to be manifestly unjust to future generations by forcing them to a much lower level of utility than earlier generations. Of course this result is dependent on the particular assumptions of the model. The paths of constant or rising consumption would be selected by using respectively a Rawlsian welfare function or an undiscounted sum of utilities. The well-known objection to the Rawlsian criterion is that it can entrap future generations at a low level of utility determined by the initial resource endowments of the economy, because it will not sacrifice a small amount of current consumption to allow capital to be accumulated. So it is unfair to future generations in a very different sense from the discounted utilitarian criterion – it denies future generations the possibility of becoming very much better off than current generations. The proposed welfare criterion would appear to overcome some of the deficiencies of the discounted utilitarian and Rawlsian criteria. The lim inf component is like a Rawlsian criterion, but applied to the long run, so it does not tie future utilities to the initial circumstances of the economy; at the same time the discounted utilitarian component prevents the utilities of current and immediately future generations from being ignored. On the face of it, the proposed criterion looks very promising.

However, as Dasgupta (1993) has emphasised, it is difficult to judge the desirability of a welfare criterion in the abstract, and it is useful to see whether the outcomes it produces in a range of models accord with our moral intuitions. After all, the discounted utilitarian criterion may *look* unfair to future generations, but in many applications it will result in future generations being substantially better off than current generations. So I now turn to the particular applications used by BCH. In both cases BCH do not present the path that would be selected by using their proposed welfare function. Rather they consider the steady states that would be selected by using only the discounted utilitarian criterion and only the lim inf criterion.

The first point I would like to make is that the Green Golden Rule outcome looks very familiar, for it involves selecting the sustainable steady state which maximises the utility function. But this is very similar to the early models of fishery economics (e.g. Gordon, 1954) in which it was assumed that the social planner selected the steady state which maximised one-period rents. Gordon recognised that this ignored the process of getting from an initial set of conditions to the steady state, but found that problem too difficult to solve, and it was left to later capital–theoretic treatments to solve the full problem. The resemblance with the conventional fisheries literature is most apparent in the special case in section 6 without capital accumulation. The Green Golden Rule yields a steady-state stock which lies always above the maximum-sustainable yield (MSY) stock for conventional reasons (in the conventional model the stock externality enters the costs of fishing; here it enters the utility function; but the arguments are the same). With discounting, but no externality effect, the steady-state stock is characterised by the condition $R'(A) = \delta$. With discounting and the externality, the steady-state stock lies between the two stocks already identified, and could lie above or below the MSY stock. Presumably the full application of the welfare criterion involving the weighted sum of the discounted utilitarian criterion and the lim inf criterion will yield a steady state between the steady states selected by the two criteria individually. As the utility discount rate tends to zero, the discounted utilitarian outcome approaches the lim inf outcome. All this is familiar. While the proposed welfare function will select a somewhat higher stock of the renewable resource than would a pure discounted utilitarian model, the latter poses no threat to the extinction of the species, for this particular example. The implication of this example would seem to be that we should simply use a rather lower utility discount rate than a conventional discounted utilitarian criterion would recommend.

I now turn to the model of renewable resources with capital accumulation. My concern here is that the particular model used has some slightly surprising features, which may not make it the most appropriate model with which to test out the proposed new welfare criterion. This is best seen in the discounted utilitarian steady state. For convenience I summarise the necessary conditions derived by BCH:

$$u_c = p + q\theta \tag{1}$$

$$\delta q = u_A + pF_A + qR'(A) \tag{2}$$

$$f'(z) = \delta + d \tag{3}$$

$$\theta A[f(z) - dz] = R(A) \tag{4}$$

$$C = F(K, A) - dK \tag{5}$$

There are two rather special features about this steady state. First, the steady-state values of the real variables, A, K, and C do not depend on preferences; to see this note that (3) can be solved for z, (4) can then be solved for A, and hence K, and then (5) can be solved for C. So, while BCH stress that an important feature of their model is that concern for the environment is represented directly by putting the stock of environmental resources, A, into the utility function, this plays no part in determining this steady state.

Second, as BCH note, an increase in the discount rate leads to an *increase* in the steady-state value of A, and indeed a high discount rate may be needed to ensure the existence of a steady state (see Corollary 1, part (c)). This seems a rather unusual feature given that the concern of BCH is with the threat that high discount rates might pose to future generations, using the conventional discounted utilitarian welfare function. It is certainly the opposite of what occurs in most conventional fisheries models, as for example the model used in section 6. As BCH note, the intuition behind the unusual result is simply that a higher discount rate leads to a lower value of the K/A ratio (see equation (3)), which requires a higher value of A.

The question then is what feature of the model used here accounts for these features, especially the second. It cannot be the fact that A enters the utility function, since the utility function does not affect the steady state. To understand what is going on let me denote by x_t what I shall call the flow rate of use of the renewable resource (or one can interpret this as the flow of pollution which damages the stock environmental resources), so that the stock of environmental resources changes according to:

$$\dot{A}_t = -x_t + R(A_t).$$

Now BCH assume that $x_t = \theta C_t$ where θ is a fixed number. I make two changes to this assumption. The first is to assume that it is not just consumption which leads to resource depletion or pollution, but rather all forms of output, so that $x_t = \theta F(K_t, A_t)$. By itself this would change little in the results of the BCH model, and indeed in their examples in sections 5 and 6 they implicitly set $d = 0$, so that in steady state there is no difference between output and consumption.

But the key feature of the above assumption is that resource use or pollution has a fixed relation to output (the linearity of this relationship is not essential). So the second change I make is to assume that there is some scope for reducing the amount of environmental resource used per unit of output (equivalently there is scope for abating pollution per unit of output), by using inputs of the other resources K and A. Rather than model this explicitly by making θ a function of inputs of K and A, and hence effectively introducing a two-sector model, I shall stick with the one-sector model by writing the aggregate production function as $G(K, A, x)$, where output is an increasing function of all its inputs. This means that, for a given level of output, it is possible to reduce the level of associated resource use/pollution by increasing inputs of K and A. One can then interpret the BCH model as taking a special case of G in which $G(K, A, x) = \min\{F(K, A), (x/\theta)\}$, i.e. there is a Leontief structure to production in which there is no possibility of substituting more inputs of K or A in order to reduce the use of x.

If one uses a more general function G which allows for substitution between all inputs, then it is straightforward to show that the first-order conditions for the steady state are now:

$$u_c = p \tag{6}$$

$$p.G_x = q \tag{7}$$

$$\delta = (u_A/q) + (G_A/G_x) + R'(A) \tag{8}$$

$$x = R(A) \tag{9}$$

$$G_K = \delta + \delta \tag{10}$$

$$C = G(K, A, x) - dK. \tag{11}$$

The new condition is (7), which sets the marginal product of x equal to its price. The remaining conditions are the analogues of the conditions of (1)–(5) for the BCH model. Now note that if $u_A = 0$ then, not surprisingly, all the real variables, x, K, A and C can be solved using (8)–(11) which do not involve preferences. Furthermore, if G was CES then (8) would become:

$$\delta = B \left[\frac{R(A)}{A} \right]^{\alpha} + R'(A) \tag{8'}$$

where B is a positive constant and $\alpha = 1/\sigma > 0$ where σ is the elasticity of substitution. Then (8') determines A, (9) determines x, (10) determines K and (11) determines C. Note that if R is everywhere concave, then (8') ensures that as δ rises, A falls. Finally note that if $u_A > 0$, then preferences for A and C will be important in determining the steady state, so that one needs to solve the full set of equations to determine the real variables;

clearly this will make the comparative statics of the effect of a change in the discount rate more complicated to calculate.

Thus if one allows for the possibility of using inputs of other resources to mitigate the amount of resource depletion/pollution associated with a given level of output, then it seems possible, at least for a particular class of production functions, to recover the traditional effects of a higher discount rate on the steady-state stock of the renewable resource when that stock does not enter the utility function, and when it does, preferences then affect the steady state, though I have not worked out the resulting comparative statics. Of course I am not claiming that the assumptions I am making are any more compelling than those made by the authors; I am merely trying to understand which feature of their model is responsible for generating their non-standard comparative static result.

To conclude, while the proposed new welfare criterion appears quite interesting, I have not found its application to the particular models in this chapter very compelling. The lim inf criterion by itself yields a steady state which is familiar from the early literature on fisheries; namely the steady state one would select if one could get immediately to that steady state from any initial conditions. The example in section 6 yields very familiar results while the more general model of the rest of the chapter has some rather special features to it which make it seem inappropriate for testing out the new criterion. I would like to see the implications of the proposed new welfare criterion worked out in a wider class of models, and in particular models of the type referred to earlier involving non-renewable resources and for which we know that the discounted utilitarian criterion with high utility discount rates gives unpalatable outcomes. If the proposed new criterion yields more palatable outcomes for those models than either the discounted utilitarian criterion or the Rawlsian criterion, then the authors will have made a very valuable contribution to the literature.

REFERENCES

Dasgupta, P. (1993) 'Optimal development and the idea of net national product' (ch. 5 in this volume)
Dasgupta, P. and Heal, G. (1979) *Economic Theory and Exhaustible Resources*, Cambridge: Cambridge University Press
Gordon, H.S. (1954) 'Economic theory of common property resources', *Journal of Political Economy*, **66**: 124–42

Part Three
Domestic policy

7 Economic policies for sustainable resource use in Morocco

IAN GOLDIN and DAVID ROLAND-HOLST

1   Introduction

Water is a distinctive resource because it constitutes a direct input to almost every economic activity, drawing a continuous thread from primary use in agriculture, through manufacturing, and into the myriad of service sectors. Despite a long economic history, water allocation stands out as one of the most significant cases of market failure in both developing and developed economies. The institutional arrangements which have governed water allocation have fostered serious resource misallocation, technological choice which is neither statically nor dynamically efficient, and an array of negative economic and environmental externalities which propagate through downstream linkages to the rest of the economy.

Historically, the relative abundance and regenerative nature of water resources have fostered inefficient water use.[1] In modern times, the clear delineation of regional boundaries limiting migration, population growth, and rising living standards have combined to intensify water use in agriculture and elsewhere, and the sustainable practices for utilising this essential resource are receiving greater scrutiny. It is only a matter of time until the reforms in water allocation, already initiated in a number of countries, are more widely applied. The essential issue is how to devise reforms which have the efficiency and incentive properties to be economically and politically sustainable. To answer this question, which is a pressing concern for many developing countries, we consider the case of Morocco. Our choice of Morocco has been facilitated by the fact that it possesses relatively sophisticated data resources and shares many common characteristics with water-scarce economies. We thus anticipate results from this case to have wider applicability.

In this chapter, we draw on Morocco to illustrate the linkages between trade and macroeconomic policies and sustainable resource use.[2] To this end, we evaluate the current state of water distribution in Morocco, distinguishing between relatively arid and moist farming regions and between rural and urban households. The available evidence suggests that the existing allocation system fosters sub-optimal and unsustainable patterns of water use and that inefficiencies arising from inappropriate pricing at the micro level have been compounded by distortions in relative prices resulting from macroeconomic and trade policies. Our analysis supports the conclusion that increased marketability of water can realise substantial static and dynamic efficiency gains in agriculture, including greater conservation. The development of an appropriate incentive framework, which includes the implementation of water tariffs which more closely approach marginal costs, is expected to contribute to demand management and conservation in irrigation, where subsidies are greatest. The adjustment of relative prices in favour of sustainable resource use will be greatly facilitated by trade reforms. These currently provide protection to agriculture; in the absence of trade reform, higher water charges would be passed through to output prices, seriously limiting efficiency gains.

In order to focus discussion of the general economic principles of sustainable resource use, we have developed a calibrated general equilibrium (CGE) model of Morocco. This captures sufficient detail in agriculture to evaluate alternative water allocation schemes. The model provides a convenient vehicle for identifying the components of domestic economic adjustment in response to various resource management policies, and allows us to assess the implications for Morocco's trade position. Conversely, the CGE model is also used to evaluate the implications of alternative trade policies for agriculture in general and water use in particular. Our results indicate that the static benefits of more efficient water allocation would be considerably magnified if the country pursued more outward oriented trade practices.

Section 2 presents an overview of Moroccan water use and policy. Section 3 contains a general conceptual discussion of efficient and sustainable water allocation. Section 4 presents the Moroccan CGE model and the data which were used to calibrate it. This is followed in section 5 with a series of simulation results evaluating the efficacy and interrelationships between water policies and trade policies. Section 6 is devoted to concluding remarks, and an appendix details the results of sensitivity analysis of the model.

2   Practical issues in Moroccan water allocation

Owing to a limited resource base and recurrent droughts, water is a scarce commodity in many parts of Morocco. The main sources of fresh water are found in the mountains, at considerable distances from urban and irrigated areas. This geographic situation necessitates storage dams and long transmission facilities, with high average cost and marginal cost rising steeply as increasingly sparse water resources are developed. The country's population is growing at over 2.6 percent annually and is expected to exceed 43 million by the year 2020. Rapid increases in water demand by agriculture, industry, and urban households are anticipated by the government. Urban migration and rising incomes are expected to lead to a 4.2 percent annual growth in urban household demand and rapid economic growth is predicated on an anticipated 5 percent annual increase in industrial demand. Meanwhile, the National Irrigation Programme aims to extend the area under irrigation by 30 percent in the next decade. Irrigation currently accounts for 92 percent of the demand for water, urban households 5 percent, and industry only 3 percent.

The availability of adequate water resources is a prerequisite for meeting the country's economic targets. Water resources are already becoming scarce in certain areas and initial projections for the year 2020, based on expected economic growth, current relative prices, and 'related water demand', clearly point to the emergence of an economy-wide water deficit. While the water balance today is largely positive in most of the North (Loukkos, Mediterranean, Sebou, and Oum Er R'bia basins), it is generally negative in the South (Souss, Zia, Rheris, and Guir basins). Although there is currently an annual overall water surplus of 1.1 billion m^3 (amounting to some 15 percent of all renewable water resources), the anticipated annual growth in demand of 4 percent is expected to lead to overall water shortages in the medium term. In addition, serious water management problems are already evident in some parts of the country. These include a severe deterioration in water quality, depletion of non-renewable groundwater resources, the increasing exploitation costs for marginal water sources, and the failure of the existing system to supply more than 10 percent of the rural population with potable water. Despite the fact that nearly all urban dwellers have safe water supplies, half the country's population is rural. Thus over 45 percent of the population lack secure water supplies.

By the year 2020, assuming current trends continue, water will still be in surplus in the Loukkos, Sebou, and Mediterranean basins in the north, but all other river basins will have negative balances. Moreover, without significant water demand management, the overall water balance will become negative (in excess of 200 million m^3 annually before 2020), which means that even nation-wide water transfers (assuming they were economically feasible) could not meet regional water deficits. The case for timely and judicious government intervention is therefore compelling. On the demand side, this might include policies to promote conservation and improved demand management in irrigation and among urban and industrial consumers. On the supply side, greater attention needs to be paid to water quality and development of additional water resources. The latter possibilities include improved secondary water capture, treatment, and recycling, desalinisation of brackish and sea water, and sustainable groundwater mining.

Appropriate pricing and incentive policies are the keys to resolving Morocco's water dilemma. A continuation of current practices implies not only growing distortions in the allocation of an increasingly scarce resource, but also an increasingly unsustainable fiscal burden. Public investments in the water sector already account for over 25 percent of the government's investment budget and, by 2020, are expected to account for up to 60 percent, reflecting the escalating costs associated with interbasin transfers and exploitation of marginal resources.[3] Meanwhile, recurrent costs are mounting with the aging of the existing water supply, irrigation, and sanitation systems. Irrigation water charges currently cover less than 10 percent of the long-run marginal cost of delivering water to agriculture, while urban water tariffs contribute less than half the cost of urban and industrial supplies.[4]

Subsidies have had a particularly distortionary effect in the agricultural sector. Low water charges (coupled with low effective collection rates on these charges) have artificially promoted production of water intensive crops. Sugar cane (which uses approximately 10,000 m^3/ha) and lucerne (15,000m^3/ha) have particularly low value added per unit of water use. The existing incentive framework does not encourage production of crops with high returns on water use. These include wheat (4000m^3/ha) and vegetables (3–4000m^3/ha).[5]

The consequences of higher water charges on patterns of production and the rural–urban terms of trade are examined in this chapter. Our primary focus is on the general equilibrium effects of water policy on relative prices and resource allocation between agricultural and nonagricultural activities. In Morocco, these sectoral effects will be intertwined with those of macroeconomic adjustment policies which are being pursued concurrently. In particular, water prices are expected to be increased at a time when output prices and other input prices are being affected by macroeconomic reforms and trade liberalisation. This calls for the analysis of water pricing issues in a framework which simultaneously includes possible changes in output and other relative prices.

Significant structural reform is currently under way in Morocco. This is expected to lead to the gradual reduction in import protection, which currently maintains the prices of sugar, cereals, oilseeds, meat and dairy products well above their opportunity cost on world markets. Gradual and broad-based agricultural trade reform is envisaged in the context of structural adjustment agreements with the World Bank. These reforms will be accelerated following a GATT agreement. The simultaneous introduction of trade and water pricing reforms would imply increased input prices and a decline in output prices. The impact on the highly subsidised sugar cane, cereals, cotton, and oilseeds sub-sectors could be particularly severe as these crops benefit from input and output subsidies which take the form of low water charges and border protection. Higher water charges in the context of macroeconomic and trade reform are expected to have significant implications for the profitability of existing agriculture, as higher charges in the context of economy-wide reforms will not be passed through into higher output prices. Thus, as shown in sections 3–5, reforms on the input and output side will reinforce one another to improve the efficiency of resource use.

3 Methodological issues

In this section, we discuss the Moroccan water distribution question from three perspectives.[6] The first of these concerns static efficiency of water allocation in Moroccan agriculture. We argue that a publicly managed system of water distribution, if it is coupled with economic incentives, could significantly improve the efficiency of water use in the country, increasing real output and incomes in the process. Secondly, we discuss how reforming agricultural water distribution can improve the intertemporal efficiency or sustainability of water use and expand the growth prospects for Moroccan agriculture. Third and finally, we discuss the important issue of how to allocate the country's water resources between rural and urban areas. Guaranteeing equitable quantities and qualities of water for household and economic use in both parts of the country will inevitably determine the political sustainability of Moroccan water policy.

3.1 Static efficiency

Historical water rights conventions represent one of the most serious market failures in traditional agriculture. As Easter (1986) and others have observed, the water rights mechanism results in a queueing allocation, where those with the original endowment use the resource at zero marginal cost and pass the remainder on to successive rights holders at zero marginal revenue. The absence of a market for water thus removes any incentive for conservation or transfer activity which might increase overall output and income. It is now widely acknowledged that some kind of institutional intervention, between the two extremes of public appropriation with uniform redistribution and completely privatised water sales, can provide the missing incentives to use water more efficiently.

Consider a simple case with two agricultural producers, identical except for their water endowments, calling one arid (A) and the other moist (M). Under the traditional scheme, M uses free water until its marginal product equals zero while A is constrained by insufficient water. Since A's marginal product for water is inevitably higher than that of M, any reallocation of water between the two would raise national agricultural output. All arguments for improving static efficiency rest on this basic productivity disparity, what remains is the incentive properties of different allocation schemes.

Assume for convenience only that water can be transferred without conveyance losses or quality degradation. If water is simply appropriated and redistributed, M and A are still unlikely to use the resource efficiently even though aggregate output rises. If, on the other hand, water were brought from M and sold to A, any price would begin to exert rational efficiency considerations on their production decisions. Water now has a real opportunity cost for M, who might change the mix of other inputs or even invest to innovate and reduce water use with minimal effects on marketable output. By the same token, a price for water would also allow A to expand factor use in the appropriate mix to most profitably use the newly available water.

Clearly, water re-allocation can increase output and market pricing of water can improve efficiency. What, then, is the role of the public sector, apart perhaps from providing initial financing? The failure of water markets is not simply due to lack of information, but results from significant problems of enforcement. Any distribution scheme of reasonable scope will cover many private holdings and perhaps even regional or national jurisdictions. In practice, it has proved difficult to guarantee the integrity of transfer agreements over significant distances and with many intervening third parties. Thus the public sector must assume a lasting supervisory role to make such an allocation scheme work. As we shall see below, public oversight may also be necessary to correct for other externalities arising in water use and allocation.

3.2   Dynamic efficiency

Water is a renewable resource, but its recurrent supply is relatively constant over the long term. Once the recurrent supply is fully utilised, the only potential for growth in the economy will come from innovations which reduce the water intensity of agricultural and other economic activities. To avoid a period of stagnation and forced adjustment, Morocco could begin now to foster the innovations which will reduce the intensity of its water use and raise its growth potential.

The literature on economic growth is replete with examples of how the correction of market failures can shift resource allocation and use to more sustainable paths. Dasgupta and Heal (1979) and, more recently, Grossman and Helpman (1991) are two prominent examples of approaches which seek to elucidate sufficient conditions for improving dynamic efficiency. Both emphasise the importance of market incentives to invest and innovate as a means of raising the sustainable trajectories of output and real income growth. It is clear, for example, that the reforms proposed above to improve static efficiency of water allocation would also improve dynamic efficiency by promoting both conservation and shifts to other inputs, including new technologies. Bringing water 'into the market' will also facilitate intertemporal appraisal of its asset value and contribute to dynamic efficiency.

3.3 Rural–urban water allocation

The growth of urban areas has occasioned water re-allocation since well before Roman times. In the last century, however, the problems of urban water insufficiency have intensified as these areas have rapidly grown in size and density and become focal points for industrial activity. In terms of public health and economic modernisation, assuring adequate quantity and quality in water supplies is one of the most serious challenges facing many developing countries.[7]

In Morocco, the challenge of balancing water use between urban and rural constituencies is complicated by the rapid growth of agriculture.[8] Agriculture has been the major consumer under the traditional rights system and the current administered system of water distribution at controlled prices. On the other hand, agricultural water use diminishes not only the quantity but the quality of water available for other uses. Water use in farming occasions a number of negative externalities, including loading of water with high mineral concentrations, fertilisers and their organic derivatives, and pesticide residues. These potential shortcomings must be weighed against the economic benefits of increased farm incomes, outputs and exports.

From the perspective of the urban sector, water is already an economic commodity, although its price rarely measures its production or opportunity cost with any meaningful degree of precision. Urban households in developing countries also have incomplete information about water quality, and intervention is usually necessary to protect the public interest. These considerations argue for a carefully designed and comprehensive approach to national water policy, one which relies on a balance between regional interests as well as between market forces and regulatory responsibility.

4   The Moroccan CGE model

The conceptual approach of section 3 was intended to clarify some basic issues. In this section, we provide a tool for policy analysis in the form of an empirical model of the Moroccan economy. As an example of its use, we report some simulation results in section 5 which evaluate the kind of water reforms discussed above.

Our Moroccan model is typical of most individual country models in the CGE literature.[9] It simulates price-directed resource allocation in commodity and factor markets, with endogenous determination of domestic consumption and production decisions. We assume that Morocco is a small importer and exporter relative to the rest of the world, and thus world prices are taken as exogenous to the model. In a given sector, demand for domestic goods and imported substitutes is characterised by a standard constant elasticity of substitution (CES) specification of product differentiation. Likewise, domestic producers supply output to constant elasticity of transformation (CET) differentiated domestic and export markets.

Table 7.1 presents the formal structural equations of the Moroccan CGE model. They are typical of one-country models of this type, except for the treatment of regional and sectoral factor allocation.[10] The agriculture sector is decomposed into two generic regions, Rainfed and Irrigated, according to method of water use. Each agricultural sub-sector chooses its factor mix and output level individually, subject to endogenous domestic prices for output, intermediate inputs, labour, and property. Property or capital is assumed to be immobile within and between agricultural sectors and mobile between other sectors. Firms are assumed to be perfectly competitive, with average cost pricing under constant returns to scale.

Water is a factor of production in this model and its use is determined by neoclassically derived factor demand criteria (equation (7) below). We assume that the supply is exogenously given and is costless in Rainfed agriculture (the small costs recorded in the social accounting matrix (SAM) in table 7.2 reflect water equipment such as wells). Water transfer between Rainfed and Irrigated agriculture, as well as between rural and urban areas, is assumed for our simulations to be effected at relative prices fixed by the government, which assumes the cost of any redistribution. To model market-directed water transfer between agricultural activities and also between rural and urban activities, a two-stage transformation frontier might be specified between Rainfed and Irrigated and between rural and urban, respectively. The non-market allocation mechanism used here most closely resembles current Moroccan policy, however, so we focus on this in the simulations below.[11]

Like the SAM to which it is calibrated, the CGE model distinguishes three types of final demand: household, investment, and government demand. In all the simulations reported below, we assume that the latter two are held constant in terms of the numéraire. This is done to facilitate welfare comparisons, but the existence of private nonconsumption goods and public goods still renders equivalent variation income comparisons meaningless. Instead, we report a variety of aggregate and household specific results to give an indication about how real output, resource use, and general purchasing power are affected by the policies considered.

Both increased water prices and reduced tariffs have direct fiscal implications, of course. In the case of water, we specify that the net change in water revenue is redistributed to households in proportion to their incomes. Otherwise, we have chosen to hold the numéraire levels of government consumption constant to minimise distortions in final demand. This leaves the government financing gap endogenous, and we assume this would be reconciled with nondistortionary taxes or transfers.

The model is calibrated to a 1985 SAM for Morocco, and herein lie two of its distinguishing features.[12] First, the Moroccan SAM distinguishes between urban and rural income groups. This is essential to evaluate the issue of social efficiency in water distribution. Second, the SAM details value added for three factors of production, labour, capital, and water. This decomposition of factors is particularly important to the modelling of agricultural sectors. The original SAM detailed 20 agricultural sectors, but for the present simulations, we have chosen a three-sector aggregation to facilitate more intensive discussion of the general policy issues. The three-sector SAM is presented in table 7.2.

To completely calibrate a CGE model of the type in table 7.1, the above data on observed economic activity must be combined with estimates of structural parameters. These include elasticities of demand (equation 4), factor substitution (6), and transformation between domestic and export markets (8). Table 7.3 details the values used in all the simulations reported in section 5. Even in an aggregate model such as this one, results are sensitive to these parameters, and we report on this in the appendix (p. 192).

Table 7.1. *Formal structure of the Morocco model*

Domestic demand

$$Q_i^C = LES(PQ_i, Y_h) = \gamma_i + \frac{\eta_i}{PQ_i}\left(Y - \sum_{j=1}^{n} PQ_j\gamma_j\right) \tag{1}$$

$$Q_i^G = s_i^G \bar{Q}^G \tag{2}$$

$$Q_i^I = s_i^I \bar{Q}^I \tag{3}$$

$$Q_i^Y = \sum_{j=1}^{n} a_{ij} X_j \tag{4}$$

Demand allocation between domestic and imported goods

$$Q_i = CES(D_i, M_i, \bar{\lambda}_i), \quad Q_i = Q_i^C + Q_i^Y, \tag{5}$$

$$\frac{M_i}{D_i} = \left[\left(\frac{a_i}{(1 - a_i)}\right)\left(\frac{PQ_i}{PM_i}\right)\right]^{\lambda_i} \tag{6}$$

Production technology and factor demands

$$X_{ik} = CES(L_{ik}, K_{ik}, W_{ik}, \bar{\rho}_{ik}) \tag{7}$$

$$F_{ik} = \left(\frac{X_{ik}}{AX_{ik}}\right)^{(1-\bar{\rho}_{ik})}\left[\beta_{Fik}\frac{TC_{ik}}{w_{Fik}}\right]^{\bar{\rho}_{ik}}, \quad F = L, K, W \tag{8}$$

Supply allocation by destination of commodities and services

$$X_{ik} = CET(S_{ik}, E_{ik}, \bar{\tau}_{ik}) \tag{9}$$

$$\frac{E_{ik}}{S_{ik}} = \left[\left(\frac{\delta_{ik}}{(1 - \delta_{ik})}\right)\left(\frac{PS_{ik}}{PE_{ik}}\right)\right]^{-\bar{\tau}_{ik}} \tag{10}$$

Composite domestic prices

$$PQ_iQ_i = PD_iD_i + PM_iM_i \tag{11}$$

$$PS_iS_i = \sum_k PS_{ik}S_{ik} \tag{12}$$

Foreign prices

$$PM_i = (1 + t_{Mi})PWM_iR \tag{13}$$

$$PE_i^k = (1 + t_{Ei}^k)PWE_iR \tag{14}$$

Domestic market equilibrium

$$S_{ik} = D_{ik} \tag{15}$$

$$PS_{ik} = PD_i \tag{16}$$

$$\sum_{i=1}^{n}\sum_k F_i^k = \bar{F}_S, \quad F = L, K \tag{17}$$

$$\bar{w}_W = w_W \tag{18}$$

$$K_i^k = \bar{K}_i^k, \quad i = Agriculture \tag{19}$$

Table 7.1 (*continued*)

Cost

$$TC_{ik} = a_{ik}^{-1} X_{ik} \left[\sum_{F=L,K,W} b_{Fik}^{\rho_{ik}} w_{Fik}^{1-\rho_{ik}} \right]^{\frac{1}{1-\rho_{ik}}} + \sum_{j=1}^{n} a_{ij} PQ_j X_{ik} \tag{20}$$

$$w_{Fik} = w_F \bar{w}_{Fik}, \quad i \neq Agriculture, \quad F \neq W \tag{21}$$

Pricing

$$PX_{ik} = AC_{ik} \tag{22}$$

Private and public income

$$Y_h = \sum_{i=1}^{n} \sum_{F=L,K,W} \theta_{hiF} \sum_k w_{Fik} F_{ik} + R\bar{r}_h + Y_G - \bar{Q}_G \tag{23}$$

$$Y_G = \sum_{i=1}^{n} \sum_k t_{ik} PK_{ik} X_{ik} R \sum_{i=1}^{n} \left[t_{Mi} PWM_i M_i - \sum_k t_{Eik} PWE_i E_{ik} \right]$$

$$+ \sum_{i=1}^{n} \theta_{giW} \sum_k w_{Wik} W_{ik} \tag{24}$$

Balance of payments

$$\sum_{i=1}^{n} \left[\sum_k PWE_i E_{ik} - PWM_i M_i \right] = \bar{B} \tag{25}$$

Numéraire

$$\frac{\sum_{i=1}^{n} PD_i D_i}{\sum_{i=1}^{n} \bar{P}D_i \bar{D}_i} = 1 \tag{26}$$

Variable and parameter definitions

Variables

AC_{ik}	Average cost of firm type k in sector i
B	Net foreign savings
D_i	Total domestic demand for output in sector i
E_i	Total exports in sector i
E_{ik}	Exports of firm type k in sector i
F_i	Total demand for factor F in sector i
F_{ik}	Factor F demand by firm type k in sector i
FC_{ik}	Fixed cost of firm type k in sector i
F_S	Economy-wide factor F supply
M_i	Total imports in sector
N_{ik}	Number of firms of type k in sector i
P_{Di}	Domestic demand price for output in sector i
P_{Ei}	Export demand price for output in sector i
P_{Eik}	Export demand price for output of firm type k in sector i
P_{Mi}	Import price in sector i

Table 7.1 (*continued*)

P_{Qi}	Composite demand price in sector i
P_{Si}	Domestic supply price in sector i
P_{Sik}	Domestic supply price for firm type k in sector i
PW_{Eik}	World export demand price for output of firm type k in sector i
P_{Xi}	Output price in sector i
P_{Xik}	Output price of firm type k in sector i
PW_{Mi}	World import supply price in sector i
Q_i	Composite (domestic and imported) domestic demand for output of sector i
Q_i^C	Composite consumption demand for output of sector i
Q^I	Aggregate real investment demand
Q^G	Aggregate real government demand
Q_i^V	Composite intermediate demand for output of sector i
R	Exchange rate
r_h	Remittance income accruing to household h
S_i	Total domestic supply in sector i
S_{ik}	Domestic supply of firm type k in sector i
t_{Eik}	Export subsidy rate for output of firm type k in sector i
t_{Mi}	Tariff rate in imports in sector i
TC_{ik}	Total cost of firm type k in sector i
t_{ik}	Sectoral producer or indirect tax rates
VC_{ik}	Variable cost per unit output
w_F	Economy-wide average price of factor F
w_{Fik}	Price of factor F paid by firm type k in sector i
W_{ik}	Water demand by firm type k in sector i
X_i	Total output in sector i
X_{ik}	Output of firm type k in sector i
X_i	Output of sector i
Y	Aggregate domestic income
Y_G	Government income
Y_h	Household income

Parameters

μ_i	CES elasticity of substitution between product varieties in sector i
δ_{ik}	Base share of exports in value of output of firm type k in sector i
ρ_{ik}	Factor substitution elasticity of firm type k in sector i
θ_{giW}	Share of water revenue going to government
θ_{hiF}	Share of factor F income from sector i going to household h
a_i	Base share of imports in domestic demand for sector i
λ_i	CES elasticity of substitution between imports and domestic goods
η_i	Marginal budget share for consumption of good i
γ_i	Subsistence consumption of good i
τ_{ik}	CET elasticity of transformation between domestic and export markets
β_{Fik}	Factor F share in value-added of firm type k in sector i
AD_i	Calibrated intercept parameter for demand
a_{ij}	Intermediate demand share for good i by sector j
AX_{ik}	Calibrated intercept parameter for production

Table 7.1 (*continued*)

Subscripts	
i	Sectors of production – Agriculture, Manufactures, Services
k	Sub-sectors, in the case of agriculture only, where the two sub-sets are Rainfed and Irrigated
F	Factors of production – Labour, Property, and Water
h	Households – Rural and Urban

Notes: Variables are denoted by English letters, structural parameters by Greek letters. An overbar denotes a base value in the case of a variable and an exogenously specified value in the case of a parameter. More than one pricing rule is specified above, although they are mutually exclusive in the simulations.

5 Simulation results

In this section, we report on the results of a few policy simulation experiments with the Moroccan CGE model. These experiments are intended to illustrate simulation methodology in the context of two important general economic issues currently facing the country, notably trade orientation and sustainability of water resources. In particular, we conducted three experiments to evaluate generic policies of trade liberalisation and water price reform. We find that the results of each policy are interesting in their own right, but that when they are implemented in concert, the economy reaps the benefits of each policy without the serious negative side effects of either.

Table 7.4 presents the aggregate results of the three experiments. In experiment 1, prices for rural irrigation water, which cover 92 percent of the country's marketed water use, are doubled from 8 to 16 percent of their urban counterpart. Experiment 2 is a trade policy simulation, entailing a complete removal of nominal Moroccan tariffs, which in 1985 averaged 21 percent across the economy and 32 percent in agriculture. Experiment 3 combines the water price and liberalisation policies of the first two simulations.

The aggregate results indicate that, other things being equal, reforming water prices in the agricultural sectors will have a contractionary effect on the economy. This is to be expected since the price increase is basically taking the form of a distortionary tax against a leading sector of the economy. Incomes and real consumption of both rural and urban households decline slightly, and real consumption falls somewhat more as increased factor prices are passed through to agricultural commodities. The government budget is affected negligibly. Thus the static effects of the policy appear to be detrimental, but a silver lining appears in the results

Table 7.2. *Social accounting matrix for Morocco, 1985 (million current DH)*

	AgRainFed	AgIrrig	Manufact	Services	Labour	Capital	Water	Tariff	ExpTax	IndTax	HHRural	HHUrban	Govt	Enterprise	CapAcct	Rdm	Total
	1	2	3	4	5	6	7	8	9	10	11	12	13	14	15	16	
1 AgRainFed	199	244	2,829	15	0	0	0	0	0	0	3,062	4,277	0	0	1,430	134	12,190
2 AgIrrig	348	298	3,458	18	0	0	0	0	0	0	3,062	5,277	0	0	1,748	613	14,771
3 Manufact	1,318	1,611	47,376	22,625	0	0	0	0	0	0	11,074	23,273	0	0	13,273	12,186	132,737
4 Services	525	642	9,516	11,542	0	0	0	0	0	0	7,591	24,851	16,399	0	23,500	3,785	98,352
5 Labour	1,555	1,901	11,219	43,258	0	0	0	0	0	0	0	0	0	0	0	0	57,933
6 Capital	5,125	6,264	11,599	14,437	0	0	0	0	0	0	0	0	0	0	0	0	37,425
7 Water	590	722	1,497	1,863	0	0	0	0	0	0	0	0	0	0	0	0	4,672
8 Tariff	598	731	7,719	0	0	0	0	0	0	0	0	0	0	0	0	0	9,047
9 ExpTax	9	10	314	0	0	0	0	0	0	0	0	0	0	0	0	0	333
10 IndTax	55	68	2,683	463	0	0	0	0	0	0	0	0	0	0	0	0	3,269
11 HHRural	0	0	0	0	7,782	12,832	0	0	0	0	0	0	306	0	0	8,589	29,510
12 HHUrban	0	0	0	0	50,151	24,593	0	0	0	0	0	0	436	0	0	1,200	76,379
13 Govt	0	0	0	0	0	0	4,672	9,047	333	3,269	583	6,420	31	0	806	663	25,823
14 Enterprise	0	0	0	0	0	0	0	0	0	0	0	0	0	0	0	0	0
15 CapAcct	0	0	0	0	0	0	0	0	0	0	4,137	12,331	3,020	0	0	21,269	40,757
16 Rdm	1,867	2,281	34,527	4,131	0	0	0	0	0	0	0	0	5,631	0	0	0	48,437
Total	12,190	14,771	132,737	98,352	57,933	37,425	4,672	9,047	333	3,269	29,510	76,379	25,823	0	40,757	48,438	

Table 7.3. *Estimates of structural parameters*

	Agriculture	Manufactures	Services
CES demand elasticity	0.9	1.4	1.4
CET supply elasticity	1.4	1.4	1.4
CES factor elasticity	0.6	0.9	1.1

Table 7.4. *Aggregate simulation results (percentage changes from base)*

	Experiment 1	Experiment 2	Experiment 3
Real GDP	− 0.65	0.79	0.11
Rural			
Income	− 0.92	8.69	8.48
Real Cons	− 1.21	8.97	8.23
Urban			
Income	− 0.92	8.58	7.77
Cons	− 1.02	8.06	7.07
Gov Bal[a]	0.59	− 35.00	− 35.00
Water use			
Rural	− 34.28	1.64	− 34.48
Urban	− 1.23	9.20	8.02
Total	− 28.66	7.53	− 4.12

[a] Change in the government budget balance as a percent of the overall budget.

for water use as the economy moves decisively toward greater sustainability. In the rural sectors, water use falls by about one-third and even urban water use is also driven down slightly by declining aggregate demand.

Trade liberalisation has more salutary effects on the static efficiency of production and real incomes. Economy-wide real GDP rises only slightly since the main factors, labour and capital, are fixed in total supply. Despite this, household incomes and real consumption post significant gains as substantial import barriers are reduced, domestic purchasing power rises, exports become more competitive, and resources are allowed more efficiently across the economy. While this typical neoclassical result supports greater initiative for Moroccan trade reform, two drawbacks are readily apparent. First, the government has foregone an important source of revenue by eliminating tariffs and a gap of about 35 percent emerges in the public budget. Secondly, the expansionary influence of liberalisation has increased domestic water use substantially. Thus the economy is on a more growth oriented, but less sustainable trajectory.

The last experiment combines the first two, and it is apparent that combining trade and water reform would confer substantial advantages on the economy, both in the medium and long term. The expansionary effects of trade liberalisation are largely retained, but reforming water prices still induces substantial reductions in agricultural (and economy-wide) water use. Although this conservation is partly offset by expanding demand in urban sectors, the net result for the economy is less water consumption. Thus the higher growth path under the combined policy is more sustainable than was the status quo. The government budget still declines appreciably with tariff revenues, but this might be offset by alternative, nondistortionary sources of revenue.

More detailed results for sectoral adjustments in the three reform experiments are given in table 7.5. Note first that agriculture in general and irrigated agriculture in particular suffer output declines in the two water price increase experiments. In experiment 1, agriculture obviously suffers from factor taxation, but in experiment 3 the expansionary effects of trade reform fail to offset this because agriculture is the most protected of the three sectors. Irrigated agriculture, where the water price increase is directly incident, contains both the most protected (e.g. sugar) and most export oriented crops (e.g. tree crops), and in this case the export expansion offsets most of the combined contractionary effects of tariff removal and higher water taxes.[13] Irrigated farming is induced to cut water use almost 50 percent in experiment 1, and more than one-third in experiment 3. In the case of experiment 2, the benefits of export expansion outweigh the costs of increased import competition, and irrigated agriculture expands slightly when water prices are constant. Rainfed agriculture manages to attract labour and expand production in both water price experiments, but loses a little ground in the balance between expanding exports and increased import penetration in the trade reform only experiment.

The other two sectors behave in predictable ways. Increased water prices and reduced real incomes reduce demand for manufactures. Since manufactures are more intensive in agricultural intermediates and therefore experience more water price transmission, both their domestic and external demand are reduced. Services thus become relatively more competitive, but the effect is barely significant. When Morocco eliminates tariffs in experiment 2, the more tradeable sectors expand output, the less so (services) contracts in the presence of economy-wide constraints on

Table 7.5. *Sectoral simulation results (percentage changes)*

Experiment 1	Output	Exports	Labour	Capital	Water	Imports
Agriculture						
Rainfed	23.84	17.36	28.23			
Irrigated	− 25.40	− 29.30	− 22.76		− 49.33	
Total	− 3.24	− 8.30	0.19	0.27	− 34.28	1.75
Manufactures	− 0.59	− 0.63	− 0.60	− 0.47	− 1.46	− 0.55
Services	0.01	0.64	0.00	0.16	− 1.05	− 0.67

Experiment 2						
Agriculture						
Rainfed	− 0.18	12.66	− 0.78			
Irrigated	0.34	13.24	− 0.77		3.65	
Total	0.10	13.19	− 0.78		1.64	17.46
Manufactures	4.01	23.25	4.18	2.96	11.23	9.32
Services	− 1.05	11.27	− 0.95	− 2.38	7.30	− 12.96

Experiment 3						
Agriculture						
Rainfed	1.03	7.22	4.57			
Irrigated	− 7.36	− 1.69	− 4.82		− 34.75	
Total	− 3.58	− 0.79	− 0.60		− 15.64	18.71
Manufactures	3.54	22.76	3.65	2.65	9.80	8.73
Services	− 1.03	12.16	− 0.97	− 2.13	6.26	− 13.70

labour and capital. In the combined experiment, the results of larger magnitude in the individual experiments prevail. In other words, agriculture and services contract for different reasons, and manufacturing expands. Indeed, the results of the two policies for nonagricultural sectors are almost additive.

6   Conclusions

Like many other developing countries, Morocco faces serious water resource constraints. The continuation of current water use practices into the next century threatens to sharply attenuate the development process. A more sustainable approach to development therefore requires that an appropriate mechanism for water production and allocation be introduced. In this chapter, we evaluate direct and indirect econmic policies to influence water use patterns, including changes in water pricing and trade reform. Our results indicate that there is considerable scope for substitution between water and other factors of production and that economic incentives to promote this can move Moroccan resource use decisively toward a more sustainable path of economic development.

To assess the country's water use policy in an economy-wide setting, we chose a CGE model. The modelling methodology is still under development and the data we have been able to assemble thus far are highly aggregated and preliminary, and our results should be interpreted accordingly. Despite this, the conclusions which emerge from the general equilibrium analysis are robust to reasonable parameter variations. Most importantly, it is apparent that increases in water prices, particularly in agriculture, can realise substantial resource savings.

The general equilibrium results suggest that agricultural water use, which constitutes 92 percent of Morocco's total use, could be reduced by more than a third if rural water prices were doubled (even though in this case they would still only reach about 16 percent of urban water prices). Taken in isolation, such a policy would secure a more sustainable basis for future income growth, but would reduce medium-term real rural incomes and Moroccan GDP. If water price reforms were undertaken in concert with more comprehensive Moroccan trade reform, the medium-term effects on incomes would be more than offset, with rural, urban, and aggregate real income rising substantially while still achieving substantial water savings. Thus the combined policies move the economy onto a path which is at once more prosperous and sustainable.

While more precise quantitative estimates await refinement of the model and more intensive data-gathering, our preliminary results demonstrate that a combination of economy-wide and sectoral policies are necessary to secure a sustainable basis for the country's future. Our results indicate that piecemeal approaches are unlikely to achieve the combined objectives of static efficiency and dynamic sustainability. The potential efficiency gains and resource savings from integrated, economy-wide policy reform are substantial and, despite the short-term adjustments they might occasion, they can increase medium-term real incomes and facilitate sustainably high real growth in the future.

Appendix: results of sensitivity analysis

Because the Morocco model is calibrated to an equilibrium SAM data set, most of its information requirements are met from direct observation of the economy under study. Although this small model is rather parsimonious, a number of its structural parameters must still be specified with

Table 7A.1. *Results for varying factor substitution elasticity*

| | Experiment 1 | | | Experiment 2 | | | Experiment 3 | | |
	Low 0.3	Central 0.6	High 1.2	Low 0.3	Central 0.6	High 1.2	Low 0.3	Central 0.6	High 1.2
All ag output	− 2.0	− 4.0	− 5.0	0.1	0.1	0.3	− 2.0	− 4.0	− 5.0
Irrigated ag output	− 5.0	− 8.0	− 12.0	− 0.1	0.3	0.8	− 5.0	− 7.0	− 11.0
Irrigated ag water use	− 22.0	− 37.0	− 58.0	2.0	4.0	8.0	− 20.0	− 35.0	− 55.0
Rural income	− 0.1	− 0.1	0.3	9.0	9.0	9.0	8.0	9.0	9.0

Table 7A.2. *Results for varying water prices*

	Experiment 1			Experiment 3		
	Low 1.5 ×	Central 2 ×	High 4 ×	Low 1.5 ×	Central 2 ×	High 4 ×
All ag output	− 2	− 4	− 8	− 2	− 4	− 8
Irrigated ag output	− 4	− 8	− 17	− 4	− 7	− 17
Irrigated ag water use	− 24	− 37	− 67	− 21	− 35	− 60
Rural income	0	0	0	8	7	6

indirect information, using econometric estimates from other sources and judgement about values which might reasonably be expected to apply. Of particular interest in the present simulations is the elasticity of substitution between productive factors in the agricultural sectors. This CES parameter (ρ in equation (7) above) is a key determinant of the adjustment in irrigated water use resulting from a price increase. Table 7A.1 above summarises the results of nine simulations we conducted to assess the CGE model's sensitivity to this parameter. We replicated each of the policy scenarios reported in section 5 (experiments 1–3) with three alternative values to bracket the experiment outcomes. Substitution elasticities in agriculture are generally conceded to be rather low, and we chose a central case of 0.6 as a reference.[14]

Note that, with only 2 exceptions in 36, the results are qualitatively consistent, and the exceptions are within a reasonable neighbourhood of zero in any case. As one would expect, the magnitudes of the results are monotone in the elasticity, indicating that greater flexibility in factor substitution yields more dramatic adjustment. Despite this, the essential endogenous variables summarised here vary much less than the elasticity parameter. From these comparisons we infer that our general conclusions about the three policies are robust. In particular, the efficacy of combined trade and water reforms, in terms of water conservation and real income growth, is consistently supported.

Another way to appraise the sensitivity of the model is to experiment with a wider range of exogenous shocks. Table 7A.2 reports the results of a variety of alternative water price increases, including increases of 1.5, 2, and 4 times current rates for irrigated agriculture. The last case corresponds roughly to an equalisation of rural and urban water prices. There are six replications, three each for experiments 1 and 3, experiment 2 being omitted since it entails only tariff reductions. The qualitative results are fully consistent within and across experiments, and their magnitudes vary in the expected direction and by about the same relative magnitude of the shock. From this we infer that water price reforms of any reasonable degree would yield significant conservation, and that a concerted effort to reform water policy and trade would achieve agricultural water saving with increased rural income.

NOTES

The views expressed here are those of the authors and should not be attributed to their affiliated institutions. We are grateful to Alan Winters and to Gene Grossman for their valuable comments on earlier drafts of this chapter.

1   Relative abundance is of course a *de facto* result of human settlement where traditional farming practices were sustainable.
2   The analysis of Morocco presented in this chapter is illustrative and preliminary and is an initial stage of a major research project which includes construction and estimation of a detailed data base on the country's economy and water use.
3   Authors' estimates based on current trends.
4   Authors' estimates based on average current water charges.
5   These estimates of water use are derived from field estimates in Morocco. They are simply indicative averages. In practice, water use varies from area to area and intensity of production, and *inter alia* depends on the rainfall, soils, and time of planting.
6   As was emphasised in section 2, trade reform also plays an important role in our empirical policy analysis. The theory and methodology on this topic are well known, however, and we omit reviewing them in this section.
7   90 percent of all fatal childhood diseases in Africa are water-borne.
8   Half the country's population lives in rural areas and these are generally the poorest segment of the population. Agriculture constitutes 15 percent of GDP, 40 percent of employment, and 30 percent of export earnings.
9   The equations of the model are listed in the appendix (p. 192).
10 See e.g. de Melo and Tarr (1992) for a more detailed exposition on models of this type.
11 The results of most of our simulations entail water savings (less transfer) and increased water revenue *vis-à-vis* the status quo. This mitigates the severity of the water mobility assumption and means that the fiscal implications of the policies examined are generally positive.
12 This SAM is estimated from one published in Mateus *et al.* (1988).
13 It would be desirable to disaggregate this and other sectors to trace the more detailed effects of these policies. This is the subject of work in progress, which includes the estimation of a 125-sector SAM for the country.
14 Recall that, in light of capital immobility in agriculture, this elasticity is actually restricted to substitution between labour and water.

REFERENCES

Arrow, K.J. and Lind, R.C. (1970) 'Uncertainty and the economic evaluation of public investment decisions', *American Economic Review*, **60**: 364–78

Boggess, W., Lacewell, R. and Zilberman, D. (1993) 'Economics of Water Use in Agriculture', in M. Osborne (ed.), *Agricultural and Environmental Resource Economics*, Oxford: Oxford University Press

Burness, H. and Quirk, J. (1979) 'Appropriate water rights and efficient allocation of resources', *American Economic Review*, **59**, 25–37

Caswell, M., Lichtenberg, E. and Zilberman, D. (1990) 'The effects of pricing policies on water conservation and drainage', *American Journal of Agricultural Economics*, **72**, 883–890

Chakravorty, U. and Roumasset, J. (1991) 'Efficient spatial allocation of irrigation water', *American Journal of Agricultural Economics*, **73**, 165–173

Clarke, C.W. (1976) *Mathematical Bioeconomics: The Optimal Management of Renewable Resources*, New York: John Wiley

Dasgupta, P. and Heal, G.M. (1979) *Economic Theory and Exhaustible Resources*, Cambridge: Cambridge University Press

de Melo, J. and Tarr, D. (1992) *A General Equilibrium Analysis of U.S. Foreign Trade Policy*, Cambridge, MA: MIT Press

Dinar, A. and Zilberman, D. (1991) *Economics of Management of Water and Drainage in Agriculture*, Norwell, MA: Kluwer Academic

Easter, K.W. (1986) *Irrigation, Investment, Technology, and Management Strategies for Development*, Boulder: Westview Press

Fisher, A.C. (1981) *Resource and Environmental Economics*, Cambridge: Cambridge University Press

Gibbon, D. (1987) *The Economic Value of Water*, Resources for the Future: Washington, DC

Grossman, G.M. and Helpman, E. (1991) *Innovation and Growth in the Global Economy*, Cambridge, MA: MIT Press

Hotelling, H. (1931) 'Economics of Exhaustible Resources', *Journal of Political Economy*, **39**, 137–175

Mateus, *et al.* (1988) 'A multisector framework for analysis of stabilization and structural adjustment policies – the case of Morocco', *Discussion Paper*, **29**, Washington, DC: World Bank

OECD (1989) Water Resource Management: Integrated Policies, Paris: OECD

Parlin, B. and Lusk, M. (1991) *Farmer Participation and Industrial Organization*, Boulder: Westview Press

Pearce, D.W. and Turner, R.K. (1990) *Economics of Natural Resources and the Environment*, Baltimore: Johns Hopkins University Press

Postel, S. (1992) *Last Oasis: Facing Water Scarcity*, New York: Norton

Reinert, K.A. and Roland-Holst, D.W. (1991) 'Structural Parameter Estimates for Trade Policy Modeling', *Discussion Paper*, Washington, DC: US International Trade Commission

Reisner, M. (1990) *Overtapped Oasis: Reform or Revolution for Western Water*, Washington, DC: Island Press

Tuluy, H. and Salinger, B.L. (1989) 'Trade, Exchange Rate Policy, and Agricultural Pricing Policies in Morocco', *Comparative Studies in the Political Economy of Agricultural Pricing Policy*, Washington, DC: World Bank

World Bank (1989) 'World Bank experience with irrigation development', vol. III: Morocco, Report **7876**, Washington, DC: World Bank

Discussion

JAIME DE MELO

In their description of the water situation in Morocco in chapter 7, Goldin and Roland-Holst expect a water shortage in Morocco in the medium term. They also point out that about 45 percent of the population lacks secure water access. From the description of the pricing of water (rural water users pay 8 percent of the price paid by urban users) those who have access to water use it until it has zero marginal product while others queue to obtain water. In their diagnosis of the problem facing Moroccan authorities in charge of designing national water policy, the authors suggest a carefully designed and comprehensive approach that relies on a balance between regional interests as well as between market and regulatory responsibility. As a first step in that process they propose a simulation analysis.

In the simulation analysis the authors assume, for every sector except rainfed agriculture, an infinitely elastic supply of water at a fixed price (in terms of the numéraire). Water enters into production as any primary factor in a standard neoclassical simulation model with first-order conditions to determine its allocation across activities. To capture the public good aspect of water use, the government receives the factor income from the sales of water, and redistributes it as a lump-sum to the representative consumer. Water does not, however, enter into the utility function. Grafted on this simple specification of water is a standard (but elaborate) treatment of foreign trade. Given these rather restrictive assumptions about the role of water, the authors examine the effects of an increase in the price of water charged to farmers and of trade liberalisations.

The authors attribute the rise in GDP in experiment 1 to the imposition of the tax on the agricultural sector that occurs when the price of water is raised. My reading is, however, different. I interpret experiment 1 as a partial removal of a factor market distortion that should raise welfare and probably GDP – although unfortunately this cannot be ascertained in this model where there is investment as well as consumption – if the use of water were held constant. However this is not the case so that GDP falls as the use of water is diminished. But this is surely a good thing since there will soon be water shortage in Morocco. The authors offer no valuation measure for this result, so one cannot really ascertain the cause behind the change in the value of GDP.

In the same vein, the authors claim that trade liberalisation has a salutory effect, because of efficiency gains. Again, this might be the case, but the way the experiment is set up, one cannot ascertain the source of the increase in the value of GDP, since water usage is not held constant.

The chapter would have benefited immensely if the authors had designed their policy experiments so that the reader could understand what was driving the results. This would have required at least a two-step procedure in which the supply of water is held fixed in the first step. Furthermore, to solve the welfare evaluation problem, the authors should have used a utility function that includes investment as an argument. Then, the authors could rely on the standard equivalent variation measure for their welfare analysis. In the present formulation, however, investment does not enter the utility function, although the authors implicitly use real GDP as one measure of welfare.

More fundamentally, could this type of analysis really shed light on the issue of water usage? Given the difficulty of getting first-hand information on the technology of agriculture with respect to factor usage, a thorough sensitivity analysis should be undertaken with respect to functional form. The use of a CET to allocate water is a useful first step in proxying for the costs of reallocating water across urban and rural sectors. It would be interesting to explore the sensitivity of the simulation results to changes in the value of the elasticity of transformation which captures this cost of reallocation. Some alternative simulations are provided in the appendix, but little effort is expended on judging their plausibility.

Understandably, the authors are interested in the level of water usage even more than in the reallocation of a given (fixed) supply of water. This will require modelling water supply explicitly. The current assumption of an infinitely elastic supply of water at a fixed price goes against the discusion in the Introduction which predicts a shortage in the medium term. Moreover, the common property aspects of water usage suggest the possibility of a negative externality that should also take into account the effect on quality of water over usage.

Finally, for further work, it would be interesting to investigate the income distribution aspects of water pricing by having several household groups, once the model were extended to include water in the utility function. If indeed, nearly half the population does not have access to water, household budget surveys to evaluate desired water consumption levels would be a necessary first step in any analysis of the effects of water pricing policies on income distribution.

In sum, the authors provide a forceful argument that Morocco will soon have a water shortage. They also give suggestive evidence that there is a severe distortion in the allocation of water because of differences in pricing across sectors. While their model represents a step in the right direction, the authors have not provided answers to most of the questions in the Introduction to the chapter.

8   Energy pricing for sustainable development in China

ROSEMARY CLARKE and
L. ALAN WINTERS

As for many other developing countries, China's plans for economic growth are likely to be achieved only at the cost of a deteriorating environment. With population predicted to grow at over 1 percent p.a. until 2000 (Hull, 1991, table 5.4) and GNP per capita of US$370 p.a. in 1990, it is under pressure to raise living standards. From 1980 to 1990, GNP grew at an average of 9.5 percent p.a. (World Bank, 1992, table 2) and China expects to sustain its current high growth rate until 2000, by which time it would exceed its goal of quadrupling 1980 GDP (Gan Ziyu, Vice Minister of the State Planning Commission, *Financial Times*, 28 February 1993). To achieve this goal it plans to double production of coal, its major energy source.

China consumes nearly 9 percent of the world's commercial energy, which makes it the world's fourth largest consumer, exceeded only by the US consuming 25 percent, the Commonwealth of Independent States (CIS) 18 percent and the EC 15 percent. Energy consumption *per capita* is low, however, at 598 kg of oil equivalent, or about 38 percent of the world average (World Bank, 1992, table 5). Unlike most other large energy users, China relies heavily on coal which provides 76 percent of its current commercial energy needs. It is fortunate in having extensive reserves of coal, much of excellent quality and available at low cost, but their use brings many environmental costs. China is currently the world's third largest emitter of carbon dioxide and one of the largest sources of methane from fossil fuels (see table 8.1). Such high rates of economic growth and heavy reliance on coal mean that carbon dioxide emissions will continue to rise and OECD projections suggest that by 2050 China will be the largest emitter in the world, contributing some 30 percent of all emissions (Burniaux *et al.*, 1992, figure 2).[1]

Energy prices in China have for many years been heavily distorted and in many cases set at levels well below the marginal costs of production. In this chapter we examine the effects of raising energy prices on economic

Table 8.1. *Greenhouse gas emissions*

	Contribution to world GHG emissions	CO₂ Emissions from industrial processes (1989)				Methane (1989)		CFCs (1989)
	% of total emissions (1)	% of total world emissions (2)	% of country total from:[a] solids (3)	liquids (4)	gas[b] (5)	% of total emissions (6)	% from fossil fuel production (7)	% of total emissions (8)
USA	18.4	22.3	37.5	42.6	19.1	13.7	35.9	22.4
ex-USSR	13.5	17.4	34.9	32.5	30.7	12.6	60.6	11.5
EC[c]	11.0	11.7	34.3	45.7	17.0	6.2	23.6	25.3
China	8.4	10.9	82.2	12.3	1.2	14.8	33.0	2.0
India	3.5	3.0	70.8	22.1	3.9	13.3	6.7	0.7
Total	54.8	65.3				60.6		61.9

Notes:
[a] Does not sum to 100 percent as excludes emissions from cement manufacture.
[b] Includes gas flaring.
[c] Includes German Democratic Republic where figures are available.
Source: World Resources Institute (1992): column (2), table 13.4; columns (3)–(5), Table 24.1; columns (6)–(8), Table 24.2.

welfare and the emission levels of several pollutants. We consider both introducing a carbon tax and rectifying various pricing distortions in energy markets. In section 1 we set out a simple model of the optimal levels of abatement. Section 2 reviews the available evidence on the major environmental costs faced by China, both those arising from global warming and those caused by sulphur dioxide, nitrogen oxides and particulates. Section 3 discusses the modelling of the abatement costs in the light of recent economic reforms while section 4 conducts some simple simulations of different approaches to abatement. Chinese policy on the level of abatement of greenhouse gases has implications both for other nations and, in its link with national air pollution, for its own citizens. Section 5 draws some policy conclusions.

1   Optimal abatement

The atmosphere is a global public good and thus the abatement of greenhouse gas emissions by any one country, such as China, confers global external benefits. From a cosmopolitan point of view, optimal abatement by China would be achieved when the marginal social benefits of reducing Chinese emissions are equal to the marginal abatement costs of doing so.

A general assumption made by most studies of greenhouse gas abatement costs is that energy markets are undistorted and that the prices paid by consumers are equal to the marginal social costs of production.[2] However, the theory of second-best suggests that the welfare effects of introducing a carbon tax could depend heavily on the existence and nature of other distortions in the economy and in energy markets in particular. Where a government subsidises a fuel, price will be less than marginal cost, consumption will be greater than optimal, and there will be welfare losses quite independent of those resulting from global warming (see Kosmo, 1987). The introduction of a carbon tax would raise the price and discourage energy consumption while at the same time reducing emissions. In these circumstances the initial units of abatement could be achieved at negative cost, i.e. raise welfare. If we represent such a case in the standard diagram of abatement costs and benefits, the intercept of the marginal abatement cost curve will lie below the origin, as shown in figure 8.1, where the abatement on the horizontal axis refers to that undertaken by China, independent of abatement by other countries.

Any reduction of Chinese greenhouse gas emissions would generate significant external benefits for other countries in addition to any possible national benefits. China has signed the convention on global warming and accepts, in principle, the need for targets, but to date it has made no

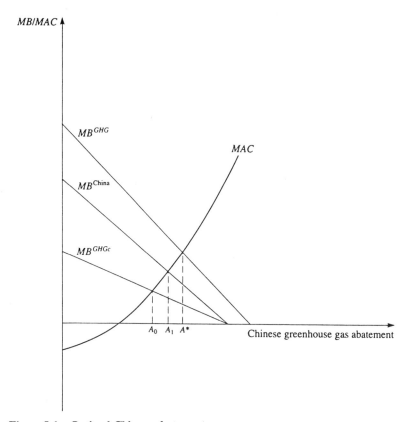

MB/MAC

MB^{GHG}

MAC

MB^{China}

MB^{GHGc}

A_0 A_1 A^* Chinese greenhouse gas abatement

Figure 8.1   Optimal Chinese abatement

specific commitment to reduce emissions (IEA, 1992a). Without a treaty, China's optimal level of abatement for greenhouse gases will be A^0, where its national marginal benefit curve, MB^{GHGc}, cuts the marginal abatement cost curve (see figure 8.1). However, Chinese abatement also yields benefits to other countries and this global externality, combined with Chinese national benefits, would result in the marginal social (global) benefit curve, MB^{GHG} and a global optimum such as A^*.

Fossil fuels, the primary source of CO_2 emissions, also emit sulphur dioxide, particulates, nitrogen oxides and carbon monoxide, resulting in air pollution and acid rain. Thus policies aimed at reducing carbon dioxide emissions will also yield secondary benefits through reductions in these emissions. Summing vertically China's marginal benefits from abating GHGs together with those from other pollutant abatement yields the schedule MB^{China}. China's national optimal level of abatement is now A_1, reducing the amount of underabatement relative to the global social optimum defined on greenhouse gases, A^*. If the externality were smaller, so that the marginal social (global) benefit curve lay below that drawn in figure 8.1, A_1 could be greater than A^*.

One complication that we have ignored in the preceding analysis is the possibility that the abatement of some emissions is not matched by abatement of others. In this study we focus on policies aimed at abating CO_2 emissions through interfuel substitution and the reduction of fossil fuel consumption. If the objective were to reduce local air pollutants, China could adopt clean technologies which permit the removal of sulphur dioxide, particulates and nitrogen oxides; however, since these processes require energy, they slightly increase carbon dioxide emissions.[3] Thus, the marginal benefit schedules, MB^{China} and MB^{GHG}, are not independent of the means adopted to abate nongreenhouse gases.

2   Marginal benefits of abatement

Information concerning the relative magnitude of the marginal benefits from abating carbon dioxide emissions and abating other air pollutants is scarce. However, preliminary evidence for other countries suggests that the latter, so-called secondary, benefits may be substantial and exceed those from carbon dioxide abatement (Glomsrød et al., 1992; Pearce, 1992; see also Shah and Larsen, 1992).

2.1   Global warming

While the regional impact of global warming is uncertain and difficult to predict, China will probably be affected by inundation of coastal areas, climatic effects on health and agriculture, and impacts on natural eco-systems (Fankhauser, 1992; Hulme et al., 1992). A study of global and regional damage costs suggests that a doubling of atmospheric CO_2 concentrations may result in China experiencing total damage amounting to 6.1 percent of GNP, compared to a world average of 1.5 percent (Fankhauser, 1992, table 15).[4] In terms of emissions, these estimates would imply an approximte marginal private damage cost for China of $0.93 per ton of carbon in 1990–2000 (this, and all other costs, have been converted to 1985 US$) rising to $2.3 in 2020–30 (Fankhauser, 1993 and personal communication). Any such estimates are, of course, tentative. It is not possible to obtain information on the relative magnitude of the global external damage costs of Chinese GHG pollution, but as, over time, China becomes the main emitter of carbon dioxide, these are unlikely to be negligible.

2.2 National environmental costs

Various categories of local environmental degradations arise from the commercial exploitation of fossil fuels. The most serious are those from emissions causing air pollution and acid rain. Sulphur dioxide emissions have risen from 13.2 million tons in 1985 to 14.9 in 1990, while those of particulates have fallen from 26 million tons in 1985 to 21.1 in 1990. Chinese NO_x emissions are currently low – about 6.1 million tons in 1986 – and come mainly from coal, unlike other countries where the main source is transport (all figures from Edmonds, 1991, table 12)[5].

Air quality in the major cities is amongst the worst in the world. In 1985 annual mean concentrations of SO_2 ranged from 13 to 225 $\mu g/m^3$ in 31 northern cities and from 8 to 504 $\mu g/m^3$ in 33 southern cities, compared with the WHO guideline of 40 to 60 $\mu g/m^3$. For particulates the figures were 333 to 1767 $\mu g/m^3$ and 224 to 821 $\mu g/m^3$ respectively, much higher than the WHO guidelines of 60 to 90 $\mu g/m^3$ (Cao, 1989, table 2; World Bank, 1992: 193). The main reasons for such high levels of emissions are the poor preparation of coal burned (only 18 percent is washed); small and medium-sized inefficient industrial boilers, domestic heaters and cooking stoves, often with low stacks; and poor atmospheric dispersion in some areas. As electricity meets only a small proportion of the country's energy needs, pollution arises mainly from industry and from the residential share of coal consumption which, at 24 percent, is higher than most other countries'.

Estimates of the damage costs of air pollutants are necessarily very imprecise, for they depend on interactions between pollutants and on imperfect scientific knowledge.[6] Moreover, lacking data on morbidity, we can consider only mortality. Particulate emissions are thought to be more harmful to health than sulphur dioxide because they can be inhaled deep into the lungs where they remain. Particulate pollution can be particularly serious indoors because of inadequate ventilation and inefficient stoves fuelled by poor quality coal or biomass fuels, including dung. Concentrations measured over the day in a wood burning kitchen have been found to be as high as 2600 $\mu g/m^3$ (Smith, 1988, table 4) while Mumford et al. (1987) found that smoky coal was more harmful than wood. As health effects depend not only on the level of emissions but also on the exposure time, these studies suggest that women, small children and the elderly, who spend less time outdoors, are particularly at risk. A Polish study found that benefits of particulate abatement exceeded costs by up to 70 percent, unlike sulphur dioxide where at no level did they do so (World Bank, 1992: 71–2).

Kinzelbach reports average lung cancer mortality in Chinese cities to be

17–31 annual cases per 100,000 compared with 4–5 per 100,000 for the country as a whole (1987: 178). Assuming that only 1 per 100,000 of these national deaths was due to cancer caused by air pollution and taking Fankhauser's value of a statistical life at $127,000 (1992), we arrive at a cost of $55.64 per ton of particulates.[7]

Sulphur dioxide is generally assumed to be a major contributor to acid rain which occurs in various regions in China (Zhao and Xiong, 1988). The worst affected are those areas to the south of the Yangtze River where rain at approximately 90 percent of sites is officially acid (pH of below 5.6). Most vulnerable are Chongqing (average rainwater pH 4.14) and Guiyang (pH 4.02) in the south-west; here metal structures have to be scraped clean of rust and repainted once every 1–3 years, and bus shells replaced every 1–2 years (Zhao and Xiong, 1988: 342 and table 10.3). Losses from metal corrosion were estimated at about US$11,000 million in 1988 (Edmonds, 1991: 20). If correct, this would indicate an average cost of $765 per ton of sulphur dioxide.

These two estimates suggest that the national benefits of reducing local air pollutants exceed those from carbon dioxide emissions by a wide margin. They can be compared with Fankhauser's estimates of $212 per ton of SO_2 (mortality and corrosion only) and $423 per ton of NO_x for low-income countries (1992: 19). Shah and Larson (1992: 34–5) assume values of $1352 per ton of SO_2 and $9735 per ton of NO_x and adjust them for purcashing power parity. Values for Pakistan are $311 for SO_2 and $2239 for NO_x; costs for China would be lower if PPP adjusted.

3   Marginal abatement costs

China's energy sector is emerging from a long period of state control involving extensive subsidy. Producer and consumer subsidies have kept fuel prices low, encouraging wasteful consumption and the continuance of inefficient technologies in both energy production and use. In recent years, economic reforms have led to the emergence of markets, where prices are determined by demand and supply, alongside state allocated quotas at state determined prices. Given the existence of two sets of prices, we must ask whether the subsidies implicit in the state prices generate any welfare loss. If all consumers meet at least some of their fuel needs through the market, market prices reflect valuation at the margin and the subsidy on any state allocated units represents a transfer, generating no welfare cost. For such consumers, provided market prices do not differ from border prices, the abatement cost of a carbon tax would be positive. If, however, some sectors receive state fuel allocations sufficient for their needs, or if inframarginal subsidies are passed on to users in terms of lower prices for their marginal purchases, then abatement in such sectors could be achieved with a welfare gain by raising prices.

The questions we must address are, therefore, whether state, market and international prices differ; what proportion of demand is met at state prices; and whether inframarginal subsidies are passed on. We start, however, by briefly describing the dual pricing system.

Three stages in price reform have been identified, reflecting a gradual evolution of markets starting in 1979. Liberalisation of the energy sector has proceeded more cautiously than in other sectors for fear of inflationary consequences (see Guo, 1992). Under the dual pricing system all state owned enterprises – energy and other – are given an annual output target and input allocations. There is compulsory state procurement of this target output and both output and input prices are set by the state. Since 1985 output quotas have also been set. Output within the quota is purchased at state determined prices while that above quota, but less than target, receives a higher 'negotiated' state price. Only output above the annual target can be sold on the free market.

The extent to which state and market fuel prices diverge differs between fuels. The greatest differences are those for coal, where in some regions market prices may be up to four times state prices, and for fuel oil. For 1985, the year of our study, coal, crude and fuel oil state prices are approximately one-third of market prices and, for oil, slightly less than one-third of international prices (see table 8.2). Kerosene and gasoline state prices are almost at international levels but diesel is about 20 percent lower. Prices for gas and electricity are centrally determined and the average electricity tariff is lower than other Asian countries, with the exception of India (World Bank, 1985: 81, n. 6). The most notable feature of the tariff is the high price to consumers.

We now consider the proportion of fuel purchases occurring at the state price. Since 1982, collectively and individually owned mines have been free to sell their coal on the open market (Guo, 1992: 70). The response from such mines has been rapid and much of the increase in output over the 1980s has come from them, the share of total output produced by central and local state owned mines having fallen from 84.5 percent in 1978 to 72.5 percent in 1984 and to 65 percent by 1989 (Byrd, 1987, table 2; Albouy, 1991: 4). The proportion of coal sold at market prices has risen from 25.7 percent in 1984 to 49.6 percent in 1985 and to 57.7 percent in 1986 (Guo, 1992, table 6.2).[8] These figures suggest that by 1985 many enterprises were purchasing marginal coal requirements at market prices. Unfortunately there is no clear indication as to the proportions of market purchases by sector.

It seems likely that in 1985, major state enterprises, such as power

Table 8.2. *Fuel prices for China, 1985*

Source	State price US$ per toe	Market price US$ per toe	International price US$ per toe
Coal	23.6	63.49	66.16
Crude oil	62.22	182.30	198.86
Fuel oil	46.82	163.17	184.13
Kerosene	239.50	n.a.	248.53
Gasoline	233.91	n.a.	242.72
Diesel	184.24	230.30	233.76
Natural gas		US$134.88 per toe	
Electricity		US$ per toe	
Residential		686.41	
Commercial and small-scale industry		347.49	
Large industry		270.25	
Agriculture		231.70	
Average		308.30	

Source: Coal, oil and electricity: state and international prices from World Bank (1985, table 3.2); market prices (for 1985–6) from Lardy (1992, table 4.3). Gas: OECD, personal communication.

generation, railways and state owned heavy industry (such as steel) received the bulk of their fuel at subsidised rates (World Bank, 1985: 72; Taplin, 1993). Other industry, and especially private enterprise which has been growing rapidly (see McMillan and Naughton, 1992: 132), probably received only a relatively small proportion of state prices. On the other hand, urban residential consumption of coal is heavily subsidised in many regions, with households buying only a very small proportion on the open market.

The persistence of state subsidies for certain fuels has introduced many distortions into the Chinese economy. Prior to the reforms, fuel prices remained unchanged over long periods, with the result that many state energy enterprises operated at a loss at different times. After 1984, national average production costs of state mined coal exceeded price (Guo, 1992: 83 and table 3.4), and by 1988 Jackson reports that losses from coal and oil producers amounted to about 56 percent of total losses (1992: 115). Until the enterprise tax system was introduced in 1983–4, all profits passed to the state, providing no incentive to cut costs and raise output. Low producer prices have meant that there have been insufficient funds for investment in expansion and modernisation of coal mines and for exploration of oil and gas. Labour productivity in coal mines is low: while some 65 percent of output at state mines is extracted mechanically (Xuan, 1993)[9] extraction at other mines is predominantly by manual labour. Allocation through state quotas often results in little attention being given to the matching of fuel quality to use.

While energy intensity has been falling in recent years, this is due more to a switch from heavy to light industry than to greater efficiency (World Bank, 1985). Energy is still used wastefully and, by western standards, power generation, industrial boilers and other types of equipment are outdated and inefficient (see World Bank, 1985; Smil, 1988). Despite the rapid growth of markets after 1985, there are many opportunities for further savings.

4   The simulations

This section simulates some of the policy issues discussed above on a schematic general equilibrium model of the Chinese economy. The model is small, the representation of existing distortions crude, the base year 1985, and the base data *very* uncertain. Hence the results can be taken as only the roughest of indications of the orders of magnitude involved. Nevertheless, they illustrate that allowing for distortions in energy markets can affect one's view of greenhouse gas abatement. They also make clear that there are no easy solutions.

The choice of 1985 as base was dictated by the availability of data. Much has happened since then – for example, a loosening of restraints on the energy sector, the introduction of managerial incentives and the partial liberalisation of prices (see Jackson, 1992) – but China is not yet a fully fledged market economy. Besides reforms take time to implement and enterprises need time to adjust, so that even if steps have been taken in the directions of our policy experiments, the economy has certainly not yet attained the long-run equilibria we derive from them.

4.1   The base data

The simulation model is based on an adapted version of the input–output table for 1985 used in GREEN (Burniaux et al., 1992). This distinguishes eight sectors (see Appendix 1) and five categories of final demand. We collapsed the latter into one domestic category (loosely called consumption) and one foreign category (exports). We did this first by adding stock-building to the intermediate demand of other industry (OTHIND) and reducing value added by that sector by the same amount. OTHIND

Table 8.3. *Shares of sales at state prices*

	Coal	Crude oil	N. gas	Refined oil	Electricity
Agriculture	0.10	0.10	1.00	0.10	0.92
Coal	1.00	1.00	1.00	0.10	0.94
Crude oil	1.00	1.00	1.00	0.50	0.94
Natural gas	1.00	1.00	1.00	1.00	0.94
Refined oil	0.00	0.50	1.00	1.00	0.94
Electricity	0.83	0.30	1.00	0.20	0.94
Energy intensive industry	0.40	0.10	1.00	0.20	0.94
Other industry	0.15	0.00	1.00	0.15	0.72
Consumption	0.55	1.00	1.00	0.25	0.63

Source: see text.

accounts for nearly 60 percent of total demand and includes food processing; 1985 stock-building was predominantly of agricultural products. Second, in order to avoid the complications of modelling dynamics, we also treated investment as an intermediate commodity demand; this is appropriate to a long-term model and is common in CGE modelling – see, for example, de Melo and Tarr (1992). We did this by adding to each column of interindustry sales the product of its total return to capital and the expenditure shares of each commodity in total investment. Capital earnings were then suppressed – they now represent intermediate flows – and the remaining excess of investment that was not allocated in this way was added into final domestic demand. It is evident that while these adjustments reduce reported national income, they leave the basic accounting identities intact.

Energy quantities corresponding to the flows in the input–output table were taken from the Asian Development Bank (1992). Given state and market fuel prices (see table 8.3), we calculated average energy prices by adjusting the sectoral shares of purchases at subsidised state prices so that the total demand values for energy generally matched the GREEN data.[10] In one or two cases (residential coal consumption and oil) our estimated average prices led to results which did not accord with GREEN estimates and we had to override these. The resulting imbalances in the input–output table were removed by scaling the value added components to ensure adding up. Our assumed prices are reported in Appendix 2, and their origins in section 4.2. Finally, we introduced subsidies of $2.5 billion and $1 billion in the coal and crude oil sectors respectively to reflect known losses. The resulting flows matrix is given in Appendix 3.

4.2   Data sources

4.2.1 Prices (see table 8.2)

There is relatively little information on prices, and in a country as large as China prices will vary by region depending on transport costs and the forces of demand and supply. Moreover the quality of coal varies by source.[11] Apart from gas, where we took OECD's price, we have relied mainly on World Bank data (1985, table 3.2) for state retail fuel prices, while market prices are taken from Lardy (1992, table 4.3) based on 'representative markets' for late 1985 and early 1986. For refined oil sectoral weighted averages were estimated taking account of the mix of products consumed by each sector using data from Asian Development Bank (1992) and *Energy Statistics Yearbook of China 1991* (1991).

4.2.2 Purchases of state prices (see table 8.3)

There is very little information on sectoral purchases of fuels. We follow Albouy (1991) on coal purchases and our assumptions on the remainder are set out in table 8.3.

We distinguish between the share of *total* sales of fuel i to sector j that occurs at state prices and the share of *marginal* sales. The former – to which the few available data and table 8.3 refer – determines the average prices of fuel i. The latter is best thought of as reflecting the proportion of purchasers in sector j who are able to buy or surrender marginal units of i at state prices. This share hardly affects the average price, but does affect behaviour because it reflects the incentives for marginal substitution in the production function.[12] We assume that the share of marginal sales at state prices is half the share of total sales given in table 8.3.

4.2.3 Emission factors (see table 8.4)

We relate emissions to economic activity by means of fixed emission factors giving emissions per unit of output. Carbon coefficients were taken from Grubb (1991). Emissions of SO_2, NO_x and particulates are technologically and/or performance related. Moreover the sulphur content of coal varies by region, that from the south of China having a higher sulphur content than that from the north. As data specific to China were not available we estimated the emission factors set out in table 8.4 by modifying UK data (Gillham et al., 1992) in the light of other available evidence. CO_2 emissions create no problems as they bear a fixed relationship to the carbon content of fuels.

Table 8.4. *Emission factors*

Fuel	CO_2 as carbon (tC/Mtoe)	SO_2 (kg/toe)	NO_x (kg/toe)	Particulates[a] (kg/toe)
Coal	1.09	31.6	12.0	31.0
Crude oil	0.82	23.8	8.0	4.5
N. gas	0.61		4.0	

Note: [a] These emission factors would represent a total of slightly less than 13 million tons. Edmonds (1991) reports particulate emissions for 1985 at 26 million tons (see table 8.2). However, windblown dust, especially from the Loess Plateau, also generates particulates and it has been estimated that dust contributes 40–60 percent of total particulates in the north, depending on the seasons, but less in the south (Zhao and Xiong, 1988). A total of 13 million tons from fossil fuel particulates would seem plausible.
Source: CO_2: Grubb (1991, table A2.3). For the other emissions, see text.

4.3   The model specification

The equations of the simulation model are given in Appendix 5. The choice of production technique is completely endogenous; all production functions are of the nested CES form, with elasticities of substitution of -0.5 at all points. First, aggregates of energy (en, comprising COAL, CROIL, GAS, ROIL and ELEC), materials (mat, comprising AG, TRANS, ENIND and OTHIND) and value added (va, comprising LAB and LAND) are created, which are then combined to get commodity output. Labour supplies are fixed in total, but intersectorally mobile, while land – a proxy for all natural resources and fixed factors – is fixed in supply and industry specific; all factor returns are endogenous. Where the input–output table reports zero inputs of a fixed factor, we shifted approximately 10 percent of value added into that category in order that every industry should have an industry specific factor.

Consumption – which here includes consumers' and government expenditure and a little investment – is modelled with an LES function. The values of necessary expenditure γ and marginal expenditure shares β are given in Appendix 4.

In international trade China is treated as a small country with differentiated products. Hence export demand curves for 'materials' commodities slope downwards with elasticities of demand of -4 or -5 (see Appendix 4). Exports and export prices for fuels are fixed exogenously, because fuel exports are small and restrictions on them are likely to continue for some time.[13] Imports demand is related to total intermediate demand in other industry (OTHIND) – i.e. we presume that only that industry imports –

with a finite elasticity of the import share with respect to relative domestic and import prices.[14]

In the main model prices are based on marginal costs of production assuming that marginal production entails buying inputs at marginal prices. Thus we equate our 'indicator price' (p_i) – a working variable introduced only to facilitate calculation and exposition – to marginal costs from equation (A5) in Appendix 5. From this define the 'market' price for consumption by adding a wedge and consumption taxes. Revenue from the former accrues to the firms, while that from the latter, naturally, accrues to the government. The wedges reflect planning instructions to firms to subsidise some sales or, in the case of electricity, to add a premium, and while in the main version of the model they have equivalent effects to taxes, that is not true in an alternative form in which firms' current accounts must balance.[15] Given the market price and an (exogenous) state price, the marginal price for consumers is calculated as a weighted average using the share of marginal consumer purchases made at state prices (cs).

The prices of interindustry flows are calculated similarly except in that the state prices, wedges and shares all potentially vary by both commodity and consuming industry, and that, for other industry, we must recognise the share of inputs that is imported. Export prices are effectively market prices – indicator prices plus wedges and taxes – except in the cases of energy commodities for which we fix them exogenously. Import prices are world prices plus the tariff.

Equation (A25) in Appendix 5 calculates firms' current accounts. The sum of the value of inputs on the left-hand side must equal the sum of the value of sales on the right-hand side. Note that these flows are evaluated using the average shares of transactions at state prices $(qa_{ij}$ and $ca_i)$ and that we introduce a slack variable into the main model, $trans_i$ (transfers into industry i), to maintain balance when pricing rules are changed.

Finally the model is closed by three aggregate constraints and definitions: the balance of trade in foreign currency, which is fixed at the calibration level, net indirect taxes including trade taxes, and aggregate effective income. The last comprises factor payments, net indirect tax revenue, foreign borrowing plus a notional transfer reflecting the difference between the average price of consumption flows and the marginal, or decision, price.

4.4   Results

4.4.1 Carbon tax and removing energy price distortions

Table 8.5 reports our principal results. We conduct two blocks of experiments – first imposing a carbon tax, column (1) and second curing certain energy pricing distortions in the Chinese economy, columns (2)–(5). Our basic message is that the removal of price distortions offers slightly less costly means to small-scale abatement, but that there is little in it. Somewhat surprisingly, there appear to be no significant 'no-regrets' policies: the reason lies in the nature of the pricing distortions which we have assumed in the calibration scenario, and our results are only as good as those assumptions. As Winters (1992) and Winters and Wang (1993) have observed, the critical requirement for modelling policy reform is estimates of the effects of the existing policies that are to be reformed. These are always hard to get to any degree of accuracy.

The traditionally measured welfare costs of the policies we consider – i.e. their costs in terms of goods and services – are somewhat smaller than those estimated for other countries or globally. For example, the global cost of halving CO_2 emissions is generally estimated at around 2–3 percent of GDP, and as requiring taxes of the order of \$100–\$200 per ton of carbon – see Boero, Clarke and Winters (1991);[16] here we obtain CO_2 emission reductions of 11 percent at a cost of 0.18 percent of total income with a tax of \$25 per ton – see column (1) in table 8.5. The tax is levied on the three primary fuels according to the emission factors in table 8.4. This is the most effective scenario in the table, and its advantage over the others is that its impact falls squarely on coal – the dirtiest of the available fuels. As a result coal consumption falls by 20 percent, output by 14 percent, and the return to coal mines by 34 percent. The carbon tax entails a loss of 0.18 percent of income but the welfare benefits of pollution abatement are significant. Based on the values discussed in section 2.2 (carbon \$1 per ton; SO_2 \$765; NO_x \$1500; particulates \$55.64), the carbon tax scenario generates abatement benefits of 0.70 percent of final demand leaving a net gain in welfare of 0.52 percent.

Emissions of the four pollutants fall by roughly the same proportions in this and in all subsequent exercises. The reason lies in the similar proportions with which the two principal primary fuels – COAL and CROIL – produce different pollutants. If there were a major shift towards natural gas, sulphur and particulates could be abated much more vigorously, but the small size of the GAS sector precludes that in the foreseeable future.

The second simulation exercise – in column (2) of table 8.5 – entails correcting the distortions in the pricing of consumption. We assume that all consumption transactions occur at marginal costs, i.e. setting the state-price shares and the consumption wedges to zero. This achieves a small welfare improvement but produces only moderate abatement of 1.6–1.9 percent, worth approximately 0.10 percent of final demand. The abolition of the allocation at state prices raises the marginal prices of coal

Table 8.5. *Simulation results*[a]

| | | Removing price distortions in: | | | |
	Carbon tax $25 per ton (1)	Consumption (2)	Production (3)	Both (4)	Both with subsidies (5)
Abatement costs:					
equivalent variation[b]	− 0.182	0.028	− 0.122	− 0.082	− 0.172
Abatement benefits[b]	0.697	0.096	0.378	0.482	0.631
Net welfare gain	0.515	0.124	0.256	0.400	0.459
Real GDP	− 0.25	0.99	− 0.15	0.84	0.73
Wage	− 1.97	− 0.02	− 2.14	− 2.14	− 3.07
Pollutants					
CO_2	− 11.26	− 1.55	− 6.15	− 7.83	− 10.26
SO_2	− 11.39	− 1.57	− 6.21	− 7.92	− 10.38
NO_x	− 11.53	− 1.59	− 6.22	− 7.95	− 10.41
Particulates	− 13.11	− 1.85	− 6.63	− 8.64	− 11.23

Percentage change from base

Note:
[a] Full simulation results may be obtained from the authors on request.
[b] As percentage of total domestic final demand. Equivalent variation allowing for changes in consumer's income is defined here as $C(U^t, p^0) - C(U^0, p^0)$, where $C(\ )$ is the expenditure function, U^0 is initial utility, U^1 post-policy change utility and p^0 initial prices.
Source: Authors' calculations.

and crude oil to consumers by 19 percent and 52 percent respectively, but at the same time the price they pay for electricity is reduced strongly (− 28 percent) as consumers are no longer discriminated against in that sector. The result is that although consumers cut back strongly on coal and crude oil, intermediate demand increases so that on balance we find only a 2 percent decline in coal use. The loss of demand is also ameliorated by the decline in the return to coalmine owners (5 percent) which allows the price of coal to industry to fall by 2 percent. The opposite occurs for electricity. The government and consumers save about $1.7 billion in transfers to industry in this scenario, but the increased cost of living absorbs most of it in welfare terms.

Column (3) in table 8.5 considers correcting the distortions in industrial energy pricing – that is, requiring all interindustry flows to occur at market prices.[17] It offers larger abatement, but at the cost of economic welfare, traditionally measured; on balance, however, it increases net welfare by 0.26 percent. The major interindustry distortions lie in the sale of crude oil to the refining industry, of coal to electricity and the onward sale of electricity. The marginal cost of refined oil rises by 2 percent, and that of electricity by 10 percent, while the marginal price of electricity to industrial users rises by between 39 and 58 percent. The result of these price changes is a dramatic fall in intermediate demand and in the return to fixed factors in the energy sector.

The reduction in welfare arises mainly from the reduction in the consumption of electricity, for which the marginal valuation far exceeds marginal cost. The net savings in transfers to industry (approximately $9.5 billion) are substantially offset by reductions in factor rewards – wages fall by over 2 percent and some specific factor returns by over 20 percent. It is notable that electricity bears, by a large margin, the largest burden in this scenario.

Column (4) in table 8.5 abolishes both consumption and interindustry distortions. It is basically the sum of columns (2) and (3), offering abatement of around 8 percent and a net welfare gain of 0.4 percent.[18]

In the calibration data we assume that coal and crude oil receive lump-sum subsidies of $2.5 billion and $1 billion respectively, but in the main model this makes no difference. Their abolition as part of a move towards market principles is just offset by increases in the endogenous transfers necessary to ensure industrial break even. Now in column (5) of table 8.5 we convert these subsidies to a per unit basis ($6.2 per toe for coal, $8.3 per toe for crude oil) and raise marginal costs correspondingly so that the initial observed price is unchanged. Then when distortions are removed, so is the subsidy, so that the net price of coal and crude oil rises further than in the previous case.

The overall effect is abatement of approximately 10 percent, generating a net welfare gain of 0.56 percent. The effect on electricity prices is much stronger than previously – it loses the benefits of subsidised inputs – but there is still a net increase in consumption. Energy intensive industry also suffers a loss of competitiveness, with the expected international trade consequences, and fixed factor owners in coal, crude oil and electricity suffer big losses. This scenario spreads more of the burden of contraction onto the primary energies, but it is still true that the largest reduction in demand falls on electricity.

From the discussion above, it is plain that one could construct packages of selective price reforms that would dominate the pure carbon tax, but to do so would not be a genuine price liberalisation. Rather we would advocate removing price distortions so far as possible – but bearing in mind any remaining distortions in trade and elsewhere – and then imposing a carbon tax to induce any further desired abatement. It is obvious from our exercise that CO_2 abatement is not an expensive policy for China once one allows for the corresponding abatement of local pollutants.

4.4.2 Scenarios assuming that sectors break even

So far we have related prices to marginal costs, and in doing so have ignored industries' flows of funds. It seems useful, however, to explore a completely different approach to pricing whereby the indicator price is chosen to ensure that sectors break even without additional transfers. Under these circumstances the prices for marginal transactions affect the shares of different goods in the bundles of consumption and inputs, but not directly the prices of outputs which are determined by the current balance requirement and thence to the average shares of transactions occurring at state prices. That is, to the extent that an industry is fortunate enough to receive subsidised inputs it is required to pass these on in terms of lower prices for its output.

Table 8.6 presents two sets of results from this alternative specification. Columns (1) and (2) correspond to column (2) of table 8.5. The former abolishes the state-price allocation for consumers both on the margin and overall. The changes in marginal incentives are as in the main exercise and induce the same changes in the consumption bundle, but now the additional revenue generated by charging full prices on all sales accrues to the firms, which must either raise costs or reduce their indicator prices to absorb it. The former adjustment increases land rents slightly, but the latter dominates with the result that the indicator, and hence the market, prices of fuels fall – most notably for coal. The consequence is that while traditionally measured welfare increases, overall welfare falls because

Table 8.6. Alternative results[a]

	Percentage change from base							
	Removing consumption price distortions				Removing interindustry price distortions			
	Break-even model		Elasticities		Break-even model		Elasticities	
	Plain (1)	Revenue adjusted (2)	Low (3)	High (4)	Plain (5)	Revenue adjusted (6)	Low (7)	High (8)
Abatement costs: equivalent variation[b]	0.050	− 0.089	0.028	0.028	0.064	− 0.136	− 0.060	− 0.181
Abatement benefits[b]	− 0.088	0.269	0.094	0.100	− 0.344	0.538	0.408	0.574
Net welfare gain	− 0.038	0.180	0.122	0.128	− 0.280	0.402	0.348	0.393
Real GDP	1.02	0.99	0.99	0.99	0.02	0.79	0.86	− 0.20
Wage	0.37	− 0.02	− 0.02	− 0.02	− 1.07	− 3.24	− 2.22	− 1.92
Pollutants								
CO_2	1.41	− 4.33	− 1.51	− 1.61	5.54	− 8.74	− 6.62	− 9.35
SO_2	1.43	− 4.39	− 1.53	− 1.64	5.62	− 8.85	− 6.70	− 9.45
NO_x	1.45	− 4.44	− 1.55	− 1.66	5.68	− 8.86	− 6.73	− 9.47
Particulates	1.67	− 5.14	− 1.81	− 1.93	6.44	− 9.43	− 7.33	− 10.10

Note:
[a] Full simulation results may be obtained from the authors on request.
[b] As percentage of total domestic final demand. Equivalent variation allowing for changes in consumer's income is defined here as $C(U^1,p^0) − C(U^0,p^0)$, where $C( )$ is the expenditure function, U^0 is initial utility, U^1 post-policy change utility and p^0 initial prices.
Source: Authors' calculations.

pollution has increased. In column (3) of table 8.6 we assume that the government prevents this perverse outcome by simultaneously levying a tax on consumption equivalent to the per unit subsidy implied by the state-price allocations. When the government intercepts the revenue effect in this way, the alternative 'break-even' model generates nearly identical results to the main one, see column (2) of table 8.5.

Columns (5) and (6) of table 8.6 offer a small sensitivity test. Returning to the main model we have recalculated the consumption and production distortion exercises with elasticities of 0.3 (low) and 0.8 (high). The latter generates rather larger effects, but the basic insights remain unchanged. In common with most modelling exercises of this kind the results are less sensitive to the assumed elasticities than to the assumed initial distortions – here the state prices and the share of sales they account for. It would have been simple to have recomputed our exercises with different values for these parameters, but this would merely have scaled our results up or down more or less *pari passu*. A different structure of initial distortions would have produced a different story – varying the above in fairly obvious ways – but we have no means of selecting among the very many alternatives.

5   Conclusions

The first and most obvious conclusion of this work is that China can achieve significant abatements of CO_2 emissions at rather low cost in terms of goods and services. Moreover, once one allows for the so-called secondary benefits of abatement in terms of reduced emissions of SO_2, NO_xs and particulates, China appears to be a modest gainer from abatement.

Second, while existing distortions in Chinese energy markets are large, their structure, to the extent that we can discover and model it on a small scale, provides no opportunities for 'generic' 'no-regrets' strategies. Thus the offsetting distortions in primary fuels and electricity mean that tackling all consumption pricing distortions or all industrial pricing distortions offers few welfare or abatement advantages: consumption offers small gains, industry small losses. 'Made to measure' policies aimed at coal that were prevented from spilling over into electricity could combine abatement and welfare gains, and to some extent this is what a carbon tax offers. Indeed, we would conclude that a carbon tax is going to be a key component of any Chinese abatement strategy.

Third, the effect of policy reform on abatement depends closely on the nature of the pricing regime. If firms respond to marginal signals the effects of abolishing subsidies could be quite different from the effects if they price primarily to break even. This implies that policies that are appropriate for countries with competitive industry structures may be less so when large state owned firms predominate, even if the latter face fierce break even conditions.

A final conclusion must be that this is all very uncertain. The factual and scientific bases of our 'data' are poor and the modelling far too aggregated to capture the full richness of the policy possibilities. What we have shown, however, is that China has opportunities for greenhouse gas abatement that would allow it to take part in global objectives at no cost to itself.

Appendix 1: definitions

Acronym	Definition	Units
AG	Agriculture	$1985
COAL	Coal, coke, etc.	toe
CROIL	Crude oil	toe
GAS	Natural gas	toe
ROIL	Refined oil	toe
ELEC	Electricity generation	toe
ENIND	Energy intensive industry (chemicals, metallurgy, building materials)	$1985
OTHIND	Other industry	$1985
LAB	Labour	$1985
LAND	Land	$1985

Appendix 2: base prices

	AG	COAL	CROIL	GAS	ROIL	ELEC	ENIND	OTHIND
Market prices to:								
Industry	60.0	62.5	200.0	135.0	[a]	600.0	133.0	133.0
Consumers	60.0	62.5	200.0	135.0	238.0	1,000.0	133.0	133.0
State prices to:								
Industry	100.0	23.6	63.2	135.0	[a]	200.0	100.0	100.0
Consumers	100.0	23.6	63.2	135.0	211.0	500.0	100.0	100.0
Exports	60.0	62.5	200.0	135.0	260.0	1,000.0	100.0	100.0
Imports	80.0	80.0	250.0	135.0	300.0	1,000.0	133.0	133.0
World	80.0	80.0	250.0	135.0	300.0	1,000.0	100.0	100.0
Indicator price	60.0	62.5	200.0	135.0	235.0	600.0	133.0	133.0
Prices for refined oil sales to industry								
Market	235.0	240.0	214.0	187.0	187.0	191.0	197.0	229.0
State	192.0	215.7	137.4	56.7	56.8	64.7	85.3	183.5

Note: [a] Varies by industry according to product mix – see below in table.

Appendix 3: flow matrix, China, 1985 ($US million)

	AG	COAL	CROIL	GAS	ROIL	ELEC	ENIND	OTHIND	Total intermed.	Imports	Consump.	Exports	Total demand
AG	37,035	355	136	9	240	5	10,200	124,629	172,609	−2,759	36,248	4,522	210,620
COAL	655	0	8	1	0	3,381	4,700	5,150	13,895	−407	3,806	372	17,666
CROIL	0	0	0	0	11,305	542	313	221	12,381	0	46	5,554	17,981
GAS	0	0	0	0	0	411	360	182	953	−40	673	19	1,605
ROIL	1,787	95	114	2	85	1,898	2,423	8,173	14,577	−119	2,383	1,635	18,476
ELEC	364	289	100	8	73	719	2,989	3,350	8,072	0	2,677	0	10,749
ENIND	15,691	648	729	50	200	135	41,242	81,463	140,158	−12,905	6,308	2,129	135,690
OTHIND	5,208	3,291	3,828	255	4,045	373	40,103	184,587	241,690	−57,038	312,794	28,521	525,967
Total	60,740	4,678	4,915	325	15,948	7,464	102,330	407,935	604,335	−73,268	364,935	42,752	938,754
LAB	88,447	9,187	451	44	2,275	736	30,024	106,229					
LAND	61,433	6,301	13,615	1,236	253	2,549	3,336	11,803					
Subsidy		−2,500	−1,000										
Availability	210,620	17,666	17,981	1,605	18,476	10,749	135,690	525,967					

Source: Authors' elaboration on table supplied by OECD.

Appendix 4: commodity demands and parameters

| | Demands (in quantity units) | | | | | Trade elasticities | | |
	Total intermed.	Imports	Consump.	Exports	Total demand	X and M	γ	β
AG	2,865.3	− 34.5	604.1	75.4	3,510.3	− 4	200.0	0.110
COAL	312.4	− 5.1	92.6	6.0	405.8	− 1	5.0	0.020
CROIL	92.1	0.0	0.7	27.8	120.6	− 1		0.000
GAS	7.1	− 0.3	5.0	0.1	11.9	− 1		0.003
ROIL	72.3	− 0.4	10.3	6.3	88.5	− 1	5.0	0.006
ELEC	27.2	0.0	3.9	0.0	31.1	− 1	2.0	0.007
ENIND	1,053.8	− 97.0	47.4	21.3	1,025.5	− 4		0.029
OTHIND	1,817.2	− 428.9	2,351.8	285.2	4,025.4	− 5	1,000.0	0.823

Appendix 5: the model

(a) Equation list

Production

$$a_{ij} = a_{ij}\left(\frac{pi_{ij}}{pij_{ik}}\right)^{\sigma_{ik}} aj_{ik} \qquad \text{(A1)} \quad j \in k \ \ k = mat, \ en, \ va$$

$$pij_{ik} = \left(\sum_{j \in k} a_{ij} pi_{ij}^{(1-\sigma_{ik})}\right)^{1/(1-\sigma_{ik})} \qquad \text{(A2)} \qquad k = mat, \ en, \ va$$

$$aj_{ik} = \left(\sum_{j \in k} a_{ij}^{\frac{1}{\sigma_{ik}}} a_{ij}^{\left(\frac{\sigma_{ik}-1}{\sigma_{ijk}}\right)}\right)^{\frac{\sigma_{ik}}{\sigma_{ik}-1}} \qquad \text{(A3)} \qquad k = mat, \ en, \ va$$

$$aj_{ik} = A_{ik}\left(\frac{pij_{ik}}{mc_i}\right)^{-\rho_i} \qquad \text{(A4)}$$

$$mc_i = \left(\sum_k A_{ik} pij_{ik}^{(1-\rho_i)}\right)^{\frac{1}{1-\rho_i}} \qquad \text{(A5)}$$

$$1 = \left(\sum_k A_{ik}^{\frac{1}{\rho_i}} a_j^{\left(\frac{\rho_i-1}{\rho_i}\right)}\right)^{\frac{\rho_i}{\rho_i-1}} \qquad \text{(A6)}$$

Factor markets

$$a_{i,land} * q_i = \overline{land}_i \qquad \text{(A7)} \qquad va$$

$$\sum_i a_{i,lab} * q_i = \overline{lab} \qquad \text{(A8)} \qquad va$$

$$pi_{i,lab} = wage \qquad \text{(A9)} \qquad va$$

Consumption

$$c_i = \gamma_i + \beta_i\left(m - \sum_l pc_l \gamma_l\right)/pc_i \qquad \text{(A10)} \qquad mat, \ en$$

Exports

$$x_i = X_i\left(\frac{px_i}{pwx_i}\right)^{ex_i} \qquad \text{(A11)} \qquad mat$$

$$x_i = \overline{x}_i \qquad \text{(A12)} \qquad en$$

Imports

$$m_i = ms_i * a_{oi} * q_o \qquad\qquad \text{(A13)} \qquad mat, en$$

where o denotes 'other industry'

$$ms_i = M_i \left(\frac{pm_i}{p_{oi}}\right)^{\varepsilon m_i} \qquad\qquad \text{(A14)} \qquad mat, en$$

Commodity balance

$$q_i = \sum_l q_l a_{li} + x_i + c_i - m_i \qquad\qquad \text{(A15)} \qquad mat, en$$

$$pcm_i = p_i + dc_i + tc_i \qquad\qquad \text{(A16)} \qquad mat, en$$

$$pc_i = (1 - cs_i) * pcm_i + cs_i * pci_i \qquad\qquad \text{(A17)} \qquad mat, en$$

$$pim_{ij} = p_j + di_{ij} + ti_j \qquad\qquad \text{(A18)} \qquad mat, en$$

$$pi_{ij} = (1 - \delta_{io} * ms_j) * [(1 - qs_{ij}) * pim_{ij} \\ + qs_{ij} * pii_{ij}] + \delta_{io} * ms_j * pm_j \qquad \text{(A19)} \qquad mat, en$$

$$px_i = p_i + dx_i + tx_i \qquad\qquad \text{(A20)} \qquad mat$$

$$px_i = \overline{px_i} \qquad\qquad \text{(A21)} \qquad en$$

$$pm_i = pwx_i + tm_i \qquad\qquad \text{(A22)} \qquad mat, en$$

$$v_{ij} = (1 - \delta_{io} * ms_j) * a_{ij} * q_i * [(1 - qa_{ij}) * pim_{ij} \\ + qa_{ij} * pii_{ij}] + \delta_{io} * m_j * pm_j \qquad \text{(A23)} \qquad mat, en$$

$$\sum_j v_{ij} + va_i + \delta_{io} * \sum_j m_j pm_j = \sum_l v_{li} - \widetilde{ti}_i \\ + [(p_i + dc_i) * (1 - ca_i) + ca_i * pci_i] * c_i \\ + (p_i + dx_i) x_i + trans_i + l_i \qquad \text{(A24)} \qquad mat, en$$

Balance of trade

$$\sum_i (x_i - m_i) pwx_i = \overline{kb} \qquad\qquad \text{(A25)}$$

Indirect taxes

$$it = \sum_i tx_i * x_i + \sum_i tm_i * m_i + \sum_i tc_i * (1 - ca_i) * c_i \\ + \sum_i \widetilde{ti}_i - \sum_i trans_i - \sum_i l_i \qquad \text{(A26)}$$

Aggregate effective income

$$m = wage * \overline{lab} + \sum_i pi_{i,land} * \overline{land}_i$$

$$+ it - kb + \sum_i (ca_i - cs_i) * (pcm_i - pc_i) * c_i \quad \text{(A27)}$$

Pollution

$$z_m = \sum_i q_i e_{mi} \quad \text{(A28)}$$

(b) Variable list
(* denotes exogenous variables, (*) exogenous for some industries)

a_{ij}	input–output coefficient of j into i
aj_{ik}	input–output coefficient of group k into i
pi_{ij}	marginal price of input–output flow i,j
pij_{ik}	marginal price of inputs of group k into i
mc_i	marginal cost
q_i	gross output
$wage$	wage
c_i	consumption
pc_i	marginal consumption price
m	'effective' income
x_i (*)	exports
px_i (*)	export price
pwx_i *	world price
m_i *	imports
ms_i	share of imports in inputs of i into 'other industry'
pm_i	import price
cs_i *	share of marginal consumption transactions made at state price
pcm_i	'market' consumption price
pci_i *	state consumption price
p_i	'indicator' price (see text)
dc_i *	consumer price wedge
tc_i *	consumption tax
px_i (*)	export price
dx_i *	export price wedge
tx_i *	export tax
tm_i *	import tax (tariff)
pi_{ij}	marginal price for flow of j into i
qs_{ij} *	share of marginal interindustry transactions made at state price
pim_{ij}	'market' price for flow of j into i
pii_{ij} *	state price for flow of j into i
di_{ij} *	industry price wedge
ti_i	industry tax

v_{ij} value of domestic industry flow of j into i

va_i value added in i

qa_{ij} *   share of all interindustry transactions made at state prices

δ_{io} *   Kronecker delta for $i =$ 'other industry'

$\widetilde{ti}_i$ total tax take on domestic interindustry flows of i

$$= ti_i * \sum_l q_l * a_{li} * (1 - qa_{li}) * (1 - \delta_{lo} ms_i)$$

ca_i *   share of all consumption taking place at state prices

$trans_i$ transfer from government to industry i

l_i *   lump-sum subsidy to i

$\overline{kb}$ *   capital balance on the balance of payments in foreign currency

it total net indirect tax revenue

z_m emissions of pollutant m

(c) Parameter list

a_{ij} CES constant for input j in aggregate k

σ_{ik} elasticity of substitution for inputs in aggregate k

A_{ik} CES constant for input aggregate k in upper level

ρ_i elasticity of substitution between aggregates at upper level

$\overline{land}_i$ fixed endowment of fixed factors for i

$\overline{lab}$ fixed endowment of labour

γ_i 'committed consumption' of i

β_i marginal income share of i

X_i constant for export function

ϵx_i elasticity of demand for exports

M_i constant for import function

ϵm_i elasticity of demand for import

e_{mi} emission coefficients, units of m per unit of i

NOTES

Research on this chapter was financed by the Economic and Social Research Council (contract Y320 25 3020). We are grateful to Joaquim Oliveira-Martins for providing us with input–output data, for help and comments from participants at the CSERGE seminar in London and at the OECD Development Centre and CEPR Conference, and from Ian Goldin, Nick Eyre, Huw Edwards, Sam Fankhauser, Katrin Millock, Stephen Newton, Ece Ozdemiroglou and Zhen Kun Wang, and to Kevin Ward for research assistance.

1 Attention focuses on carbon dioxide because, relative to other greenhouse gases, it is both the largest contributor to global warming in terms of emissions and because it takes longer to break down in the atmosphere (Nordhaus, 1991, table 1).

2 Burniaux *et al.* (1992) explores the effect of energy market distortions.

3 For example, flue gas desulphurisation removes over 90 percent of sulphur but

increases carbon dioxide emissions by approximately 5 percent, representing 2 percent increased energy consumption and 3 percent carbon in the resulting gypsum.

4 The Chinese figure reflects a high average agricultural loss. As the possible range of welfare change in this sector is wide – including the possibility that climatic effects will be beneficial – this estimate could vary from 2.6 to 9.6 percent of GNP (Fankhauser, 1992: 23).

5 The figures for sulphur dioxide may be even higher: Ross reports emissions of 18.5 million tons (1988: 134).

6 For example, in addition to contributing to global pollution, oxides of nitrogen interact with tropospheric ozone – with probable substantial health effects – and with sulphur dioxide in forming acid rain. SO_2, NO_x and ozone all cause respiratory problems, and NO_x and particulates are believed to cause cancer.

7 $(11,390.6 * £127,000)/26.0$ Mt particulates.

8 China announced that most coal will be sold at market prices from 1993. The China National Coal Corporation reported that some 57 percent of 1993 production would be sold at market prices compared with 20 percent in 1992 (*Financial Times*, 4 January 1993). This suggests that some coal from state mines will continue to be allocated centrally.

9 99 percent of extraction in the US is mechanical.

10 The exception was for coal where the OECD table underestimates total demand by $12 billion in their estimation and by $7 billion in ours.

11 State prices vary widely depending on quality and transport costs: from $10.5/toe for local raw coal to $48.65/toe for washed coal (World Bank, 1985, table 3.2, n. g).

12 Strictly we should consider marginal decisions at *either* state or market prices and combine the resulting quantities demanded, but with five fuels this would require 32 different sets of marginal conditions, so we use the short cut of applying average marginal prices to a single representative allocation exercise.

13 Besides it is peculiarly unhelpful to consider solutions to Chinese greenhouse gas emissions in terms of China exporting its crude oil and coal to be burned elsewhere.

14 Given the small share of imports, this is very nearly identical to the traditional CES import function.

15 The consumption wedges could, for example, be the 'tax equivalent' of quantitative rations – which clearly still persist in China, but which could not be satisfactorily incorporated into such a simple and aggregated model as this.

16 With energy inputs accounting for only about 4–5 percent of the gross value of output, these orders of magnitude are not surprising.

17 Prices for refined oil continue to differ between sectors, however, because different mixes of products are purchased by different sectors.

18 Welfare still falls relative to the base situation because trade taxes and restrictions still persist.

REFERENCES

Albouy, Y. (1991) 'Coal pricing in China: issues and reform strategy', World Bank, *Discussion Paper*, **138**, China and Mongolia Department Series, Washington, DC: World Bank

Asian Development Bank (1992) *Energy Indicators of Developing Member Countries of ADB*, Manila: Asian Development Bank

Boero, G., Clarke, R. and Winters, L.A. (1991) *The Macroeconomic Consequences of Controlling Greenhouse Gases: A Survey*, Department of the Environment, Environmental Economics Research Series, London, HMSO

Burniaux, J.-M. *et al.* (1992) *The Costs of Reducing CO_2 Emissions: Evidence from GREEN*, OECD, Working Paper, **115**, Paris: OECD

Byrd, W.A. (1987) 'The impact of the two-tier plan/market system in Chinese industry', *Journal of Comparative Economics*, 11: 295–308

Cao, Hongfa (1989) 'Air pollution and its effects on plants in China', *Journal of Applied Ecology*, **26**: 763–73

de Melo, J. and Tarr, D. (1992) *A General Equilibrium Analysis of US Foreign Trade Policy*, Cambridge, MA: MIT Press

Edmonds, R.L. (1991) *China's Environment: Problems and Prospects*, paper presented at University of Keele (17 December)

Energy Statistics Yearbook of China 1991 (1991) Beijing: Chinese Statistics Bureau

Fankhauser, S. (1992) *Global Warming Damage Costs: Some Monetary Estimates*, CSERGE, *Working Paper*, GEC 92–29, London: CSERGE

—— (1993) *Evaluating the Social Costs of Greenhouse Gas Emissions*, Draft CSERGE GEC, *Working Paper*, 93– (May), London: CSERGE

Gillham, C.A., Leech, P.K. and Eggleston, H.S. (1992) *UK Emissions of Air Pollutants 1970–1990*, National Atmospheric Emissions Inventory, *LLR 887 (AP)*, London: Department of the Environment

Glomsrød, S., Vennemo, H. and Johnsen, T. (1992) 'Stabilization of emissions of CO_2: a computable general equilibrium assessment', *Scandinavian Journal of Economics*, **92(1)**: 53–69

Grubb, M. *et al.* (1991) *Energy Policies and the Greenhouse Effect*, vol. 2, Dartmouth: The Royal Institute of International Affairs

Guo, J.-J. (1992) *Price Reform in China, 1979–86*, New York: St Martin's Press

Hull, T.H. (1991) 'China's population in the eighties', in Jiye Wang and Terrence H. Hull (eds.), *Population and Development Planning in China*, North Sydney: Allen & Unwin

Hulme, M. *et al.* (1992) *Climate Change due to the Greenhouse Effect and its Implications for China*, *WWF Report*, Gland, Switzerland

International Energy Agency (IEA) (1992) *Climate Change and Policy Initiatives*, Paris: OECD

—— (1992b) *Energy Statistics and Balances of Non-OECD Countries 1989–1990*, Paris: OECD/IEA

Jackson, S. (1992) *Chinese Enterprise Management Reforms in Economic Perspective*, Berlin and New York: Walter de Gruyter

Kinzelbach, W.K.H. (1987) 'Energy and environment in China', in Bernard Glaeser (ed.), *Learning From China? Development and Environment in Third World Countries*, London: Allen & Unwin

Kosmo, M. (1987) *Money to Burn? The High Costs of Energy Subsidies*, Washington, DC: World Resource Institute

Lardy, N.R. (1992) *Foreign Trade and Economic Reform in China, 1978–1990*, Cambridge: Cambridge University Press

McMillan, J. and Naughton, B. (1992) 'How to reform a planned economy: lessons from China', *Oxford Review of Economic Policy*, **8(1)**: 130–43

Mumford, J.L.K. *et al.* (1987) 'Lung cancer and indoor air pollution in Xuan Wei, China', *Science*, **235**: 217–20

Nordhaus, W.D. (1991) 'To slow or not to slow: the economics of the greenhouse effect', *Economic Journal*, **101**: 920–37

Pearce, D.W. (1992) *The Secondary Benefits of Greenhouse Gas Control*, CSERGE, *Working Paper*, **92–12**, London: CSERGE

Ross, L. (1988) *Environmental Policy in China*, Bloomington and Indianapolis: Indiana University Press

Shah, A. and Larsen, B. (1992) *Carbon Taxes, the Greenhouse Effect and Developing Countries*, World Development Report 1992, Background Paper, **6**, Washington, DC: World Bank

Smil, V. (1988) *Energy in China's Modernization: Advances and Limitations*, Armonk, NY: M.E. Sharpe

Smith, K. (1988) 'Air pollution: assessing total exposure in developing countries', *Environment*, **30(10)**: 16–35

Taplin, J.H.E. (1993) 'Economic reform and transport policy in China', *Journal of Transport Economics and Policy*, **27(1)**: 75–86

Winters, L.A. (1992) 'Integration, trade policy and European footwear trade', ch. 7 in L.A. Winters (ed.), *Trade Flows and Trade Policy After "1992"*, Cambridge: Cambridge University Press: 175–209

Winters, L.A. and Wang, Z.K. (1993) *Eastern Europe's International Trade*, Manchester: Manchester University Press, forthcoming

World Bank (1985) *China: The Energy Sector*, Annex 3 to *China: Long-Term Development Issues and Options*, Washington, DC: World Bank

   (1992) *World Development Report 1992: Development and the Environment*, Washington, DC: World Bank

World Resources Institute (1990) *World Resources 1990–91*, New York and London: Oxford University Press

   (1992) *World Resources, 1992–93*, New York and London: Oxford University Press

Xuan, Z. (1993) *Environmentally Sound Coal Technologies and China*, paper presented at Economic and Social Commission for Asia and the Pacific, Regional Workshop, Bangkok (7–10 April)

Zhao, D. and Xiong, J. (1988) 'Acidification in Southwestern China', in H. Rodhe and R. Herrer (eds.), *Acidification in Tropical Countries*, 1988 SCOPE, New York: John Wiley

Discussion

ATHAR HUSSAIN

With its huge population and rapid economic growth in recent years, China raises special concern about its impact on global warming. This concern is further heightened by the fact that China is a very inefficient, as well as being the largest, user of coal. Its emission of grams of carbon per dollar of GNP is many times that for any country, though *per capita* emission still remains very small compared to those in developed economies (Whalley and Wigle, 1991). Clarke and Winters' chapter 8 is the first systematic attempt to deal with the important policy issue of how China might lower its air pollution. Although 'sustainable development' appears in the chapter's title, the analytical framework of the chapter is static, focused on the impact of one-shot fuel price rationalisation and carbon taxation. The chapter has three main messages:

1. The cost of CO_2 abatement in China appears to be low and possibly negative if secondary benefits of abatement are taken into account.
2. The removal of distortion in energy prices seems to yield relatively small benefits.
3. Carbon taxation has substantial benefits and should be the central component of environmental and energy policy in China.

These conclusions, as Clarke and Winters emphasise, are based on slender and uncertain evidence. The conclusion that a carbon tax would be the central component of environmental policy is perhaps not surprising given that reducing carbon emission is taken to be the policy aim and price rationalisation and a carbon tax are the only policy instruments that are considered. To broaden the discussion of the pattern of energy consumption and its impact on the environment, I focus on two questions:

1. Are there policies which, in the short run, merit priority over an energy tax?
2. Accepting the reduction of atmospheric pollution to be the aim, is carbon emission the appropriate policy target?

Much of my Discussion will concentrate on quantitative restrictions which the authors mention but do not incorporate into their analysis. Such restrictions are still pervasive and have a significant impact on the scale and composition of energy consumption in China. To bring out their importance, let me draw attention to the following two features of primary energy consumption in China over the reform period (1978–92) (both based on TJN, 1993):

−   From 1978–92, while national income at constant prices grew by around 9 percent per year, energy consumption (measured in terms of coal tons) rose by only 5 percent, which gives an income elasticity of 0.6.
−   The share of coal amongst primary energy sources (others being oil, hydro-electricity and natural gas) has increased steadily, and stood at 75 in 1992.

The income elasticity of consumption of primary energy is surprisingly low by international standards and does not fit in with the low prices of fuel, which is singled out for emphasis in the chapter and much of the literature on China. It raises the obvious question 'why?'. There are three possible explanations, which are not mutually exclusive. First, the growth of energy consumption is underestimated relative to the growth of national income. Second, the consumption of energy per unit of GNP has fallen due to increased efficiency in energy use or a shift in structure of GNP away from energy intensive sectors. Third, quantitative restrictions have kept consumption from rising as it otherwise would have. The first is plausible given price distortions and the growth of nonstate owned and household coal mining in the North-West, which is likely to be underestimated. The second is discussed in detail in Lin (1992), which concludes that efficiency in energy use has risen over the 1980s. But the low income elasticity would also seem to be due to numerous quantitative restrictions:

- Coal and petroleum products are not always available even at higher nonplan prices; quantity rationing in the margin has been more or less a permanent feature since 1978.
- Planned and unplanned electricity outages are a commonplace and households are usually supplied low amperage electricity to discourage the use of household electrical appliances. The countryside, where most of the Chinese population lives, has a limited supply of electricity.
- Space heating of public buildings in winter is banned south of the Yangtze, even though average winter temperature can be lower than that in South-East England, and only allowed for a limited period of the year north of the river.
- International trade in energy is controlled by the central government and national self-sufficiency in energy has until now been the policy, which limits the use of oil and natural gas.

Drawing on the analysis of rationing by Neary and Roberts (1980), these quantitative restrictions are equivalent to an 'implicit' energy tax levied at rates varying with the use and the fuel. Given multiple prices and the coexistence of administrative and market allocations, the schedule of the 'implicit' energy tax is complicated. Generally speaking, households face a higher 'implicit' tax than industrial users and oil and natural gas are taxed at a higher rate than coal (see below). An analysis of the impact of carbon taxation without the consideration of quantitative restriction begs the question of what is being assumed about them. The impact of the tax will be very different depending on whether these restrictions remain or disappear. In their calculations, Clarke and Winters assume that supply and demand is equated by the higher nonplan price, and the lower plan price acts like a proportional intramarginal subsidy to all users. As it were, the nonplan price is equivalent to the 'virtual price' (Neary and Roberts, 1980) – i.e. the price at which unrationed demand will be the same as the rationed demand. And the lower plan price is not associated with the preferential allocation of energy to some users; in fact, the price at the margin varies and many of the profligate users of energy per unit of value added, such as heavy industry, may face a lower price. In sum, in China there is both an 'implicit' price subsidy on intramarginal units and also an 'implicit' tax on marginal units due to quantitative restrictions.

A discussion of energy taxation makes little sense without the abolition of lower plan prices and also in time the quantitative restrictions. The abolition of multiple prices and the conversion of the implicit tax into an explicit tax should have priority over the introduction of a carbon tax, and is a 'no-regrets' policy in the sense that it would lead to a more efficient allocation of energy to various uses.

Turning to the composition of primary energy sources, the high share of coal and its steady rise since 1978 is not all due to the low coal price but also to quantitative restrictions. For example, the use of oil for power generation is subject to strict administrative control and is banned in most cases. This is on top of a special tax on fuel oil levied on enterprises at varying rates (STB, 1993). Moreover, the share of natural gas is very low (around 2 percent) because the domestic output has been low and reliance on imports has been ruled out; it does not seem to be due to the high price of natural gas relative to coal. There are strong reasons to believe that the removal of restrictions on international trade in energy alone would lead to a large switch in favour of natural gas and oil for heating and electricity generation, especially in the coastal region, and thus have a significant impact on atmospheric pollution without any energy tax. The coastal region depends heavily on coal mined in the North-West and transported over a long distance on a severely congested railway network. Thus, besides a rationalisation of domestic energy prices and removal of quantitative controls, a relaxation of restrictions on energy imports is another 'no-regrets policy'. China's international trade regime is not as immutable as Clarke and Winters believe; it has already undergone a massive change in recent years and a further removal of quantitative restrictions is planned as part of China's drive to rejoin GATT.

As pointed out by Clarke and Winters and emphasised in a number of studies, the conversion ratio of coal into energy in China is low and coal burning is associated with a large discharge of particulates. This is not due simply to pricing, but also to technology, including the treatment of mined coal before burning. The argument that technology choice is influenced by the price does not apply to China in the same way as it does in a market economy. Much of the capital stock relevant to energy use embodies technology which was initially borrowed from the former Soviet Union and locally developed. Restrictions on imported technology still remain, though they are much weaker than in the prereform period. The argument is that low price alone has not been responsible for the technology choice and thus for the air pollution associated with it. A carbon tax will facilitate a switch to best-practice technology, but it is neither the only nor the most effective means of achieving the aim. A carbon tax would encourage a higher conversion ratio of coal into useable energy, but not necessarily a reduction of particulates and secondary emissions, which are of immediate concern. What is also needed is a set of policies which have a direct impact on technology embodied in the new capital stock and the speed of replacement of the old capital stock, such as a subsidy on investment embodying cleaner technology. An upgrading of coal boilers and the washing of coal before use would seem to be far more relevant than a carbon tax.

Turning to the wider issue of targeting carbon emissions, the risk of global warming lies far into the future. Its timing and economic impact are surrounded with uncertainty. The economic consequences of global warming for China mentioned in the chapter are little more than speculations, and provide a slender basis for a policy which imposes costs now in return for benefits in the distant future. However, as documented by Clarke and Winters, air pollution associated with the use of energy is already a serious problem in China and increasingly perceived as such by the Chinese leadership. But air pollution with an adverse impact now and carbon emissions are not perfectly correlated, and the indices of atmospheric pollution which Clarke and Winters mention raise the issue of what should be the target of China's environmental and energy policy. The chapter assumes this to be carbon emissions, but the grounds for targeting particulates, SO_2 and other gases appear to be far stronger. The switch in the policy target opens up the issue of relevant policies. An energy tax would still remain an important policy, though not the only policy, but there is no reason for such a tax to be based on carbon content or emissions.

I turn finally to the data and information on which the chapter is based. China is not as much of *terra incognita* as may be imagined. Information on China is not merely available from Western sources and international agencies; the Chinese authorities publish a huge amount of statistics, a fair amount of which are in English and the ones in Chinese are useable after the translation of headings into English, which needs no more than a few hours of research assistance by a Chinese student. Apart from a mention of the *Energy Statistics Yearbook of China 1991*, the chapter is marked by an absence of references to Chinese material, including the widely available *Statistical Yearbook of China*. Had Clarke and Winters consulted it, they would have discovered that domestic use accounts for 15 percent of coal use (TJN, 1993: 479) not 24 percent as in the chapter. By not consulting Chinese material, Clarke and Winters have unfortunately reduced the value added of their effort. They rely on the input–output table for 1983 even though the 117-sector table for 1987 has been available since 1991, and the use of the table would have avoided some of the arbitrary assumptions in the chapter.

NOTE

This discussion draws on research work on 'Public Finance in Transitional Economies: China and Poland', supported by ESRC (Grant No. R000 23 3425).

REFERENCES

Energy Statistics Yearbook of China 1991 (1991) Beijing: State Statistical Bureau
Lin, X. (1992) 'Declining energy intensity in China's industrial sector', *The Journal of Energy and Development*, **16(2)**: 195–218
Neary, P. and Roberts K. (1980) 'The theory of household behaviour under rationing', *European Economic Review*, **13**: 25–42
STB (State Tax Bureau) (1993) *Current Taxation System in the PRC*, Beijing: State Tax Bureau, mimeo
TJN (1993) *Tongji Nianjian 1993 (Statistical Yearbook of China 1993)*, Beijing: State Statistical Bureau
Whalley, J. and Wigle, R. (1991) 'The international incidence of carbon taxes', in R. Dornbusch and J. Poterba (eds.), *Global Warming: Economic Policy Response*, Cambridge MA: MIT Press

Part Four
International policy coordination

9 Carbon abatement, transfers and energy efficiency

JEAN-MARC BURNIAUX, JOHN
P. MARTIN, JOAQUIM
OLIVEIRA-MARTINS and DOMINIQUE
VAN DER MENSBRUGGHE

1 Introduction

The concept of 'sustainable growth' is rather fuzzy but, as many of the chapters in this volume have emphasised, it involves a concern with the earth's environmental resources. The earth's atmosphere is one important example of such a resource. In recent years, there has been a growing awareness of the potential threat to the atmosphere posed by global warming. The phenomenon of global warming is associated with the accumulation in the atmosphere of so-called 'greenhouse gases', of which carbon dioxide (CO_2) is the most important man-made gas. While there is great uncertainty about the likelihood of global warming, the risk is now being taken seriously, as evidenced by the fact that many OECD countries are promulgating targets for curbing their emissions of greenhouse gases, with a particular focus on CO_2.

Previous work[1] with the OECD GREEN model has shown that an international agreement involving all the major CO_2 emitting countries is necessary to tackle the problem of climate change. However, devising an international agreement and developing strategies for its implementation and enforcement are likely to prove daunting tasks. For example, it would be highly desirable for any agreement to be cost-effective. But in order for any agreement to be cost-effective, CO_2 abatement must be undertaken by both OECD *and* nonOECD countries, with the largest burden being borne by the coal intensive low income lesser developed countries (LDCs) such as China and India (see chapter 8 in this volume). Thus, a key question for policy makers is: how can one design a cost-effective and equitable international agreement which could commit all the key CO_2 emitting countries to curb their emissions?

One possible avenue to achieve such an agreement could be the creation of an international market for tradeable emission permits. Under certain conditions, this would produce a least-cost allocation of emission curbs across countries, and the revenues raised from selling permits could serve to compensate the losers. But this raises the crucial problem of the initial allocation of permits across countries and how this could be varied over time in such a way as to ensure adequate compensation for the losers among the LDCs.

Another possible avenue was followed by the Framework Convention on Climate Change which was approved at the Earth Summit in Rio de Janeiro in June 1992. This treaty endorsed the principle of *joint implementation*. This implies that the OECD countries should compensate for the carbon abatement costs incurred by LDCs by providing them with 'new and additional resources'. In addition, it has been argued that the OECD countries should engage in technology transfers to the nonOECD countries, with a view to raising their energy efficiency.

This chapter will use GREEN to explore this second avenue by simulating the impact of a direct transfer mechanism between the OECD and the nonOECD countries. This financial transfer will be tied to new investment in order to promote energy efficiency in the LDCs; in this way it can be regarded as a proxy for technology transfers. The aim will be to assess the potential scope for curbing CO_2 emissions via such technology transfers. Several scenarios will be presented to highlight different aspects and likely consequences of this policy action, with a special emphasis on issues related to energy efficiency.

2   Brief overview of GREEN

The key dimensions of GREEN, a multi-country, multi-sector, dynamic applied general equilibrium (AGE) model, are set out in table 9.1. The current version of the model runs over a 65-year time horizon from 1985 to 2050, using time intervals of five years between 1985 and 2010 and 20 years thereafter. It consists of 12 *regional* sub-models: for OECD regions – US, Japan, EC and Other OECD – and eight nonOECD regions – the former USSR, the Central and Eastern European Countries (CEECs), China, India, the Energy exporting LDCs, the Dynamic Asian Economies (DARs), Brazil and the Rest of the World (ROW). The remainder of this section outlines briefly the model structure.[2]

2.1   Supply and demand

There are 11 producing sectors in GREEN. 8 sectors cover the supply and distribution of energy: coalmining, crude oil, natural gas, refined oil, electricity, gas and water distribution[3] and three back-stop technologies. Three back-stop alternative energies (i.e. available in infinitely elastic

Table 9.1. *Key dimensions of the GREEN model*

Producer sectors	Consumer sectors
(1) Agriculture	(1) Food, beverages and tobacco
(2) Coalmining	(2) Fuels and power
(3) Crude oil	(3) Transport and communication
(4) Natural gas	(4) Other goods and services
(5) Refined oil	
(6) Electricity, gas and water distribution	
(7) Energy intensive industries	
(8) Other industries and services	
(9) Carbon-based back-stop (coal, oil and gas)	
(10) Carbon-free back-stop (coal, oil and gas)	
(11) Carbon-free electric back-stop	

Regions	Primary factors[a]
(1) United States	(1) Labour [1]
(2) Japan	(2) Sector specific 'old capital' [8]
(3) EC	(3) 'New' capital [1]
(4) Other OECD[b]	(4) Sector specific fixed factors for coal, crude oil and gas [3]
(5) Energy exporting developing countries[c]	(5) Carbon-free fixed factor for electricity [1]
(6) China	(6) Land in agriculture [1]
(7) The former USSR	
(8) India	
(9) Central and Eastern Europe countries (CEECs)[d]	
(10) Dynamic Asian Economies[e]	
(11) Brazil	
(12) Rest of the World (ROW)	

Notes:
[a] Figures in [brackets] represent the number of each primary factor in each regional sub-model.
[b] This grouping excludes Iceland and Switzerland.
[c] This grouping includes the OPEC countries as well as other oil exporting, gas exporting and coal exporting countries.
[d] Bulgaria, Czech and Slovak Federal Republic, Hungary, Poland, Romania and former Yugoslavia.
[e] Hong Kong, Philippines, Singapore, South Korea, Taiwan and Thailand.

supply and at a given price) – a carbon-based back-stop, a carbon-free back-stop and a carbon-free electric back-stop – are assumed to come on stream in all regions by the year 2010. The remaining sectors are broad aggregates: agriculture, energy intensive industries and other industries and services.

All sectors are assumed to operate under constant returns to scale and cost optimisation. Production technology is modelled mainly by a nesting of constant-elasticity-of-substitution (CES) functions (see figure 9.1). There are a few exceptions to the CES nesting: all inputs are assumed to be used in fixed proportions in the production of fossil fuels (coal, crude oil, natural gas), petroleum products and the back-stop technologies.

In each period, the supply of primary factors listed in table 9.1 is usually predetermined. However, supplies of agricultural land, the carbon-free electric resource (nuclear, hydro and geothermal), oil, natural gas and coal are all assumed to be sensitive to their contemporaneous prices.

Coal and gas prices are determined by the supply elasticity of their respective fixed factor. The real world price of crude oil is endogenous in GREEN.[4] This is implemented by introducing a supply equation for oil in the energy exporting LDCs. All other oil producers are assumed to be price-takers.

The prices of back-stop technologies are exogenous and identical in all regions; they were taken from the Stanford-based Energy Modeling Forum Study no. 12 (EMF 12) entitled 'Global Climate Change: Energy Sector Impacts of Greenhouse Gas Emission Control Strategies'.[5] By definition, back-stop technologies, once they come on stream, are available in all regions in unlimited quantities at constant marginal costs (see Manne and Richels, 1992). As a consequence, this rules out any incentive to trade in 'new' energy sources between regions.

A single representative consumer is assumed to allocate optimally his disposable income among the four broad consumer goods (food and beverages, fuel and power, transport and communication and other goods and services) and saving. The consumption/saving decision is completely static: saving is treated as a 'good' and its amount is determined simultaneously with the demands for the other goods, the price of saving being set arbitrarily equal to the average price of consumer goods.[6]

The government collects carbon or energy taxes, income taxes and indirect taxes on intermediate inputs, outputs and consumer expenditures. Carbon tax revenues are recycled to households by assuming revenue-neutrality: the tax-induced changes in the government budget are automatically compensated by changes in marginal income tax rates. Government expenditures are exogenous in real terms, growing at the same rate as GDP.

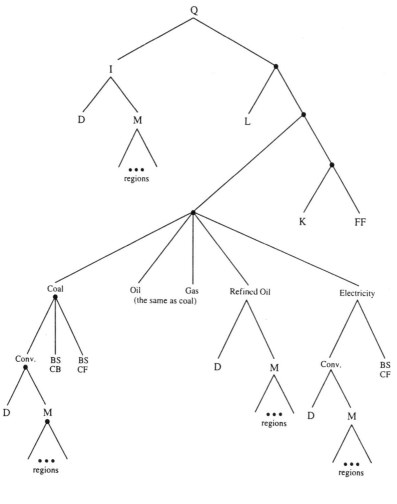

I: Intermediate Inputs   M: Imported
L: Labour   C: Conventional source
K: Capital   BS/CB:Carbon-Based Back Stop
FF: Specified Fixed Factor   BS/CF: Carbon-Free Back Stop
D: Domestic

Figure 9.1   Production functions of GREEN

Each region runs a current account surplus (deficit) which is fixed in nominal terms. The counterpart of these imbalances is a net outflow (inflow) of capital, which is subtracted from (added to) the domestic flow of saving. In each period, the model equates gross investment to net saving (equal to the sum of saving by households, the net budget position of the government and foreign capital inflows). This particular closure rule implies that investment is driven by saving.

The basic assumption with regard to trade flows between regions is that imports originating in different regions are imperfect substitutes. This specification of imports – called the Armington specification – implies that each region faces downward-sloping demand curves for its exports. This specification is implemented for all goods except crude oil, which is assumed to be a homogeneous commodity across regions, implying a unique world oil price.

2.2   Dynamics, technical progress and energy efficiency

GREEN has a simple recursive dynamic structure as agents are assumed to be myopic, basing their decisions on static expectations about prices and quantities. Model dynamics originate from two sources: (i) depletion of fossil fuel resources; and (ii) accumulation of productive capital.

In GREEN, time is treated through a sequence of static equilibria. Given the myopic nature of expectations, there is no unique balanced growth path along which the model runs from base to terminal years depending on the values of its parameters, as would be the case with a fully intertemporal model. This does not mean that economic growth in GREEN is a purely exogenous process; in fact, it combines endogenous stock dynamics – capital stock accumulation and exhaustion of fossil fuel reserves – with exogenously defined technical parameters, such as the rates of labour and capital-augmenting technical progress and the rates of Autonomous Energy Efficiency Improvement (AEEI). The rest of this section describes how these coefficients intervene in the vintage structure of the model.

The production structure of GREEN assumes a putty/semi-putty technology: technologies associated with new and preexisting capital vintages are characterised by different levels of substitutability among inputs.[7] At the first level, various energies are combined into a composite energy bundle, given an exogenous productivity index (the AEEI coefficients). At the second level, the composite energy good is aggregated with capital expressed in efficiency units given the rate of capital-augmenting technical progress. Output is then produced by the composite 'energy–capital' good and labour expressed in efficiency units given the rate of labour-augmenting technical progress.

When corresponding factor demand functions are derived, it can be shown that the exogenous technical progress parameters serve to lower the producer price of the nonenergy good and to raise real income (see the appendix on p. 260). The rates of labour and capital-augmenting technical progress also serve to calibrate the Business-as-Usual (BaU) scenario along a balanced growth path: this requires that the BaU scenario reproduces GDP growth targets for each region, with the labour-to-capital ratio (in efficiency units) constant over time.[8] In counterfactual scenarios, these indices are held constant and GDP varies endogenously in line with alternative paths of capital accumulation (and exhaustion of reserves in the case of industries extracting fossil fuels).

By affecting the aggregate demand for energy, the AEEI parameter plays a crucial role in GREEN as it does in the majority of other models which address the climate change issue. But there is much controversy in the literature about the likely magnitude of the AEEI.[9] In the standard specification of GREEN, energy productivity indices for old and new capital vintages are given equal values, and it is also assumed that the AEEI is the same across regions. However, these assumptions may be too pessimistic since one might expect new capital to be more energy efficient especially when there is a stated policy priority to improve energy efficiency. It also seems plausible that there may be some form of technological 'catch-up'. This would imply that countries with low energy efficiency could benefit from higher AEEI growth than countries with relatively high energy efficiency. In this chapter we explore the possibility that a multilateral agreement involving capital transfers from OECD countries to the LDCs could lead to an increase of the AEEI in the developing regions.

3   The role of the AEEI parameter in the BaU scenario

3.1   The BaU scenario

Given a set of assumptions about population, GDP *per capita* and oil and gas reserves,[10] the model simulates a BaU scenario where no actions are taken to restrain CO_2 emissions. In this reference case, global carbon emissions are projected to grow at an annual average rate of around 2 percent a year: the level of world emissions increases from 5.3 billion tons of carbon in 1985 to 21.5 billion tons in 2050.

The BaU scenario highlights a major shift in the projected distribution of world emissions. The OECD countries' share of global emissions is roughly halved between 1985 and 2050. On the other hand, China's share of global emissions increases from 9.5 percent in 1985 to 25.5 percent in 2050, and India's share increases from 2.4 to almost 8 percent (table 9.2). The breakdown by fuels shows that coal burning is the main energy source in these two countries; this partly explains why the share of coal in world primary energy demand is projected to almost double between 1985 and 2050.

The counterpart of larger reliance on coal at the world level is a marked decline in crude oil consumption. This fuel switch occurs in response to increasing real oil prices generated by the depletion of oil reserves which becomes binding after 2030.[11] Because world coal reserves are virtually infinite, the supply of coal is very elastic and the increase in real oil prices translates into a large shock in relative energy prices, shifting demand towards coal.

3.2   Impact of different values of the AEEI parameter

The AEEI coefficient plays an important role in the BaU scenario, because, given compounding, it induces a large energy conservation effect in the long run. In order to test the sensitivity of the BaU scenario with respect to this parameter, we ran two scenarios: in the first, the AEEI in intermediate and final demand was set equal to 0.5; in the second, both the AEEI in intermediate and final demand was raised to 2 per cent per year.

Figure 9.2 shows the impact of these alternative specifications on world emissions. The results illustrate the key role of the AEEI parameter. The level of global carbon emissions in the year 2050 varies across scenarios from 16 to 24 billion tons. The straight line in figure 9.2 represents the level of 7 billion tons of carbon emissions annually, roughly the target announced by the 1988 Toronto Conference on Climate Change. According to the IPCC (1990), this level of global emissions could serve to stabilise climate change by the middle of the next century.

We used GREEN to simulate the value of AEEI necessary to stabilise global emissions at 7 billion tons by the year 2010. This required a common value of AEEI in all regions of 3.5 percent in 2010, rising to 6.8 percent in 2050. A striking result with this counterfactual simulation is that the required growth of AEEI is much larger than the growth rate of emissions in the BaU scenario (around 2 percent per annum). The reason for this apparent counterintuitive result is related to the link between technical progress, output prices and real income. Indeed, as shown in the appendix, the rise in energy productivity tends to lower the relative price of energy, thereby generating a substitution effect from nonenergy towards energy goods. In the aggregate the increase in autonomous energy efficiency also generates a real income gain that leads to higher consumption of both energy and nonenergy goods. The net result is that emissions do not decrease in the same proportion as the AEEI increase because the energy conservation effect is partly compensated by the relative price and income effects.

Table 9.2. *World carbon emissions by region and type of fuel, BaU scenario (% of world emissions)*

Year 1985	USA	Japan	EEC	Other OECD	Energy-exp. LDCs	China	Former USSR	India	CEECs	DAEs	Brazil	ROW	Total
Coal	8.4	1.5	4.7	1.7	1.5	8.2	6.8	1.8	4.1	0.7	0.2	2.5	42.0
Crude oil	11.4	3.0	7.5	2.6	4.5	1.2	5.9	0.6	1.2	1.1	0.7	2.5	42.2
Natural gas	4.5	0.4	2.2	0.8	1.3	0.1	5.1	0.0	0.8	0.0	0.0	0.4	15.8
Back-stop synthetic fuels	0.0	0.0	0.0	0.0	0.0	0.0	0.0	0.0	0.0	0.0	0.0	0.0	0.0
Total	24.3	5.0	14.4	5.1	7.3	9.5	17.7	2.4	6.1	1.9	0.9	5.4	100.1

Year 2050	USA	Japan	EEC	Other OECD	Energy-exp. LDCs	China	Former USSR	India	CEECs	DAEs	Brazil	ROW	Total
Coal	5.7	1.7	2.5	1.3	2.6	23.1	11.1	7.4	4.2	1.2	0.2	3.1	64.1
Crude oil	1.2	0.5	0.7	0.5	3.2	0.1	1.1	0.6	0.4	0.7	0.9	0.4	10.4
Natural gas	1.4	0.3	1.3	0.4	2.9	0.2	1.6	0.0	0.4	0.1	0.1	0.5	9.2
Back-stop synthetic fuels	4.2	2.1	2.6	0.6	0.6	2.0	0.0	0.0	0.1	1.0	0.9	2.2	16.3
Total	12.6	4.5	7.0	2.8	9.3	25.5	13.8	8.1	5.1	2.9	2.1	6.2	100.0

Note:
Memorandum items:
World carbon emissions in 1985 = 5,254 million tons of carbon.
World carbon emissions in 2050 = 21,517 million tons of carbon.

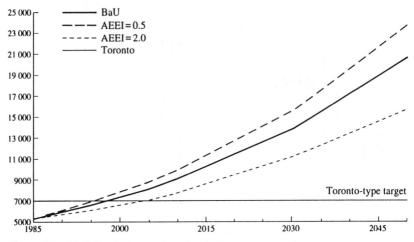

Figure 9.2   World emissions under alternative AEEI assumptions, 1985–2050 (million tons of carbon)

4   Energy productivity and catch-up

4.1   Energy productivity trends

A comparison of the levels of energy input per unit of GDP, as computed from the GREEN data base, reveals a wide dispersion across the regions. Figure 9.3 shows the ratio between GDP and Total Primary Energy (TPE) consumption in the BaU scenario. Japan has the highest level of energy efficiency in 1990 with around $95,000 of GDP per TeraJoule of TPE, followed closely by the DAEs. The other OECD regions have approximately 70 percent of Japanese levels.[12] The low income, coal intensive LDCs – like China and India – and the former USSR are in the lower part of the chart, with energy produtivity levels almost five times lower than Japan. There is some degree of 'catch-up' in the GREEN BaU scenario, but this is mainly confined to the DAEs and Brazil. This convergence process is driven by price mechanisms, given that all regions are assumed to have the same AEEI of 1 percent per year in all periods.

The above patterns of energy productivity can be used as a basis for designing a counterfactual scenario where an action is taken at the international level to reduce global emissions by increasing the rate of energy technological catchup in the energy intensive nonOECD regions. A very rough calculation enables one to derive the required rate of AEEI increase in the nonOECD regions which would enable them to reach the level of energy productivity in Japan at a certain point in time, say 2030.

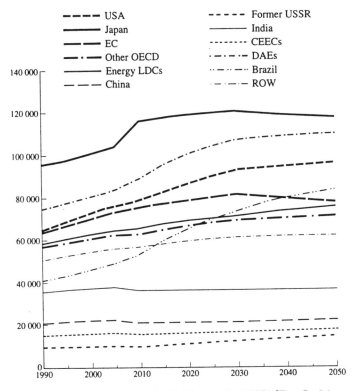

Figure 9.3   Energy production levels, BaU scenario (1985$/TeraJoule)

The level of energy productivity in Japan is projected in GREEN to be around $120,000 (at constant 1985 prices) per TeraJoule by the year 2030. The average level of energy productivity in the energy intensive nonOECD regions is around $20,000 per TeraJoule, i.e. six times lower. Given this gap, a technological catch-up process over the period up to 2030 would require an average AEEI of 4.1 percent per year in these regions.

4.2   Establishing a link between transfers and energy efficiency

The next step is to link the increase of the AEEI to international action aiming to target an improvement of energy efficiency in the nonOECD regions. According to the Rio Framework Convention, the principle of 'joint implementation'[13] of a carbon restriction in all regions could take the form of the OECD regions transferring part of their carbon tax revenues to the nonOECD regions.

Along these lines, let us suppose that the revenues of a carbon tax imposed in OECD regions alone are recycled towards investment in the nonOECD regions, with the explicit aim of raising energy efficiency in the latter. The problem now is how to link the level of transfers with the improvement of energy efficiency. In this chapter we adopt a pragmatic approach by assuming that there is a function relating the share of foreign transfers in total investment to the AEEI of the following form:

$$\lambda_E = f(\text{Transfers/Investment}), \quad \text{with } f' > 0, \text{ and } f'' < 0 \qquad (1)$$

where λ_E is the annual rate of AEEI. This function is calibrated in such a way that, if the ratio Transfers/Investment is zero (i.e. no Transfers), then λ_E is equal to 1 percent and there is no change in the exogenous rate of technical progress relative to the BaU scenario. Conversely, if the ratio Transfers/Investment is equal to 1 (i.e. all domestic investment is financed by foreign capital), the economy will tend to catch-up at the rate of AEEI required for complete convergence to the level of energy productivity in Japan. The negative second derivative reflects the assumption of the marginal decreasing return to transfers in terms of increasing the AEEI.

We experimented with several functional forms and parameterisation of $f(.)$ and we finally opted for a logistic-type function which corresponds to one of the most optimstic scenarios of catch-up. Accordingly, $f(.)$ is defined as follows:

$$\lambda_E = \frac{\bar{\lambda}_E}{1 + (\bar{\lambda}_E - 1).exp(-a.(T/I))} \qquad (2)$$

where T, I, are respectively Transfers and Investment and $\bar{\lambda}_E$ the required catch-up rate defined above. In the simulations presented here, $\bar{\lambda}_E$ is equal to 4.1 percent per year and the parameter a of the logistic function was set to 5. Of course, none of these assumptions is written in stone and can be changed. Nonetheless, the results which emerge from the simulations are rather robust *vis-à-vis* alternative specifications.

5   Two scenarios of international recycling of carbon tax revenues

We simulated a scenario of international recycling of carbon tax revenues corresponding to the imposition by OECD regions of an equivalent $10 per barrel carbon tax (approx. $80 per ton of carbon).[14] This tax is then recycled towards nonOECD regions to the extent of 80 percent of its revenue. The share of each donor region corresponds roughly to a balanced rule within the OECD group, with the US and Japan accounting for equal shares of 25 percent, the EC 30 percent and the Other OECD 20 percent, whereas the recipient shares of receiving regions are allocated according to their emissions in the BaU scenario.

The choice of BaU emissions as reference for the shares of the recipient regions implies that there is a shift in the respective shares of China, India and the former USSR. This leads to an increasing flow of transfers towards the countries which are projected to be the major CO_2 emitters at the horizon of 2050. For example, China and the former USSR are assumed to receive, respectively, 26 and 38 percent of total transfers by 2000. These shares are reversed by 2050.

Table 9.3 gives the summary results of this simulation. The imposition of a carbon tax in OECD regions leads to a 42 percent reduction in OECD emissions relative to the BaU by 2050. In the same year, GDP and household real income decrease by 1.5 and 3.6 percent, respectively. Income losses are particularly large because, given the closure rule of the model, the transfers correspond to a flow of revenue directly from OECD households to the investment sector in the recipient nonOECD regions. The increase in energy efficiency induced by these transfers leads to a decrease in emissions relative to BaU in China and India of 7–8 percent by 2050. By contrast, in the former USSR, the effect of emission reduction appears only by 2050. Up to this date emissions actually increase relative to BaU because the transfers give rise to large income gains which increase energy use and this tends to cancel the effect of higher energy efficiency. In the aggregate, this scenario leads to a reduction of around 15 percent of world emissions by 2050. But this achieves only a small proportion of the Toronto target which requires a cut of around 65 percent by the year 2050.

Table 9.4 contains three summary statistics that explain the reasons for the limited impact of the international recycling strategy on global emissions. While the simulated amounts of transfers are sizable, as they increase from 150 to 280 billion US$ between 1995 and 2050, their share of total investment in the recipient countries never exceeds 17 percent. The implied improvement in energy efficiency is from 1.0 to 1.63 percent per year in the early periods, declining to 1.36 per year by 2050. Such a small increase in the AEEI could not, by itself, achieve a substantial emission abatement.

The conclusion from this experiment is that the impact of transfers aiming to achieve energy efficiency gains via nonprice mechanisms is likely to be small. This suggests the desirability of exploring the possibility of combining price and nonprice mechanisms in a global carbon abatement strategy.

One possible avenue to achieving energy efficiency through a price mechanism could be the removal of the large distortions affecting energy markets, especially in the nonOECD regions. Some empirical evidence[15] and previous work with GREEN suggest that there are a substantial

Table 9.3. *Summary statistics for the international recycling of carbon tax revenues scenario*

GDP (percent deviations relative to BaU)

	USA	Japan	EEC	Other OECD	Energy-exp. LDCs	China	Former USSR	India	CEECs	DAEs	Brazil	ROW	Total
1995	-0.2	-0.4	-0.3	-0.4	-0.9	0.6	1.7	0.5	2.1	0.1	1.0	0.7	-0.1
2000	-0.4	-0.9	-0.6	-1.1	-1.3	1.6	6.2	1.2	5.9	0.1	2.9	1.9	0.1
2010	-0.7	-1.4	-1.0	-1.8	-1.8	2.8	11.4	2.0	10.6	0.0	5.2	3.3	0.3
2050	-1.0	-1.8	-1.7	-2.7	-0.1	4.6	14.8	3.3	14.7	0.0	5.7	4.5	0.9

Household real income (percent deviations relative to BaU)

	USA	Japan	EEC	Other OECD	Energy-exp. LDCs	China	Former USSR	India	CEECs	DAEs	Brazil	ROW	Total
1995	-1.4	-3.4	-2.9	-5.0	-1.6	3.9	6.6	3.3	6.1	-0.1	2.6	2.0	-1.2
2000	-1.6	-3.5	-3.0	-5.4	-2.7	5.2	12.2	4.5	11.0	-0.1	5.1	3.3	-0.9
2010	-1.8	-3.6	-3.1	-5.7	-3.6	6.2	17.3	5.1	15.8	-0.1	7.6	4.9	-0.5
2050	-2.7	-3.5	-4.4	-6.3	1.2	8.8	20.0	5.6	18.9	0.5	8.3	6.9	0.8

Carbon emissions (percent deviations relative to BaU)

	USA	Japan	EEC	Other OECD	Energy-exp. LDCs	China	Former USSR	India	CEECs	DAEs	Brazil	ROW	Total
1995	-14.9	-12.0	-12.4	-17.7	-0.1	-4.0	4.9	-1.4	-2.7	1.8	3.0	-0.3	-6.2
2000	-20.9	-16.0	-16.8	-24.4	-0.7	-5.5	8.0	-2.6	-1.8	1.7	5.8	+0.5	-8.1
2010	-30.6	-21.6	-23.7	-33.4	-1.5	-8.3	5.5	-6.0	-2.8	1.7	7.5	-1.9	-11.8
2050	-47.8	-31.4	-37.1	-48.9	-0.1	-7.0	-3.7	-7.9	-3.6	1.2	2.5	-1.5	-15.0

Table 9.4. *Transfers and AEEI in the recycling of an OECD carbon tax scenario*
Transfers (in millions 1985 US$)

	1995	2000	2010	2050
USA	− 39,706	− 40,684	− 43,577	− 70,646
Japan	− 39,649	− 40,625	− 43,683	− 70,769
EC	− 47,682	− 48,633	− 52,417	− 84,924
Other OECD	− 31,751	− 32,470	− 34,950	− 56,614
Energy-exp. LDCs	—	—	—	—
China	39,697	42,225	51,484	127,367
Former USSR	61,914	61,719	59,945	56,605
India	9,525	11,366	13,697	36,789
CEECs	20,665	21,120	20,553	22,643
DAEs	—	—	—	—
Brazil	6,342	6,469	6,848	8,490
ROW	20,633	19,501	22,262	31,130
Total transfers	158,775	162,399	174,689	283,025

Note: A negative sign indicates a donor region, a positive sign a recipient region.

Transfers/GDP ratio (in %)

	1995	2000	2010	2050
USA	− 0.8	− 0.7	− 0.6	− 0.4
Japan	− 2.3	− 2.0	− 1.7	− 1.0
EC	− 1.6	− 1.4	− 1.3	− 1.1
Other OECD	− 3.1	− 2.8	− 2.6	− 2.2
Energy-exp. LDCs	—	—	—	—
China	5.8	5.1	4.5	2.5
Former USSR	8.2	7.7	6.7	3.4
India	2.7	2.6	2.3	1.5
CEECs	6.2	5.8	5.0	2.8
DAEs	—	—	—	—
Brazil	2.1	1.7	1.3	0.4
ROW	2.0	1.6	1.4	0.7

Note: A negative sign indicates a donor region, a positive sign a recipient region.

Table 9.4 (*continued*)

Transfers/Investment ratio (in %)

	1995	2000	2010	2050
USA	− 4.8	− 4.1	− 3.4	− 2.1
Japan	− 7.2	− 5.9	− 4.4	− 2.1
EC	− 7.0	− 6.0	− 4.9	− 3.2
Other OECD	− 13.6	− 11.9	− 10.0	− 6.9
Energy-exp. LDCs	—	—	—	—
China	15.3	14.4	13.3	8.7
Former USSR	16.9	15.9	13.8	7.6
India	13.4	13.8	12.8	9.7
CEECs	15.3	14.0	11.3	5.8
DAEs	—	—	—	—
Brazil	10.0	8.3	6.3	1.9
ROW	10.2	8.5	7.3	3.6

Note: A negative sign indicates a donor region, a positive sign a recipient region.

AEEI in the nonOECD regions (in % growth per year)

	1995	2000	2010	2050
Energy-exp. LDCs	1.0	1.0	1.0	1.0
China	1.7	1.6	1.6	1.4
Former USSR	1.8	1.7	1.6	1.3
India	1.6	1.6	1.6	1.4
CEECs	1.7	1.6	1.5	1.2
DAEs	1.0	1.0	1.0	1.0
Brazil	1.4	1.4	1.3	1.1
ROW	1.4	1.4	1.3	1.1

number of subsidies distorting energy prices, mainly in some nonOECD regions. The removal of these subsidies could lead to a significant improvement in welfare in these regions. This would also cut emissions through a decline of energy demand and higher efficiency.[16]

In this chapter we consider another possibility by simulating a scenario where all countries are assumed to reach an agreement to impose a *global* carbon tax. As in the previous experiment, part of the carbon tax revenue raised in the OECD regions is assumed to be recycled towards investment in the nonOECD area. This transfer mechanism could both compensate the nonOECD region for their losses after the imposition of a carbon tax and improve their energy efficiency through the link between the amount of transfers and the AEEI.

Along these lines, we ran a scenario imposing a $50 carbon tax in all regions throughout the period. The transfer scheme is the same as the previous simulation. Tables 9.5 and 9.6 give the impact on GDP, welfare and emissions. As expected, GDP and real income losses in the OECD group are more moderate than in the previous scenario where only the OECD regions were assumed to impose the tax. Nonetheless, some nonOECD regions continue to record net gains, namely the former USSR, CEECs, Brazil and ROW. China and India suffer GDP losses, but record a net increase in household real income. This suggests that a cost-efficient and equitable taxation *cum* transfer scheme could be designed in order to compensate the losers and induce them to participate in a global agreement to levy carbon taxes. The key point with this scenario is that the amount of world emission reduction achieved is substantial: almost 50 percent compared with BaU levels, with emissions being stabilised at around 10 billion tons per year. This would still fall some way short of achieving the Toronto target of 7 billion tons.

Table 9.6 gives the amount of transfers involved in the recycling of OECD carbon tax revenues and its share in investment and the implied improvement of energy efficiency. Finally, figure 9.4 shows the evolution of energy productivity levels in this scenario. It shows that there is some degree of catch-up among regions relative to Japan. In the first group, the DAEs and the US reach the energy productivity level of Japan by 2050. Another group is formed by the other OECD and nonOECD regions, with the exception of China, the former USSR and the CEECs. For China, energy efficiency is on an upward trend but the degree of convergence is still limited. The former USSR and the CEECs remain in the lower bound because their levels of energy prices – which include the price distortions observed in the benchmark year – are still very low compared with other regions.

Table 9.5. *Summary statistics for the implementation of a global carbon tax scenario*

GDP (percent deviations relative to BaU)

	USA	Japan	EEC	Other OECD	Energy-exp. LDCs	China	Former USSR	India	CEECs	DAEs	Brazil	ROW	Total
1995	-0.1	-0.1	-0.1	-0.2	-1.0	-0.5	-0.2	-0.1	0.7	-0.1	0.2	-0.1	-0.2
2000	-0.2	-0.2	-0.2	-0.4	-1.7	-0.5	0.3	-0.2	2.0	-0.2	1.0	0.3	-0.3
2010	-0.3	-0.4	-0.3	-0.7	-2.3	-0.3	1.2	-0.2	3.6	-0.2	1.8	0.7	-0.3
2050	-0.6	-0.8	-0.7	-1.1	-0.7	-0.2	3.8	-0.2	5.1	-0.7	1.3	0.7	-0.3

Household real income (percent deviations relative to BaU)

	USA	Japan	EEC	Other OECD	Energy-exp. LDCs	China	Former USSR	India	CEECs	DAEs	Brazil	ROW	Total
1995	-0.4	-0.8	-0.8	-1.6	-2.6	0.8	3.4	1.9	2.0	0.1	1.5	0.0	-0.5
2000	-0.5	-0.8	-0.8	-1.9	-3.9	0.3	3.4	1.3	3.5	0.1	2.6	0.3	-0.6
2010	-0.7	-1.0	-0.9	-2.0	-4.8	0.0	4.1	1.2	5.3	0.2	3.9	1.1	-0.7
2050	-1.4	-1.6	-1.9	-2.6	0.2	-0.2	6.6	0.4	5.9	-0.9	1.6	0.7	-0.6

Carbon emissions (percent deviations relative to BaU)

	USA	Japan	EEC	Other OECD	Energy-exp. LDCs	China	Former USSR	India	CEECs	DAEs	Brazil	ROW	Total
1995	-10.7	-6.9	-7.7	-12.5	-10.5	-30.2	-27.0	-24.0	-22.1	-8.8	-6.7	-17.1	-16.5
2000	-15.4	-8.9	-10.7	-17.6	-14.0	-42.2	-37.8	-35.2	-29.9	-12.1	-7.5	-22.7	-23.2
2010	-23.3	-13.1	-16.0	-25.0	-19.2	-56.6	-46.6	-50.1	-38.6	-16.5	-8.2	-31.9	-32.9
2050	-39.9	-21.4	-26.9	-39.6	-25.7	-67.7	-49.3	-66.4	-47.7	-24.5	-13.9	-47.9	-47.3

Table 9.6. *Transfers and AEEI in the implementation of a global carbon tax scenario*
Transfers (in million 1985 US$)

	1995	2000	2010	2050
USA	− 13,322	− 13,907	− 15,109	− 27,159
Japan	− 13,320	− 13,821	− 15,216	− 27,284
EC	− 15,964	− 16,513	− 18,259	− 32,741
Other OECD	− 10,642	− 11,050	− 12,177	− 21,826
Energy-exp. LDCs	—	—	—	—
China	13,307	14,386	17,895	49,094
Former USSR	20,750	21,003	20,874	21,817
India	3,191	3,873	4,767	14,178
CEECs	6,941	7,199	7,157	8,728
DAEs	—	—	—	—
Brazil	2,126	2,156	2,382	3,273
ROW	6,925	6,637	7,750	11,996
Total transfers	53,240	55,256	60,824	109,086

Note: A negative sign indicates a donor region, a positive sign a recipient region.

Transfers/GDP ratio (in %)

	1995	2000	2010	2050
USA	− 0.3	− 0.2	− 0.2	− 0.2
Japan	− 0.7	− 0.6	− 0.6	− 0.4
EC	− 0.5	− 0.5	− 0.4	− 0.4
Other OECD	− 1.0	− 0.9	− 0.9	− 0.8
Energy-exp. LDCs	—	—	—	—
China	2.2	2.0	1.8	1.1
Former USSR	3.6	3.4	2.9	1.5
India	1.0	1.0	0.9	0.7
CEECs	2.5	2.4	2.0	1.2
DAEs	—	—	—	—
Brazil	0.7	0.6	0.5	0.2
ROW	0.7	0.6	0.5	0.3

Note: A negative sign indicates a donor region, a positive sign a recipient region.

Table 9.6 (*continued*)

Transfers/Investment ratio (in %)

	1995	2000	2010	2050
USA	− 1.5	− 1.4	− 1.1	− 0.8
Japan	− 2.2	− 1.9	− 1.5	− 0.8
EC	− 2.2	− 2.0	− 1.7	− 1.2
Other OECD	− 4.3	− 3.8	− 3.3	− 2.5
Energy-exp. LDCs	—	—	—	—
China	6.2	5.8	5.5	3.9
Former USSR	7.8	7.2	6.2	3.5
India	5.5	5.6	5.2	4.3
CEECs	6.6	6.0	4.8	2.6
DAEs	—	—	—	—
Brazil	3.7	3.0	2.3	0.8
ROW	3.8	3.1	2.7	1.5

Note: A negative sign indicates a donor region, a positive sign a recipient region.

AEEI in the nonOECD regions (in % growth per year)

	1995	2000	2010	2050
Energy-exp. LDCs	1.00	1.00	1.00	1.00
China	1.25	1.23	1.22	1.15
Former USSR	1.32	1.30	1.25	1.14
India	1.22	1.22	1.21	1.17
CEECs	1.27	1.24	1.19	1.10
DAEs	1.00	1.00	1.00	1.00
Brazil	1.15	1.12	1.09	1.03
ROW	1.15	1.12	1.11	1.06

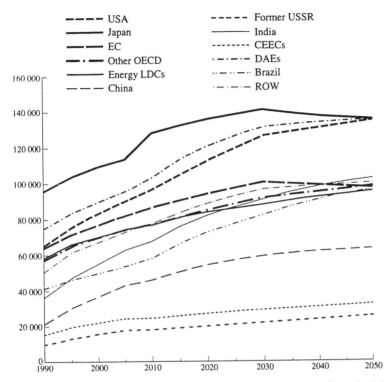

Figure 9.4 **Energy productivity levels, global tax scenario (1985$/TeraJoule)**

6 Conclusions

In recent years, there has been a growing awareness of the potential threat to the earth's atmosphere posed by global warming. While there is great uncertainty about the likelihood of global warming, the risk is now being taken sufficiently seriously that many OECD countries are promulgating targets for curbing their emissions of greenhouse gases, especially carbon dioxide (CO_2). Previous work with the OECD's GREEN model has shown that actions by the OECD countries alone to restrict their CO_2 emissions are unlikely to have a large impact on global emissions. An effective international agreement to curb global emissions must involve the major CO_2 emitting countries outside the OECD area such as China, India and the Newly Independent States of the former USSR. But as actions to restrict CO_2 emissions in the nonOECD countries are likely to be costly, they would require compensation in order to entice them into implementing an agreement. This chapter uses GREEN to simulate the impact on emissions and welfare of a direct transfer mechanism between the OECD and the nonOECD countries. The novel point is that the transfer is tied to new investment with the explicit aim of promoting greater energy efficiency in the nonOECD countries.

The main conclusions are as follows:

(1) The autonomous energy efficiency improvement parameter plays a key role in determining base-line levels of emissions. However, very high and implausible rates of technical progress would be needed in order to stabilise CO_2 emissions by the middle of the next century.

(2) Implementing a transfer scheme under which OECD carbon tax revenues are recycled towards investment in the nonOECD area is likely to have only a moderate impact on both energy efficiency and emissions. The reason is that, despite the large amount of transfers, the latter are likely to account for only a small share of investment in the nonOECD countries in the next decades. This suggests that pure nonprice mechanisms implemented in the nonOECD area may be insufficient to deal with the climate change problem.

(3) A scenario in which a global carbon tax is combined with a transfer mechanism tied to an energy efficiency mechanism could achieve a sizable reduction of world emissions without imposing an excessive burden on the real income of all nonOECD regions participating in the agreement.

Appendix: energy efficiency, emissions and real income in GREEN

This appendix illustrates how the AEEI coefficient influences carbon emissions and real income in GREEN. For sake of clarity, we use a simplified partial equilibrium specification which mimics most of the properties of the supply schedule of GREEN.

Consider a set of inputs, involving several energy sources, labour and capital, which are combined through three levels of aggregation. At the bottom level, a composite energy good (E) is made up of several types of energy sources. The inner level aggregates the composite energy good and capital (K). Finally, at the top level, labour is combined with the 'energy–capital' bundle to produce final output. The energy efficiency improvement coefficient (λ) is introduced at the bottom level as a disembodied technical progress coefficient which converts the composite energy good into efficiency units. This three-level production function is written as follows:

$$Q = \left[\gamma \left(a \cdot \lambda^{-\rho_1} \left(\sum_i \epsilon_i \cdot E_i^{-\rho_e} \right)^{\frac{\rho_1}{\rho_e}} + \beta \cdot K^{-\rho_1} \right)^{\frac{\rho_1}{\rho_2}} + \delta \cdot L^{-\rho_2} \right]^{-\frac{1}{\rho_2}}. \quad (A1)$$

The usual first-order conditions yield the demands for the ith energy source:

$$\bar{E}_i = \epsilon_i^{\sigma_e} \cdot \left(\frac{pe_i}{\overline{PE}}\right)^{-\sigma_e} \bar{E} \qquad (A2)$$

where $\bar{E}_i$ is total demand for energy; $\bar{E}$ is total demand; and $\overline{PE}$ is the price of the composite energy good, all expressed in physical units. $\bar{E}$ and $\overline{PE}$ are the usual CES aggregates. The price of the composite energy good in efficiency units is:

$$PE = \lambda^{-1} \overline{PE} = \lambda^{-1} \left(\sum_i \epsilon_i^{\sigma_e} \cdot pe_i^{1-\sigma_e}\right)^{\frac{1}{1-\sigma_e}}. \qquad (A3)$$

That is the ratio of the composite price in 'physical' units and the technical progress coefficient. Using the similar relationship for energy demand in efficiency unit (E),[17] $E = \lambda \bar{E}$, we can verify that individual energy demands vary proportionally with AEEI:

$$E_i = \lambda^{-1} \cdot \epsilon_i^{\sigma_e} \cdot \left(\frac{pe_i}{\overline{PE}}\right)^{-\sigma_e} E. \qquad (A4)$$

We turn next to the upper levels of the production function. Leaving aside the effect from substitution between energy sources with different carbon contents, emissions are proportional to the aggregate demand for the composite energy good in physical terms $(\bar{E})$. Therefore, the way the AEEI coefficient ultimately affects emissions depends on how the aggregate nominal energy expenditure varies in line both with the effect of λ on the price PE and with substitution effects through the upper nestings. The aggregate demand for energy in physical terms can be determined as follows:

$$\bar{E} = s_e \cdot s_{ke} \cdot \lambda^{\sigma_1 - 1} \cdot \overline{PE}^{-\sigma_1} \cdot P_{ke}^{\sigma_1 - \sigma_2} \cdot P^{\sigma_2} \cdot Q \qquad (A5)$$

where s_c and s_{ke} are distribution shares; P_{ke} the price of the composite 'energy–capital' bundle; and P the aggregate output price.

Equation (A5) shows that the energy coefficient λ has a proportionate decreasing effect on energy demand to the extent that there is no substitution between capital and energy $(\sigma = 0)$.[18] For strictly positive substitution elasticities, the emission reduction will be compensated by a substitution effect in favour of energy demand. When substitution elasticities are greater than unity, an AEEI greater than one should lead to an increase of emissions.

The impact of AEEI on energy demand (and emissions) is further complicated by the fact that, in GREEN, substitution elasticities vary over the medium to the long term as a result of the vintage structure of the production system.

NOTES

The opinions expressed in this chapter are our own and cannot be held to represent the views of the OECD or its Member governments. We would like to acknowledge helpful comments on an earlier draft from Gene Grossman, Lucrezia Reichlin and Alan Winters. Thanks are also due to Christophe Complainville for expert research assistance.

1 See Martin *et al.* (1992); Oliveira-Martins, Burniaux and Martin (1992).
2 See Burniaux, Nicoletti and Oliveira-Martins (1992) for a much fuller discussion of the specification, parameterisation and calibration of GREEN.
3 Because of data constraints, it was impossible to isolate the electricity sector from the gas and water distribution sectors.
4 The real world price of oil is computed with respect to a weighted average of real exchange rates in the OECD regions. In each country, the real exchange rate is defined as the ratio of a weighted average of domestic primary factor prices to the numéraire of the model, which is the price of labour in the US.
5 The prices of the back-stop energies are as follows: $50 per barrel for the carbon-based back-stop, $100 per barrel for the carbon-free back-stop and 75 mills per Kwh for the electric back-stop option.
6 The demand system used in GREEN is a version of the Extended Linear Expenditure System (ELES) which was first developed by Lluch (1973). The formulation of the ELES used in GREEN is based on atemporal maximisation (see Howe, 1975). In this formulation, the marginal propensity to save out of supernumerary income is constant and independent of the rate of reproduction of capital.
7 The interested reader is referred to Burniaux, Nicoletti and Oliveira-Martins (1992) for a full description of the specification of production functions in GREEN.
8 This implies that the Harrod-neutral technical progress in the capital input is calculated as the difference between the exogenous growth of GDP and the endogenous accumulation of the capital stock in physical terms. This is a standard calibration procedure in dynamic AGE modelling (see Ballard *et al.*, 1985).
9 See for example Manne and Richels (1992, chapter 9); Dean and Hoeller (1992).
10 For details of these assumptions and their sources, see Martin, Burniaux, Nicoletti and Oliveira-Martins (1992).
11 The effective supply of crude oil in the energy-exporting LDCs is constrained by potential supply after the year 2030.
12 It is noteworthy that in GREEN all variables are expressed in constant 1985 US$. By using Purchasing Power Parities (PPPs), the base levels of energy productivity would be substantially modified. However, the qualitative picture described in the text would still remain.
13 See Coppel (1993) for a discussion of the issues involved in the concept of 'joint implementation' of a global carbon abatement target.
14 Given the conversion rule that 1 barrel of oil = 0.11855 tons of carbon, a $10 per barrel of oil tax equivalent translates into a tax of $84.36 per ton of carbon. The EC Commission suggested that an energy *cum* carbon tax equivalent to $10 per barrel of oil could stabilise EC emissions at 1990 levels by the year 2000.
15 See Larsen and Shah (1992).

16 Previous simulations with GREEN suggest that the removal of distortions could lead to a 20 percent carbon abatement relative to BaU by 2050, see Burniaux, Martin and Oliveira-Martins (1992).

17 By definition expenditure is identical whether we work in physical efficiency units:

$$PE \cdot E = (\lambda^{-1} \cdot \overline{PE}) \cdot (\lambda \cdot \bar{E}) = \overline{PE} \cdot \bar{E}$$

18 λ has an effect on the aggregate energy demand through the composite prices P_1 and P depending on the share of energy in the 'energy–capital' aggregate and in total output. For simplicity, we assume that this is a second-order effect.

REFERENCES

Ballard, C.L., Fullerton, D., Shoven, J.B. and Whalley, J. (1985) *A General Equilibrium Model for Tax Policy Evaluation*, Chicago: Chicago University Press

Burniaux, J.-M., Martin, J. and Oliveira-Martins, J. (1992) 'The effect of existing distortions in energy markets on the costs of policies to reduce CO_2 emissions', *OECD Economic Studies*, **19**: 141–65

Burniaux, J.-M., Nicoletti, G. and Oliveira-Martins, J. (1992) 'GREEN': a global model for quantifying the costs of policies to curb CO_2 emissions', *OECD Economic Studies*, **19**: 49–92

Coppel, J. (1993) 'Implementing a global abatement policy: some selected issues', OECD, Economics Department, mimeo

Dean, A. and Hoeller, P. (1992) 'Costs of reducing CO_2 emissions: evidence from six global models', *OECD Economic Studies*, **19**: 16–47

Fullerton, D. (1983) 'Transition losses of partially mobile industry-specific capital', *Quarterly Journal of Economics* (February): 107–25

Howe, H. (1975) 'Development of the extended linear expenditure system from simple saving assumptions', *European Economic Review*, **6**: 305–10

Intergovernmental Panel on Climate Change (IPCC) (1990) 'Policy makers' summary of the scientific assessment of climate change', New York: WMO and UNEP

Larsen, B. and Shah, A. (1992) 'World energy subsidies and global carbon emissions', Public Economic Division, Washington, DC: World Bank, mimeo

Lluch, C. (1973) 'The extended linaer expenditure system', *European Economic Review*, **4**: 21–32

Manne, A.S. and Richels, R.G. (1992) *Buying Greenhouse Insurance: The Economic Costs of CO_2 Emission Limits*, Cambridge, MA: MIT Press

Martin, J.P., Burniaux, J.-M., Nicoletti, G. and Oliveira-Martins, J. (1992) 'The costs of international agreements to reduce CO_2 emissions: evidence from GREEN', *OECD Economic Studies*, **19**: 93–121

Oliveira-Martins, J., Burniaux, J.M. and Martin, J.P. (1992) 'Trade and effectiveness of unilateral CO_2 abatement policies: evidence from GREEN', *OECD Economic Studies*, **19**: 123–40

10 Policy coordination for sustainability: commitments, transfers, and linked negotiations

CARLO CARRARO and DOMENICO
SINISCALCO

1 Introduction

In a world of transnational or global pollution, the optimal protection of the environment requires an international, and sometimes a global, coordination of emission control policies. Hence, the analysis of sustainable growth, and of the related optimal environmental policy, must take into account the international dimension of the environment. Define as 'sustainable' a growth path which accounts for the various functions of environmental resources (in production and consumption). Even if all countries solve the intertemporal optimisation problem, and define a domestic emission path which can ensure the environmental sustainability of economic growth, the existence of transnational and global externalities leads to a suboptimal outcome through various forms of free-riding behaviour.

On the one hand, the global effects of some forms of pollution jeopardise the unilateral attempts at reducing emissions; on the other, the appropriability of a cleaner global environment by all countries provides an incentive not to join global environmental agreements, undermining the attempts at cooperation through free-riding. Hence the need for international coordination.

In principle, the required coordination of emissions could be obtained through a set of global regulations, implementing an optimal management of emissions. However, in the existing institutional setting, there is no authority which can impose supranational environmental policies, and emissions coordination has to be obtained through voluntary agreements among sovereign countries.

In the real world, a large number of international environmental agreements are currently in force. The recent ones, in particular, seem to share some features: they usually involve only a subgroup of the negotiating countries as signatories (partial cooperation); and they tend to use other policy instruments, such as development aid or technological co-operation, as a key instrument for increasing the number of signatories (recent examples are the Climate Change Convention or the agreements on CFCs' emissions control).

The literature on the protection of the international environment is still trying to grasp the characteristics of the international agreements mentioned above, in order to analyse their inner structure and to identify appropriate mechanisms to design and enforce new agreements implementing a suitable coordination of environmental policies.

Recent work on the subject explores alternative ways to characterise the emergence of environmental cooperation. A class of models characterise international environmental negotiations as one-shot games, where countries bargain over emissions. Another class of models characterise environmental agreements as infinitely repeated games. Both classes of models show that various mechanisms can lead to coalitions involving a small number of countries, which yield inadequate environmental protection when the number of countries is large (for a recent discussion, see Barrett, 1992). Whatever incentive to sustain environmental cooperation is quickly dominated by the incentive to free-ride. This result seems to be robust as it is invariably obtained in different models (unless strong positive externalities in the abatement technology are introduced, see the discussant's comments and Heal, 1993).

Starting from the above consideration, our intuition is that we must 'add some elements' to environmental negotiations, in order to sustain co-operation. As mentioned above, in some recent negotiations the control of emissions is linked to other policy issues, in order to increase the number of signatories. This chapter analyses the possibility of creating and expanding environmental coalitions, i.e. of increasing the number of cooperating countries, by means of two alternative, but related, mechanisms.

Drawing on previous work (Carraro and Siniscalco, 1991, 1992; Heal, 1993), we first discuss the situation in which small environmental coalitions exist, and are sustained by any endogenous mechanism. Starting from this situation, in which a coalition is stable, we explore the possibility of expanding it by means of self-financed cash transfers. These expanded coalitions are shown to be profitable, but their stability requires some degree of commitment by a subset of the signatory countries.

Second, we extend the analysis to consider the case in which large environmental coalitions can be achieved by linking optimally environmental agreements to other agreements which involve a positive and partially excludable externality (such as an agreement on technological cooperation).

The two mechanisms are related, but the difference is substantial and easy to grasp. In the case of transfers and commitments, the gains from partial environmental cooperation are used to expand the existing coalition, by inducing other countries to cooperate through self-financed transfers. To sustain broader coalitions by means of transfers, however, a minimum degree of commitment must be introduced into the game. The various forms of commitment proposed are less demanding than a commitment of cooperation by all players, since they may involve only a fraction of the cooperating countries. The resulting game is halfway between noncooperative and cooperative. Partial commitment and transfers can even lead to cooperation by all countries.

In the second case, we link two negotiations in order to offset the incentive to free-ride on the environmental agreement. In the example we provide, environmental negotiations are linked to R&D cooperation, which involves an excludable positive externality and increases the joint coalition welfare. In this way, the incentive to free-ride on the benefit of a cleaner environment (which is a public good fully appropriable by all players) is offset by the incentive to appropriate the benefit stemming from the positive R&D externality (which is excludable and therefore fully appropriable only by the signatory countries). The latter incentive can create a bandwagon effect which increases the profitability and the stability of the joint agreement, substitutes for the need of a partial commitment, and may lead, under appropriate conditions, to environmental cooperation by all countries. In the latter case, the optimal protection of the environment is achieved.

The chapter is divided into four main sections. In section 2, we introduce the general framework and discuss the main results on stable coalitions; in section 3, we analyse the possibility of expanding a stable coalition by means of transfers and commitments; in section 4, we discuss the rationale of linking different negotiations and describe an example where an environmental agreement is linked to technological cooperation. The final section 5 contains some concluding remarks.

2   Stable environmental coalitions

This section presents a general framework to assess the profitability and stability of international agreements to protect the environment; it defines the conditions for the existence of stable environmental coalitions; it recalls some recent literature which shows that, under fairly general conditions on the country's welfare functions, small coalitions exist.

2.1   Players, payoffs, strategies

Consider n countries ($n \geq 2$) that interact in a common environment, and bargain over emission control of a specific pollutant. Each country i benefits (economically) by using the environment as a factor of production and as a receptacle for emissions. The welfare of each country, however, is negatively affected both by its own emissions e_i and by other countries' emissions $\mathbf{e}_{-i}$, where $\mathbf{e}_{-i}$ is the vector $(e_1, \ldots, e_{i-1}, e_{i+1}, \ldots, e_n)$.

Country i's benefit and damage can be represented by the welfare function $P_i(e) = B_i(e_i) - D_i(e_i, \mathbf{e}_{-i})$, where $B_i(e_i)$ denotes benefits arising from the use of the environment for production and consumption activities; $D_i(e_i, \mathbf{e}_{-i})$ denotes damages (welfare losses) resulting from pollution emissions; and $\mathbf{e} \equiv (e_1 \ldots e_n) = (e_i, \mathbf{e}_{-i})$ is the vector of all countries' emissions.

Countries consider one pollutant at a time. Let δ_i be the maximum level of pollution emissions for country i. It is computed by maximising environmental benefits $B_i(e_i)$ without taking into account the associated costs evaluated through the function $D_i(.)$. Moreover, δ_i can be seen as a measure of a country's size and level of development. The 'emission game' between the n countries is defined by a triple (N, S, P), and by appropriate rules: as usual, $N = \{1 \ldots n\}$ is the set of players, $S = S_1 \times \ldots \times S_n$, where $S_i = [0, \delta_i]$, is the strategy space, and $P = (P_1(e) \ldots P_n(e))$ is the payoff vector. Complete information is assumed.

By taking into account reciprocal externalities, a country may decide whether or not to cooperate with other countries in order to reduce total emissions. At this stage, we assume that cooperative agreements are not binding. The decision regarding whether or not to cooperate is the outcome of a 'metagame' in which each country anticipates the choice (cooperative or noncooperative) of the other countries, and the relative outcomes in terms of emission levels.[1]

Let us begin by analysing the outcomes of the game under alternative strategic combinations. First, we assume that countries play simultaneously and noncooperatively. Thus, country i's optimal level of emissions is determined by equating marginal benefits with marginal costs, given the emission levels set by the other countries. The solution of the system of first-order conditions determines the Nash equilibria of the game. For simplicity's sake, we assume the equilibrium to be unique. The Nash equilibrium of the noncooperative game can also be determined by computing the fixed point of countries' best-reply functions. Let $R_i(\mathbf{e})$, $e = (e_1 \ldots e_n)$, be country's i's best-reply function, where $R_i(\mathbf{e}) = \{e_i : P_i(e_i, \mathbf{e}_{-i}(\geq P_i(s_i, \mathbf{e}_{-i}))$, for all $s_i \in S_i\}$. The noncooperative equilibrium e^0 is defined by $e^0 = R(e^0)$, where $R(e) = (R_1(e) \ldots R_n(e))$.

Alternatively, countries can decide to set emissions cooperatively. In this case, we assume that a bargaining process takes place in order to achieve a Pareto optimal outcome. The bargaining process may lead to the formation of a coalition among j countries, where j goes from 2 (the smallest feasible coalition) to n (when all countries set emissions by taking into account reciprocal externalities). We define 'full cooperation' as a situation in which a coalition formed by n countries emerges, while 'partial cooperation' is a coalition formed by $2 \le j < n$ countries. In this work, we determine the cooperative outcome of the game by using the Nash bargaining solution.[2] Moreover, we use the noncooperative equilibrium $e^0 = (e^0_1 \ldots e^0_n)$ as the threat point of the bargaining process.[3] Stated more formally, j countries will act cooperatively when they set emissions maximising the joint product of the difference between $P_i(e)$ and P^0_i, where P^0_i denotes the noncooperative welfare.

Before setting emission levels, each country must therefore decide whether or not to act cooperatively. This decision can be modelled by defining a 'metagame' in which countries choose between the cooperative and the noncooperative strategy by anticipating the outcomes of the related emission game.[4]

2.2   Profitability and stability of coalitions

Let $P_i(j)$ be country i's welfare when it decides to cooperate, and $j - 1$ other countries also cooperate, whereas $Q_i(j)$ is its welfare when country i does not join the coalition formed by j countries. Moreover, let J stand for the set of cooperating countries, and J_0 the set of countries that play noncooperatively. Let us suppose, for simplicity, that all countries are symmetric, i.e. the welfare function is not country specific. We do not therefore index the welfare functions P and Q and their parameters.

A minimum requirement must be met for an environmental coalition to be formed: the welfare of each country signing the cooperative agreement must be larger than the noncooperative welfare. In other words, country i gains from joining the coalition, with respect to its position when no countries cooperate, if $P(j) > P^0$. This leads to Definition 1.

Definition 1: A coalition formed by j players is profitable if $P(j) > P^0$ for all countries belonging to J.

Of course, this only represents a minimum requirement that may not suffice to induce many countries to sign a cooperative agreement. The main problem preventing the formation of any coalition is the possibility of free-riding by some countries. Free-riding can be explained as follows: since one country can profit from the reduction of emissions by co-operating countries, it has an incentive to let other countries sign the cooperative agreement. If all countries are symmetric, it may happen that no cooperation takes place. In this case, the 'metagame' in which countries choose between cooperation and noncooperation is represented as a Prisoners' Dilemma. As we will see, however, this representation of countries' strategic choice may not be appropriate.

The problem can also be stated more formally. For each country, the crucial comparison is between $P(j)$, the country's payoff for belonging to the j coalition, and $Q(j-1)$, the country's payoff when it exits the coalition, and lets other $j-1$ countries sign the cooperative agreement. Let $Q(j-1) - P(j)$ be a country's incentive to defect from a coalition formed by j players, whereas $P(j+1) - Q(j)$ is the incentive for a non-cooperating country to join a j coalition (which, consequently, becomes a $(j+1)$ coalition). Thus, a stable coalition can be defied as in Definition 2.

Definition 2: A coalition formed by j players is *stable* if there is no incentive to defect, i.e. $Q(j-1) - P(j) < 0$, for all countries belonging to J, and there is no incentive to broaden the coalition, i.e. $P(j+1) - Q(j) < 0$, for all countries belonging to J_0.

This definition corresponds to that of cartel stability presented in the oligopoly literature (see D'Aspremont and Gabszewicz, 1986. A similar definition is also used in Barrett, 1991).

It has been shown that under fairly general conditions stable coalitions exist (see Donsimoni *et al.*, 1986). However, this does not satisfactorily address the problem of protecting international commons because, as it has been demonstrated both in the oligopoly and in the environmental literature (see, for example, D'Aspremont and Gabszewicz, 1986; Hoel, 1991; Barrett, 1992; Carraro and Siniscalco, 1991, 1992), stable coalitions are generally formed by $j \leq n$ players, where j is a small number, for any number of players, A few exceptions are the works by Barrett (1991) and Heal (1993) which consider a positive externality sharing in the abatement technology and obtaining wider coalitions.

3   Expanding coalitions through transfers and commitment

The existence of small coalitions, which are inadequate for the protection of the global commons, leads to the attempt to increase the number of cooperating countries through different mechanisms. Many papers, and some actual negotiating attempts, have explored the possibility of using welfare transfers to induce cooperation among the noncooperating countries.

3.1   Transfers without commitment

Suppose we start from a stable j coalition which, by definition, has already exploited all the endogenous incentives to cooperate. Suppose this coalition is too small to achieve sustainable development, so that the j countries wish to expand it: can the j cooperating countries expand the coalition through self-financed welfare transfers to the remaining players? Given the previously stated rules of the game, the answer is no. This is demonstrated by Proposition 1.

Proposition 1: Suppose no countries can commit to the cooperative strategy. Then, in this case, no self-financed transfer T from the j cooperating countries to the other noncooperating countries can successfully enlarge the original coalition.

Proof: For the transfer to be self-financed, it cannot be larger than the gain that the j players obtain from moving to a $(j + 1)$ coalition. Furthermore, in order to add one player to a j coalition, the transfer T must be larger than the loss incurred by the $j + 1$ player by entering it. These two conditions yield:

$$[P(j + 1) - P(j)] \geq T > Q(j) - P(j + 1). \tag{1}$$

This condition makes it possible to self-finance an enlarged coalition. However, is this broadened coalition stable? The $j + 1$ player does not defect if the transfer is larger than $Q(j) - P(j + 1)$. However, by definition of stable coalitions, $P(j + 1) > Q(j)$: the j players of the original coalition have therefore an incentive to defect, their incentive being greater because of the transfer made to the $j + 1$ player. Hence, the $(j + 1)$ coalition is unstable.

QED

The intuition behind this result is simple. Welfare transfers to noncooperating countries decrease by T the payoff of the countries belonging to the j coalition, preserving profitability (transfers are self-financed), but creating instability. The instability has to be dealt with by some form of commitment. As we anticipated in the Introduction, the various forms of commitment we analyse are less demanding than the commitment by all players assumed in cooperative games.

Summing up, welfare transfers from countries belonging to a stable coalition to noncooperating countries cannot be used to expand the initial coalition, unless the rules of the game are changed. There are various rules that can lead to the formation of larger stable coalitions. We focus our attention on the role of commitment. If all countries were committed to cooperation, obviously no free-riding would exist. There are several, less demanding forms of partial commitment which, if associated with appropriate welfare transfers, can lead to large stable coalitions.

3.2 Schemes of commitment

Following Carraro and Siniscalco (1991, 1992), we propose some different schemes of commitment, that could serve as possible blueprints for environmental cooperation (of course, other types of institutional mechanisms could be proposed as well). The types of commitments are:

(1) *Stable coalition commitment:* only the j countries belonging to the stable coalition commit to cooperation.
(2) *Sequential commitment:* the j countries are committed to cooperation and any new signatory, as soon as it enters the expanded coalition, must commit to cooperation as well.
(3) *External commitment:* a subset of noncooperating countries commits to transfer welfare in order to induce the remaining nonsignatories to cooperate, and to guarantee the stability of the resulting coalition.

Finally, by appropriate calculations we compute, as a benchmark, the minimum number of committed countries which is necessary and sufficient to induce all other countries to cooperate, by transferring to them all the gains from cooperation.

As far as transfers are concerned, a nontrivial analysis is required to impose constraints on the amount of resources to be transferred: were the transfers unconstrained, all nonsignatories could be bribed, but the mechanism would not be credible.

The constraints we impose are:

(1) Transfers must be *self-financed*, i.e. the total transfer T must be lower than the gain that the committed countries obtain from expanding the coalition.
(2) The move to a larger coalition must be *Pareto improving*, i.e. all countries must increase their welfare *vis-à-vis* the situation preceding the coalition expansion, and *vis-à-vis* non-cooperation (the larger coalition must be profitable).
(3) Committed countries choose the transfer in order to *maximise the number of signatories* (given the above two constraints).[5]

Given the different schemes of commitment and the above restrictions, Carraro and Siniscalco (1991, 1992) analyse the formal conditions to expand coalitions, and carry out a few examples with symmetric countries.

First of all, a general conclusion emerges from such analysis: both the existence of stable coalitions, and the possibility of expanding them, depend on the pattern of interdependence among countries, as described by the slope of their best-reply function. The reason that lies behind this result is intuitively simple. The best-reply functions reflect, *inter alia*, the marginal damage produced by foreign countries' emission increase when the domestic country reduces its own emissions. Suppose countries bargain over emission levels in order to achieve an optimal aggregate outcome, taking into account reciprocal externalities. As is well known, cooperation among all countries is profitable and optimal, but is intrinsically undermined by free-riding, as reflected by the best-reply function of a country which does not belong to the partial coalition. If this best-reply function is negatively sloped, the noncooperating country will expand its emissions if the coalition restricts them, offsetting the effort of the cooperating countries. If, on the contrary, the best-reply functions are orthogonal or near-orthogonal, the free-riders will simply enjoy the cleaner environment without paying for it, but will not offset the emission reduction by the cooperating countries, leaving scope for coalitions and for their expansion.

A second set of results concern the possibility of expanding stable coalitions through transfers and commitments:

(1)   Starting from a stable coalition formed by j country, the commitment of their members induces, through appropriate transfers, other r countries to join the initial coalition; in general, r is larger, the larger the gain from moving to the wider coalition, and the lower the incentive to defect from it. As previously emphasised, such incentive is strictly related to the pattern of interdependence among countries. Hence r is larger, the steeper are countries' best-reply functions (i.e. when such functions are orthogonal or near-orthogonal).

(2)   The instability problem is further reduced by adopting the 'sequential commitment' scheme. Such form of commitment is more demanding than the 'stable coalition commitment' described above, because it rules out the problem of granting the coalition stability. However, full cooperation cannot always be achieved because there may exist values of r for which the gain from further broadening the coalition is lower than the loss incurred by the entering country, i.e. the transfer would not be sufficient to induce one more country to join the coalition.

(3)   In the case of 'external commitment', r additional countries can be induced to cooperate, and the $j + r$ coalition is stable, if the remaining $n - j - r$ noncooperating countries commit to carry on appropriate transfers to the $j + r$ cooperating countries. The dimensions of the resulting coalition increase as the incentive to defect from the $j + r$ coalition decreases, and as the gain that non-cooperators achieve from moving to a $j + r$ coalition increases. Notice that noncooperators gain when the cooperative agreement is expanded because they receive fewer emissions. Hence, a subset of them find it profitable to induce other nonsignatories to enter the coalition, and to guarantee its stability.

Just to give an idea of the magnitudes involves, the main results which were obtained in the example with symmetric countries can be summarised.

(1)   First, even in the most favourable case (near orthogonal best-reply functions) stable coalitions tend to be small (at most three countries join the coalition, whatever n). Nonetheless, this implies that the metagame describing the environmental negotiation is not a Prisoners' Dilemma, but rather a Chicken Game.

(2)   Second, the number of signatory countries can be substantially increased through self-financed transfers to noncooperating countries, provided some form of commitment takes place. In the proposed example, with near orthogonal best-reply functions, the 'stable coalition commitment' about doubles the size of the coalition; the 'sequential commitment' can lead towards full cooperation; the number of committed players which can ensure full cooperation is about 60 percent of the negotiating countries; the 'external commitment' can produce stable coalitions that involve more than a half of the negotiating countries (see Carraro and Siniscalco, 1992).

In the less favourable case (negatively sloped best-reply functions), on the contrary, stable coalitions may not even exist; hence, there are no gains from cooperation to expand them.

Some reflections on the empirical nature of the benefit and damage functions seem to show that, in most cases of transnational or global pollution, the best-reply functions should be near-orthogonal and that the emission reduction by some countries should not be offset by greater emissions elsewhere (think of CFCs, acid rain, and CO_2 whenever the so-called 'carbon leakage' is not too high). This issue needs further investigation on empirical grounds. However, if it proves correct, the analysis of cooperation carried out so far may become relevant for policy discussion.

4   Linking environmental negotiations

Let us consider an alternative route to expand an environmental agreement, namely the link between separate negotiations. This mechanism, too, offers interesting intuitions for the protection of the global commons.

4.1   A general framework

Let us start from the environmental game described in section 2. After having exploited all the mechanisms to expand the coalition by bargaining solely on emissions (i.e. on abatement costs and environmental benefits), suppose again that the environmental coalition is too small to attain a satisfactory protection of the environment. Moreover, assume that no country can commit to cooperation, which implies that the strategic behaviour proposed in section 3 cannot be used to expand the coalition.

In this section, we therefore take a step further and propose a mechanism which 'breaks the wall' between environmental negotiations and other policy issues, by linking the environmental agreement, which is profitable but unstable, to another agreement which is profitable and stable (because it produces a positive externality which is excludable). Consider, as an example, an agreement on R&D cooperation which shares the innovation costs and produces an appropriable benefit by the signatories (e.g. a patent on a new production process). In this case, the excludable benefit of the agreement on R&D cooperation can be used to increase the stability of the environmental agreement, thus increasing the overall welfare.

Linking two negotiations has the following meaning: two negotiations are said to be linked when signing the first agreement is conditional on signing the other one, and vice versa. Notice that the linkage changes the rules of the game, its strategy spaces and payoff functions *vis-à-vis* the case of two separate negotiations. Hence, in order to evaluate the profitability and stability of the joint agreement, we need to redefine the payoffs in the different cases.

Let $P^1(j^*_1)$ be the payoff of the j^*_1 countries which join the first (environmental) agreement, whereas $Q^1(j^*_1)$ is the payoff of the nonsignatories. Similarly, define $P^2(j^*_2)$, and $Q^2(j^*_2)$ for the second agreement. Assume now that the two negotiations are linked. The payoff of the countries signing the joint agreement is $P^u(j^*_u)$, whereas the nonsignatories achieved $Q^u(j^*_u)$. Notice that, given the stability condition proposed above (see Definition 2), j^*_k, $k = 1, 2, u$, is defined by

$P^k(j^*_k) - Q^k(j^*_k - 1) = 0$, $k = 1, 2, u$, i.e. j^*_k defines the number of countries belonging to the stable coalition. Moreover, $P^k(j^*_k) \geq 0$, $k = 1, 2, u$ (see Definition 1). Finally let J^1, J^2, J^u be the sets of signatory countries in the three cases described above, whereas J^1_0, J^2_0, J^u_0 are the sets of nonsignatories. As we are analysing the possibility of expanding the environmental coalition, we only consider the case $J^1 \in J^u$.

Notice that:

Definition 3: Linking two negotiations increases the dimension of the stable environmental coalition if $j^*_u > j^*_1$. The move to a larger stable coalition is profitable for the j^*_1 countries belonging to the stable environmental coalition if:

$$P^u(j^*_u) \geq P^1(j^*_1) + P^2(j^*_2) \quad \text{when } J^1 \in J^u, J^1 \in J^2. \tag{2a}$$

$$P^u(j^*_u) \geq P^1(j^*_1) \quad \text{when } J^1 \in J^u. \tag{2b}$$

The definition specifies the incentives to link the two agreements. The linkage can occur when it increases the welfare of the signatories, *vis-à-vis* the separate negotiations. Notice that the linkage may not be Pareto optimal. Countries which do not sign the joint agreement may lose with respect to the situation in which they belong to one of the two separate negotiations. As the goal of the proposed mechanism is to expand the environmental coalition, $J^1 \in J^u$, we consider the signatories of the second agreement.

Definition 4: The welfare of countries which do not belong to the environmental agreement, but belong to the other one, does not decrease when the joint coalition is formed if:

$$P^u(j^*_u) \geq P^2(j^*_2) \quad \text{when } J^2 \in J^u. \tag{3a}$$

$$Q^u(j^*_u) \geq P^2(j^*_2) \quad \text{when country } i \in J^2, i \notin J^u. \tag{3b}$$

Furthermore, in order to achieve Pareto optimality, the joint coalition must not decrease the welfare of those countries who did not belong to any coalition. Let Q_0 be the payoff of these countries before the joint coalition is formed. Moreover, J_0 denotes the set containing them. We then have Definition 5.

Definition 5: Linking two negotiations is Pareto optimal if conditions (2) and (3) hold and if:

$$P^u(j^*_u) \geq Q_0 \quad \text{when } J_0 \in J^u. \tag{4a}$$

$$Q^u(j^*_u) \geq Q_0 \quad \text{when country } i \in J_0, i \notin J^u. \tag{4b}$$

Notice that this definition has an interesting implication:

Proposition 2: If n, the number of negotiating countries, is the dimension of J^2 and J^u (i.e. all countries sign the second and the joint agreement), and if $P^u(n) \geq P^1(j^*_1) + P^2(n)$, $j^*_1 < n$, then the linkage of the two negotiations expands the environmental coalition and is Pareto optimal.

Proof: By assumption $j^*_1 < n = j^*_u$, which implies that the linkage expands the environmental coalition. Moreover, $P^k(j^*_k) \geq 0$, $k = 1, 2, u$, by the profitability condition. Hence, $P^u(n) \geq P^1(j^*_1) + P^2(n) > 0$. Finally, $J^u = J^2$, J^u_0 is empty (there exists no nonsignatory). Hence, (3b) and (4) are irrelevant, whereas (2a), (2b) and (3a) are satisfied.

QED

Proposition 2 is useful to discuss the results of a simple economic model that we describe in section 4.2 to illustrate the mechanism proposed above.

4.2   Technological cooperation and environmental agreements

The general conditions proposed above suggest that the linkage of two negotiations can help expand the environmental coalition. In order to provide an economic application of the previous theoretical analysis, we consider the case in which technological transfers and R&D cooperation are linked to the environmental negotiation.

The example that we are going to present explicitly considers the interactions between the government and domestic firms, and among governments in different countries. Firms maximise profit; countries maximise their own welfare, which includes profits, domestic consumer surplus and environmental quality.

Let us begin with firms. Consider an oligopolistic industry with n firms facing an inverse demand function $p = D^{-1}(Y)$, where $Y = y_1 + y_2 + \ldots + y_n$ is the total quantity produced, and p is its price. Each firm has a cost of production $C_i(y_i, x_i, \mathbf{x}_{-i})$, which is a function of its own production y_i, of the amount of research x_i that it undertakes, and the amount $\mathbf{x}_{-i} = (x_1, x_2, \ldots x_{i-1}, x_{i+1}, \ldots x_n)$ that its rivals undertake. The relationship between the cost of firm i and the R&D undertaken by other firms captures the existence of positive R&D externalities or spillovers, i.e. we assume that some benefits of each firm's R&D flow without payment to other firms. In particular, the external effect of firm j's R&D is to lower firm i's unit production cost. One interpretation is that successful innovations of rivals can be imitated, and that imitation is cheaper than innovation.[6]

Firms' strategies consist of a level of R&D and production. These two variables are set simultaneously and noncooperatively by the n firms. Each firm is assumed to be located in a different country and subject to a country specific environmental legislation. The n firms are supposed to sell to a single global market. For simplicity, neither transportation, nor other additional costs of selling the good abroad, are considered.

Each government negotiates over two issues: emission reduction and R&D cooperation. In other words, governments choose, either cooperatively or noncooperatively, two strategic variables: the abatement level which is imposed on firms (e.g. an emission standard), and the degree of spillovers occurring in the production of innovations. If a government joins an R&D coalition, the spillover is equal to one, i.e. all firms belonging to countries in the coalition benefit from the R&D performed in these countries. If a country does not join the R&D coalition, the benefit is equal to the 'technological leakage' (which is normalised to zero for simplicity's sake). Hence, benefits from R&D are excludable. If a government joins an environmental coalition, it benefits from a cleaner environment, and pays for the emission abatement. If it does not join the environmental coalition, the country can profit from the cleaner environment without paying the cost.

The basic idea of the model is to link R&D and technological cooperation as defined above, with environmental protection. Through such linkage, countries belonging to an environmental coalition can induce other countries to cooperate, as technological cooperation, if conditional on environmental cooperation, provides an extra incentive to join the agreement.

As discussed in section 2, the environmental problem is global. Hence, the environmental damage depends on the emissions produced by all firms. The damage function can thus be written as: $D_i(E) = \delta(e_1 + e_3 \ldots e_n)$, $i = 1, \ldots, n$, where $E = e_1 + e_2 \ldots e_n \geq 0$ are total global emissions. Hence, the environmental negotiations are undermined by the free-riding problem, i.e. coalitions are hardly stable (see section 3). Vice versa, we assume R&D cooperation to be stable, i.e. the net benefit from joining the R&D coalition is assumed to be larger than the net benefit from choosing a different strategy (either noncooperation, or joining a different R&D coalition), whatever the number of countries in the R&D coalition.

In each country the government, or a regulatory agency, takes two decisions. The first one is whether or not to join the environmental and/or the R&D coalition. This decision is taken by anticipating that all countries which do not cooperate cannot profit from the innovation spillover. The second decision concerns the environmental standard, i.e. the abatement level to be imposed on the firms. These two decisions are taken by maximising a social welfare function defined as the sum of the domestic firm's profits, the domestic consumers' surplus, minus the environmental damage borne by the country. The sequence of decisions is the following: first the government decides whether or not to cooperate, and which coalition to join; then, given this decision, it sets the optimal environmental standard (abatement level); finally, all firms decide simultaneously and noncooperatively their R&D expenditure and production.

Suppose the two negotiations are linked, i.e. countries can benefit from the R&D spillovers only if they sign the environmental agreement. As in previous sections, $P^u(j)$ denotes the payoff of cooperating countries when the coalition is formed by j governments, whereas $Q^u(j)$ denotes the payoff of noncooperating countries.

As shown in Carraro and Siniscalco (1993), $P^u(j)$ and $Q^u(j)$ are defined by three components: $P^u(j) = P^u_r(j) + P^u_a(j) + P^u_e(j)$ and $Q^u(j) = Q^u_r(j) + Q^u_a(j) + Q^u_e(j)$.

(1)   The production effect: $P^u_r(j)$, $Q^u_r(j)$. This component captures the effect of the coalition on the domestic firms' profits and consumers' surplus. As the coalition reduces unit production costs, it increases production, thus increasing the firms' profit and market share, and the consumers' surplus. However, as j approximates n, the effect on the market share tends to zero (when $j = n$, the oligopoly is symmetric again); hence, the production effect first increases, and then decreases, showing a humped shape. In any case, $P^u_r(j) \geq Q^u_r(j)$, for all $j \leq n$, which implies $j^*_r = n$. Hence, this component of the welfare function tends to stabilise the coalition.

(2)   The abatement effect: $P^u_a(j)$, $Q^u_a(j)$. This is the part of the welfare function which is commonly used in the environmental literature (e.g. Hoel, 1991; Barrett, 1992; Carraro and Siniscalco, 1992). It is composed of two effects: the positive effect of abatement levels on emission control (a cleaner environment), and the negative effect of the abatement costs. As emphasised in section 3, $P^u_a(j) \geq Q^u_a(j)$ only for small values of j ($j \leq 3$). This is therefore the unstable component of the welfare function.

(3)   The emission/output technological effect: $P^u_e(j)$, $Q^u_e(j)$. This additional component of the welfare function derives from the negative effect of production on emissions. Such negative effect can be reduced by firms' R&D, which changes the environmental features of the production technology, and therefore the emission/output ratio. This component is the most ambiguous. On the one side, joining the coalition increases production and therefore emissions, thus reducing welfare; on the other side, joining the

coalition reduces emissions (increases welfare) through a lower emission/output ratio. Carraro and Siniscalco (1993) show that these two effects tend to offset each other, i.e. $P^u_e(j)$, and $Q^u_e(j)$ are small and approximately equal for all $j \leq n$.

It is now possible to discuss the size of the profitable and stable coalitions. Most literature on stable environmental coalitions only considers the second component, i.e. $P^u_a(j)$ and $Q^u_a(j)$, of the welfare functions. In this case, the profitability of any coalition is easily proved, because $P^u_a(j) > 0$ for all $2 \leq j \leq n$. Moreover, the stable coalition is generally defined by $j^*_a \ll n$, for n large (see Barrett, 1992). In particular, using linear damage function and a quadratic abatement cost function, $j^*_a \leq 3$, whatever n. This result was first proposed in the cartel stability literature (D'Aspremont et al., 1983), and can be found in Hoel (1991), Carraro and Siniscalco (1991, 1992), and Barrett (1992). As stated in section 2 of the chapter, the result is quite strong. Profitable and stable coalitions exist, but they tend to be small, whatever the number of countries. Hence, their contribution to environmental protection is generally small.[7]

The important thing to be stressed is the following: $P^u_a(j)$ and $Q^u_a(j)$ are the payoffs of the game in which countries negotiate solely on emissions. Hence, given the additivity of the welfare function, $P^u_r(j) + P^u_e(j)$ and $Q^u_r(j) + Q^u_e(j)$ are the payoffs of the game describing the negotiation on R&D cooperation. Finally, $P^u(j)$ and $Q^u(j)$ are the payoffs of the joint agreement. It is therefore possible to analyse whether the linkage of the two negotiations expands the stable environmental agreement, and increases the welfare of the members of the joint one.

Let us analyse first the R&D agreement alone. As stated above, $j^*_r = n$, and $P^u_e(j) - Q^u_e(j - 1)$ is negligible. Hence, n is also the number of countries joining the R&D coalition. The intuition behind this result is that the benefits from R&D cooperation are excludable. Hence no free-riding take place, and all countries would like to join the coalition (in order to reduce their production costs). The question is therefore the following: how many countries sign the joint agreement? Carraro and Siniscalco (1993), using linear demand and damage functions, and quadratic abatement and R&D cost functions, show that there exist reasonable values of the parameters of the model such that $j^*_u > j^*_a$. In particular $j^*_u = n$.

The explanation is again that the benefit from R&D cooperation, which derives from the innovation spillovers on the production cost, is appropriable, i.e. the coalition can exclude noncooperating countries from such benefit. By contrast, the abatement effect, i.e. the benefit from a cleaner environment, is not excludable, i.e. all countries profit from the coalition higher abatement levels. The linkage induces all countries to sign both agreements, in order not to lose the benefits stemming from R&D cooperation.

The Pareto optimality of linking the negotiations about R&D and environmental cooperation can easily be proved because $j^*_u = j^*_r = n$ (see Proposition 2). In this case, signatories achieve both the benefits of the R&D coalitions (which could be achieved anyway, because stable for all $2 \leq j \leq n$) and the benefits of the environmental coalition (which is unstable, but it is stabilised by linking the two negotiations).

5   Conclusions

The chapter starts from the obvious remark that the analysis of sustainable growth, in the presence of transnational and global pollution, requires an explicit consideration of the international coordination of environmental policy.

The literature on the international protection of the environment shows that the incentive to free-ride on environmental cooperation is very strong. Coordination of environmental policy does not necessarily correspond to a Prisoners' Dilemma (Carraro and Siniscalco, 1991); however, wide environmental cooperation is highly problematic, since the global environment is a public good, and since the environmental externalities seem to be substantial. Accordingly, stable environmental coalitions exist, but may be small, as the incentive to free-ride easily dominates the incentive to cooperate, when the number of cooperating countries increases.

We therefore propose to abandon the idea of negotiating only on emission reductions and explore two mechanisms to sustain wider environmental cooperation.

In sections 2 and 3 of the chapter, we analyse a mechanisms which is still confined to environmental policy. A stable coalition implies gains from cooperation for the signatory countries. These gains are transferred to noncooperating countries to induce them to join the environmental agreement. The transfer, however, subtracts welfare from the stable coalition, thus hampering stability. This is why the mechanism requires some kind of commitment by the cooperating countries. Various forms of partial commitment substantially increase the number of signatories, and can even lead to cooperation by all countries.

In section 4 of the chapter, we take a step further and present an alternative mechanism which 'breaks the wall' between environmental negotiations and other policies. In our example, environmental policy is linked to technological cooperation. By making technological cooperation conditional upon environmental cooperation, it is possible to expand the stable environmental coalition, increasing the welfare of its members. The environmental agreement and technological cooperation can be analysed as two separate negotiations. The environmental coalition is profitable but unstable; technological cooperation is profitable and stable. The joint negotiation is more profitable and more stable than the two separate negotiations, as it uses the gains from technological cooperation to offset the environmental free-riding incentives and to reach full cooperation both on technology and on the environment.

NOTES

The authors are grateful to Geoff Heal, Marcus Miller, Lei Zhang, Alan Winters, and the participants of the OECD Development Centre and the CEPR Conference for their comments. The usual disclaimer applies.

1 We restrict our analysis to one-shot games. In terms of additional equilibrium outcomes, analysing repeated games would be fruitful only if appropriate trigger or stick/carrot strategies could sustain cooperation as an equilibrium outcome. The level of emissions, however, can hardly be conceived as a trigger variable which can be increased strategically, in response to other countries' defection. Some reasons are the following: first, emission reduction, in cases such as CO_2 or CFC, involves substantial and irreversible investments. Secondly, expanding emissions as a retaliation could generate environmental damage primarily to the triggering country. Finally, an increase in emissions can hardly be used as a selective punishment. Other effective punishments (e.g. trade protectionism) could be even more costly for the triggering country and, therefore, not credible. For these reasons, we believe that trigger or stick/carrot strategies are not particularly helpful in sustaining cooperation.

2 This assumption is not crucial because, in the rest of the analysis, all countries will be assumed to have the same benefit and damage functions. In this case, any bargaining solution in the literature would give the same result.

3 In a two-player game, this means interpreting Rubinstein's alternating offers model as a model in which players face a risk that, if the agreement is delayed, then the opportunity they hope to exploit jointly may be lost (see Binmore, Rubinstein and Wolinsky, 1986).

4 Most environmental studies model this 'metagame' as a one-shot Prisoners' Dilemma, in which noncooperation is the dominant strategy.

5 Notice that transfers enter a country's payoff in an additive way. Otherwise, each cooperating country would maximise its payoff with respect to both emissions and transfers. This would be the case if transfers were carried out using policy instruments which interact with other economic variables, and with emissions in particular. Such extension of the analysis is discussed in section 4 of the chapter.

6 The literature on R&D cooperation and innovation spillovers is quite large. Our assumptions are the standard ones in this literature. See Katz (1986); Katz and Ordover (1990); Suzumura (1990); Wu and De Bondt (1991); Motta (1992).

7 Of course, this conclusion depends on the assumption of symmetric countries.

Were countries different, the coalition of the largest ones could produce significative effects on emissions. Moreover, it excludes the presence of strong positive externalities in the abatement technology, as proposed by the discussant of this chapter, and in Heal (1993).

REFERENCES

Barrett, S. (1991) 'The paradox of international environmental agreements', London Business School, mimeo
   (1992) 'Self-enforcing international environmental agreements', *CSERGE Working Paper*, GEC **92-34**, London: CSERGE
Binmore, K., Rubinstein, A. and Wolinsky, A. (1986) 'The Nash bargaining solution in economic modelling', *Rand Journal of Economics*, **17**: 176–88
Carraro, C. and Siniscalco, D. (1991) 'Strategies for the international protection of the environment', CEPR, *Discussion Paper*, **586**; *Journal of Public Economics*, **52**: 309–28 (1993)
   (1992) 'Transfers and commitments in environmental negotiations', paper prepared for the ESF Task Force 3; forthcoming in K.-G. Mäler (ed.), *International Environmental Problems: An Economic Perspective*, Dordrecht: Kluwer Academic
   (1993) 'R&D cooperation for the stability of international environmental agreements', Fondazione Matteo, Milan, mimeo
D'Aspremont, C.A. and Gabszewicz, J.J. (1986) 'On the stability of collusion', in G.F. Matthewson and J.E. Stiglitz (eds), *New Developments in the Analysis of Market Structure*, New York: Macmillan Press: 243–64
D'Aspremont, C.A. and Jacquemin, A. (1988) 'Cooperative and non-cooperative R&D in duopoly with spillovers', *American Economic Review* (December): 1133–7
D'Aspremont, C.A., Jacquemin, A., Gabszewicz, J.J. and Weymark, J. (1983) 'On the stability of collusive price leadership', *Canadian Journal of Economics*, **16**: 17–25
Donsimoni, M.P., Economides, N.S. and Polemarchakis, H.M. (1986) 'Stable cartels', *International Economic Review*, **27**: 317–27
Heal, G. (1993) 'International negotiations on emission control', in C. Carraro (ed.), *Trade, Innovation, Environment*, Dordrecht: Kluwer Academic
Hoel, M. (1991) 'Global environmental problems: the effects of unilateral actions taken by one country', *Journal of Environmental Economics and Management*, **20(1)**: 55–70
Katz, M.L. (1986) 'An analysis of cooperative research and development', *Rand Journal of Economics*, **17(4)**: 527–43
Katz, M.L. and Ordover, J.A. (1990) 'R&D cooperation and competition', *Brookings Papers on Economic Activity*, Microeconomics: 137–91
Motta, M. (1992) 'Cooperative R&D and vertical product differentiation', *CORE DP*, **9128**; forthcoming in *International Journal of Industrial Organization*
Suzumura, K. (1990) 'Cooperative and non-cooperative R&D in oligopoly with spillovers', Institute of Economic Research, Hitotsubashi University
Wu, C. and De Bondt, R. (1991) 'On the stability of R&D cooperation', *DTEW*, Katholieke Universiteit Leuven

Discussion

MARCUS MILLER and LEI ZHANG

1   Outline and summary

How to expand the size of international coalitions for protecting the environment? This is the challenging issue tackled by the authors of chapter 10. They assume that coalition members take account of the social cost of emissions and agree to implement measures for abatement, so as coalition size increases more and more of the external effects of emissions are internalised: this is socially efficient. But, with the rising cost of abatement, the incentive to 'free-ride' becomes progressively more attractive: that is the problem. (Free-riders ignore transnational effects and set low abatement levels.)

To help sustain environmental coalitions, two solutions are considered. First, *cash transfers* for new entrants (financed by gains from environmental cooperation); second, *linking environmental coordination to cooperation in other fields* where there are positive externalities. In the economic model outlined in section 4.2, it is the opportunity to cooperate in industrial R&D which acts as the inducement to join the coalition. Indeed, if, as in Carraro and Siniscalco (1993), a specific linear-quadratic formulation is adopted, they find that the sustainable coalition can even expand to include all countries!

The first thing we do in our Discussion is to take precisely this linear-quadratic formulation (which for convenience we refer to as the CS model) and to extend it by including positive externalities *in the abatement technology* itself. In this case we find that a global environmental coalition can in principle be self-sustaining *without any linkage* to cooperation in other fields.

The second point we make is to recommend the imposition of charges for emissions – something that seems to be omitted from the CS model. (For the convenience of the reader, some salient features of the linear-quadratic formulation reported in Carraro and Siniscalco, 1993, are summarised briefly below.)

2   Key features of the CS model

1   Both industry demand and damage functions are linear; costs for abatement and R&D are quadratic.

2   The maximum coalition sustained simply by the gains in cooperation to abate is only 3.
3   But cooperating to protect the environment induces cooperation in R&D which generates two sets of external benefits. The first is the impact of R&D cooperation in reducing private industrial costs of production; the second is the effect in reducing rates of emission.
4   Both of these two externalities are taken into account when a country decides to join a coalition, but it appears from the simulation results that it is the former, the cost-saving effect, which is far and away the more significant.
5   For 'reasonable parameter values', R&D cooperation sustains a global environmental coalition.
6   While countries agree on abatement measures, and cooperate on R&D, they make no effort to charge for emissions.

3   Externalities in abatement

The key idea of the chapter is that positive externalities from coordination can sustain large coalitions. This can, we believe, be most directly seen by considering the possibility of a positive externality in the technology of abatement itself! We find any positive externality of this form raises the size of the coalition; and when it reaches a critical value the coalition becomes global.

To see this, we need consider only the abatement effects (using the terminology and the linear-quadratic structure of the CS model). For a member country this effect can be written as

$$A(j) = \delta(jq_j + (n + j)q_h^0) - \tfrac{1}{2}\Phi q_i^2 + \beta' \sum_j q_j, \tag{1}$$

where the externality is captured by the parameter β'. The abatement effect for a noncooperative country, which does not benefit from the externality, is simply

$$A^0(j) = \delta(jq_j + (n - j)q_h^0) - \tfrac{1}{2}\Phi q_h^{0^2}. \tag{2}$$

The optimal abatement policy for a cooperative country is thus

$$q_i = \frac{\delta j + \beta'}{\Phi}, \tag{3}$$

while the optimal abatement policy for a noncooperative country is

$$q_h^0 = \frac{\delta}{\Phi}. \tag{4}$$

Substituting (3) and (4) into (1) and (2) yields

$$A(j) = \frac{1}{2\Phi} \{(\delta j + \beta')((\delta + 2\beta')j - \beta') + 2\delta^2(n - j)\}, \tag{5}$$

$$A^0(j) = \frac{1}{2\Phi} \{2\delta j(\delta j + \beta') + \delta^2(2(n - j) - 1)\}. \tag{6}$$

The key to defining the largest sustainable coalition, namely the incentive to join a coalition rather than 'free-ride', can therefore be written as:

$$A(j) - A^0(j - 1) = \frac{\delta(2\beta' - \delta)}{2\Phi}$$

$$\cdot \left(j + \frac{2\delta^2 - \delta\beta' + \beta'^2 - \sqrt{\delta^4 + 4\delta^3\beta' + \beta'^4}}{\delta(2\beta' - \delta)} \right)$$

$$\cdot \left(j + \frac{2\delta^2 - \delta\beta' + \beta'^2 + \sqrt{\delta^4 + 4\delta^3\beta' + \beta'^4}}{\delta(2\beta' - \delta)} \right) \tag{7}$$

This can be written more concisely as

$$\Delta A(j) = \frac{\delta(2\beta' - \delta)}{2\Phi} (j - j_1)(j - j_2), \tag{8}$$

where $\Delta A(j)$ denotes the incentive to join a coalition of size j, where

$$\beta' = r\delta,$$

and the roots of (8) can be expressed as

$$j_1 = \frac{2 - r + r^2 - \sqrt{1 + 4r + r^4}}{2r - 1}, \tag{9}$$

$$j_2 = \frac{2 - r + r^2 + \sqrt{1 + 4r + r^4}}{2r - 1}, \tag{10}$$

The possible forms taken by this function (and the maximum coalition sizes it generates) are shown in figure D10.1, for various values of β', the coefficient measuring the abatement externality. For $\beta' = 0$, of course, the function has roots 1 and 3, just as in CS; i.e. the maximum sustainable coalition is only 3. As β' rises to 0.3δ and 0.4δ, however, the larger root rises to approximately 8 and 17 as shown in figure D10.1. But as the externality coefficient tends to a critical value of 0.5δ, the upper root tends to $+\infty$, that is, *the maximum coalition size rises to include all countries.* (For $\beta' > 0.5\delta$, the 'bandwagon' effects are of course even more pronounced.)

Formally one may calculate the marginal effect of β' on the maximum size of the coalition j_2 as

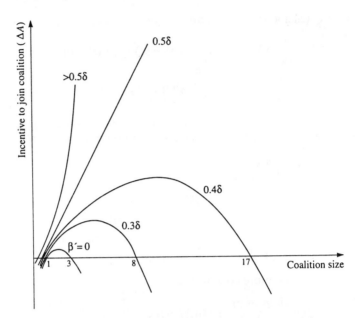

Figure D10.1   Abatement externalities and the incentive to cooperate

$$\frac{dj_2}{dr} = \frac{1}{(2r-1)^2}\left\{3 + 2r - 2r^2 - \frac{2(2r-1)(1+r^3)}{\sqrt{1+4r+r^4}} + 2\sqrt{1+4r+r^4}\right\} > 0,$$

for $r \le \frac{1}{2}$. $\hspace{4cm}$ (11)

In figure D10.2, we show how j_2 rises with β'. It is evident from this highly simplified example just how powerful externalities can be; and specifically how by creating a bandwagon effect they can sweep all countries into a global coalition. (Note that the critical value of externality required here for a global coalition, $\beta' = 0.5\delta$, seems to be small relative to that assumed for R&D expenditure in the CS model.)

A natural question posed by our example is: why should the externalities be outside the technology of environmental protection? Can one not keep the bandwagon effect and drop the linkage to cooperation in non-environmental fields? The answer will clearly depend on the likely extent of abatement externalities.

4   Charging for emissions

To restrict damage to the environment, coalition governments in the CS model are prepared to impose costly abatement requirements upon

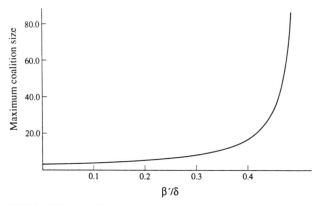

Figure D10.2   How coalition size increases with the externality

private firms. But meanwhile no charges are made upon emissions themselves; so there is no economic incentive for firms to reduce pollution. This is doubly unfortunate; first because extra R&D effort would (according to their model) be capable of reducing the emission to output ratio, and second because there are positive externalities to be had here too! So why not harness these incentives, particularly when the alternative is excessive use of abatement regulations?

One could presumably calculate optimal emission taxes to be used in conjunction with the abatement technology. Since these taxes would raise costs and reduce output, they would however work against the sustainability of the coalition. Two points can be made here: first is the argument in the chapter – namely that by linking cooperation on the environment to other forms of cooperative activities, there are considerable gains to be had (which will offset the negative consequences of environmental taxes). But second it would appear that, at least in principle, a set of production subsidies and lump-sum taxes could be used to generate the same sort of results, even without the linkage.

The argument runs as follows. Ignore the R&D aimed at reducing production costs; but retain the R&D which cuts emission charges. Tax emissions so that firms have the incentive to carry out this R&D, and so generate the externality. Subsidise production to offset the cost effect; and use lump-sum taxes to balance the budget. Formally, it *seems* that one could in this way generate both efficient emission rates *and* enjoy a bandwagon effect, without any reference to linkage outside the field of environmental cooperation.

5   Conclusions

Why will individual countries spend the resources necessary to protect the global environment in the absence of global measures for enforcement? The answer provided in the formal model of the chapter is that coordinating to protect the environment can be linked to positive industrial externalities; and this linkage will make environmental coalition work, with possibly strong bandwagon effects.

Clearly, powerful positive externalities can sustain sizable coalitions – a point we underline by considering externalities *in abatement technology itself*. Our example suggests the need for further study of the technology of abatement; see for instance Heal (1993) who stresses the public good aspect of initial lump-sum investments in abatement technologies which have declining average costs. But the authors instead choose to stress a presumed linkage between deciding to cooperate on environmental protection and enjoying substantial externalities from cost-saving R&D, which has no direct connection with the environment. This seems possible, but one could well ask: if there are such gains to be had, why have they not been reaped already? Why not, in any case, start by focusing specifically on the gains to coordination arising from the technology of environmental protection? And consider also the role of emission taxes?

The authors have, at a theoretical level, succeeded in linking together the economic literature on R&D externalities and the discussion of environmental protection. But whether they have convincingly demonstrated that efforts at environmental protection must henceforth be studied in harness with more general technical cooperation is more doubtful. What is far more likely is that environmental issues will feature in international trade negotiations. This is the link that is provocatively analysed in Daniel Esty's *Greening the GATT*. The specific institutional solution he proposes, both to adjudicate on environmental aspects of trade disputes and to coordinate environmental policies more generally, is the creation of an International Environmental Organisation – a twin sister to the GATT itself.

REFERENCES

Carraro, C. and Siniscalco, D. (1993) 'R&D cooperation for the stability of international environmental agreements', Fondazione ENI Enrico Mattei, Milan, mimeo
Esty, D. (forthcoming) *Greening the GATT: Making Trade and Environmental Policies Work Together*, Washington, DC: Institute for International Economics
Heal, G. (1993) 'Formation of international environmental agreements', Columbia University, Graduate School of Business, March, mimeo

11 Industrial competitiveness, environmental regulation and direct foreign investment

RAVI KANBUR, MICHAEL KEEN and
SWEDER VAN WIJNBERGEN

1 Introduction

Environmental sustainability of economic growth hinges on the pollution intensity of output. If that intensity declines as growth progresses, through active policy or otherwise, economic growth within the confines of a limited resource base becomes at least possible. Recent econometric analysis has come up with intriguing results on this issue. For pollutants where most of the damage is done in the country where the pollution originates, intensities decline starkly after a particular level of *per capita* income is reached. However, for those pollutants where the costs fall on people living far away from the place where the pollution is caused, no such turning point can be observed (Grossman, 1994). When a significant part of the benefits of regulation accrues to people not contributing to the cost of the regulation, rules are difficult to put in place. Thus resolving the difficulties of bringing about international agreements on environmental standards, the topic of this chapter, may well be the key to resolving any conflict between economic growth and environment quality that may exist.

Such difficulties have been on prominent display recently. The typical pattern is for rich countries to insist on global harmonisation on tough western standards, with poorer countries baulking at the costs or likely impact on economic growth. Side payments, a possible solution to this conflict, create obvious budgetary and monitoring problems and are thus not on offer on a significant scale. As a consequence, little progress has been made in, for example, resolving the environmental problems of Eastern Europe's nuclear reactors, or the wide range of environmental issues that were on the table during the UN's environment conference in Rio de Janeiro in 1992. The key result of this chapter is that such problems are unavoidable when harmonisation is chosen as a coordination strategy, but can be avoided if minimum standards are used instead.

The strategic issues that environmental regulation raises in an international setting are similar to those brought up by 'tax competition' that have long been studied in the public finance literature: see, for instance, Gordon (1983) and Mintz and Tulkens (1986). This literature's finding that taxes on interjurisdictionally mobile factors will be inefficiently low in a noncooperative equilibrium of the interjurisdiction game suggests a parallel fear of wasteful competition in relaxing environmental standards. Yet the distinctive concerns that arise in the environmental context have received little attention.[1]

Our analysis focuses on two features that have become central to international negotiations in this area. One is the link between environmental concerns on one hand and movements towards closer economic integration on the other. This issue has come to the foreground in the recent discussions on the North American Free Trade Agreement (NAFTA). Environmental groups have argued that increased integration will facilitate evasion of the strict environmental controls applied in the US, since firms could simply move to Mexico, where standards are much more loosely applied, and export their products back to the US. The other feature we focus on is the potential asymmetry in both behaviour and interests between large countries and small ones; which means, to a very considerable extent, between the industrial North and the South. This asymmetry has already loomed large in the political arena. Here we will see that size matters in the international game of environmental regulation. We will also see that some coordination strategies offer a better prospect of overcoming the ensuing problems than do others.

Section 2 describes the model, and section 3 characterises the noncooperative equilibrium. Section 4 evaluates and compares two policies for the international coordination of environmental standards: harmonisation to some common level, and the imposition of an agreed minimum. Section 5 draws some conclusions.

2   The basic model

This section[2] develops a very simple model designed to bring out the various international aspects of environmental regulation mentioned above. Assume two countries, contiguously located on the interval $[-1,1]$. The border is at point 0, with the foreign country located to the left and the home country to the right. Firms are characterised by their location s in this interval. Within each country, firms are uniformly distributed. The number of firms, however, may differ between the two: there are h home firms and H foreign firms (capital letters refer to the foreign country and lower case letters to the home). The relative size of the two economies, as measured by relative number of firms, $\theta = h/H$, is a key parameter.

Firms have two options: they can either decide to produce at home or they can produce abroad, just over the border, and export back to their original location. Relocating and exporting back is assumed to be more costly the further the firm needs to move; thus if unit costs are λ, then for a firm located at s total costs are $s\lambda$. These costs summarise transport costs, trade barriers, barriers to direct foreign investment and the like. For brevity, we refer to them as relocation costs. The parameter λ is also of central importance in what follows: it is a measure of integration, with lower λs corresponding to more openness.

To sharpen our focus on the relocation decision, we assume that a firm either produces one unit of output or nothing at all. Profits are taxed on a source basis.[3] If production takes place at home (resp., abroad), profit taxes of an amount γ (Γ) are paid. The firm produces pollution as a byproduct; costs increase, and therefore after-tax profits π (Π) decrease, as less pollution is produced. For simplicity we assume a simple linear relation between profits π (Π) and pollution produced, δ (Δ):

$$\Pi = a_0 + a_1\Delta - \Gamma$$
$$\pi = a_0 + a_1\delta - \gamma. \tag{1}$$

Foreign and domestic firms have access to the same technology, so the profit function parameters a_i are identical across countries. To simplify notation, we set $a_1 = 1$; we furthermore set a_0 sufficiently large that we can neglect the possibility of firms going out of business.

Environmental regulation takes the form of an upper limit on the amount of pollution that a firm may emit in the country where production takes place. In the home (foreign) country, this cap is set at d (D). Since profits increase in Δ (δ), profit maximisation implies:

$$\Delta = D, \quad \delta = d. \tag{2}$$

Note that an increase in d means a reduction in environmental quality (i.e. more pollution).

Firms will decide to relocate abroad if either lower taxation or less stringent environmental regulation is sufficiently attractive to offset the relocation costs incurred. It is straightfoward to show that, because of the linearity of relocation costs, all firms between zero and s^* will move to the other country, where:

$$s^* = \frac{(D - d) - (\Gamma - \gamma)}{\lambda}. \tag{3}$$

At s^*, the attractions of more lenient environmental standards and/or lower taxes elsewhere just offset relocation costs; at distances to zero less than $|s^*|$, these advantages strictly dominate relocation costs and firms will move across the border. Figure 11.1 illustrates for the case where $s^* > 0$. The essence is straightforward: the higher is domestic taxation compared to abroad, the more stringent is environmental regulation compared with that abroad, and the lower relocation costs, the more firms will relocate to the foreign country.

The government in each country values tax revenues but dislikes pollution; in this section we assume identical preferences for both governments. We also assume, for the present, that pollution does not cross international boundaries: to emphasise that strategic behaviour induces inefficiencies even without the international spillovers that have been much emphasised in the literature, we defer consideration of the latter until section 3. Without much loss of generality we assume linearity and marginal utility of revenue and of pollution equal to 1 and -1 respectively, so home and foreign welfare *per firm* operating in the country are simply:

$$w^* = \gamma - d$$
$$W^* = \Gamma - D. \tag{4}$$

The home country's objective function equals the welfare derived from each firm operating in the country times the number of such firms. From (4) and the discussion of location choice above, this is given by:

$$w(d,d) = \begin{cases} \text{If } s^* \geq 0 \\ \quad w = h(1 - s^*)(\gamma - d) \\ \qquad = h\left(1 - \left\{\dfrac{(\gamma - d) - (\Gamma - d)}{\lambda}\right\}\right)(\gamma - d) \\ \text{If } s^* \leq 0 \\ \quad w = (h + H(-s^*))(\gamma - d) \\ \qquad = \left(h + H\left\{\dfrac{(\Gamma - d) - (\gamma - d)}{\lambda}\right\}\right)(\gamma - d). \end{cases} \tag{5}$$

A similar expression obtains for $W(D,d)$, the foreign country's welfare criterion.

3   Environmental competition: the Nash equilibrium

Suppose now that each country sets out to maximise its own welfare by choice of environmental regulation, in a noncooperative Nash setting.

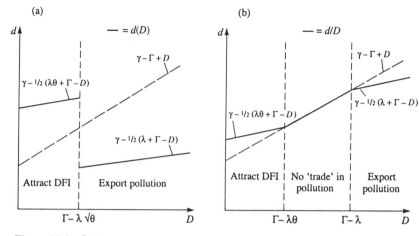

Figure 11.1   Best responses
(a) $\theta < 1$
(b) $\theta > 1$

The profit tax levels γ and Γ are taken as fixed throughout the analysis. Given the foreign country's regulation level, D, the home country therefore chooses d to maximise (5). The analysis of the problem is complicated by the fact that the objective function has a different structure in the two regimes shown: that in which the home country plays host to foreign firms, and that in which home firms go abroad to take advantage of lax environmental regulation and/or lower taxation. Which of these regimes it is optimal for a country to be in depends not only on the other country's regulation level, but also on the relative sizes of the two economies (θ). The best response function of the home country is defined as:

$$d(d) = \mathrm{argmax}_d(w(d,d)). \tag{6}$$

Kanbur *et al.* (1993) show in a similar model that, if $\theta \leq 1$, (6) yields:

$$d(d) = \begin{cases} \gamma - \tfrac{1}{2}(\lambda + \Gamma - d); & D \geq \Gamma - \lambda\sqrt{\theta} \\ \gamma - \tfrac{1}{2}(\lambda\theta + \Gamma - d); & D \leq \Gamma - \lambda\sqrt{\theta} \end{cases} \tag{7}$$

for the home country, while if $\theta \geq 1$ then

$$d(d) = \begin{cases} \gamma - \tfrac{1}{2}(\lambda + \Gamma - d); & D \geq \Gamma - \lambda \\ \gamma - \Gamma + D; & \Gamma - \lambda\theta \leq D \leq \Gamma - \lambda \\ \gamma - \tfrac{1}{2}(\lambda\theta + \Gamma - d); & D \geq \Gamma - \lambda\theta. \end{cases} \tag{8}$$

The intuition behind these best responses, which are illustrated in figure 11.1, is as follows. Take first the case where $\theta \leq 1$, so that the home country is the smaller of the two; this case is shown in figure 11.1a. Then, at very high levels of the pollution cap in the foreign country (that is, very lenient environmental standards and a high d), it is optimal for the home country to have tighter regulations. Some firms are lost to the foreign country, but regulations there are so lax that it is not worth matching them given the domestic welfare costs of pollution: the optimal policy is to 'export pollution'.

As the foreign country tightens its regulations (D falls), it is at first optimal for the home country to follow suit – equation (7) gives the exact amount by which the home country should reduce its pollution cap. However, as the foreign country continues to tighten its environmental regulation – lower D – there comes a point (when $D = \Gamma - \lambda\sqrt{\theta}$) where the home country can gain by switching to offering lower environmental standards than the foreign ones. In doing so it loses from an increase in domestic pollution, but the revenue gains from the relatively large number of firms who move in from the (large) foreign country more than make up for this. For this range of foreign environmental standards, the optimal policy is to attract inward Direct Foreign Investment (DFI) by offering relatively lax environmental standards, or, in other words, to actually 'import pollution'.

This incentive to lower standards at home in response to tighter standards abroad does not exist when the home country is the larger of the two. In this case, as the foreign country tightens its regulations, the optimal response for the (now large) home country is always to tighten its own regulations too, since the number of firms that can be attracted by undercutting standards is relatively small.

To investigate the Nash equilibrium, now assume, without loss of generality, that $\theta \leq 1$. The foreign country's reaction is then given by interchanging lower and upper case letters in (8) and replacing θ by $1/\theta$:

$$d(d) = \begin{cases} \Gamma - \frac{1}{2}(\lambda + \gamma - d); & d \geq \gamma - \lambda \\ \Gamma - \gamma + d; & \gamma - \lambda/\theta \leq d \leq \gamma - \lambda \\ \Gamma - \frac{1}{2}(\lambda/\theta + \gamma - d); & d \leq \gamma - \lambda\theta. \end{cases} \tag{9}$$

In spite of the discontinuity in the home country's best-response function, it can be shown that there exists a unique Nash equilibrium, as indicated in figure 11.2 (cf. Kanbur et al., 1993, for a formal proof). One can show that in that equilibrium, the respective pollution caps at home and abroad are given by:

$$d^N = \gamma - \lambda[\tfrac{1}{3} + (\tfrac{2}{3})\theta]$$
$$D^N = \Gamma - \lambda[\tfrac{2}{3} + (\tfrac{1}{3})\theta]. \tag{10}$$

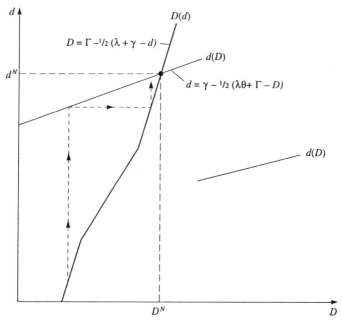

Figure 11.2 The Nash equilibrium

One central feature of the noncooperative equilibrium is immediate: from (9),

$$d^N - \gamma > D^N - \Gamma.$$

Firms thus move from the large country to the small one. More particularly, if profit taxes are the same in the two countries, the environmental standards will be weaker in the small country. The reason is intuitively clear. When the small country undercuts the larger one by setting a higher pollution cap, it increases pollution domestically through its own firms (which are relatively few in number) but experiences a net gain (revenue minus pollution costs) from foreign firms (which are relatively large in number) that are now attracted to produce in the small country. The small country thus has the greater incentives to set lax environmental standards.

The international competition in environmental regulation characterised and examined above is clearly Pareto inefficient. In particular, starting at the noncooperative equilibrium, a small tightening of standards by both parties will leave both better off. To see this, note that the effect on home welfare of a small multilateral reform is:

$$dw = w_d dd + w_D dD,$$

The subscripts indicate derivatives. When evaluated at the Nash equilibrium, $w_d = 0$, while from (5), recalling that in equilibrium $s^* < 0$, and from (10) one gets:

$$w_D = -(\gamma - d^N)\frac{H}{\lambda} = -H[\tfrac{1}{3} + \tfrac{2}{3}\theta] < 0.$$

By an analogous argument, $W_d < 0$ also. Thus a small joint tightening of environmental standards is mutually beneficial.

Moreover, international spillovers exacerbate this problem. To see this, suppose now that a fraction ϕ_D of the pollution produced by each firm in the foreign country spills over to the home country and, similarly, that a fraction ϕ_d of the pollution produced by a firm located in the home country spills over to the foreign country. Note that ϕ_D and ϕ_d may differ: French mining waste drifts North through the Rhine but, unlike spawning salmon, Dutch pollutants do not swim upstream to return the favour. Assuming for brevity's sake that $s^* < 0$, the objective functions of the two countries are now:

$$
\begin{aligned}
w(d,d) = {} & (\gamma - d)\left(h + H\left\{\frac{(\Gamma - d) - (\gamma - d)}{\lambda}\right\}\right) \\
& - \phi_D DH\left(1 - \left\{\frac{(\Gamma - d) - (\gamma - d)}{\lambda}\right\}\right) \\
W(D,d) = {} & (\Gamma - d)H\left(1 - \left\{\frac{(\Gamma - d) - (\gamma - d)}{\lambda}\right\}\right) \\
& - \phi_d d\left(h + H\left\{\frac{(\Gamma - d) - (\gamma - d)}{\lambda}\right\}\right).
\end{aligned}
\tag{11}
$$

To see the effects of the spillovers on the incentives to choose tighter standards, differentiate w and W with respect to d and D, respectively:

$$
\begin{aligned}
\frac{\partial w}{\partial d} = {} & (\gamma - d)\frac{H}{\lambda} - \left(h + H\left\{\frac{(\Gamma - d) - (\gamma - d)}{\lambda}\right\}\right) \\
& - \phi_D D\frac{H}{\lambda} \\
\frac{\partial W}{\partial D} = {} & (\Gamma - d)\frac{H}{\lambda} - H\left(1 - \left\{\frac{(\Gamma - d) - (\gamma - d)}{\lambda}\right\}\right) \\
& - \phi_d d\frac{H}{\lambda}.
\end{aligned}
\tag{12}
$$

Compared to the no-spillover case analysed above ($\phi_D = \phi_d = 0$), incentives thus move unambiguously in the direction of laxer standards as ϕ_D and ϕ_d increase. The reason is simple: since a firm's pollution in the foreign country in any case spills back across the border, the home country might as well attract it over so as to derive some benefits by taxing its profits. The argument is symmetric for both capital importer and capital exporter, with the result that standards will be more lax in the Nash equilibrium.

4 International coordination of environmental regulation

The results presented so far provide a characterisation of beneficial marginal reforms: a small reform is Pareto improving if it involves tighter standards in both countries. But in practice the policy debate has been about reforms that are anything but marginal. Two possible coordination strategies have been prominent in the public debate. One is the harmonisation of environmental standards as currently advocated by many in the EEC.[4] In terms of our model, harmonisation implies imposing $D = d = d^*$, say. The other proposal involves imposition of minimum standards, as proposed, for example, by Cumberland (1979, 1981); in the context of our model this takes the form of an upper bound on the pollution caps d and D. The framework developed so far can be used to shed light on these alternatives. In order to bring out the issues sharply, we assume in the rest of this section that $\gamma = \Gamma$, so that environmental standards are the sole consideration in location decisions.

We analyse the harmonisation strategy first. Clearly the implications depend on the level at which the common standard is set. Starting from the noncooperative equilibrium, it seems reasonable to concentrate on levels somewhere in between d^N and D^N. Our central result of harmonisation is that convergence to any such level is bound to harm the small country. The explanation of this powerful result is surprisingly simple.

Consider first harmonisation at the lower of the two caps, $d^* = D^N$, that is with both countries adopting the (relatively tight) standard of the large country. This is bound to make the small country worse off than in the noncooperative equilibrium, since in the unconstrained game its optimal response to D^N was not D^N but the more relaxed standard d^N. Now imagine increasing the common cap d^* above D^N. The small country is harmed even more – it suffers greater pollution as d^* goes up, but without attracting any DFI (since standards remain harmonised and profits taxes are assumed identical). It follows, therefore, that in the absence of compensating international transfers, *the small country will always object to harmonisation.*

The large country, however, may benefit from harmonisation, depending on the level at which the common standard is set. To see this, notice that the only effect of harmonisation to its own tight standard is to force a higher standard on the foreign country, and thus to stem the outflow of large country firms. Thus, with the same pollution level as in the noncooperative equilibrium, and less capital outflow, harmonisation at the tighter of the two noncooperative Nash standards makes the large country better off – it keeps all the pollution benefits and does not lose firms to the small country.

As the harmonised standard is progressively loosened, however, the large country is harmed by the higher pollution levels although, since harmonisation prevails, it does not suffer capital outflows. Finally, when the harmonised standard reaches that of the small country, the large country is bound to fare worse than in the Nash equilibrium, since its optimal response to d^N is not d^N but D^N. Thus for a tight enough harmonised standard the large country does better than in the Nash equilibrium; but if the harmonised standard is too lax (perhaps in deference to the small country's standards), both countries are immiserised relative to the noncooperative equilibrium!

Harmonisation thus emerges in a very unfavourable light. It is never *Pareto* improving: without compensating transfers, the smaller country always loses out on harmonisation. One can show, however, that it is potentially improving in aggregate if the common standards are sufficiently tight. This then poses a delicate political problem. For it implies that whilst all countries might gain from harmonisation of their environmental standards, large countries will have to transfer resources to the smaller ones if the latter are to share in their benefits. Without such transfers, all benefits accrue to the larger country. Experience, not least that of the Rio Summit, does not leave one sanguine about the feasibility of negotiating international compensation payments of the kind required.

Consider next minimum standards. Here the strategy is to impose d, $D \leq \mu$: pollution caps may not exceed the minimum standard μ, but countries can choose stricter standards if they wish. To have any bite, the minimum standard must of course be tighter than the most lenient standard set in the noncooperative equilibrium: $\mu < d^N$. To distinguish the strategy from one of harmonisation, we also impose $\mu > D^N$. The detailed analysis of such a constraint is somewhat complex. By an argument similar to that in Kanbur *et al.* (1993), however, one can show that if a Nash equilibrium exists in his amended game then (in obvious notation) environmental standards become:

$$d^m = \mu$$
$$D^m = \Gamma - \tfrac{1}{2}(\lambda + \gamma - \mu) \qquad\qquad (13)$$
$$= \tfrac{1}{2}(\mu + \gamma - \lambda);$$

the latter equality follows since $\Gamma = \gamma$ by assumption. (13) indicates that the small country thus tightens its standards to exactly the minimum permissible. Standards also improve (pollution caps tighten) in the large country, even though it is not directly affected by the minimum standard constraint: the raising of environmental standards across the border diminishes the prospect of outward investment in response to the protection of its own environment. Standards thus rise in both countries. As one would expect, they rise more (pollution caps are reduced more compared to the Nash levels) in the small country than they do in the large; and hence capital flight from the latter to the former diminishes.

It is clear that the large country benefits from the minimum standard: it is enabled to reduce the pollution damage from firms in its jurisdiction, *and* enjoys a return of outward investment. By the same token, it might at first seem that the effect on the small country is ambiguous: pollution is reduced, but inward investment lost. This apparent ambiguity, however, can be resolved. Remarkably, the first, beneficial, effect dominates, and the small country also gains. A formal proof of this can be constructed along similar lines as in Kanbur and Keen (1991). Here we give only the intuition, which is again surprisingly simple for such a strong result. One can imagine the unconstrained noncooperative equilibrium of section 3 being established as the outcome of a dynamic process in which, starting with relatively tight environmental standards (low d and D), competitive pressures lead a monotonic loosening of standards in both countries (as indicated by the arrowed lines in figure 11.2).

Since each country's maximum attainable welfare falls as the other relaxes its standard,[5] welfare in each also falls monotonically on the path to (d^N, D^N). Imposing a minimum standard, however, puts a brake on his downward spiral as soon as the small country's best response reaches μ, and so spares each country the additional welfare loss that it would otherwise suffer in converging to the noncooperative equilibrium. Harmonisation, of course, also blocks the competitive degradation of standards. But it does more than this: in imposing uniformity, and so destroying the asymmetry of the noncooperative equilibrium, it ignores the fundamental (size) asymmetry between the countries involved.

The surprising conclusion that the country with the laxer environmental regulation gains from the imposition of a binding minimum standard stems, it should be emphasised, entirely from the strategic interaction between the two countries. If standards did not change in the large country after the imposition of a minimum environmental quality standard, the small country would certainly lose, since all that would happen in that case is that it would be forced away from its best response in welfare terms. It gains, however, because the large country, less concerned now about loosing footloose firms, tightens standards too. The attractions of imposing a minimum standard thus derive from its effect on precisely those countries that will *not* find the minimum a binding constraint.

5   Summary and conclusions

The difficulty of coordinating environmental policy between nations may well be the most serious threat to the environmental sustainability of economic growth. Where pollution damage strikes the very country that causes the pollution to begin with, evidence suggests that measures will be taken to reduce the pollution intensity of economic production. But where the damage strikes people in countries other than the one from which the pollution originates, coordination and incentive problems have so far thwarted attempts at effective international regulation.

An additional difficulty stems from the fact that environmental regulation, through its impact on industrial costs, undermines the international competitiveness of domestic industries and so may become a weapon in international strategic rivalries. Industrialists complain about unfair competition from rivals exporting from countries with laxer environmental standards. Environmentalists point to outward investment as a vehicle for industry to circumvent environmental controls.

The results of this chapter support these arguments, although not the remedies those groups typically propose. We have seen that, even when pollution does not spill across national boundaries, noncooperative behaviour generates wasteful competition, tending towards a general lowering of environmental standards. Both sides in the end allow more pollution than either would have preferred.

Size differences exacerbate the extent of this wasteful competition: small countries bordering large neighbours can attract a great deal of foreign investment at relatively low cost by loosening their environmental standards. This in turn forces the larger country to respond and a downward spiral results. Increased economic integration, by lowering the costs of relocation abroad and exporting goods back, reduces the national cost of environmental competition and therefore produces more of it. Moreover, these two effects interact in a damaging manner: the more unequal in size are the two countries, the more closer economic integration between them leads to inefficient degradation of environmental standards. We show that the common response to such problems, harmonising on a common standard, is unlikely to succeed. When countries are of unequal size, harmonisation of environmental standards will *always* leave the small country worse off, irrespective of the level at which standards are harmonised. And the larger country will also lose if the common standard is set too low. As a consequence, no harmonisation strategy is likely to be agreed upon without some sort of international compensation mechanisms.

We also show, however, that a different strategy of coordinating international responses offers more promise: the imposition of a minimum standard of environmental control, leaving each side free to impose tighter standards. The smaller country will adhere to the minimum while the larger country will set its standards somewhat tighter; the destructive tit-for-tat generated by strategic interactions is thus forestalled. As a consequence, international agreements on the basis of a minimum standard should be substantially easier to reach and implement. And success in reaching such agreements should, in turn, lead to substantially more optimism on the issue of whether environmental sustainability is compatible with sustained economic growth.

NOTES

The views expressed in this chapter are our own and do not necessarily reflect those of the institutions we are affiliated with. Thanks are due to Alan Winters for his comments on this chapter which draws on the more extensive analysis contained in Kanbur, Keen and van Wijnbergen (1993).

1 For an exception see Oates and Schwab (1988).

2 This section draws on Kanbur *et al.* (1993).

3 Formally, the residence principle is more common. But deferral until profits are actually transferred and limits on tax credits mean that the reality is often closer to source taxation; see for instance, Devereux and Pearson (1989).

4 This is the view behind the much-quoted claim of environmental dumping, raised most often in the case of trade with the newly reforming economies in Eastern Europe. It is an open question, of course, whether the lofty environmental ideals merely serve as a cover for old-fashioned protectionism.

5 It is easiest to see this by establishing the converse, that each country gains if the other tightens its standards: for one option is simply to tighten domestic standards by the same amount, so leading to lower pollution damage and unchanged location decisions.

REFERENCES

Cumberland, J.H. (1979) 'Interregional pollution spillovers and consistency in environmental policies', in H. Siebert *et al.* (eds.), *Regional Environmental Policy: The Economic Lines*, New York: New York University Press

(1981) 'Efficiency in interregional environmental management', *Review of Regional Studies*, **2**: 1–9

Devereux, M. and Pearson, M. (1989) *Corporate Tax Harmonisation and Economic Efficiency*, London: Institute for Fiscal Studies

Gordon, R.H. (1983) 'An optimal taxation approach to fiscal federalism', *Quarterly Journal of Economics*, **98**: 567–86

Grossman, G.M. (1994) 'Pollution and growth: what do we know?', ch. 2 in this volume

Grossman, G.M. and Krueger, A.B. (1991) 'Environmental impacts of a North American Free Trade Agreement', *Discussion Paper*, **158**, Woodrow Wilson School, Princeton University; now published in P. Garber (ed.), *The US–Mexico Free Trade Agreement*, Cambridge, MA: MIT Press (1993)

Kanbur, R. and Keen, M. (1991) 'Tax competition and tax coordination when countries differ in size', *American Economic Review*, **3(4)**: 877–92

Kanbur, R., Keen, M. and van Wijnbergen, S. (1993) 'Stratetic aspects of environmental regulation in open economies', Tinbergen Institute, *Working Paper*, TI **93-198**

Mintz, J. and Tulkens, H. (1986) 'Commodity tax competition between member states of a federation: equilibrium and efficiency', *Journal of Public Economics*, **29**: 133–72

Netherlands Centraal Plan Bureau (1992) *Long Term Economic Consequences of Energy Taxes*, *Working Paper*, **43**, The Hague (in Dutch)

Oates, W.E. and Schwab, R.M. (1988) 'Economic competition among jurisdictions: efficiency enhancing or distortion inducing', *Journal of Public Economics*, **35**, 333–54

Discussion

JEAN-CLAUDE BERTHÉLEMY

An important issue at the nexus of environmental and trade policies concerns the negative impact that an environment protection policy could have on a nation's welfare, through lessening its competitiveness and consequently the level of its economic activity. Then, in a noncooperative game, all countries will tend to adopt lax environmental policies, for fear of losing industrial competitiveness and employment to other countries.

We have here a classic example of suboptimal Nash equilibrium; here, noncooperation among actors leads to excessive pollution. The argument is of course reinforced if one introduces transfrontier pollution, which obviously needs to be taken into account within an international coordination framework.

Kanbur, Keen and van Wijnbergen's chapter 11 (hereafter KKW) provides an elegant illustration of this issue, based on a simple two-country model. Their model assumes that each country maximises a utility function depending positively on income provided by economic activity (profit taxes collected by the government in the KKW framework) and negatively on pollution, which is a result of economic activity itself.

There is nothing new in the result that the Nash equilibrium of the game considered is suboptimal. It is defined as the crossing point of two rising reaction curves, defined in terms of pollutant emission (d and D). These reaction curves result classically from utility maximisation, with iso-utility curves, of the home countries represented as in figure D11.1. In such a context, it is clear that the noncooperative Nash equilibrium is suboptimal.

The model presented by KKW has, however, an original feature, because they introduce an asymmetry among the two countries. This asymmetry is based in KKW's model on differences in country size, the small (home) country being, at the Nash equilibrium, more prone to accept pollution. This feature of the model is then used to show that a coordinated 'harmonisation policy' cannot be Pareto improving, because it would worsen the welfare of the small country. It is worth examining this 'powerful result' (to use KKW's words), in order to check its robustness *vis-à-vis* the various simplifications introduced here.

As a matter of fact, this result is fairly general, as long as one considers only one policy instrument per country (D, d). This is shown in figure D11.1. In this figure, all 'harmonisation policies' considered by KKW belong to segment AB. We can assume without loss of generality that, as it appears in the KKW example, point A is the best point of segment AB, from the home country point of view. As shown graphically, point A is also obviously worse, from the home country point of view, than the Nash equilibrium N (QED). The basic reason for this result is that any policy which implies more pollution activities in the foreign country (D greater than D^N) impacts negatively on the home country's welfare. Of course, coordinated policies that would go beyond A (between O and A in the bisector) could be potentially Pareto improving, for a symmetric reason. These results are to a large extent independent of the model specification. In particular, they do not depend on the origin of the asymmetry among countries nor on the specification of profit and utility functions.

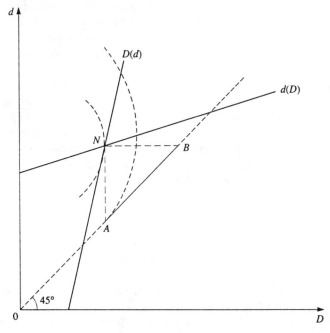

Figure D11.1   Nash equilibrium in environment policy

A similar geometrical demonstration can be provided for the last result reported by KKW, namely that a 'minimum standard' policy could be Pareto improving. Through such a policy, the home country's welfare can now be improved, through a reduction (rather than an increase) of the foreign country emission of pollutants, which itself results from the home country's reduction of pollution below the cap.

The reason why the above discussion was worth carrying out is that it helps understand why the results advertised by KKW may collapse in a more complete framework. Up to now, only one single policy instrument has been considered, a quantitative control of pollution. However, it might be preferable to consider the environmental policy from a different perspective:

– It may be based on taxes rather than on regulation.
– It may be designed *together* with the overall tax policy (γ, Γ).

Assume first that policy makers prefer to use tax incentives rather than regulation to curb pollution (which seems to be a reasonable assumption for an economist). Then, if the foreign country increases its pollution D, through reduced taxation on pollutant emissions, it might have to increase profit tax rates Γ as well; this will happen if the foreign country has set a fiscal objective in terms of a constant total taxation rate. As a consequence, a harmonisation of environmental policies might have ambiguous effects on the home country: on the one hand, its welfare is reduced by an increase in D, but on the other hand, it is improved by a decrease in Γ. If the home country is less affected by the foreign country's pollution (because, for instance, it is upstream on the Rhine river, to take KKW's example), then we might find a Pareto improving harmonisation policy, the home country enjoying the consequences of increased taxation in the foreign country, and the foreign country enjoying reduced transfrontier pollution from the home country. Of course, such an example cannot be exhibited directly in the simplified KKW framework, but this is due only to the oversimplification of their model.

The previous discussion suggests that one cannot consider the environmental policy in isolation from other policy instruments which affect the results of the game. In KKW's framework, the tax policy is exogenously given. This is due to a peculiarity of their model, in which $d\,(D)$ and $-\gamma$ $(-\Gamma)$ play a symmetrical role. As a consequence, the only variable for which their model can be solved is $d - \gamma\,(D - \Gamma)$, and they have simply chosen to fix $\gamma\,(\Gamma)$. Now, assume that the utility function of the government is a bit more complex than the linear one postulated by KKW. Then, one can optimise for $\gamma\,(\Gamma)$ as well as for $d\,(D)$, and one has to consider a game in which, as in the real world, each country manipulates at the same time more than one independent policy variable. Here we have an environmental policy $d\,(D)$ and a taxation policy $\gamma\,(\Gamma)$.

For instance, if the utility function, per unit of output, is something like:

$$w^* = \gamma^a d^{-b}$$

then, at the equilibrium, there is some proportionality equation between d and γ. Again, this might enable the existence of a Pareto improving environmental harmonisation policy. If the foreign country has to relax its environmental standards (D) due to harmonisation, then it will also increase its tax rate on profits (Γ). If the home country welfare function is more sensitive to the latter effect than to the former, a harmonisation policy may be beneficial to it. Again, the foreign country may benefit as well, if for instance it receives transfrontier pollution from the home country, and then is more affected by changes in d rather than changes in γ.

In sum, the argument of KKW, though sensible and relevant in quite a wide range of model specifications, becomes blurred when one tries to expand it in a context where environmental policy would be designed together with other policies such as taxation. For this reason its relevance to real-world policy discussion should not be overestimated.

NOTE

The views expressed here do not necessarily reflect those of the OECD Development Centre.

Index

Note: 'n.' after a page reference indicates the number of a note on that page.

abatement 52, 59, 60–2, 71, 77
  China: marginal benefits 204–6; marginal
    costs 206–9
  and coalitions 277, 278, 284–6
  technologies 75, 76
accounting (shadow) prices 123, 124–5,
  126, 127, 132–3
  valuation problem 128–30
acid rain
  China 206
  and income growth 34
  sources 32, 33
Aerometric Information Retrieval System
  24
age profile of population 64, 65
agricultural sector
  incipient pollution 59–60
  water use 181, 182–3, 187–91, 197:
    elasticity of substitution 194–5
Ahmad, E. 125
air quality
  China 205, 234
  data sources 23–5
  estimation methods 25–6
  and income levels 66–70
  large-scale pollution 33–5
  population growth 72–3
  urban and local air pollution 27–33
airborne lead 29–31
Albouy, Y. 207, 211
algae 40
Anand, S. 124
Anderson, D. 115, 137, 138
Anderson, K. 3
aquifers 114–15
Arens, P. 138
Armington specification 244

Arrow, K.J. 119, 122, 126, 138
arsenic 37, 38, 39, 45n.8
Asian Development Bank 210, 211
Autonomous Energy Efficient
  Improvement (AEEI) 244–50, 252–3,
  254–61

Ballard, C.L. 262
Barbier, E. 87, 116, 150, 151
Bariloche model 147, 150
Barrett, S. 265, 269, 278, 279
Barro, R. 74
Becker, G. 55, 57, 138
Beckerman, W. 84, 91, 92
Begemann, L. 137
Behrens III, W.W. 91, 92, 93, 148
Beltratti, A. 157, 160
Binmore, K. 281
Binswanger, H. 137
biodiversity 66
biological oxygen demand (BOD) 40–1, 42
birth rates 53–5, 64–6, 67, 71
Blackhurst, R. 3
blue whales 129
Boero, G. 214
Brazil 248, 249, 259
Broome, J. 148
Brown, G. 138
Brundtland Report 111, 143, 147, 150
Burniaux, J.-M. 200, 209, 227, 262, 263
Business-as-Usual (BaU) scenario 245–55
Byrd, W.A. 207

cadmium 37, 38, 39
calibrated general equilibrium (CGE)
  model, Morocco 176, 182–7, 192
Cao, H. 205

capital market 114
capital stock, natural 87, 109, 150–1, 153
carbon
    and oxygen regime 40
    taxation: China 202, 213–15, 219, 231–4,
        254; revenue transfers 249–59
carbon dioxide
    emission levels 24, 43, 201: China 200,
        204, 211–14, 231; and income levels
        66–9; and population 70
    global warming 34–5: costs 94
    GREEN model 245, 246–8, 259–60:
        international abatement 239–40
carbon monoxide
    concentration 30
    sources and effects 32–3
Carraro, C. 265, 269, 271, 272, 273, 278,
    279, 280, 283
Carson, R.T. 138
cash-cropping 113
Cashdan, E. 103
catastrophes 88–90
Chakravarty, S. 118
Chapman, T. 137
chemical oxygen demand (COD) 40–1, 42
chemicals, toxic 37–8
Chichilnisky, G. 147, 148, 149, 153, 157,
    160, 162, 164
Chichilnisky criterion 149–50, 153–4
China
    carbon tax 202, 213–15, 219, 231–4, 254
    demographic transition 66, 76
    energy pricing 200–2, 219–27, 230–5:
        abatement 202–9; simulations 209–19
    energy productivity 248, 249, 258–9
    GREEN model 245
    Mongol invasions 98
chlorination of water 35
chloro-fluorocarbon (CFC) emissions 201
Clark, C.W. 137, 138
Clarke, R. 214
Cline, W.E. 94, 148
coal
    China 207, 209, 211, 214–16, 230–4
    GREEN model 242, 245–6
coalitions, environmental 265–81, 283–8
Cobb, J.B. Jr 84, 120
Code of Federal Regulation (CFR) 29
Cole, H.S.D. 91
coliform 36–7
commitment to cooperation 271–3
competition, environmental 292–7
composition of economic activity 19–20,
    29, 31
    incipient pollution 60
Conservation Foundation 31–2, 37

contingent valuation methods (CVMs)
    138n.23
Cooper, R. 138
Copeland, B. 62
Coppel, J. 262
cost–benefit analyses 2–3
    social 119–21
Cowen, T. 120
credit markets 114, 145
crude oil
    China 214–16
    GREEN model 242, 246
Cumberland, J.H. 297
current-value Hamiltonian 126

D'Aspremont, C.A. 269, 279
Daly, H.E. 2, 19, 51, 84, 120, 148, 150
Dasgupta, P. 2, 111, 114, 119, 120, 122,
    123, 125, 133, 136, 137, 138, 139, 148,
    151, 152, 153, 163, 167, 181
De Bondt, R. 281
de Melo, J. 195, 210
Dean, A. 262
death rate 53–5, 64–6, 67, 71
defence expenditure 90
deforestation 66, 115
demographic transition 53–8, 63–6, 69–71
    policy implications 74, 76
    sustainability 73
Denison, E.F. 88
Devereux, M. 301
direct foreign investment (DFI) 294, 297,
    300
discount rates
    intergenerational 148–9, 169
    and well-being 117–20
dissolved oxygen 40–1, 42
Dixon, J.A. 137
domestic animals 114, 145
Donsimoni, M.P. 269
dual pricing system, China 207
'dumping', environmental 43
Dutta, P. 154
dynamic efficiency of water allocation
    180–1

East Germany 99
Easter, K.W. 179
ecologic transition 52, 59–63, 66–71
    policy implications 74
    sustainability 73
Economides, N.S. 269
Edmonds, R.L. 205, 206, 212
education
    expenditure 124, 125
    and fertility 55: policy implications 74–5

efficiency
  energy 260–1
  water allocation 179–81
Eggleston, H.S. 211
Ehrlich, A. 112, 113, 115
Ehrlich, P. 112, 113, 115, 136
Eisner, R. 85
electricity
  China 207, 216–17, 232
  India 207
Energy Statistics Yearbook of China 211, 234
enterprise tax system 208
equity, intergenerational 147–9
Esty, D. 288
existence value 129
extinction, risk of 90, 122

faecal coliform 36–7
faecal discharge
  and oxygen regime 40
  pathogenic contamination from 35–7
Falkenmark, M. 137
Falloux, F. 137
Fankhauser, S. 204, 206, 228
fertility rate
  demographic transition 53, 55–8: policy
    implications 74–5
  environmental resources 114
Fieldhouse, D.K. 100, 101
fires 90
Fisher, A.C. 122, 138
flue gas desulphurisation 227n.3
food supplies 95–6
foreign direct investment 294, 297, 300
forests 66, 115
  net national product 131
fossil fuels
  emissions 203
  environmental costs 205–6
  shortages 93
  stocks 115
free-riding 264, 265, 269, 272, 285–6
  research and development cooperation
    266, 277
Freeman, C. 91
fuelwood valuation 128
Fullerton, D. 262

Gabszewicz, J.J. 269, 279
gasoline 31
Germany, East and West 99
Ghana 100, 101
Gigengach, A.R. 137
Gillham, C.A. 211
Global Environmental Monitoring System
  (GEMS) 23–4

global warming
  China 204, 234
  costs 94
  long-term nature 96–7
  second-best optima 121–2
  sources 34–5
Glomsrød 204
Golden Rule of economic growth 151, 158
Goldin, I. 3
Goodland, R. 51
Gordon, H.S. 168
Gordon, R.H. 290
governments 96–102, 103–4
  implementability of environmental
    policy 145
GREEN 239, 240–61
Green Golden Rule 151–64, 168
greenhouse gas emissions 201
  China 202–4
  see also carbon dioxide; global warming
Gross, D.R. 113
Grossman, G.M. 23, 24, 25, 26, 27, 29, 31,
  32, 43, 45, 52, 63, 181, 289
Grubb, M. 211, 212
Guo, J.-J. 207, 208

Hahn, F.H. 122
Hamilton, L.S. 115
Hammond, P.J. 150
Hanemann, M. 138
happiness 84
Hartwick, J. 136
Heal, G.M. 2, 119, 120, 122, 123, 125, 136,
  137, 139, 148, 149, 151, 152, 153, 157,
  160, 163, 164, 167, 181, 265, 269, 282,
  288
health, public 124, 125
heavy metals 37–40
Helpman, E. 181
Henry, C. 122, 138
Herrera, A.O. 147, 148
Heston, A. 28, 37, 38, 42, 74, 77
Hettige, H. 60
Hicks, J.R. 85
Hobbes, Thomas 102–3
Hoel, M. 269, 278, 279
Hoeller, P. 262
Hoff, K. 137
Holdren, J. 112, 113, 115
Holtz-Eakin, D. 24, 34, 63, 66–9
Hong Kong 100
Hotelling, H. 148
household production 128–9
Howarth, A. 120
Howe, H. 262
Hull, R.H. 200

Hulme, M. 204
human capital 55–8, 74–5
Hyde, W. 3

imports, pollution-intensive goods 43,
   47–50
incipient pollution 52, 59–60, 61, 71, 77
income
   and aggregate well-being 123–4
   and air quality 27–9, 30–1, 32, 33, 43
   carbon tax revenues 251, 254, 255
   China 231–2
   demographic transition 55, 56, 64–6, 67,
      69–71
   ecologic transition 59, 60, 62–3, 66–71,
      78–9
   and environmental demands 21
   GREEN model 260–1
   meaning 85, 88–90
   need for growth 71–3
   and water consumption 198
   and water quality 36, 38, 41
India
   carbon tax 254
   demographic transition 66, 76
   electricity tariffs 207
   energy productivity 248, 249, 259
   GREEN model 245
industrial sector
   environmental damage 21
   incipient pollution 60
   water use 190–1
infant mortality 55, 56
innovations, water use 180–1
insurance market 90, 114
Intergovernmental Panel on Climate
   Change (IPCC) 246
International Energy Agency (IEA) 203
intrinsic worth 129
investment
   carbon tax 250
   changing nature of 102–3
   effects 106, 107–8
   meaning 86
   and saving 244
   and taxation 98, 109
   water sector, Morocco 178, 198
   yields 91
Investment Programme Contour (IPC) 107
irreversibility of accounting prices 129
irrigation 113
   Morocco 177, 178, 190: subsidies 176

Jackson, S. 208, 209
Jacquemin, A. 279
Jahoda, M. 91

James, D.E. 137
Japan
   carbon tax revenues 250
   economic performance 100
   energy productivity 248–9, 258–9
Johnsen, T. 229
Jones, E.L. 97–8

Kanbur, R. 294, 298, 299, 301
Kannai, Y. 154
Kaser, M.C. 99
Katz, M.L. 281
Keen, M. 294, 298, 299, 301
Kennedy, E. 113
King, P.N. 115
Kinzelbach, W.K.H. 205–6
Knudsen, O. 3
Koopmans, T.C. 117, 118, 137
Korea, North and South 99–100
Kosmo, K. 202
Krautkraemer, J.A. 151
Krueger, A.B. 3, 23, 24, 25, 26, 27, 29, 31,
   32, 43, 45, 52, 63
Kurz, M. 119, 126, 138

Laity, J.A. 25, 26, 31, 45
Lal, D. 108
Landry, A. 77n.1
Lane, R.E. 84
Lardy, N.R. 208, 211
Larsen, B. 204, 206, 262
Lauwers, L. 149
lead
   air pollution 29–31
   water pollution 37, 38, 39
Leech, P.K. 211
Levhari, D. 122
Lewis, W.A. 84, 85
liberalisation, trade 189–90, 197–8
life expectancy 53, 55, 56
Lin, X. 232
Little, I.M.D. 100, 125, 137
Lluch, C. 262
local air pollution 27–33
Low, P. 3
Lucas, R.E. 60, 106
lung cancer 205–6

Mabbut, J. 137
McGuire, C.B. 138
McMillan, J. 208
MacNeill, J. 51
Magrath, W. 138
maintenance costs
   changing nature of 102–3, 109
   levels 13–14, 91, 94–6

meaning 85–6
Majumdar, M. 132, 139
Malaysia 28
Mäler, K.-G. 111, 114, 125, 129, 136, 138, 150
Malthus, Reverend Thomas 72
Mankiw, G. 75
Manne, A.S. 242, 262
manufacturing sector *see* industrial sector
Marer, P. 99
Marglin, S. 125, 133, 137
Markandya, A. 87, 116, 150, 151
Martin, J.P. 262, 263
Mateus, A. 195
Meade, J.E. 158
Meadows, D.H. 91, 92, 93, 148
Meadows, D.L. 91, 92, 93, 148
men and technological adaptation 127–8
mercury 37, 38, 39
meteorites 90
methane emissions 201
Mexico 290
Meyer, A. 114
mineral shortages 93
Mintz, J. 290
Mirrlees, J.A. 118, 119, 122, 125, 137
Mitchell, R.C. 138
Morocco
  air quality 28
  water allocation 175–99
Motta, M. 281
Mukendi, A. 137
Mulder, P. 137
Mumford, J.L.K. 205
Mundlak, Y. 106
Murphy, K. 55, 57
Musgrave, R. 124

National Irrigation Programme 177
natural capital stock 87, 109, 150–1, 153
natural gas
  China 233
  GREEN model 242
Naughton, B. 208
Neary, P. 232, 233
negotiations, linking 274–80
Nelson, R. 137
Nerlove, M. 114
net national product (NNP) 111
  biases 127–8
  in dynamic economy 130–6
  Hamiltonian 126
  measurement 124–5
Netherlands Centraal Plan Bureau 92, 93, 95, 96
Newcombe, K. 138

nickel 37, 38, 39
Nicoletti, G. 262
Nigeria 100, 101
nitrates 41, 42
nitrogen 40
nitrogen dioxide
  concentration 30
  sources and effects 33
nitrous oxides
  acid rain 34
  China 205, 206, 211–12
  emission levels 43
  monitoring stations 45n.2
  Pakistan 206
  sources and effects 33
non-linear dose-response relationships 112
Nordhaus, W.D. 84–5, 88, 95, 121, 122, 143, 227
Norgaard, R. 120
North American Free Trade Agreement (NAFTA) 290
North Korea 99

Oak Ridge National Laboratory 24
Oates, W.E. 301
oil
  China 214–16, 233
  GREEN model 242, 246
Olewiler, N. 136
Oliveira-Martins, J. 262, 263
Olsen, W.K. 137
Oniang'o, R. 113
option values 130, 144
Ordover, J.A. 281
Organisation for Economic Cooperation and Development (OECD) 33, 93–4
overuse of land 112
oxygen regime 40–1, 42

Pakistan 206
Parfit, D. 117, 120
pathogenic contamination from faecal discharge 35–7
Pavitt, K.L.R. 91
Pearce, D.W. 2, 87, 116, 150, 151, 204
Pearl–Verhulst logistic model 153
Pearson, M. 301
per capita income *see* income
permits, emission 239–40
Phelps, E.S. 122, 151, 158
phenols 45n.9
phosphorus 40
Polemarchakis, H.M. 269
policies
  demographic and ecologic transitions 58, 74–5

policies (*cont.*)
  implementability 145
  and income growth 43
  pressures for change 14
  social 14
  water allocation 187, 191–2
Portes, R. 137
productivity, energy 248–9, 258–9
profitability
  and coalitions 268–9, 275
  and pollution 291
property rights 20, 21–2
prosperity *see* income
protectionism 14, 301n.4
  Morocco 176, 178
public services 124

Radetzki, M. 19, 22
Ramsey, F. 117, 148
Ramsey Rule 119
Randers, J. 91, 92, 93, 148
Ravallion, M. 124
regenerative capacity of environment 112
  Green Golden Rule 151–2, 153, 156
  pollution levels 20
regulations
  air quality 29
  costs 93–5
  focus 22
  international 289–91, 294, 297–301,
    303–4
  water quality 38, 40
Reij, C. 137
relocation costs 291–2
renewable natural resources 112
Repetto, R. 113, 138
research and development (R&D) 266, 274,
    276–80, 284, 287–8
Richels, R.G. 242, 262
risk 122
Roberts, K. 232, 233
Robinson, J. 158
Romer, D. 75
Romer, P.M. 106
Rosenzweig, M.R. 137
Ross, L. 228
Roughgarden, J. 136
Rubinstein, A. 281

salinisation 113
savings 242
scale of economic activity 19–20
  air pollution 31
  water pollution 41
Schiff, M. 3
Schwab, R.M. 301

Scolnik, H.D. 147, 148
Scott, M.F.G. 83, 85, 86, 88, 91, 106, 170,
    108, 109
sea level, rise in 89
security issues 14
Sefton, J. 138
Selden, T.M. 24, 28, 32, 33, 34, 63, 66–9,
    77
Sen, A. 124, 125, 133, 137
Senegal 101
service sector
  environmental damage 21
  incipient pollution 60
  water use 190–1
sewage
  and oxygen regime 40
  pathogenic contamination from 35–7
shadow (accounting) prices 123, 124–5,
    126, 127, 132–3
  valuation problem 128–30
Shah, A. 204, 206, 262
Sherman, P.B. 137
Shoven, J.B. 262
Singapore 100
Siniscalco, D. 265, 269, 271, 272, 273, 278,
    279, 280, 283
Smil, V. 209
Smith, K. 205
social accounting matrix (SAM), Morocco
    182–3, 188
social choice problem 149
social policy 14
soil degradation 66, 109, 112–13
  and evaporation rate 114
Solorzano, R. 127, 138
Solow, R.M. 116, 120, 23, 126, 137, 148,
    150, 159, 163
Song, D. 24, 28, 32, 33, 63, 69, 77
South Korea 99
specialisation, international 47–50
Spence, A.M. 129
Squire, L. 125
Srinivasan, T.N. 122
State and Local Air Monitor System
    (SLAMS) 25
State Tax Bureau (STB) 233
static efficiency of water allocation 179–80
Stern, N. 125
Stiglitz, J.E. 137, 139
structural adjustment, Morocco 178–9
Sub-Saharan Africa 100–2, 112–14
subsidies
  fuel 202: China 208, 210, 216–17, 219,
    233
  and water allocation 176, 178, 179
  and welfare 258

sulphur dioxide
  acid rain 34, 206
  China 205, 206, 211–12, 234
  concentration 29, 30
  monitoring stations 23
  Pakistan 206
  sources and effects 31–2
Summers, L. 144
Summers, R. 28, 37, 38, 42, 74, 77
suspended particulate matter (SPM)
  China 205, 211–12, 233–4
  concentration 29, 30
  sources and effects 27–9
Suzumura, K. 281
Syrquin, M. 21

Taiwan 100
Tamura, R. 55, 57
Taplin, J.H.E. 208
tariffs
  electricity 207
  water 176, 178, 187, 190
Tarr, D. 195, 210
taxation 286–7
  carbon: China 202, 213–15, 219, 231–4,
    254; revenue transfers 249–59
  China 208, 232–3, 234
  environmental competition 293, 295,
    304–5
  GREEN model 242–4
  and investment 98, 109
  relocation costs 291–2
Taylor, S. 62
technology
  back-stop 240–2
  China 233–4
  cooperation 276–81
  and growth 21
  improvements 19–20, 44, 75–7: biases
    127–8; costs 88; effects 106, 107
Tietenberg, T. 136, 150
TJN 231, 235
Tobey, J.A. 43
Tobin, J. 84
toxic chemicals 37–8
transfers, welfare 270–1
Tulkens, H. 290
Turner, R.K. 2, 87

uncertainty 122–3, 135–6
  and accounting prices 129
Underwood, B.A. 113
Union of Soviet Socialist Republics
  carbon tax 254
  energy productivity 249, 259
United Nations 99, 113

United Nations Environment Programme
  137
United States of America
  air quality 30–1, 32, 33: carbon dioxide
    concentration 94; data sources 24–5;
    estimation methods 26
  carbon tax revenues 250
  energy productivity 249, 259
  maintenance costs 94, 95
  North American Free Trade Agreement
    290
  urban areas
    air pollution 27–33
  water allocation 181
Uruguay Round 3
US Congress 3
Usher, D. 101
utilitarianism 153–7, 162–3, 167–8

Valdes, A. 3
van der Mensbrugghe, D. 3
Van der Taak, H. 125
van Liederkierke, L. 149
van Wijnbergen, S. 294, 298, 301
Vennemo, H. 229
von Amsberg, J. 116–17
von Braun, J. 113

wages 134
Wang, Z.K. 214
wars 90, 102
water
  allocation, Morocco 175–99
  quality: data sources 23–4; estimation
    methods 26; heavy metals and toxic
    chemicals 37–40; oxygen regime
    40–1, 42; pathogenic contamination
    from faecal discharge 35–7; problems
    66
  valuation 128
Weale, M. 38
Weil, D. 75
Weitzman, M.L. 137, 150
welfare state 109
welfare transfers 270–1
well-being 116–19, 123–4
  net national product 126, 132, 134–6
West Germany 99
Weymark, J. 279
whales 129
Whalley, J. 231, 262
Wheeler, D. 60
Wigle, R. 231
Wilen, J.E. 153
Winters, L.A. 3, 214
Wolinsky, A. 281

Wolpin, K.I. 137
women 127–8
World Bank 3, 19, 31, 32, 64, 92, 93, 94,
    100, 114, 200, 205, 207, 208, 209, 211,
    228
World Commission on Environment and
    Development 111, 147
World Health Organisation 28
World Resources Institute 24, 35, 40, 51,
    59, 96, 102, 201

Worldwatch Institute 27, 29
Wu, C. 281

Xiong, J. 206, 212
Xuan, Z. 209

Yosida, K. 164

Zambia 101
Zhao, D. 206, 212